DOCUMENTARY HISTORY SERIES

For Want of a Lighthouse

BUILDING THE LIGHTHOUSES
OF
EASTERN LAKE ONTARIO
1828–1914

MARC SEGUIN

2015

Order this book online at www.trafford.com
or email orders@trafford.com

Most Trafford titles are also available at major online book retailers.

Cover design by Dan Seguin
danseguindesigns@telus.net

All profits from the sale of this book will go towards the preservation of the remaining lighthouses on the shores of eastern Lake Ontario.

Print information available on the last page.

ISBN: 978-1-4907-5673-8 (sc)
ISBN: 978-1-4907-5672-1 (hc)
ISBN: 978-1-4907-5671-4 (e)

Library of Congress Control Number: 2015904018

Trafford rev. 04/23/2015

 www.trafford.com

North America & international
toll-free: 1 888 232 4444 (USA & Canada)
fax: 812 355 4082

The beacon light, the beacon light,
How sweet thy parting beams

There is a point on which the eye of the beholder lingers the latest
And on which it fixes the soonest
A point of farewell to the outward bound
And of greeting to the home bound

It is the light house

Storms may howl around
And blend ocean, sky and land in a seeming chaos
The clouds may be torn asunder by tremendous whirlwinds
And run, rugged and frightful, close under the ice of a pitiless
horizon Yet, unmoved and calm and bright through all
The light house sends out its rays of hope
Amidst the black darkness and wild commotion

[Anonymous. *Hallowell Free Press.* Jan. 29, 1833]

CONTENTS

PART III   EPILOGUE

APPENDICES

PREFACE

When gazing from the mainland at the crumbling ruins of the distant Scotch Bonnet Island lighthouse, or viewing up-close the boarded-up Point Traverse lighthouse, I've often wondered... Why were these and other lighthouses along these shores built? Who built them, and who maintained them? Why were most of these lighthouses demolished, and what will become of those lighthouses that remain?

I've long been curious about how past events and people are connected with the houses, barns, barracks, churches and other structures which they've built and which are still standing as enduring monuments to their energy and vision. Historic documents and written accounts can help to connect us with our past; as can old maps, paintings and photographs. However, it's only the three-dimensional, tangible objects, especially buildings, that evoke in me a strong connection with those people and events that have preceded us.

It's with this mindset that I started to delve into the history of the few lighthouses that are still standing in the area where I live, at the eastern end of Lake Ontario on the shores of Prince Edward County in Ontario, Canada. Through my research, I found that, prior to 1914, there had been no fewer than twelve lighthouses constructed in Prince Edward County, and that these dozen towers were really part of a much larger, closely connected network of lighthouses stretching over one hundred kilometers along the Canadian shore of Lake Ontario and through the Bay of Quinte from Presqu'ile Point in the west to Kingston harbour in the east.

I soon realized that to restrict my examination of lighthouses to the limited boundaries of this one county was to ignore the larger historical and geographical context which led to the establishment of what I discovered was one of the world's largest concentrations of lighthouses. By expanding my research, I found that more than forty-five lighthouses and light towers had been built on the Canadian shores of eastern Lake Ontario in the period from 1828 to 1914.

In an attempt to present a comprehensive record of the building of these lighthouses and to provide a resource for others who may be inspired to do further research, I've compiled this documentary history relying heavily on primary sources; especially contemporary newspaper articles and official government reports from which I've quoted extensively. In so doing, I've tried to place these documents — this raw historical data — into a broader context to show why these lighthouses were important to 19th and 20th Century mariners, and how they made a significant contribution to Canada's history.

Over the decades, as transportation patterns changed and aids to navigation evolved, most of the lighthouses and light towers of eastern Lake Ontario were discontinued, demolished or replaced by simpler, more efficient lighting systems. Today, only seven of the original forty-five towers are still standing. It's my hope that, by documenting the history of all of the lighthouses which were once part of this remarkable network of fixed aids to navigation, I might be able to contribute, in some small way, to saving these last few pieces of our built marine heritage; these last remaining physical links to an important part of our past.

Marc Seguin
Prince Edward County, Ontario
February, 2015.

ACKNOWLEDGEMENTS

My sincerest thanks to those individuals who, through their financial contributions and general encouragement, have made this book possible:

Thayer B. Cluett

Robert Cluett IV

Philip and Loretta Seguin

I am also indebted to a number of persons who provided hands-on support for the creation of this book:

Marjorie C. Seguin, my wife, editor and chief supporter

David Rowney, my friend and publicist

Dan Seguin, by brother and designer of the book cover

My sons Philip and Daniel, for their photography work

In compiling this documentary history, numerous libraries, archives, online collections and individuals have provided valuable materials, information and advice, all of which have made this book possible. Among them are:

Amanda Hill, archive.org, Archives of Ontario, Aubrey Johnson, Bay of Quinte Yacht Club, Belleville Public Library, The British Library, Canadian Coast Guard, canadiana.org, Chance Brothers, Cobourg Public Library, David Rumsey Map Collection, Deseronto Archives, Ernest Margetson, Hastings County Archives, Hastings County Historical Society, John Lyons, Kingston Public Library, Krista

Richardson, Library and Archives Canada, Marine Museum of the Great Lakes, Prince Edward County Mariners Park Museum, maritimehistoryofthegreatlakes.ca, New York Public Library, NOAA, Orland French, ourontario.ca, Prince Edward County Public Library and Archives, Queen's University Archives, Sue Fraser, The Naval Marine Archive The Canadian Collection, Toronto Marine Historical Society, Toronto Public Library Baldwin Room, U.S. Patent Office.

Thanks to all for your contributions.

Marc Seguin, April 2015

NOTES TO THE READER

Quotations

Extensive quotations from original sources have been included in this work. Every effort has been made to reproduce these original passages as accurately as possible. In most cases, words or place names that are misspelled or that use spellings or capitalization that are not generally accepted today have not been corrected. In order to clarify any spellings which may be misleading or confusing, comments or clarifications within square brackets [...] have been added by the author. Portions of quotations in round brackets (...), are part of the original quotation. Names of all ships and all published works appear in *italics*.

Dates

There is often confusion over the precise date that a particular lighthouse was constructed. Some sources quote the date that construction of a lighthouse was begun. Other sources quote the date that the main lighthouse tower was completed. Still others quote the date that the lighthouse was first put into active service when its lamps were first lit. I have chosen to standardize on this last date, the date that the lighthouse was first activated for use as a functioning aid to navigation.

Lighthouse Names and Place Names

In some cases, there is very little consistency from source to source in the naming of the lighthouses and the naming of the geographical locations where they were built. This is often the result of a lack of a standard geographical naming convention; a condition that existed throughout the 19th Century and still exists in some cases today in spite of attempts to normalize geographic names after the Geographical Board of Canada was established in 1897. [See: Natural Resources Canada. http://www.nrcan.gc.ca/earth-sciences/geography-boundary/geographical-name/search/11084]

For instance, throughout the 19th Century, the south-eastern point of Prince Edward County was usually referred to as South Bay Point, and the lighthouse there was initially called the South Bay Point lighthouse. Since 1932, the official name of the point where the lighthouse is located has been Prince Edward Point [See: Natural Resources Canada. http://www4.rncan.gc.ca/search-place-names/unique.php?id=FCIMX] and the official name of the lighthouse is now the Prince Edward Point lighthouse. Some historical sources however, refer to this as the Point Traverse lighthouse and local residents always refer to this as the Point Traverse lighthouse even though the geographic feature officially named Point Traverse is more than a kilometer north of the lighthouse.

For the sake of consistency and to avoid confusion, the most current official name of lighthouses and place names is generally used in the narrative. The official names of lighthouses are taken from the 2009 edition of the Canadian Coast Guard's *List of Lights Buoys and Fog Signals* [See: http://www.notmar.gc.ca/go.php?doc=eng/services/list/inland-waters-2009]. Official place names are taken from Natural Resources Canada's "Canadian Geographical Names Database" [See: http://www.nrcan.gc.ca/earth-sciences/geography/place-names/search/9170]. In quotations, the official name appears in square brackets [...] where it differs from the quoted name.

A complete list of lighthouses and their alternate names can be found in Appendix 1.

Measurements

For distances over water, I have used nautical miles: 1 nautical mile = 1.85 km.

In quotations, any distances over water stated in kilometers or statute miles have been converted to nautical miles and surrounded by square brackets [NN nautical miles].
1 kilometer = 0.54 nautical miles
1.15 statute miles = 1 nautical mile

For distances over land, I have used kilometers (kms): 1 km = 0.62 miles. In quotations, any distances over land stated in miles have been converted to kilometers and surrounded by square brackets [NN kms].
1 mile = 1.61 kms

Other distances appearing in quotations have been converted to meters, kilometers or nautical miles as appropriate.

For water depths and ship dimensions, I have used feet: 1 foot = 0.3 meters. In quotations, any measurements stated in meters or fathoms have been converted to feet and surrounded by square brackets [NN feet]. For the sake of clarity, in some cases, multiple units of measure are shown. Illustrative nautical charts marked with depths in meters or fathoms have not been altered.
1 meter = 3.28 feet = 0.55 fathoms
1 foot = 0.17 fathoms = 0.30 meters
1 fathom = 1.83 meters = 6.00 feet

For speeds over water, I have used knots: 1 knot = 1.85 kilometers per hour (kph).
In quotations, any speeds over water stated in kilometers per hour or miles per hour have been converted to knots and surrounded by square brackets [NN knots].
1 kilometer per hour = 0.54 knots
1.15 miles per hour = 1 knot

Lighthouse Terminology

Aid to navigation
Any technology used to assist mariners in the navigation of their vessels. These include <u>lighthouses</u>, buoys, beacons, fog signals, radio systems, computers and satellites.

Base
The lowest point of the <u>tower</u> above grade or above high-water that rests on the <u>foundation</u> or pier.

Buoy
A floating <u>aid to navigation</u> often used to mark channels and underwater obstructions.

Catoptric light
Type of lighting apparatus used to reflect the light from a lamp by means of one or more parabolic dishes.

Dioptric light
Type of lighting apparatus used to focus the light from a lamp through a cut glass or molded glass lens. Also called a Fresnel lens or lenticular apparatus.

Focal plane height
The measurement from the surface of the water to the centre of the <u>light</u>. This usually differs from the <u>overall height</u>.

Foundation
The structure, usually below grade, upon which the <u>tower</u> is built. On a marine site, the foundation is often a timber pier or crib filled with stones.

Gallery
The narrow walkway around the outside of the <u>lantern</u>, usually surrounded by a railing.

Lightkeeper
The person responsible for lighting the <u>lighthouse</u> lamp(s) and generally maintaining the lighthouse and the related equipment and grounds. Also referred to as the keeper.

Lantern
The glassed-in structure at the top of the <u>lighthouse</u>, often a small room up to 10 feet across and 10 feet high, inside of which the lighting apparatus is placed. Usually square, octagonal or 12-sided.

Light
The lamp(s) and equipment used to project a beam across the water. Also the term used for any lighted aid to navigation including a <u>lighthouse</u> itself.

Light tower
A fixed <u>aid to navigation</u> usually consisting of an open framework of iron or steel and usually lighted by a weatherproof lamp, often with no <u>gallery</u> or enclosed <u>lantern</u>.

Lighthouse
Historically, a lighthouse was a tall, enclosed <u>tower</u> built as a fixed <u>aid to navigation</u> with a <u>light</u> placed at the top that was enclosed by a <u>lantern</u> surrounded by a <u>gallery</u>. It also had enough space inside to provide living accommodations for at least one <u>lightkeeper</u>. Therefore the lighthouse was both a dwelling and a navigational aid combined.

In Canada, very few lighthouses were constructed to accommodate a keeper within the walls of the <u>tower</u> itself. No lighthouses of this type were ever built on Lake Ontario. Instead, the keeper's dwelling was either a building that was completely separate from the lighthouse or it was attached directly to the <u>tower</u> even though the <u>tower</u> itself was never used as living space.

Over time, as building technology and lighting technology evolved, lighthouses changed form. The early <u>towers</u> were cylindrical or polygonal stone structures. Later, enclosed wood-framed <u>towers</u> became common. Finally, concrete <u>towers</u> were built. In addition, there were other forms that often bore little resemblance to a traditional lighthouse. These forms included partially enclosed wood-framed <u>towers</u>, open steel framework (skeleton) <u>towers</u> and partially enclosed steel framework <u>towers</u>. All of these types of fixed <u>aids to navigation</u> that lacked a <u>gallery</u> and enclosed <u>lantern</u> are referred to here as <u>light towers</u> rather than lighthouses. Some types of navigational lights are not included here, particularly lighted buoys, navigational lights on bridges, and lights on other buildings that were not built specifically as aids to navigation, such as a light on a church steeple.

Overall height
This is the *official* height of the <u>lighthouse.</u> Theoretically, this is the height as measured from the <u>base</u> to the vane (the top portion of the ventilator on the roof of the <u>lantern</u> marking the highest point of the <u>lighthouse</u>). This official height often only measures the <u>tower</u> and excludes the <u>lantern</u>. As a result, this measurement can be less than the actual height of the entire structure. Also, the <u>overall height</u> usually differs from the <u>focal plane height</u>.

Platform
The top of the <u>tower</u> upon which the <u>lantern</u> and <u>gallery</u> are placed.

Tower
The main vertical structure of the <u>lighthouse</u>.

Watch room
Usually the room in the <u>lighthouse</u> directly below the <u>lantern</u>. This is traditionally where the <u>lightkeeper</u> stayed at night to "watch" the light. Many <u>lighthouses</u> in Canada did not have a watch room.

Vessel Types

Barge
Any vessel used primarily for transporting bulk cargo. A barge may be powered by sail or steam (see <u>Steam barge</u>), or it may be towed by another ship.

Barque (or Bark)
A large square-rigged sailing ship. Barques were the largest commercial sailing vessels used on the Great Lakes.

Bateau
A flat-bottomed boat used to carry cargo, powered primarily by oars or poles, but could be rigged with a sail to run with the wind. Used extensively on the St. Lawrence River before it was canalized. Superseded by the larger <u>Durham boat</u>.

Canaller
A late 19th Century term for any steam-powered cargo ship that was small enough to fit through the Welland Canal (less than 270 feet over all, and drawing less than 12 feet of water).

Dredge
A vessel adapted to dig a channel to make a waterway navigable by ships.

Durham boat
A flat-bottomed boat used to carry cargo, powered primarily by oars or poles, but could be rigged with a sail to run with the wind. Durham boats had a greater capacity than <u>bateaux</u>.

Laker
A late 19th Century term for any steam-powered cargo ship that was too big to fit through the Welland Canal, so it could only sail the upper lakes and Lake Erie as far as Port Colborne.

Propeller
A steam-powered ship fitted with a propeller, instead of paddlewheels.

Schooner
A sailing ship with two or more masts whose principal sails were rigged fore-and-aft. Schooners were the most common type of commercial sailing ships on the Great Lakes throughout the 19th and early 20th centuries.

Sloop
A small, single-masted sailing ship.

Steam Barge
Any steam-powered vessel used primarily for transporting bulk cargo.

Steamboat
Any steam-powered vessel, usually referring to one fitted with paddlewheels.

Steamer
Any steam-powered vessel, usually referring to one fitted with a propeller.

Steamship
Any steam-powered ship.

Tug
Any steam-powered vessel used primarily for towing other vessels or for marine salvage work.

CHRONOLOGY

Pre-history	First Nations peoples establish settlements throughout the Great Lakes region.
1678	French launch the barque *Frontenac* on Lake Ontario.
1755-60	Seven Years' War in North America.
1760	The French garrison at Fort Frontenac (Kingston) surrenders to the British.
1763	Canada becomes a British possession.
1775-83	American War for Independence
1784	Loyalists arrive in what is now Ontario.
1791	Old Province of Quebec split into Upper Canada (west of Montreal) and Lower Canada.
1792	Toronto renamed York, capital of Upper Canada.
1804	First lighthouse on the Great Lakes built at Niagara (demolished 1814).
1808	Lighthouse built at Gibraltar Point at entrance to York (Toronto) harbour.
1812-14	War of 1812.
1825	Erie Canal completed by the State of New York, from Buffalo to the Hudson River.
1829	False Ducks Island lighthouse activated. First ship passes through the Welland Canal.

1832	Rideau Canal completed between Bytown (Ottawa) and Kingston.
	Ohio and Erie Canal completed from Cleveland, Ohio, to the Ohio River.
1833	Point Petre lighthouse activated.
	Welland Canal improved.
	Nine Mile Point lighthouse activated.
1834	Ottawa River canals completed.
	Town of York becomes the City of Toronto.
1835	Private wharf light erected by Billa Flint in Belleville harbour.
1837-38	Rebellion in Upper and Lower Canada.
1840	Presqu'ile Point lighthouse activated.
1841	Upper Canada becomes Canada West and Lower Canada becomes Canada East as part of the new United Province of Canada.
1845	2ⁿᵈ Welland Canal completed.
1846	Kingston incorporated as a city.
	Kingston Harbour lighthouse activated.
1847	St. Lawrence canals completed from Montreal to Prescott:
	Lachine Canal (1825)
	Cornwall Canal (1843)
	Beauharnois Canal (1845)
	Williamsburg canals (1847).
1851	1ˢᵗ Belleville Harbour lighthouse activated.
	Two Presqu'ile Range lights activated.
1855	First canal at Sault Ste. Marie Canal completed by the State of Michigan.
1856	Scotch Bonnet Island lighthouse activated.
1858	1ˢᵗ Snake Island Shoal lighthouse activated.
1862	Erie Canal deepened from 4 feet to 7 feet.
1866	Pleasant Point lighthouse activated.

1867	Confederation of Nova Scotia, New Brunswick, Canada East and Canada West to form the Dominion of Canada. Canada East becomes the Province of Quebec and Canada West becomes the Province of Ontario.
1870	1st Pigeon Island lighthouse activated.
	Telegraph Island lighthouse activated.
	Manitoba becomes a province.
1871	Salmon Point lighthouse activated.
	British Columbia becomes a province.
1873	Prince Edward Island becomes a province.
1876	Two Wellers Bay Range lights activated.
1879	Calf Pasture Shoal Range light replaces the Presqu'ile Bay rear range light.
	1st Belleville Harbour lighthouse destroyed by fire.
1880	1st Portsmouth Harbour lighthouse activated.
1881	2nd Belleville Harbour lighthouse activated.
	Prince Edward Point lighthouse activated.
	3rd Welland Canal completed.
1885	Deseronto Harbour lighthouse activated.
1887	2nd Portsmouth Harbour lighthouse activated.
1890	Centre Brother Island lighthouse activated.
	Murray Canal opens.
	1st Murray Canal East and West Pier lights activated.
1891	Three Brighton Range lights activated replacing the Presqu'ile Range lights.
1892	Two Barriefield Common Range lights activated.
	Potters Island light activated.
1894	The Narrows Shoal lighthouse activated.
	Potters Island light discontinued.
1895	Sault Ste. Marie Canal completed by the Government of Canada.
1899	2nd Murray Canal East and West Pier lights activated.

1900	2nd Snake Island Shoal lighthouse activated.
	Private light at Bath activated (c.1900).
	Private light at Garden Island activated (c.1900).
1903	State of New York begins construction of the Erie Barge Canal.
1905	Two Trenton Range lights activated.
	Alberta and Saskatchewan become provinces.
1909	2nd Pigeon Island lighthouse activated.
1911	Onderdonk Point lighthouse activated.
1912	Two Portsmouth Range lights activated.
1913	Construction commenced on the 4th Welland Canal.
1914	Outbreak of World War I
	Main Duck Island lighthouse activated.

REFERENCE MAPS

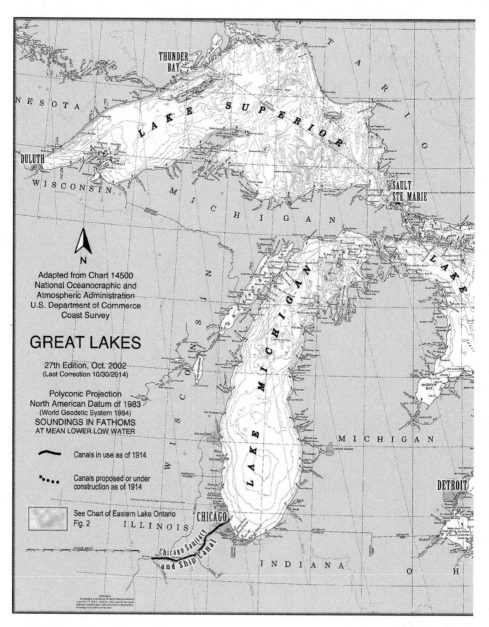

(1) Map of the Great Lakes region. Adapted from U.S. Coast Survey Chart of Lake Ontario, 2014.
[Courtesy of U.S. National Oceanic and Atmospheric Administration - NOAA]

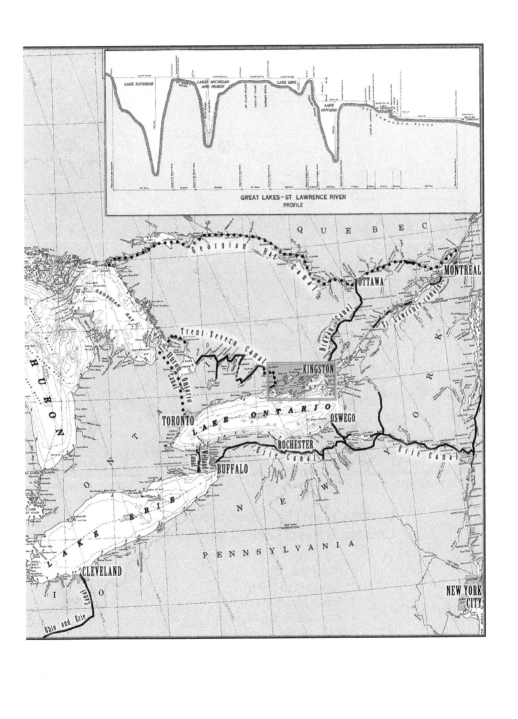

GREAT LAKES – ST. LAWRENCE RIVER
PROFILE

(Fig. 2) Adapted from: *Chart 2000 Lake Ontario*. Canadian Hydrographic Service   (Scale is approximate.)

Lighthouses and Light Towers on the Canadian Shores of Eastern Lake Ontario

1. Point Petre (1833)
2. Salmon Point (1871)
3. Scotch Bonnet Island (1856)
4. Presqu'ile Point (1840)
5 to 12 - see Fig. 3 overleaf
13. Narrows Shoal (1892, 1894)
14. Belleville Harbour (1835, 1851, 1881)
15. Telegraph Island (1870)

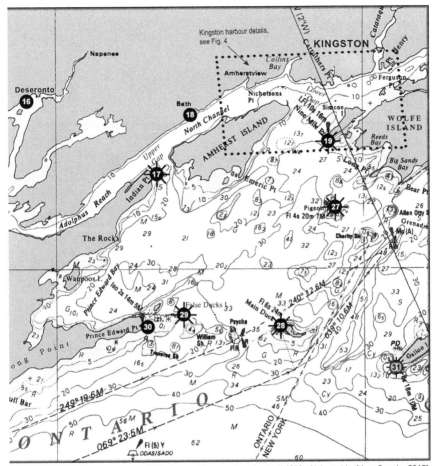

Fisheries and Oceans Canada, April 1998. [Adapted by Marc Seguin. 2015]

 Lake light   ● Harbour light or Passage light

16. Deseronto Harbour (1885)
17. Pleasant Point (1866)
18. Bath (C.1900)
19. Nine Mile Point (1833)
20 to 26 - see Fig. 4 overleaf
27. Pigeon Island (1870, 1909)
28. Main Duck Island (1914)
29. False Ducks Island (1829)
30. Prince Edward Point (1881)

31. Galloo Island, New York State (1820)

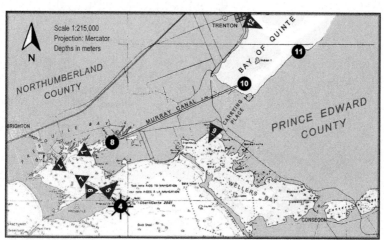

(3) Presqu'ile Bay detail. Adapted from *Chart 2059, Scotch Bonnet Island to Cobourg.*
Canadian Hydrographic Service, Fisheries and Oceans Canada, July 1998. (scale is approximate)

Lake light   ●Harbour light or Passage light   ▼Range light

4. Presqu'ile Point (1840)
5. Presqu'ile Range (2 lights, 1851)
6. Calf Pasture Shoal (2nd Presqu'ile Range rear, 1879)
7. Brighton Range (3 lights, 1891)
8. Murray Canal Pier West (1890, 1899)
9. Wellers Bay Range (2 lights, 1876)
10. Murray Canal Pier East (1890, 1899)
11. Onderdonk Point (1911)
12. Trenton Range (2 lights, 1905)

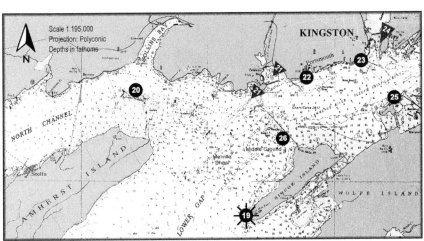

(4) Kingston harbour detail. Adapted from *Chart 2064, Kingston to False Ducks Islands*. Canadian Hydrographic Service, Fisheries and Oceans Canada, March 1999. (scale is approximate)

Lake light   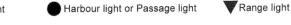Harbour light or Passage light   ▼Range light

19. Nine Mile Point (1833)
20. Centre Brother Island (1890)
21. Portsmouth Range (2 lights, 1912)
22. Portsmouth Harbour (2 lights, 1880, 1887)
23. Kingston Harbour (1846)
24. Barriefield Common Range (2 lights, 1910)
25. Garden Island (C. 1900)
26. Snake Island Shoal (1858, 1900)

For Want of a Lighthouse

Building the Lighthouses
of Eastern Lake Ontario
1828-1914

INTRODUCTION

The want of a light house at the eastern extremity of the lake
has often been complained of.

["The Loyalist", December 16th, 1826]

For most of its length and breadth, the deep, open waters of Lake Ontario, the most easterly of the Great Lakes, have long been easily navigated by sailing ships, steamboats and steamships. However, from Presqu'ile Point near Brighton, Ontario, to the entrance of the St. Lawrence River at Kingston, the north-eastern quadrant of the lake has always presented numerous hazards to mariners. This sixty-five nautical mile stretch is dominated by the irregular-shaped peninsula of Prince Edward County which protrudes out into Lake Ontario from the Canadian shore like a giant, misshapen anvil awaiting the hammer-blows of fierce storms to smite ships against its rocky reefs and sandy shoals. For much of the 19th Century, ship captains had no choice but to navigate around this protruding land mass and, as there were no sheltered harbours along its Lake Ontario shore, they were forced to sail much of the distance knowing that there would be no refuge should a storm suddenly develop.

A number of geographical, geological, hydrographical and meteorological factors converge in this quadrant of the lake to compound the dangers presented by the protruding Prince Edward peninsula, one of which is a line of shoals, reefs and rocky islands reaching right across Lake Ontario from Prince Edward County's southeastern point to the shores of New York State, forming a further series of obstacles to ships sailing to and from Kingston and the entrance to the St. Lawrence River. Along this line, known by hydrographers as the Duck Galloo Ridge, the otherwise deep lake suddenly becomes shallower and narrower, thereby magnifying the effects of storms which resulted in such a large number of ship sinkings and shipwrecks in the 19th Century that this area became known as "the graveyard of Lake Ontario"[1].

This same Prince Edward peninsula also has a calmer, gentler side in the form of a sheltered "Inside Passage" along its northern and eastern edge where there are dozens of safe harbours. This Inside Passage is centered on the relatively smooth waters of the Bay of Quinte; a wide, meandering waterway providing more than forty nautical miles of generally easy sailing from Pleasant Point at the Upper Gap off of Prince Edward County's eastern tip, to The Carrying Place at the narrow isthmus separating the Bay of Quinte from Lake Ontario via Wellers Bay and Presqu'ile Bay. With the opening of the Murray Canal across this isthmus in 1890, a complete waterway connection from the Bay of Quinte directly to the open lake was established. Eastward from the Upper Gap, the North Channel in the lee of Amherst Island extends the Inside Passage to the mouth of the Cataraqui River where Kingston's harbour is sheltered from Lake Ontario's worst storms by Simcoe Island and Wolfe Island at the entrance to the St. Lawrence River.

It was on these shores of eastern Lake Ontario that a network of more than forty-five lighthouses and light towers was constructed "for the safety and convenience of navigation" in the period 1828 to 1914. These aids to navigation were a key element in a general transportation policy that was gradually developed by successive colonial and Canadian governments throughout the 19th and early 20th centuries.

This policy recognized that shipping on the Great Lakes, and the improvement of this great natural inland water route that connects with the St. Lawrence River and the Atlantic Ocean, was absolutely essential to Canada's developing economy.

The primary focus of this inland transportation policy was the digging of canals. From the 1820's through to the 1950's, canals were constantly being dug, improved, expanded and upgraded to allow ships eventually to sail non-stop from the head of Lake Superior to the Atlantic Ocean. As a direct response to the Americans' Erie Canal — running from Lake Erie, across New York State to the Hudson River and constantly threatening to divert much of the shipping trade to New York City — the Welland Canal and St. Lawrence canals were established. In addition, the Rideau, Ottawa River, Trent, Murray and Sault Ste. Marie canals were also part of this policy to improve internal transportation and to keep much of the carrying trade in Canadian waters.

Secondarily, the transportation policy focused on establishing harbours, building roads to connect the backcountry with the harbours, and constructing lighthouses to guide ships safely from harbour to harbour. Through a combination of dredging river mouths and building extensive breakwaters, harbours were created on Lake Ontario and along the shores of the other Great Lakes wherever rivers emptied into them. These harbours provided ships with the ports that they needed to load and unload their cargoes. From the harbours, rudimentary roads were cleared to the back country so that raw materials could be moved down to the ports, and finished goods brought in by ship could be moved back to the towns and villages that were developing in the hinterland.

As the population around Lake Ontario increased, more canals were dug and improved, more harbours were dredged and more ships were built. Before the War of 1812, the combined population of the Great Lakes region including Upper Canada, western New York State, Ohio and Michigan Territory was less than 200,000.[2] There were only six harbours of note on Lake Ontario: three on the Canadian side; at Kingston, York (renamed Toronto in 1834), and Niagara, and three on the American side; at Sackets Harbor, Oswego and Charlotte. In all, there were less than 50 ships on the Great Lakes.[3]

By the beginning of the 20th Century, the population of the Great Lakes region had ballooned to more than 10,000,000,[4] and the number of commercial vessels plying the Lakes had increased more than eighty-fold to some 4,400 ships.[5] With the opening of the Welland Canal in 1829 and the Sault Ste. Marie Canal in 1855, all of the Great Lakes were connected together as one continuous navigable waterway. By 1900, hundreds of ports dotted the shores of these inland seas. On the Canadian side of eastern Lake Ontario alone, the number of ports had increased from one, at Kingston, to more than a dozen including Wellington, Consecon, Trenton, Belleville, Deseronto, Picton, Bath and Portsmouth.

As more ships carried more cargo and more passengers to more ports, the want of lighthouses on the Great Lakes was increasingly felt. The construction of lighthouses was recognized as one of the few contributions that the government could make to help keep ships on course so that they might arrive at their destinations with their hulls and cargoes intact, and their crews and passengers safe. As the 19th Century progressed, ship captains and ship owners demanded that more and more lighthouses be built, especially in the north-east quadrant of Lake Ontario where the numerous navigational hazards coincided with some of the busiest shipping routes.

In response to these demands, a remarkable network of lighthouses developed along the Canadian shores of eastern Lake Ontario. By the early 20th Century, a total of more than forty-five lighthouses and light towers had been erected along this sixty-five nautical mile stretch over the course of some eighty-five years. The result was one of the greatest concentrations of lighthouses anywhere in the world.

This is the story of the building of those lighthouses.

PART I

THE SETTING

PART I – THE SETTING

CHAPTER 1

Lake Ontario

Everywhere beset with ducks and drakes.

(Sir Richard Bonnycastle, 1846)

Long before any lighthouses were built on the Great Lakes, the first commercial trading vessels on these inland seas were undoubtedly the canoes of the First Nations peoples. The first European sailing ship on Lake Ontario appeared in the late 17th Century when the French launched the *Frontenac* at Cataraqui (now Kingston) in 1678.[1] By the mid-18th Century, both the French navy and Britain's Royal Navy had small fleets of bateaux, sloops and schooners built to support the fur trade around Lake Ontario.[2] Until 1788, only government-owned ships, mostly naval vessels, were allowed on the Great Lakes. With the increase in population on the Canadian side of Lake Ontario due to the settlement of Loyalists displaced after the American War for Independence, the first privately owned sailing ships were permitted to sail the Great Lakes for purely commercial purposes:

An Ordinance, For promoting the Inland Navigation.

Whereas present circumstances do not require that the transport of merchandize and peltries over the upper lakes should be carried on solely by vessels belonging to His Majesty, and the thriving situation of the new settlements of loyalists in the Western-country [west of Montreal, in what is now the Province of Ontario], makes it expedient under certain restrictions, to facilitate the transport of a variety of other articles across those Lakes, which will tend to increase the exports of this Province, and consequently to augment its commerce, be it therefore enacted ... that it shall and may be lawful for all his Majesty's good and liege subjects trading to the Western-country by the way of the great Lakes, who shall have taken out the usual pass conformable to the law, to cause such their effects and merchandize as shall be specified in the said pass, to be waterborne in any kind of vessel under the burthen of ninety tons, if the same be built and launched in any part or place within his Majesty's government, and all the owners of the bottom and cargo, and the captain, conductor, crew and navigators shall (since the first of May, 1783.) have taken the oath of allegiance to his Majesty....

And be it also enacted by the same authority, that nothing in this Act shall be construed to affect any small vessels under the burthen of five tons, found navigating the river St. Lawrence and the bay of Quinty [Quinte], on the North-eastern side of Lake Ontario, for the convenience of the loyalists and others in their settlements....[3]

This law recognized the economic reality that where there are settlements there is commerce and trade, and that trade was highly dependent on the efficient transportation of goods. With the absence of passable roads, it was the lakes and rivers of the interior of the country, especially the Great Lakes and the St. Lawrence River, that were the most practical transportation routes available.

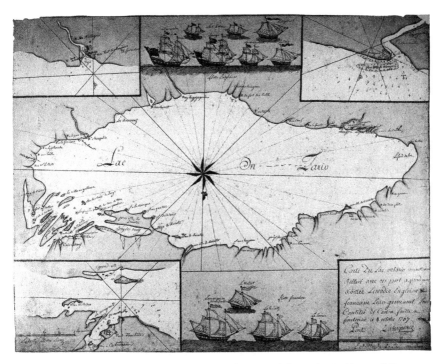

(5) French map of Lake Ontario 1757. Note that North is at the bottom of the map.
Carte du Lac Ontario by Labroquerie.
Seven ships of the British fleet on Lake Ontario are shown at top. The French fleet on the lake is shown at bottom. The inset at lower left shows Cataraqui (Kingston).
[Courtesy of The British Library]

When the old province of Quebec was divided to form Upper Canada and Lower Canada in 1791, only bateaux and a few British government ships could be found sailing Lake Ontario. The first commercial merchant ship, the *York*, was launched in 1793.[4]

Three years later, a traveler from Dublin, Ireland, Isaac Weld, observed that:

> Several decked merchant vessels, schooners, and sloops, of from fifty to two hundred tons each, and also numberless large sailing bateaux, are kept employed on Lake Ontario. No vessels are deemed proper for the navigation of these lakes but complete sea boats, or else flat bottomed vessels, such as canoes and bateaux, that can safely run ashore on an

3

emergency. At present the people of the United States have no other vessels than bateaux on the lake....[5]

The same year that Weld was travelling through Upper Canada, Jay's Treaty, the "Treaty of Amity, Commerce and Navigation", between the United States and Great Britain, came into effect and the handful of commercial vessels plying the Great Lakes were then able, for the first time since the end of the American War for Independence, to openly transport goods across the international boundary to and from ports on both sides of Lake Ontario:

> <u>Article III</u>
>
> It is agreed that it shall at all times be free to his majesty's subjects, and to the citizens of the United States, and also to the Indians dwelling on either side of the said boundary line, freely to pass and repass by land or inland navigation, into the respective territories and countries of the two parties, on the continent of America ... and to navigate all the lakes, rivers, and waters thereof, and freely to carry on trade and commerce with each other.[6]

Not only did Jay's Treaty open opportunities for trade between the American Great Lakes states and Upper Canada — the first American ship on Lake Ontario being launched in 1797[7] — but the treaty stipulated the removal of the British garrisons from the forts at Michilimackinac, Detroit, Niagara, and Oswego, and this lead to an influx of American settlers into Michigan, Ohio and western New York state. By 1800, this region of the United States had a population of more than 100,000 people.[8]

While the population of Upper Canada was slower to increase, steady arrivals of immigrants from Britain and Ireland as well as from the United States continued to add to the number of settlers on the Canadian side the Great Lakes. Weld commented that,

Already are there extensive settlements on the British side of Lake Ontario, at Niagara, at Toronto, at the Bay of Canti [Bay of Quinte], and at Kingston, which contain nearly twenty thousand inhabitants; and on the opposite shore, the people of the states are pushing forward their settlements with the utmost vigour.[9]

By 1806, the population of Upper Canada was estimated at more than 70,000.[10]

Commerce kept pace with this population growth and more ships — the link vital to sustain the growth of this young economy — were built on the Great Lakes to satisfy the demand for the transportation of goods and people, especially on Lake Ontario near whose shores most of Upper Canada's population lived. In 1800, the number of sails that could be counted on Lake Ontario was only a few dozen, and many of those were naval vessels; but by the 1820's, there were virtually no naval vessels on the lake due to the Rush-Bagot Treaty,[11] and the number of commercial vessels exceeded one hundred, including a number of steamboats. By the 1830's, as a result of the construction of the Welland Canal to bypass the Niagara Falls and allow ships to sail between lakes Erie and Ontario, several hundred ships had access to Lake Ontario and were transporting cargoes to Kingston and other Lake Ontario ports from as far away as Buffalo, Cleveland, Detroit and Chicago.[12]

In the late 18th and early 19th centuries, large ships from Britain and Europe regularly crossed the Atlantic Ocean carrying imported goods and immigrants up the St. Lawrence River as far as Montreal. Beyond that point, their further passage to Upper Canada was effectively blocked by a series of rapids beginning with those at Lachine and including several others to just above the Galops rapids where the towns of Prescott, Ontario and Ogdensburg, New York were established. At Montreal, the cargoes and passengers were transferred onto bateaux or onto larger Durham boats for the difficult passage up the rapids of the upper St. Lawrence River. At Kingston, situated at the extreme north-eastern corner of Lake Ontario where the waters of the lake funnel into the St. Lawrence, freight forwarders would warehouse the goods and forward them onward to ports on Lake Ontario and beyond in company with passengers aboard larger schooners and steamboats capable of navigating the waters of the Great Lakes.

Raw materials and partially manufactured goods including lumber, wheat, flour and potash as well as other cargo destined for overseas markets were likewise trans-shipped at Kingston or Prescott for the return trip down the St. Lawrence. Even after railroads began to slowly develop starting in the mid-19th Century, sloops, schooners, and other sailing ships, and later side-wheeler steamboats and propeller-driven steamships, still provided the most efficient and cost-effective mode of transport for cargo and passengers.

On Lake Ontario, there was also a substantial cross-lake shipping trade between the United States and Canada. Salt from Syracuse and later coal from Pennsylvania as well as manufactured goods were shipped north to Toronto, Belleville, Deseronto, Kingston and other Canadian ports, while barley from Prince Edward County, apples from Northumberland County and lumber from mills all across the north shore of Lake Ontario were shipped south to Rochester's port at Charlotte as well as to Oswego and other ports on the U.S. side of the lake. As canals were dug, improved and expanded and as populations throughout the Great Lakes region increased, the amount of cargo, the variety of goods and the number of ships sailing on Lake Ontario increased throughout the 19th Century.

For much of the 19th Century, Kingston was the most important port on the lake. As the primary trans-shipment point for cargoes passing up and down the St. Lawrence River, most ships sailing Lake Ontario would eventually sail into Kingston harbour. After the completion of the Welland Canal, and later the St. Mary's Canal at Sault Ste. Marie, vessels hailing from every major port on the Great Lakes would call at Kingston. However, mariners faced numerous difficulties while transporting goods and passengers by ship to and from this busy port at the eastern end of Lake Ontario. The dangers that made these waters so hazardous were a function of a curious combination of geography, geology, hydrography and, most of all, the weather.

Many early writers penning observations of their journeys made reference to weather conditions while sailing on Lake Ontario. As early as 1788, Deputy Surveyor-General John Collins, commented on the lake and the type of ships suitable for its navigation:

> Vessels sailing on these waters being seldom out of sight of land, the navigation must be considered chiefly as pilotage, to which the use of good natural charts are essential and therefore much wanted. Gales of wind, or squalls, rise suddenly upon the lakes, and from the confined state of the waters, or want of sea-room (as it is called), vessels may in some degree be considered as upon a lee shore, and this seems to point out the necessity for their being built on such a construction as will best enable them to work to windward. Schooners should, perhaps, have the preference, as being rather safer than sloops.... [13]

A "lee shore" is the nearby shore towards which a vessel is being blown by the wind and upon which the vessel could be easily wrecked. In all but a wind directly from the east, vessels sailing the waters of eastern Lake Ontario were almost always on a lee shore.

Isaac Weld tells of his experience sailing on Lake Ontario from Kingston to Niagara in June 1796, and it seems to have been a pleasant and uneventful one:

> Lake Ontario is the most easterly of the four large lakes through which the boundary line passes, that separates the United States from the province of Upper Canada.... This lake is less subject to storms than any of the others, and its waters in general, considering its great expanse, are wonderfully tranquil. [14]

Other writers, however, experienced Lake Ontario very differently. Sailing from Kingston to York in May, 1795, Elizabeth Simcoe, wife of the Lieutenant-Governor, recorded in her journal:

Tues. 12th — I went on board the *Onandaga*, the Government schooner, but the wind coming ahead, we could not sail.

Fri. 15th — We weighed anchor at twelve. After sailing five miles a head wind and a stiff gale arose; we returned to the harbour. At two the wind changed and we sailed again; a wet afternoon.

Sat. 16th — Unpleasant, cold weather, little wind.

Sun. 17th — About 5 p.m. we were off Gibraltar Point at York [Toronto]. It blew extremely hard from the shore....[15]

After having waited three days for a favourable wind, Mrs. Simcoe had spent twenty-seven very rough and wet hours sailing some 140 nautical miles to get back to her home at York.

It was not just sailing vessels that had to contend with the weather. Steamboats first made their appearance on the Great Lakes in 1816 with the construction of the *Frontenac*, captained by James McKenzie, built at Finkle's Shores near Bath. These ships too were subject to storms on Lake Ontario as reported by *The Kingston Chronicle* in September 1820:

The Steam Boat *Frontenac*, which sailed on Monday for York [Toronto] after proceeding as far as Long Point [in Prince Edward County], was compelled by the violence of the gale to return to Kingston on Tuesday evening. She sailed again early yesterday morning, but went no further than the Nine Mile Point [on Simcoe Island, near Kingston], and returned about nine o'clock. The wind for the past two days has blown very strong from the South West. The Steam Boat *Sophia*, which arrived here on Wednesday, is still detained in port by the weather, as well as the *Frontenac*.[16]

The Steam-Boat

FRONTENAC,

JAMES MACKENZIE, Master,

Will in future leave the different Ports on the following days—
VIZ.

Kingston, for York, on the 1st, 11th and 21st days of each month.
York, for Queenston, 3d, 13th and 23d days of each month.
Niagara, for Kingston, 5th, 15th and 25th days of each month.

(6) Steamboat Frontenac. *The Kingston Gazette.*
This newspaper advertisement presents a stylized view of the *Frontenac*, the first steamboat on the Great Lakes. Built at Ernestown (Bath) in 1816, she sailed Lake Ontario until destroyed by fire at Queenston in 1827. Most early steamboats, including the *Frontenac*, were also fully-rigged sailing ships, a detail missing in this engraving. The ship's captain, James McKenzie, would play a role in the construction of the first lighthouses in eastern Lake Ontario. [From *The Kingston Gazette*, October 22, 1819]

Another traveler, Edward Talbot, wrote of Lake Ontario in 1824, that:

> … It is often visited with violent storms, which render its navigation peculiarly dangerous; and though none except experienced seamen ought to be entrusted with the management of the craft which sail upon its wide but deceitful bosom, yet many fellows have obtained the command of vessels who are utterly ignorant of every thing connected with navigation.[17]

The late-season storms were often especially severe at the eastern end of the lake and were a threat to any ship trying to make one last voyage in November or December before winter weather closed navigation until the following spring. The *Kingston Chronicle* described one such December storm on eastern Lake Ontario:

> The [schooner] *Mary Ann* left Kingston in a storm of sleet on Thursday the 9th. instant, laden with goods for York [Toronto], and with a great number of passengers, Having passed the Duck Islands, she was proceeding with a fair wind, though against a heavy sea raised by a previous gale from the westward, when a series of disasters befel her which effectually prevented her from reaching her destined port.
>
> The sleet which in falling, adhered to every part of the sails and rigging, soon rendering them unpliant and the ship became unmanageable.
>
> The jib, foresail and mainsail were successively torn to pieces by the wind, the mainmast was sprung in three places and finally went over the side, carrying with it the greater part of the foremast. In this crippled state the vessel was left totally at the mercy of the elements, and was driven towards the south shore about three miles above Oswego ....
>
> The fate of the *Mary Ann*, is another added to the many, former proofs of the risks attending the navigation of Lake Ontario at this late period, when gales of wind are as frequent as they are violent, and are moreover often accompanied by storms of snow or sleet which becoming encrusted upon the sails and rigging render them unmanageable on the change of wind, and nautical skills useless.
>
> We lament to learn a report, that three other vessels were wrecked in the gale of the 10th inst. on the United States shore.[18]

Relying on all of his skill and experience, Captain Mosier, master of the *Mary Ann*, had set all of his anchors in his attempt to prevent a total wreck. The anchors held and the ship, crew, passengers and cargo were all saved. Other ships however were not so fortunate, and as increased trade due to increased population led to an increase in the number of ships sailing Lake Ontario, so too did the number of wrecks increase along with the tragic loss of life and property.

Had Mosier and other captains been able to better predict the storms that resulted in the loss of so many ships and lives, they might have postponed their departures from the safety of sheltered harbours, and these losses may have been reduced. However, weather forecasting in the early 19th Century was, at best, a crude art. Armed only with a barometer and a thermometer, and with a sharp eye to the speed and direction of the wind, ship captains could only guess at what the weather conditions might be once underway and many miles from a harbour of refuge. Meteorology as a science was still in its infancy by the middle of the 19th Century, and it was not until the 1870's that governments, first in the United States and then in Canada, established the first rudimentary meteorological services to forecast storms and to communicate their predictions to ports on the Great Lakes.[19]

(7) Scene on Lake Ontario, c. 1840. Detail of sketch, Light Tower Near Cobourg, by W.H. Bartlett.
This fanciful sketch shows a steamboat, a sailing ship and a fishing boat dealing with the boisterous nature of Lake Ontario.
[Author's collection]

But it was not the weather alone that made the waters of eastern Lake Ontario so hazardous for mariners. A quick glance at a map of Lake Ontario reveals that its most prominent geographical feature is the Prince Edward peninsula which juts out into the lake and provides no safe harbours for ships sailing an east-west course close to the Canadian shore. From Presqu'ile Bay along the irregular Prince Edward County shoreline to just west of Salmon Point, enormous Ice-Age deposits of sand have created beautiful sand beaches and long stretches of dunes, the most popular of which are known locally as The Sandbanks.[20] While these beaches are very attractive to summer tourists, they are also a sign of dangerously shallow waters that have stranded numerous ships and taken many lives. Further east, beyond Salmon Point and along the shore to False Ducks Island, the sand beaches quickly become rocky limestone reefs and the near-shore waters are littered with dangerous shoals.

For more than forty nautical miles along this coast, there are no sheltered bays or harbours of refuge where ships can wait out a storm. Until the opening of the Murray Canal in 1890 which cut across the narrow neck of the Prince Edward peninsula to connect the open waters of Lake Ontario with the sheltered Inside Passage through the Bay of Quinte, it was only at Presqu'ile Bay and Wellers Bay to the west of the Prince Edward County, and at South Bay on the eastern side of the County, that a ship could find any deep-water shelter from the sometimes severe weather. To sail those forty treacherous miles, the average schooner, given fine weather and a favourable wind, would be at risk for nearly ten hours. Only an experienced captain with a very fast schooner running before a strong breeze might be able to round this dangerous coast in less time.

The *Kingston Gazette* noted that Captain Mosier of the *Mary Ann* averaged a remarkable speed of seven knots in the spring of 1817 (two years before his near-fatal encounter with a December storm) when he sailed the 140 nautical miles from York to Ernestown:

> On Thursday at 3 o'clock P.M. arrived at Ernest Town [Bath], in the Bay of Quinte, the Schooner *Mary Ann*, Capt. J. Mosier, in 20 hours from York [Toronto] .... This is the

seventh voyage which this excellent vessel has made this season, to the great credit of her Master.[21]

At that speed, the *Mary Ann,* might have been able to pass the dangerous Prince Edward shore in as little as six hours.

Early steamboats were less reliant on the direction and speed of wind and currents. Captain McKenzie's *Frontenac,* could reach speeds of up to nine knots as reported by passenger John Howison in 1821:

> The steamboat *Frontenac,* when the wind is favourable, sails nine knots an hour with ease. We fortunately had a strong breeze directly astern, which soon brought us in sight of York, the seat of government, and the capital of Upper Canada.[22]

Like all early steamboats, the Frontenac had not only a steam engine to propel her, but she was a fully-rigged sailing ship. This speed was most likely achieved with the engine operating near full power while running with the wind with all sails flying.

By the 1830's, more reliable and more powerful steam engine technology allowed shipbuilders to dispense with sails altogether. In 1832, the *Montreal Gazette* reported:

> We hear that the new steamer *William IV* was completed last week and started from Gananoque on Saturday last. The first trial of the engine was very satisfactory, reaching the extraordinary speed of from fifteen to sixteen miles per hour.[23]

At sixteen miles per hour — the equivalent of more than 14 knots (26 km/hr) — a very fast steamboat like the 100 horsepower *William IV* could, under ideal conditions, cut the trip around the Prince Edward peninsula to as few as three hours.

Regardless of the type of ship, transit time past Prince Edward County's dangerous shores was considerable. Under adverse conditions with the wind and current running counter to the course of the ship, and with no prospect of seeking refuge in a safe harbour, even the most powerful steamboats would have to wait out a storm at one end of the peninsula or the other, or risk foundering in the open lake or being wrecked on a lee shore.

Most of Lake Ontario, with an average depth of more than 280 feet and up to 46 nautical miles wide, is generally safe to sail in all but the severest of storms. Not so at the eastern end of the lake where, in addition to reefs, sandbars and a lack of harbours along the treacherous Prince Edward shore, a string of islands and shoals stretching right across the lake from Prince Edward Point to Stony Point in New York State present an even more formidable set of hazards for ships. The assessment of the Canadian Hydrographic Service, the government agency responsible for charting Canada's waterways, is that:

> ... in general, Lake Ontario is free from outlying shoals and dangers; the only shoals dangerous to navigation being those found in the vicinity of Prince Edward County, off the Canadian shore, and amongst the islands in the northeastern part of the lake...[24]

The principal islands on the American side of this string of obstacles include Stony Island and Galloo Island, while on the Canadian side there is Main Duck Island, False Ducks Island (also known as Swetman Island) and Timber Island which are collectively known at "The Ducks". Modern bathymetric and hydrographic research has shown that these islands guarding the approaches to the St. Lawrence River are situated on a ridge which follows the edge of an underwater shelf along a line where the deepest part of Lake Ontario suddenly rises up and becomes considerably shallower. This feature is known as the Duck Galloo Ridge.[25] Parts of the ridge rise up abruptly from the lakebed to form rocky, underwater shoals; other portions rise up further to form barely submerged reefs; and at a few spots the ridge is exposed above the lake's surface to form low, rocky islands. Similar, submarine ridges running out into Lake Ontario from the Prince Edward peninsula — Scotch Bonnet Ridge, Salmon Point Ridge and Point Petre Ridge — combine to create often difficult, sometimes dangerous and occasionally deadly sailing conditions.

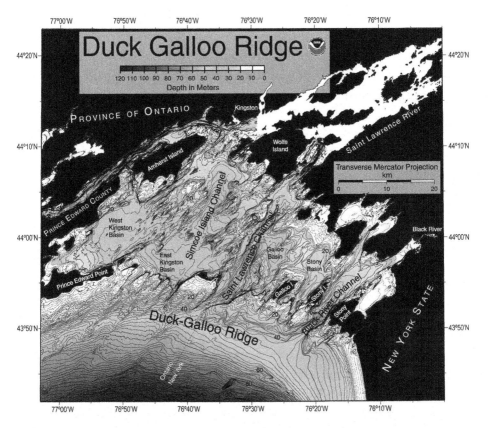

(8) Bathymetry of the Duck Galloo Ridge, 1999. NOAA Great Lakes Environmental Research Lab with the Canadian Hydrographic Service and NOAA National Ocean Service.

This chart shows how Lake Ontario gets narrower and shallower along the line of islands extending from Prince Edward County, Ontario, to New York State. [Courtesy of U.S. National Oceanic and Atmospheric Administration, National Geophysical Data Center - NOAA]

The abrupt west-to-east shallowing of Lake Ontario in the vicinity of the Duck Galloo ridge — from 500 feet to 60 feet over a distance of only sixteen nautical miles — is compounded by the sudden narrowing of the lake to barely twenty-five nautical miles between Prince Edward Point and Stony Point. With Lake Ontario's general east-west orientation, and the prevailing winds coming from the west, this long fetch of the lake often results in extreme conditions at the eastern end. This geography creates a significant funneling effect of the weather in eastern Lake Ontario where waves of up to six meters high have been measured.[26]

All of these factors are further compounded by the annual onslaught of severe gales as described by the U.S. National Oceanographic and Atmospheric Administration (NOAA):

> Gales are most likely from October through December and blow out of the southwest through northwest. This is particularly true at the east end of the lake, where a funneling effect may occur with west and southwest winds, which prevail throughout most of the year. As these winds encounter land, on either side of the lake, near the Thousand Islands, they are accelerated. A moderate blow in midlake often becomes a dangerous gale in this restricted area.... The strongest sustained measured wind on the lake was west-north-westerly at 50 knots. This short period record (17 years) occurred in November. Since extremes along the shore range from 50 to 65 knots, it could be expected that an extreme on the lake could reach 90 knots.[27]

Contemporary, anecdotal accounts reveal that a large number of ships were lost on Lake Ontario at the end of the annual eight-month shipping season, especially in November and December, when storms were usually at their worst and captains and owners of vessels were desperately trying to deliver one or two more loads before ice formed in the harbours. These accounts are corroborated by an analysis of some of the only statistical evidence available, courtesy of researcher David Swayze who has compiled comprehensive Great Lakes shipwreck data from documentary sources.[28]

The data indicates that between 1799 and 1929, of the 415 ships that were lost on Lake Ontario (excluding those sunk in harbours, or temporarily stranded or grounded), 38% of them were lost in the last five weeks of the shipping season, in November and the beginning of December. Of these 158 late-season losses, almost one-third occurred in the area between Presqu'ile Point and The Ducks. Most of the lost vessels were sailing ships, but perhaps surprisingly, more than one-quarter of them were steamboats of various types.[29]

These heavier losses at the end of the season often occurred during snowstorms, many of which were quite severe and sometimes the result of what is known now as "lake-effect snow". This weather condition can be summarized as:

> A distinctive type of winter weather found in relatively few places. It's native to some but not all areas bordering the Great Lakes....
>
> Snowbelt maps reveal several key ingredients in the recipe for lake-effect snow, most notably a leeward location. Because winds across the region are generally from the west or northwest, snowfall is likely in areas immediately east and southeast of the Great Lakes whenever frigid air sweeps down from Canada and picks up moisture as it crosses a large, relatively warm lake. Large inland lakes are huge reservoirs of heat that warm up slowly in summer and cool down gradually in late fall and winter....
>
> Because the lake surface is much warmer, typically by more than 20 Fahrenheit degrees, extensive evaporation occurs when a moving air mass is in contact with the lake for a substantial distance. Although its speed across the lake might shorten or prolong the transfer of moisture, a significant lake-effect snowstorm typically requires relatively long contact distance, or fetch....

Lake Ontario, with average and maximum depths of 282 and 802 feet, respectively, stores much more heat and remains largely open to evaporation throughout the winter. In most years, no more than 21 percent of its surface freezes over.

Not surprisingly, the heaviest snows occur when the lake is relatively warm and evaporation more intense.[30]

Captain Mosier was one of those unfortunate mariners who experienced, first hand, the effects of this type of weather when the *Mary Ann* narrowly escaped being wrecked during a lake-effect snowstorm in 1819. A similar storm hit eastern Lake Ontario in 1860 and left more than thirty-five ships damaged, ashore, or wrecked with at least sixteen lives lost.[31] The November gale was described briefly in the Kingston newspaper, *The Daily British Whig*:

> The violent gale and accompanying snow-storm of Friday and Saturday ... have been attended with serious disaster in this locality. The high wind of Saturday abated somewhat on Sunday, but the weather was sufficiently boisterous to create apprehension for the safety of vessels afloat....
>
> Masters of vessels describe the gale as being one of the most furious ever known in this quarter. Never were so many vessels known to be ashore in this locality. The wind calmed down on Monday morning, but in the afternoon it again rose to a gale from the South, accompanied with snow.[32]

Further compounding the dangers resulting from this combination of geographical features and meteorological patterns was another factor which persisted throughout much of the 19th Century: the lack of navigational charts.

Even though many of the early ship captains had been trained on ships at sea and so brought with them to the Great Lakes their experience of ocean voyages and a familiarity with the use of charts, navigation on Lake Ontario for much of the 19th Century was accomplished without the use of this important tool. Instead, captains relied almost entirely on their compass and on "dead-reckoning" which was based on many years of experience and knowledge handed down from captain to mate.

This mindset was described by D.D. Calvin III, name-sake and grandson of the 19th Century ship-salvager and lumber merchant of Garden Island:

> There are two fundamental differences between navigation on the Great Lakes and at sea; both arise from the relatively restricted area of the lakes. One is that on the lakes all navigation is on compass courses and by "dead reckoning"; positions are never determined by observation with instruments, as at sea. The other is that a lake vessel must be thought of as always on a lee shore; at sea, a ship may run before a gale for days, but a few hours is the most that can be hoped for on the lakes....
>
> The typical lake captain is a man who has come up from the lower deck. There are no training ships for lake officers: they get their training in the University of Hard Knocks.... A man begins as deckhand, becomes watchman, then wheelsman, gets his mate's papers and finally his master's certificate. He has no knowledge of navigation in its salt-water sense, his knowledge is rather that of the highly specialized technique of the lakes — of navigating big steamers in crowded waters, day and night, and of using every minute of time to advantage.[33]

Typically, as a captain sailed out of a harbour, he would take a bearing with his compass, set his ship on the correct heading, and then order the crew to keep a vigilant lookout for known landmarks as they neared islands or the mainland. Once a landmark was spotted, another bearing would be taken and the ship's heading adjusted as necessary. For instance, when sailing from Oswego to Kingston, a course towards The Ducks of N. ¾ W. (North, three-quarter West, or 348°45'0") would be set.[34] Within two hours, the ship would be out of sight of land and, in favourable weather, after sailing another four hours on the original heading, the lookouts would hope to spot in the distance Main Duck Island off the starboard bow and the low shoreline of Prince Edward County's Long Point to port. Along the way, the experienced captain would have been adjusting his course by dead-reckoning to correct for any leeway due to the normal westerly crosswind and the west-to-east current. In addition, he may have been using a distance-log (either a chip log or later a patent-log with an impellor) to verify how many miles his ship had sailed as well as a hand-lead to take soundings at any points where the depth of the water was questionable.

Captain Howard Patterson's *Illustrated Nautical Dictionary,* published in 1891, is a useful reference for these nautical terms:

> Dead-reckoning. Finding the track which the ship has made and the distance thereon by correcting the courses sailed for leeway, variation, and deviation.... [p. 270]
>
> Hand Lead. A conical shape length of lead weighing from 7 to 14 pounds, used for sounding in water of less than 20 fathoms.... The cavity in the end of the lead is to be filled with tallow or soap, so that a sample of the bottom may be obtained. [p. 84]
>
> Lee-way. The amount a vessel loses by being forced sideways through the water owing to the pressure of the wind on the vessel's sails, side, and rigging. [p. 198]
>
> Log. The old-fashioned log is an apparatus employed for ascertaining the ship's rate of sailing. It consists of the log-line, log-chip, reel, and two sand-glasses of 14 and 28 seconds respectively. [p. 114][35]

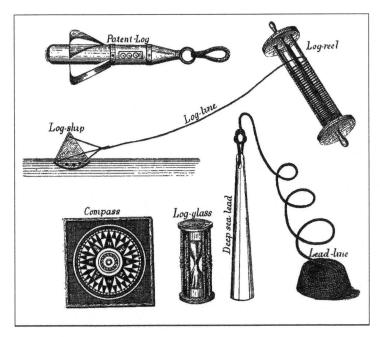

(9) 19ᵗʰ Century navigation instruments. Illustrations by Harper, Harper, Outing and Paasch.
Navigation on the Great Lakes relied mostly on the ship captain's experience combined with his use of the compass to determine course and heading, the log-line to determine distance travelled, and the lead-line to determine water depth.
[From *Patterson's Illustrated Nautical Dictionary*, 1891]

After passing Main Duck and Galloo islands, the captain would set a course that would take the ship near the low-lying outcropping of rock known as Pigeon Island and then on to the next landfall at Simcoe Island's Nine Mile Point, the entrance to the outer harbour at Kingston. From there, carefully avoiding the shoals around Snake Island as well as those closer into the wharves, the ship would arrive at her destination.

For much of the 19ᵗʰ Century, navigating in this manner on the Great Lakes was common practice. It was also common enough for ships to be grounded or wrecked because of the captain's inexperience or because of a dead-reckoning miscalculation. Also, during a gale or a snowstorm, or at night or in a fog, navigating in this way was usually impossible. Even after land had been sighted, it was often difficult to determine the ship's precise position unless a well-known landmark were readily discernable. In the example of the ship bound Oswego for Kingston, a heavy blow from the east could easily sweep the ship well west of Main Duck Island and bring her perilously close to the dangerous shoals known as Harris, Williams and Psyche, or even onto False Ducks Island itself. Likewise a heavy blow from the west could wreck the ship on Galloo Island or on Charity Shoal. Without a proper chart to help him determine his position, the captain would have to keep sailing in the general direction of his intended destination until a known landmark was sighted and only then could the ship's course be corrected.

While many maps of Lake Ontario had been in existence since the 17th Century, none of them showed any hydrographic details that would be useful to mariners. The first known hydrographic survey of the lake had been made by Augustus Ford, a merchant seaman from Rhode Island. At age nine during the American War for Independence, Ford served aboard an American blockade runner sailing to the West Indies to take on provisions for General Washington's Continental Army. After the war, he was a crewmember on the first U.S. ship to sail to China.[36] It was on these voyages that Ford would have learned the importance of nautical charts.

At age twenty-five, he settled at Oswego on Lake Ontario. For the following twelve years, as described in a letter he wrote later, he sailed the lake recording depth soundings and compass bearings wherever he went:

> I arrived at Oswego on the 7th July in 1797 one year after the British had evacuated Fort Ontario at that place, I took charge of the first vessel on the American side of the lake. I was entirely ignorant of the lake, having no chart or course or distance from one port to another, and no pilot to be found and a lake of 200 miles in length and from 40 to 55 miles wide most all bard harbors [blocked by sand bars] and great many dangerous shoal. I then commenced keeping a journal by taking the soundings by keeping the hand lead in constant use when there was a chance, and examined all shoals taking the bearings and distances from

the main land and courses from one point to another by different angles. I not only sounded all the British side and American but through the middle of the lake and this a constant employ for 12 years.[37]

In 1810, Ford was commissioned as an officer in the U.S. Navy, and during the War of 1812 he drafted copies of his chart for use by Commodore Chauncey, commander of the U.S. fleet on Lake Ontario. Although Chauncey promised on several occasions during the war to have Ford's chart published at government expense, it was not until more than two decades later, in 1836, that his *Chart of Lake Ontario from Actual Survey* was engraved and published at New York and distributed commercially. This was the first comprehensive navigational chart of Lake Ontario.

Immediately after the War of 1812, other charts showing small portions of the Canadian side of the lake had been prepared for the British Admiralty from the hydrographic surveys of Captain William Fitz-William Owen and his assistant, Lieutenant Henry Wolsey Bayfield[38] of the Royal Navy, who together had made a detailed survey of the upper St. Lawrence River and the north-eastern shore of Lake Ontario as far as the Presqu'ile peninsula. Even as late as 1898, the British Admiralty had published only four hydrographic charts which included very small portions of Lake Ontario.[39] Ford's navigational chart, however, was the first one that included depth soundings of near-shore waters around the entire lake as well as accurate measurements of distances from harbour to harbour.

The publication of this chart should have been an achievement cheered by every mariner sailing on Lake Ontario. An accurate chart showing distances, bearings and water depths should have been seen as an essential tool to be coveted by every shipmaster and ship owner. However, it seems that many mariners, especially those on the American side of the lake, clung to their old habits of sailing by dead-reckoning and compass bearings alone, for very few even bothered to obtain a copy of Ford's chart. This fact was lamented by an anonymous writer in a letter to the editor of the *Oswego County Whig* in 1838:

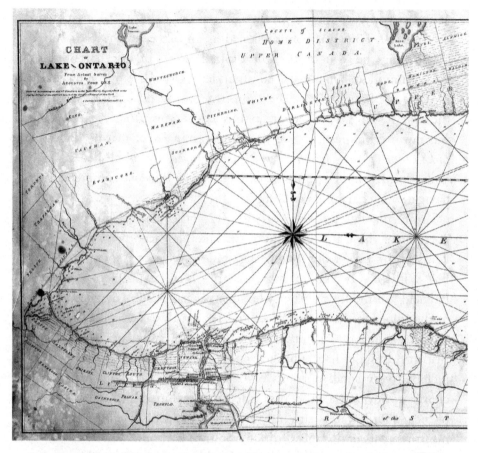

(10) Augustus Ford's Chart of Lake Ontario, 1836. Lithographed by N. Currier, New York.

This was the first hydrographic chart of Lake Ontario published. In spite of being produced in 1836, this chart does not show the Point Petre lighthouse which had been built three years earlier, but it does show the False Ducks Island lighthouse (1829) and the Nine Mile Point lighthouse (1833). Original is 24" x 55".

[Courtesy of Library and Archives Canada, NMC11314]

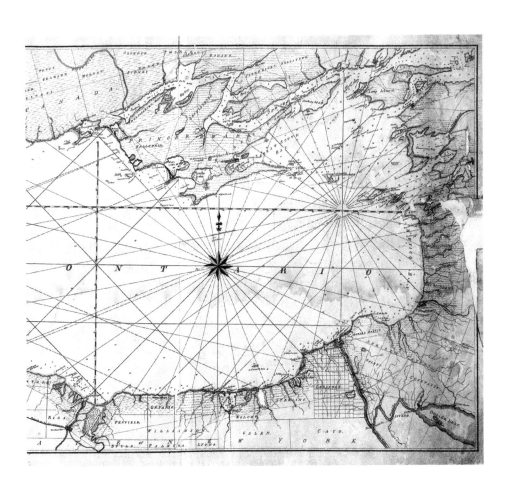

Chart of Lake Ontario — The following communication is upon a very important subject to that part of the community which navigate our lake, or do business upon its waters. The chart here alluded to, by every one who has examined it, is spoken of in the highest terms, and is afforded at so trifling a sum as to place it within the reach of all. We understand that on the other side, so convinced are they of its utility, that scarcely a Canadian captain is without one; and we are at a loss to account for the tardiness of our own captains and others in providing themselves with this preservative from danger. There is such a thing as being "a penny wise, and a pound foolish," and this looks very much like it. The charts can be obtained at the book store of James Sloan in this village, and we should think the editors in the different ports on Lake Ontario, would subserve the public interest by directing the attention of captains and ship owners to this subject.

FOR THE OSWEGO COUNTY WHIG.

Sir - I am an old sailor, have had much practical experience, and for twenty-five years have navigated Lake Ontario. I have had my mind upon a subject for a long time, that I wished to call the attention of Masters and owners of vessels to; and I shall ask the use of your columns to do so, as it is a matter in which the public, too, are very interested.

I have carefully examined a *Chart of Lake Ontario*, made by Capt. Augustus Ford of the U. S. Navy, and cannot but express my great surprise that this Chart is not used on board of every vessel upon the Lake; and I should think that every person who owns a vessel or is in any way concerned with the navigation of Lake Ontario, would have one of these Charts hanging in his counting-house, or some other place where constant reference might be had to it. I have examined it very particularly with regard to its correctness, and I have no hesitation in saying that the courses, distances, soundings, harbors, shoals, and islands, are very correctly laid down. This I say from my own knowledge and observation, and I have heard many of the Lake Captains make the same remark.

I have been out five or six days together in a thick fog, sometimes wind blowing heavy and again light and variable - then I found use for a chart. I was once out in a violent snow storm two days, bound from Niagara to Kingston. The first land we saw after leaving Niagara, was the east end of the False Ducks, not more than a cable's length [180 meters] from the Island. Had we had a Chart on board we should not have been so near losing the vessel, and perhaps our lives, as we were. Capt. Murky, of the schooner *York*, from Toronto, bound to Kingston, was castaway on the Devil's Nose [in 1799]. Afterwards, Capt. Murky was lost on board the *Washington*, with all hands [in 1806]. Captain Parker, of the *Speed* [H.M. Schooner *Speedy*], was lost with 23 souls on board, off Prosaic Isle [Presqu'ile, in 1807]. There is no doubt in my mind, that if the masters of these vessels had been provided with Capt. Ford's Chart, not only one of these terrible disasters and loss of lives would have happened. I could give a great many more instances.

My object is to call the attention of masters and owners of vessels to the use of these Charts. I believe a great amount of property and many lives would be saved if they were more used and better understood. I have been informed that Capt. Ford has been to great pains and expense in making this Chart, and that it has cost him much time and money. They are offered for sale at the trifling price of three dollars. I should think every man who is in any way concerned in the navigation of the Lake should have one for every day reference. (unsigned)

Oswego, May 25, 1838.[40]

It would be almost forty years before another comprehensive and detailed chart of Lake Ontario would be produced. In the meantime, a number of cruising guides were privately published describing the ports and harbours around the lake and providing sailing directions from port to port. The first of these guides was *The Harbours and Ports of Lake Ontario* compiled in 1857 by Toronto resident and yachtsman, Dr. Edward Hodder, commodore of the Royal Canadian Yacht Club.[41] Hodder's intention for producing his guide was, as he stated in the book's dedication:

> For the Members of the Royal Canadian Yacht Club... in the hope that it may not only interest, but also excite and encourage in them a taste for that invigorating, truly British pastime, and manly sport, Yachting....
>
> May it also be useful to them, by giving such sure and accurate information relative to the various Harbours and Ports on Lake Ontario, as may create in them a fondness for cruising, from the conviction, that in any weather they can speedily reach some haven of refuge where their gallant little Barks may, in shelter and in safety, ride out the fiercest storm.[42]

Hodder's guide appears to have been quite accurate as much of it was based on the earlier hydrographic surveys of Fitz William Owen together with Hodder's own observations. While it contained much information that would be of interest to commercial mariners, including detailed sketches showing the plan of many harbours, there is no indication that his guide was used by anyone other than private yachtsmen.

This book was followed some fifteen years later by a similar guide, *Atkin's Pocket Compass of the Harbors, Ports, Lighthouses, and Buoys of Lake Ontario and River St. Lawrence*, published in 1871 by Francis F. Atkin of Oswego, New York. From his comments in the preface of the book, it appears that Atkin wrote his guide specifically for the shipping trade:

The need of a reliable pocket manual as a book of reference, for the convenience of those whose business is closely connected with the navigation of Lake Ontario, has long been felt.... We are not aware that there is in existence a single work upon the subject, of sufficient dimension to be carried upon the person. The object of this little work, is to supply this long felt need....

The aim of the author has been to furnish all of the necessary general information, pertaining to the navigation of Lake Ontario, which is absolutely required, in the smallest possible space....

The work is submitted to the navigators of Lake Ontario with full assurance of its correctness, and the consciousness of its ability to supply the wants of such a work so long looked for.[43]

Atkin relied heavily on Augustus Ford's chart which had been published thirty-five years earlier. Unlike Hodder's guide, Atkin's book contained no harbour sketches but only written descriptions of the harbours around Lake Ontario.

Ford's chart remained the only comprehensive navigational chart of the lake until the U.S. Army Corps of Engineers published a new chart of Lake Ontario in 1877. The United States Congress had established the U.S. Lake Survey in 1841 when the Corps of Topographical Engineers was directed to begin hydrographic work on the Great Lakes beginning with a survey of Lake Michigan.[44] The Corps of Topographical Engineers was later amalgamated with the U.S. Army Corps of Engineers and it began a hydrographic survey of Lake Ontario in 1857.[45] However, the survey was not completed until 1875 and the comprehensive chart of Lake Ontario was finally published in 1877.[46]

This was the first chart that both described the most common navigational routes or sailing directions, and also graphically depicted these "shipping lanes" crossing Lake Ontario from port to port.

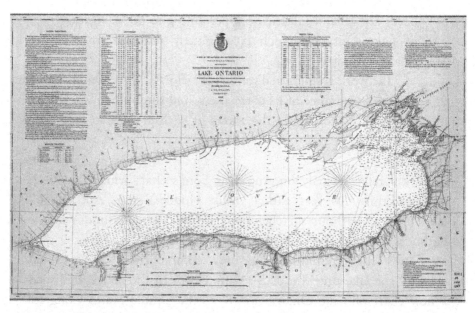

(11) U.S Lake Survey, Chart of Lake Ontario, 1877. Survey of the Northern and Northwestern Lakes – Lake Ontario, by the U.S. Corps of Engineers.

This was the second comprehensive hydrographic chart of Lake Ontario to be published.

[Courtesy of NOAA's Office of Coast Survey Historical Map & Chart Collection http://historicalcharts.noaa.gov, LC00061_00_1877_LS]

By the beginning of the 20th Century, reliable navigational charts and comprehensive guides of Lake Ontario were readily available. Nevertheless, even if these charts were used regularly, one additional factor complicated the navigation of Lake Ontario still further: a number of relatively strong magnetic anomalies in the eastern Lake Ontario region which caused compass needles to deviate substantially from Magnetic North so as to throw any navigator well off course.

All navigators would have been familiar with magnetic variation: the difference in the compass reading between magnetic North and true North; and most would have known about magnetic deviation caused by cargoes like iron ore or railroad rails carried on board their ship. Patterson defines magnetic deviation in his *Illustrated Nautical Dictionary* as, "The deflection of the compass needle from the magnetic meridian owing to the attraction of the ship's iron, or elements of magnetism in the cargo."[47] However, until the end of the 19th Century most mariners would have had no understanding whatsoever of the significant magnetic deviation resulting from localized, in-ground iron ore deposits, and there were a number of these magnetic anomalies in the eastern Lake Ontario region.

In 1894, a surprising discovery of substantial magnetic deviation was made at Kingston:

> MAGNETIC DISTURBANCE has been found to exist at several places along the shores as well as on lake Ontario itself. Observations made at and near Kingston, Ont., by Major J.B. Cochrane, Assistant Director of Military Surveys, Department of Militia and Defence, then professor at the Royal Military College, Kingston, show ... that over a considerable area the compass variation varies from 16º E. to 30ºW. The observations were made during the months of March and April of 1894 and 1895 with a solar compass.[48]

The significance of this discovery was highlighted by the United States Hydrographic Office in 1895 when they issued the following notice:

It is very plain that vessels navigating at the eastern end of Lake Ontario cannot rely closely on their compass bearings. In the neighborhood of the Main Duck Islands, it has been frequently observed that there is a great deviation of the compass, sometimes as much as a point at a time. This renders navigating very uncertain in thick weather. This deviation is due, most probably, to numerous superficial deposits of iron ore. An examination of the magnetic observations that have been made in Ontario shows that there are numerous localities in the region immediately above Lake Ontario where there are considerable local irregularities. The dips at Kingston and Belleville, at the foot of Lake Ontario and at Prescott, on the St. Lawrence River, are among the most irregular recorded on the Magnetic Survey of Canada, and it is certain that both the compass and the dipping needle will be subject to notable and irregular local influences in the eastern portion of the lake.[49]

Until these magnetic anomalies became better understood so that navigators could compensate for them, they added to the hazards of sailing the waters of eastern Lake Ontario.

(12) Ship's compass. Illustration by Harper, Harper, Outing and Paasch. [From *Patterson's Illustrated Nautical Dictionary*, 1891.]

The overwhelming effect of all of these factors combined — weather, geography, hydrography and geology — was the loss of many ships in eastern Lake Ontario in the 19th and early 20th centuries.

The dangerous reputation of this part of the lake was well known by mariners and often reported in newspapers around the Lakes. One such dramatic, although exaggerated statement appeared in Belleville's *Daily Ontario* newspaper in 1879:

> Two-thirds, or more of the shipwrecks that occur on Lake Ontario take place between Point Petre and the Main Ducks. This reference holds good on both sides. Sailors dread the terrible sweep of wind and wave that beset them there, especially towards the close of navigation. Owing to frequent shallows sailing is treacherous and the motion of the water difficult to contend with.[50]

While there is insufficient evidence to support the newspaper's claim of such a high proportion of shipwrecks in these waters around Prince Edward County, there is no doubt that hundreds of ships grounded, stranded, wrecked or foundered around the Prince Edward peninsula with considerable loss of lives, cargo and vessels over the last two centuries. Willis Metcalf, in his important reference work, *Canvas and Steam on Quinte Waters*, lists more than sixty shipwrecks in these waters,[51] while the dive organization "Save Ontario Shipwrecks", claims to have identified more than fifty sunken vessels in the area.[52] David Swayze cites eighty or so wrecks that were total losses in these waters,[53] not including hundreds of ships that were temporarily grounded or stranded and later recovered, and not accounting for many ships that simply "sailed through a crack in the lake" and disappeared without a trace.

As early as 1803, the government of Upper Canada had realized that lighthouses, already successfully established on seacoasts in many parts of the world, would be a benefit to shipping on the Great Lakes. These aids to navigation were a proven technology that could help guide ships to and from the three harbours that were then in use on the Canadian side of Lake Ontario: Niagara at the mouth of the Niagara River, York on the north shore of Lake Ontario, and Kingston at the entrance to the St. Lawrence River. Accordingly, the provincial legislature authorized the construction of three lighthouses:

*An Act... to establish a FUND
for the erection and repairing of LIGHT HOUSES
(5th March, 1803)*

... And whereas it will be necessary and essential to the safety of vessels, boats, rafts and other craft passing from Lake Ontario into the river Niagara and passing by the Isle called Isle Forest [Simcoe Island], and likewise into the Port of York [Toronto]...

The Government of this Province is hereby authorized... to lay out and expend, or cause to be laid out and expended, in the erection and keeping in repair, and other incidental charges attending three Light-Houses, one to be erected and built upon the south-westernmost point of a certain island called Isle Forest, situated about three leagues [nine statute miles] from the town of Kingston, in the Midland District; another upon Mississagua point, at the entrance of the Niagara River, near to the Town of Niagara [Niagara-on-the-Lake], and the other upon Gibraltar Point.[54]

Upon careful reading of this early statute, it appears that the legislators were motivated as much by a desire to increase scarce provincial revenues through the collection of lighthouse duties as they were by concerns for the safety of the ships and their crews, passengers and cargoes. Nevertheless, the legislation did lead to the construction of the first lighthouses on the Great Lakes; one on Mississauga Point at the mouth of the Niagara River in 1804, and another on Gibraltar Point at York in 1808.

The third lighthouse, the one proposed for eastern Lake Ontario on Isle Forest (also called Gage Island, and later renamed Simcoe Island), at the entrance to the outer harbour at Kingston, was somehow overlooked at that time, and almost twenty years would pass before the question of building a lighthouse at the eastern end of the lake would again come before the provincial legislature. This grave oversight contributed to the loss of many ships, many tons of cargo, and many lives in this region where the effects of unforgiving geography and horrific weather were compounded by a lack of charts and the navigational disorientation caused by local magnetic anomalies.

THE ISLAND LIGHTHOUSE, 1808.

(13) Gibraltar Point Lighthouse, York (Toronto), erected 1808. Artist unknown. This was the second lighthouse established on the Great Lakes. As of 2015, this lighthouse is still standing on the Toronto Islands and it is the oldest remaining Great Lakes lighthouse.
[From *Robertson's Landmarks of Toronto*, Vol. 2. 1896]

While 19th Century mariners may not have been able to articulate all of the details of the geographical, meteorological, hydrographical and geological factors which combined to make the waters of eastern Lake Ontario an extremely dangerous place to sail a ship, they certainly would have known from their own experience that there were considerably more navigational hazards in this region than almost anywhere else on the Great Lakes. In an attempt to mitigate these dangers, ship owners and captains continually clamoured for the construction of lighthouses to improve the "safety and convenience of navigation".

The result was that over the course of almost a century, a dozen lake lights were built on the shores of eastern Lake Ontario to guide ships around the Prince Edward peninsula and past The Ducks. By providing ships with safer passage through these treacherous waters, these lake lights in turn provided the impetus for increased trade into and out of numerous harbours which were established all along the Canadian shore, and particularly along the "Inside Passage" where ports flourished and where an additional thirty harbour lights and passage lights were built as an integral part of this extensive network of eastern Lake Ontario lighthouses.

CHAPTER 2

The Inside Passage

A safe and commodious harbour
(George Heriot, 1805.)

The sprawling Prince Edward peninsula which presents so many hazards to navigation on its dangerous Lake Ontario side, also has a calmer, safer, more welcoming side. This is the Bay of Quinte; a long, meandering channel of generally smooth sailing, which is at the centre of a relatively safe "Inside Passage" of sheltered waters connecting Kingston harbour with Presqu'ile Bay.

Many early chroniclers described the virtues of this tranquil Inside Passage:

> Having passed Ernest-town [west of Kingston], the bay of Quinte commences with Fredericksburgh, to the north at its entrance, and Marysburgh, to the south.
>
> This bay, which may be considered throughout as a harbour, is formed by a large peninsula consisting of the townships of Ameliasburgh, Sophiasburgh, and Marysburgh, extending easterly from an isthmus, where

there is a portage, at the head, or west end of the bay, to Point Pleasant [Pleasant Point], the easternmost extremity of the peninsula, opposite to Amherst Island. [William Smyth, 1799][1]

The bay of Quinté .... affords, throughout its winding extent, a safe and commodious harbour, sheltered from the storms by which the lake is frequently agitated. [George Heriot, 1805][2]

A little to the westward of Kingston is the Bay of Quinté, very singularly formed between the irregular peninsula of Prince Edward county on the south, and the main land of the Midland district on the north. This inlet affords to vessels safe shelter from the heavy gales frequently experienced on the lake. [Joseph Bouchette, 1831][3]

(14) Scene on the Bay of Quinte, c. 1830. Watercolour on paper, Bay of Quinte, by Thomas Burrowes.
The stone mills at Glenora in Prince Edward County are on the left. The Adolphustown shore In Lennox & Addington County is on the right.
[Courtesy of Archives of Ontario]

In his book, *Canada and the Canadians*, Sir Richard Bonnycastle gave one of the most extensive descriptions of the Inside Passage when he wrote about his voyage of several days along this waterway in 1846:

> I left Kingston in autumn, ... and embarked on board the *Prince Edward* steamboat, [in command of] Captain Bonter, for the mouth of the river Trent, in the Bay of Quinte. First you steam along the front of the famous city of Kingston, which now presents something of an imposing front, from the waters of the St. Lawrence, which here leave Lake Ontario and contract into two channels between which are Long Island [Wolfe Island] and some others....
>
> A few miles above Kingston, you enter the Bay of Quinte by passing between the main land and Amherst Isle, or the Isle of Tanti, ...on which are now extensive and flourishing farms. At the east end of the Isle of Tanti are the Lower Gap and the Brothers, two rocky islets famous for black bass fishing and for a deep rolling sea, which makes a landsman very sick indeed in a gale of wind. After passing this..., the bay[the North Channel], an arm rather of Lake Ontario, becomes very smooth and peaceable for several miles, until you leave the pleasant little village of Bath....
>
> After passing Bath, the Upper Gap... gives you another tremendous rolling in blowing weather, and the expanse of Lake Ontario is seen to the left, with the tortuous bay of Quinte again to the right; this arm of the lake being made for fifty or sixty miles more by the fertile district of Prince Edward, an island of great extent, and one of the oldest of the British settlements in Upper Canada....
>
> The vessel calls at several small settlements, and stops for the night at Hallowell or Picton, for the village has both names. This is a most picturesque locality, in a nook of the bay, with undulating hills and sharp ravines, a handsome church and other public edifices, and a large and thriving population.... and after sleeping there, go on to Belleville....

Belleville, the county town of the Victoria district, is situated on the shores of this bay, and, from an insignificant village in 1837, has risen in 1846 to the rank of a large and flourishing town, the main street of which surprised me not a little by its extent, the beauty of its buildings, and the display of its shops....

We steamed on to the Trent river through a glorious corn and apple country, and arrived there in time to meet my young friend, and to proceed in our waggon to Brighton, a few miles westward on the Toronto road, where we slept.

Trent Port, or Trent village, is situated on both banks of the exitus of the Trent river into the Bay of Quinte, and is remarkable for two things: as being the intended outlet of one of the finest back countries in Canada, by a gigantic canal [the Trent Canal], which was to open Lake Huron to Ontario, through a succession of inland lakes and rivers, but which noble scheme was nipped in the bud after several of the locks had been excavated, and very many thousands of pounds expended. It is now remarkable only for its long, covered wooden bridge, and the quantity of lumber, i.e... deals, plank, staves, square timber, and logs floating on the tranquil water for exportation.

Brighton is a little pleasant high-road hamlet, with two inns, and no outs, as it is not a place of trade, excepting as far as a small sawmill is concerned; but this will change, for it is near Presqu'ile, the only natural harbour on Lake Ontario's Canada shore, from Toronto to Kingston, or from one end to the other. Here the Bay of Quinte approaches the lake so close, that a canal of four or five miles only is requisite, through a natural level, in order to have a safe and sheltered voyage from Kingston without going at all into the real and dangerous lake, which is every where beset with "ducks and drakes," as its rocky and treacherous islets are called.

This canal, which may be constructed easily for about five and twenty thousand pounds, must soon be made, and the bar of Presqu'ile Harbour deepened, so as to ensure a shelter for vessels in the furious gales of October and November.[4]

Sir Richard's extensive narrative not only describes the entire route of the Inside Passage, including the scenery and many of the growing towns that had created harbours in the sheltered waters of the Bay of Quinte, but he also refers to the necessity of digging a canal across the isthmus at The Carrying Place. This is where the Prince Edward peninsula is connected with the rest of the mainland and where the headwaters of the Bay of Quinte are a separated from Wellers Bay and its outlet to Lake Ontario, a mere two and a half kilometers away. For most of the 19th Century, this was the one significant obstacle that prevented the Inside Passage from being used as a regular shipping lane along the north shore of Lake Ontario.

In the late 18th Century, an early settler at The Carrying Place, Asa Weller, had established a profitable portage service across the isthmus as described in 1810:

Most of the traders, with small vessels who go from Kingston to York, Niagara, or Detroit, pass up this bay to the head which is only 1 mile and 3 quarters from a small lake called Willow's Lake [Wellers Bay] that puts into Lake Ontario, and here, the vessels are carried across by means of wheels and oxen. The road is quite level and sandy. Those traders which come down Lake Ontario generally cross this carrying place into the bay....[5]

Weller had built a simple wooden railway on which a wagon pulled by a team of oxen could carry a bateau, a Durham boat, or a load of lumber across the isthmus. Asa's cousin, William from Cobourg, ran a stagecoach business to transport passengers and limited amounts of freight along the main road from The Carrying Place to York.[6] The road, like all early roads in the province, was generally in very poor condition and normally passable only in the driest part of mid-summer or by sleigh in frozen mid-winter.[7] It was the lack of a short canal at The Carrying Place that forced ships sailing between York or Niagara and Kingston to risk the open waters of Lake Ontario in order to get past the Prince Edward peninsula.

For many decades, there was talk of completing this "Inside Passage" by digging a canal across this isthmus to connect the Bay of Quinte with either Presqu'ile Bay or Wellers Bay, both of which had openings into Lake Ontario. Often referred to as the Simcoe Canal, or Murray Canal, it had been marked on maps as early as 1800.[8] However, it was not until 1882 that the Government of Canada finally allocated the funds to build the Murray Canal, and it was eight years later before the canal was fully opened to shipping.

As a result of this delay of nearly a century, ships had to continue to navigate the perilous route around the Prince Edward peninsula in the open waters of Lake Ontario, and a number of those ships were lost as a result. It is impossible to determine how many ships were lost on the lake because of the long delay in digging the Murray Canal. Certainly any ship sailing between the St. Lawrence River and Toronto or Niagara would have benefitted from the completion of this Inside Passage, as would ships sailing from Charlotte or Oswego to most ports on the Bay of Quinte. An analysis of David Swayze's extensive data shows that, of the fifty-eight ships documented as total losses due to storms on Lake Ontario between Presqu'ile Point and Nine Mile Point from 1798 to 1889, at least seventeen of them would likely have been spared, along with fifty-five lives, had the Murray Canal been in operation at the beginning of the 19th Century instead of at its end.[9]

Well before the canal was begun, settlements were established on many of the rivers where they emptied into the Bay of Quinte. These settlements grew into towns such as Trent Port (later named Trenton), Belleville, Northport, Mill Point (later named Deseronto), Napanee, Hallowell and Picton as well as Bath and Portsmouth situated further along the Inside Passage towards Kingston. These towns prospered as their natural harbours were improved to provide ports for the

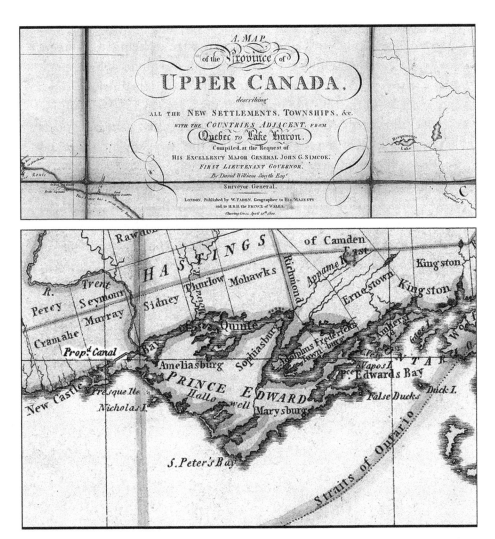

(15) Location of the proposed Murray Canal, 1800. Detail from *A Map of the Province of Upper Canada* by David William Smyth.

A canal connecting the western end of the Bay of Quinte with Lake Ontario had been proposed by Lieutenant-Governor John G. Simcoe as early as 1796. Marked on this map as "Propd. Canal", land between the Bay of Quinte and Presqu'ile Bay had been reserved for canal purposes. Digging of the canal did not start until 1882.

[Courtesy of David Rumsey Map Collection]

increasing number of schooners and steamboats whose safe passage from all across the Great Lakes would be facilitated by the building of lighthouses to guide them through eastern Lake Ontario's most dangerous waters. Eventually, lighthouses were in demand all along the Inside Passage itself for use as passage lights to guide ships through tricky narrows, and as harbour lights to direct ships the final few miles into port. With the opening of the Murray Canal in 1890, this Inside Passage allowed mariners to forgo the shoals, reefs, gales and other hazards of the open lake, and traffic along this waterway increased and still more lighthouses were built to further facilitate this commerce.

For the want of lighthouses along the Canadian shores of eastern Lake Ontario, many ships were lost along with their crews, passengers and cargoes. As a result, hardly a year would go by for almost a century that ship owners, ship captains, town councils, members of Parliament and commercial associations did not ask the government to erect lighthouses on the shores of Lake Ontario or along the Inside Passage to guide ships to safe harbours and to help keep their crews, passengers and cargoes safe. This was the setting in which a remarkable network of lighthouses and light towers was constructed. By 1914, more than forty-five of these essential aids to navigation had been built along the Canadian shores of eastern Lake Ontario "for the safety and convenience of navigation".

PART II

THE LIGHTHOUSES

After the first lighthouses on Lake Ontario had been erected on Mississauga Point at the mouth of the Niagara River in 1804, and on Gibraltar Point at the entrance to York harbour in 1808, no lighthouses were built anywhere on the lake for more than a decade. During that decade, there were many changes around Lake Ontario and in the entire Great Lakes region. Following the War of 1812, populations on both sides of the lake continued to increase. More people meant more commerce and trade and hence more shipbuilding to provide vessels to transport goods to their markets.

By the 1820's, the population of Michigan, Ohio and western New York State had increased five-fold to more than 1,000,000,[1] while the population of Upper Canada had doubled and was approaching 150,000.[2] In addition, increased commercial shipbuilding on Lake Ontario had doubled the number of commercial vessels sailing the lake to well over one hundred ships, including at least ten steamboats.[3]

By then, the European obsession with canal building had reached North America where canals were seen as the solution to the problems of transporting goods and immigrants thousands of kilometers inland from the ocean to where new settlements were developing, and returning to tidewater with the raw materials which those hinterlands held in abundance. In 1817, the State of New York had begun digging the Erie Canal through which canal boats could transport cargoes from Lake Erie to the Hudson River, down which the boats could be floated to the Atlantic Ocean at New York City. This marked the beginning of a 140-year inland transportation rivalry between the U.S. Erie Canal route and the Canadian waterway that would eventually be developed via the Welland Canal, Lake Ontario, and the St. Lawrence River to allow ships to transport goods to and from Montreal. This rivalry would last until the completion of the St. Lawrence Seaway in 1959.

(16) Barges on the Erie Canal. Watercolour on paper, "View on the Erie Canal", by J.W. Hill, 1831.
The canal was opened 1825 and connected Lake Erie with the Hudson River and New York City. Draught animals walking along the towpath would tow barges carrying passengers and cargo. Competition between the Erie Canal-Hudson River route and the Welland Canal-Lake Ontario-St. Lawrence River route lasted well into the 20th Century.
[Courtesy of New York Public Library]

In 1821, preliminary steps were taken toward developing this Canadian waterway when the "Board of Commissioners for the Improvement of the Internal Navigation" was established by the provincial legislature of Upper Canada to look into the feasibility of building canals throughout the province.[4] The commission, headed by prominent Kingston resident John Macaulay, concentrated its efforts on examining routes for canals in three areas: between Lake Erie and Lake Ontario via the Grand River and Burlington Bay; from Kingston to Montreal along the Cataraqui, Rideau and Ottawa rivers, and directly to Montreal along the St. Lawrence River from Kingston.

While the Internal Navigation commissioners were still studying various canal routes and making countless recommendations, the

New Yorkers completed their Erie Canal in 1825, and eventually a northward extension from Syracuse to Lake Ontario at Oswego, New York, would be opened in 1828. Following New York's lead, the State of Ohio had begun digging a canal in 1825 that would eventually allow cargo to be carried from Lake Erie to New Orleans, Louisiana, via the Ohio and Mississippi rivers.[5]

As a result of the colonial government's inability to commit funds for the construction of the canals proposed by Upper Canada's Internal Navigation commission, William Hamilton Merritt of St. Catharines organized the privately financed Welland Canal Company,[6] and by 1825, work had begun on the canal that would bypass the arduous portage route around Niagara Falls. The following year, the British military began work on the strategically sited Rideau Canal to connect Lake Ontario with the deep-water port at Montreal as an alternate to the more direct St. Lawrence River route that ran along the Canada/ U.S. border.

(17) Ship in the old Welland Canal. Sketch by L.R. O'Brien.
The first Welland Canal was opened for use by small sailing ships in 1829. The canal was upgraded numerous times to accommodate larger and larger vessels.
[From Grant, *Picturesque Canada*, 1882]

The first ships would pass through the Welland Canal in 1829, and by 1833 an improved canal would be completed from Port Colborne on Lake Erie to Port Dalhousie on Lake Ontario. By then, the Rideau Canal would be nearing completion as would canals on the Ottawa River to connect Montreal with the northern terminus of the Rideau at Bytown (later named Ottawa).

With Kingston as the Rideau Canal's planned southern terminus, this harbour, already a busy freight-forwarding port, became busier than ever. The Oswego Canal would open further opportunities for increased trade of American manufactured goods into Canadian ports. The Welland Canal would allow ships from lakes Michigan, Huron, and Erie to sail as far as Kingston where their cargoes could be trans-shipped onto steamboats passing through the Rideau Canal or onto barges headed directly down the St. Lawrence River to Montreal.

With all of these canals connecting with Lake Ontario, the number of ships sailing the Great Lakes increased dramatically, and by the 1830's there would have been several hundred vessels with access to Lake Ontario. By then, the population of Michigan, Ohio and western New York State would exceed 1,500,000,[7] while the population of Upper Canada would be approaching 200,000.[8]

In the midst of all of these developments, the Upper Canada Legislature turned their thoughts once again to the matter of the "safety and convenience of navigation" on Lake Ontario.

CHAPTER 3

First Light

A good and sufficient lighthouse.
(An Act to provide for the Erection of a Light House, on
the False-Ducks Island, in Lake Ontario. 1828)

In December, 1826, Upper Canada's *Loyalist* newspaper had commented that, "The want of a light house at the eastern extremity of the lake has often been complained of. The subject may probably present itself to the attention of Parliament."[1] By then, four lighthouses had already been put into operation by the United States Government on the New York side of eastern Lake Ontario. On the Canadian side of the lake, only the Gibraltar Point lighthouse still guided mariners to York harbour — the lighthouse initially erected on Mississauga Point at Niagara had been demolished in 1814 to make way for new fortifications.

False Ducks Island Lighthouse (1829)

In January, 1827 a committee of the Legislature of Upper Canada met at York to examine "... the petition of ship owners and others, praying for a light-house upon the False Ducks Island".[2] Chairing the committee was John Beverly Robinson. Robinson was the attorney-general of the province and elected member of the Legislative Assembly for the town of York. He was also a central figure in the "Family Compact", a group which would dominate politics in Upper Canada until 1840.

The term Family Compact often was used by members of the Reform opposition in the legislature to describe derisively a conservative group of politicians, administrative officers and government supporters who were bound together by friendships and common interests.[3] For more than a decade, decisions made by members of the Family Compact, who dominated both the Legislative Council (the Upper House of the Parliament of Upper Canada) and the Executive Council (the Lieutenant-Governor's advisory body) would affect the progress of lighthouse construction along the shores of eastern Lake Ontario.

The lighthouse location under consideration by Robinson's committee, False Ducks Island, is part of a grouping of two small islands and a number of reefs off the south-eastern tip of Prince Edward County. In the 19th Century, these islands were also known as the Lesser Drakes, as distinguished from Main Duck Island (sometimes referred to as the Real Duck) located seven nautical miles further out into the lake. The nearby wave-swept reef, often referred to as The Ducklings or Gull Island, is now called Gull Bar. These are part of the string of islands running across eastern Lake Ontario from Prince Edward County to Stony Point in New York State that form the highest points of the underwater Duck Galloo Ridge.

The 1827 report of the Committee was based largely on the testimony of Captain Charles Macintosh, and included a summary of his recommendations:

REPORT

Of the Select Committee to whom was referred the petition of certain ship owners and others, praying for a light-house upon the False Ducks Island, with the evidence laid before said committee.

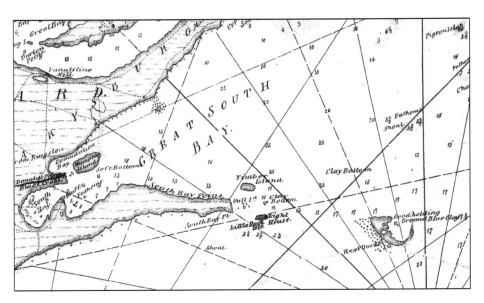

(18) Location of False Ducks Island (marked as "Little Duck Isle"). From Augustus Ford's *Chart of Lake Ontario*, 1836 (detail).
To the right is Main Duck Island marked as "Real Ducks". To the left is Waupoos Island marked as "Wampoos Island" where some of the stone for the lighthouse was quarried.
[Courtesy of Library and Archives Canada, NMC11314]

CHARLES MACINTOSH, captain of the schooner *Superior*, examined

Has navigated Lake Ontario, between York and Kingston, for nine or ten years, and is well acquainted with the track.—A light house on the south east point of the False Ducks would tend greatly to the safety and convenience of navigation.

The *Hibernian*, a schooner, was totally wrecked there, and her cargo lost about six years ago: and vessels are now frequently obliged to lie to at night, at great risk, when they might otherwise run in.—Considers it by far the most dangerous point of the lake.[4]

A cursory examination of the proceedings of the provincial legislature over the prior decade shows that Captain Macintosh was often used as an "expert witness" and supplied testimony to numerous committees concerned with marine matters in Upper Canada. He was one of five brothers, all of whom captained their own ships.[5] Charles was undoubtedly an experienced mariner whose opinion held some weight with government officials and members of the legislature.

The ship that Macintosh refers to as the "Hibernian" was the *Hibernia*, a schooner that was wrecked at the False Ducks in November, 1822, during a voyage from Kingston to York. The *Kingston Chronicle* published a brief account of that incident:

On the morning of Sunday the 17th inst. the schooner *Hibernia*, of this port, bound with a valuable cargo of goods to York, ran upon the False Duck's in a fog, and was wrecked. The crew, who are saved, managed to get all the goods, with the exception of some casks of sugar, landed on the beach, but more or less damaged by the water. In attempting to bring away the cargo, two boats, one belonging to the Dock yard, the other a Durham boat, have also been unfortunately lost, in consequence of the exposed situation of the wreck, and the stormy weather lately experienced. The vessel we understand, is gradually going to pieces.[6]

Given that the *Hibernia* was wrecked on a foggy night, it is questionable whether or not the presence of a lighthouse could have prevented this accident. Depending on the thickness and extent of the fog, it is likely that the light from any lighthouse would have been difficult to see at any appreciable distance. Fog horns, fog bells, and fog whistles only came into widespread use at light stations on the Great Lakes later in the 19th Century.

Nevertheless, the False Ducks was known to be a dangerous place. Another late season storm had nearly wrecked the schooner *Mary* there in 1816:

> Kingston Gazette, December 7, 1816 — The Schooner *Mary* of Oswego, Capt. Trowbridge, from the Genesee [Charlotte, New York], bound for Ogdensburg, freighted with about 600 barrels of Flour and Pork, struck on a rock in a gale, last Tuesday, at the False Ducks. - Soon after she struck, the Captain and three men went ashore in a boat, leaving two men on board, who were taken off yesterday by Capt. Mosier, of the schooner *Mary Ann* of this port, together with the Captains trunk &c., at the imminent risk of his life. We are informed by a passenger, who went on shore with the captain, that he is now in the Bay of Quinte, endeavoring to procure boats to save as much of the property on board as possible. It is feared however, that by this time she is a complete wreck.[7]

Fortunately, no lives were lost and the *Mary* was eventually refloated.[8]

A detailed hydrographic survey conducted by Captain William Fitz William Owen of the Royal Navy in 1815 and 1816 shows the many shoals and reefs in the vicinity of False Ducks Island.[9] Augustus Ford's *Chart of Lake Ontario* (figure 18) based on soundings he took in the same area some years earlier, also shows a number of shoals near the False Ducks (see also figure 72 for a later chart).

One might reasonably ask then — since the location of these shoals was known from the early years of the 19th Century, why did ship captains not steer well away from them?

The simple answer is that this is exactly what ship captains did. They kept as far away as they could from these dangerous shoals and reefs. Often, however, gales, snowstorms, fog and the then-unknown effect of local magnetic anomalies on a compass bearing could easily result in a ship deviating from its intended course. Even an experienced captain using his well-honed dead-reckoning skills was no match for eastern Lake Ontario under such adverse conditions.

The Committee of the Upper Canada legislature continued its examination of Captain Macintosh:

> [Macintosh] knows the False Duck Island: It is about thirty miles from Kingston, and about one and a half from Timber Island. The False Duck Island is about three miles in circumference, contains hard wood timber, and some cedar, and some good soil. - Has stone upon it fit for making the light house, though not of a good description of building stone. Good stone might be got on the main land, about eleven miles from the Island. — Has conversed with Mr. Kennedy, a stone mason, about it, and from his information, a good light house, exclusive of lamps, would cost about £750....
>
> He says, that it may be estimated that at present about twenty schooners, and three steam-boats would enter and clear Kingston for the upper part of Lake Ontario, and this is besides American vessels, which would benefit by it, not only in sailing to and from Kingston, but in their passage to Ogdensburg.
>
> Has conversed particularly with Capt. McKenzie of the *Frontenac*, and is sure that he perfectly agrees with him as

to the necessity of a light house on the False Ducks, and the situation for it.[10]

It is clear that Captain Macintosh had carefully consulted with other experts, including a stone mason and another experienced ship captain, before testifying before the committee.

Together with Mr. Kennedy, the stone mason, Macintosh suggested that the contractor hired to build the lighthouse could make do with the stone found on False Ducks Island, even though it was not of the best quality. The stone masons who were eventually hired to build the lighthouse found the stone on the island completely unsuitable for building the tower and they had to go as far as Waupoos Island and the town of Bath in order to find their building materials.[11]

Macintosh also mentions Captain James McKenzie, an experienced sailor who knew the waters of Lake Ontario well. By 1827, McKenzie had already been captain of the steamboat *Frontenac* for ten years, and had recently been appointed to command the new steamboat *Alciope*. McKenzie had started his marine career in the British merchant service and later joined the Royal Navy where he rose to the rank of Sailing Master, serving first against Napoleon's navy in European waters and later against the Americans on the Great Lakes during the War of 1812.[12]

Robinson's committee's recommended that the legislature allocate £1,000 to build the lighthouse:

> Your Committee has no doubt that a light-house upon the south east point of the False Ducks would be a very important advantage to navigation; and, as they think the sum of one thousand pounds, and perhaps a less sum, would defray the charge of its erection, and of the necessary lamps, they recommend that it be provided for according to the prayer of the petition; — that commissioners be appointed to fix upon the proper site, and to contract for and superintend its erection, and that such light house fees

be imposed as may gradually reimburse the public treasury, and furnish the means of supporting the light.[13]

In the March 1828 session of the legislature, the assembly approved the recommended expenditure for the construction of the False Ducks Island lighthouse and passed the following act:

AN ACT to provide for the Erection of a
Light House,
on the False-Ducks Island, in Lake Ontario.
Passed 25th March, 1828.

WHERAS it would tend greatly to the safety and convenience of Navigation upon Lake Ontario, if a Light House were constructed upon the Island commonly called the False-Ducks Island in the said Lake:

Be it therefore enacted, by the King's Most Excellent Majesty, by and with the advice and consent of the Legislative Council, and Assembly of the Province of Upper Canada...

That it shall be made lawful ... immediately after the passing of this act ... to appoint Three Persons to be Commissioners for Erecting a good and sufficient Light House upon such part of the Island commonly called the False-Ducks Island, in Lake Ontario, as they shall judge the most proper, and for procuring the necessary apparatus for lighting the same.

And be it further enacted by the authority aforesaid, That from and out of the Rates and Duties now raised, levied, and collected ... there be granted to His Majesty, the Sum of One Thousand Pounds, to enable His Majesty to defray the expense of Erecting the said Light House, and furnishing the same....[14]

The three commissioners appointed were James McKenzie, Michael Spratt and John Macaulay. Since Upper Canada had no civil service as such, commissioners were appointed on an ad-hoc basis to oversee public works projects. Those appointed were usually well connected with the government, which meant they were either members of the Family Compact or closely associated with that group.

All three commissioners were residents of Kingston. As we have already seen, James McKenzie was a well-known ship captain. Michael Spratt was Master Attendant of the Naval Yard in Kingston and, as such, was probably acting as the Royal Navy's representative on the advice of Commodore Robert Barrie, the ranking naval officer in the Canadas.[15] Not coincidentally, Spratt was also a shareholder in the Cataraqui Bridge Company (incorporated in 1827),[16] so he would have been well acquainted with some of the most prominent residents of Kingston, many of whom were connected closely with the government. One of his fellow shareholders was John Macaulay, the third commissioner.

Macaulay was an apt choice as a lighthouse commissioner. For the previous seven years, he had been head of the Internal Navigation Commission looking into improving transportation throughout the province by digging canals and developing harbours. He was the eldest son of one of Kingston's most successful merchants, Robert Macaulay. John's father died when he was young and he was raised by his mother and his uncle, John Kirby. The young Macaulay had attended Reverend John Strachan's school in Cornwall along with his brother William. There, they met and became friends with John Beverly Robinson, George Markland, and other men who would later rise to prominence in Upper Canada and form the core of the Family Compact.

John Macaulay followed in this father's footsteps and, with the help of his uncle, John Kirby, established himself as a merchant in Kingston. Later, he became publisher of the *Kingston Chronicle*, and often published editorials favourable to the government and administration controlled by the Family Compact. In 1821, Macaulay was appointed President of the Board of Commissioners for the Improvement of the Internal Navigation. At a time when transportation of goods was largely by water, this was a very important position. He was also postmaster for Kingston and briefly held the post of Collector of Customs. He later became Inspector General of Upper Canada and was appointed a member of the Province of Canada's Executive Council, posts he held until his death in 1857.[17]

(19) Portrait of John Macaulay, 1857. Pastel on paper by G.T. Berthon.
Macaulay was one of the lighthouse commissioners responsible for the construction of the first three lighthouses built in eastern Lake Ontario.
[Courtesy of Queen's University Archives]

Being well-connected with members of the government, many of whom were former school chums, he enjoyed the benefits of these numerous political appointments. In turn, he used his influence to have family and friends appointed to various positions. His brother, Reverend William Macaulay, was a minister of the Church of England and a prominent resident of Prince Edward County where he owned a large estate and was rector of St. Mary Magdalene church. John was undoubtedly instrumental in having William appointed as chaplain to the Legislative Assembly of Upper Canada after Reverend

John Strachan stepped down from that post to join the Lieutenant-Governor's Executive Council.[18]

It may have been on John Macaulay's recommendation that the other two commissioners were appointed to help him oversee the construction of the False Ducks Island lighthouse. As noted earlier, Michael Spratt was a fellow shareholder in the Cataraqui Bridge Company, while James McKenzie had originally been appointed captain of the steamship *Frontenac* by the ship's first owners who had included Macaulay's uncle, John Kirby.[19]

Upon receiving their appointments in May, 1828, the lighthouse commissioners immediately set about their task. First, they hired an architect to draw a set of plans and to act as construction supervisor. The architect chosen was fellow Kingstonian, Thomas Rogers. Rogers had recently designed Kingston's new St. George's Church under the direction of the church's building committee which had included church wardens John Macaulay and John Kirby. Rogers also designed the Cataraqui Bridge for the Cataraqui Bridge Company of which lighthouse commissioners John Macaulay and Michael Spratt were shareholders. Later, at the request of Reverend John Strachan, he designed the second St. James Church at York, as well as the Parliament buildings of Upper Canada.[20]

On May 8, 1828, Rogers and the commissioners sailed out to False Ducks Island to determine the best building site for the new lighthouse. Following that, in order to understand the true nature of the structure they were entrusted to build, they sailed to Galloo Island where the United States government had erected a lighthouse in 1820. The tower on Galloo island must have confirmed in Macaulay's mind the type of lighthouse to be built on False Ducks Island for, on his return to Kingston, he wrote, "We have an idea of building a round tower, nearly in the proportion of a Tuscan column, and as small in its diameter as may be consistent with its solidity, in order to save materials."[21]

With the commissioners' approval, Rogers would have been responsible for determining the detailed construction specifications for the lighthouse and drafting the tender documents. For his work on the lighthouse, Rogers was paid a flat fee of £3 for the drawings of the tower as well as a commission of three percent for superintending the construction, for a total income amounting to £20.17s.6d.[22]

The commissioners' report from 1828 provides many of the details of the progress of construction of the False Ducks Island lighthouse:

> Report of the Commissioners
> appointed to superintend
> the erection of a Light House
> on the False Ducks Island, in Lake Ontario.
>
> We the undersigned Commissioners appointed under the authority of an act passed at the last session of the provincial parliament, entitled "An Act to provide for the erection of a Light House on the False Ducks' Island, in Lake Ontario"
>
> Most respectfully beg leave to report:
>
> That, immediately after we had received official notice of our appointment in the month of May last, we met at Kingston, where after an attentive inspection of the light house erected by the Government of the United Sates on the Gallop Island [Galloo Island], and obtaining other general information respecting the nature of the duties imposed on us, we advertised for tenders for building the tower of the Light House, on a spot which we had fixed on at the South eastern point of the False Ducks' Island.[23]

In June, the tenders were reviewed and the work for the construction of the stone tower was awarded to four stone masons: William Allan, John McLeod, William Scott and Robert Matthews. It is probably not coincidental that Robert Matthews was one of the masons selected for the lighthouse project as he had worked alongside Thomas Rogers during the construction of St. George's Church.[24]

The commissioners' report gives the general specifications for the tower:

The building was to be circular in form — sixty feet in height from the ground line — ten feet in diameter within walls, which were to be four feet in thickness at the bottom — and gradually diminishing to a thickness of two feet at the top. The floor of the platform for the reception of the Lantern, was to be of cut lime stone well jointed and cemented, and supported by a substantial brick arch — The outer face of the Tower was to be rough cast in a neat and durable manner.— The contractors who were respectable mechanics, undertook to prepare the building for the reception of the lantern on the fifteenth day of September, when they were to be paid for their work the sum of five hundred and forty six pounds.[25]

On a technical note, the masonry finish on the tower's exterior, known as "rough casting", was a type of triple-layered stucco or parging intended to protect the stonework from the elements. As described in the book *Practical Masonry* published in 1841...

Rough-Casting, is an outside finishing.... The materials used for rough-casting are fine gravel well washed, until completely free from all particles of earth or clay, mixed with pure lime and water, until the whole is in a semi-fluid state.[26]

Over time, this rough-cast finish would prove to be inadequate. After a number of years, the parging began to fall off the tower and it had to be replaced many times, adding considerably to the long-term cost of maintaining the lighthouse.

Soon after the contract was awarded for the stonework, the masons arrived at False Ducks Island to begin their work. However, they quickly found that the stone available on the island was not suitable for their purposes:

When the masons commenced their work it was their impression, as well as our own, that the Island itself would afford an ample supply of stone, fit for building as well as for making lime. In this respect we were disappointed, and it consequently became necessary to obtain materials from quarries at Mill creek, near Bath, and at Wapoos' Island, in Prince Edward's bay. The vessel employed in bringing those supplies of stone and lime was frequently detained on the way and prevented by the weather from unloading with regularity at the False ducks' Island, which, it is well known, affords no shelter or protection from the winds. The masons thus lost much time, and instead of completing the tower according to contract, on the fifteenth day of September, they did not put up the platform of the lantern, until the latter end of October—a period so late in the season that we would not allow them to proceed and rough cast the exterior lest the severe frosts of the winter coming on before the work was dry, should damage it and cause the mortar to fall off....[27]

During the summer, the commissioners had made several inspection visits to False Ducks Island courtesy of Captain Whitney of the steamboat *Queenston* and Captain Mosier, former captain of the schooner *Mary Ann,* now commanding the steamboat *Niagara.* Now, at the end of October, the stone-work on the tower was completed and the commissioners proudly reported that:

> The tower, which is actually about sixty two feet in height from the ground line to the top of the platform, is neat in its proportions, and we may add that, as a piece of mason-work, we think it will vie in point of strength with any similar structure in America.[28]

The lighthouse's lantern, the large, glass-enclosed room at the top of the lighthouse, and the lighting apparatus inside the lantern were not included in the contract with the stone masons. The commissioners had set out earlier to procure those components separately.

Given the commissioners' association with Upper Canada's Family Compact which always looked to the Mother Country, Great Britain, for any manufactured goods and which retained a great deal of anti-American sentiment in the aftermath of the War of 1812, they most likely had a preference to source the lantern and lighting apparatus from a British supplier. The lighthouse on Green Island (Ile Verte) in the Gulf of St. Lawrence had been supplied with such equipment, and the commissioners made inquiries about the lantern obtained for that lighthouse.

The Ile Verte lighthouse had been built two decades earlier by Lower Canada's lighthouse authority, the Quebec Trinity House, and it had been fitted with a top quality lantern and lamps that had been imported from Britain. However, budgetary considerations were paramount in the minds of the commissioners from Upper Canada:

> We next turned our attention to the Lantern, and the necessary apparatus for lighting it; which we understood might either be procured in England or in the United States.
>
> We were induced in the first instance to ascertain on what terms we might be provided with the lighting apparatus from England and with this view, we entered into correspondence with a gentleman resident at Quebec, from whom we obtained information which satisfied us that importation from that quarter could not be attempted. The apparatus for fitting up the light on Green Island [Ile Verte] in the Gulph of Saint Lawrence, with thirteen lamps, reflectors, &c. including the frame and roof of the lantern, packing, &c. cost, in 1809, according to the London invoice, upwards of fourteen hundred pounds, sterling, a sum far exceeding the whole amount appropriated for erecting as well as furnishing the Light House on the False Ducks.[29]

The records of the Legislature of Lower Canada indicate that the exact amount paid for the Ile Verte lantern alone was £1222 4s. 5p.[30]

The cost of this single component significantly exceeded the entire £1000 budget for the False Ducks Island lighthouse. As a result, the commissioners had no choice but to obtain the necessary items from American sources:

> We were, therefore, obliged to address ourselves to the person who has for many years had a contract for fitting up and supplying the light houses of the United States. From this person we purchased ten lamps and ten reflectors, with other necessary materials including glass of double thickness for the windows of the lantern....[31]

The person that the commissioners turned to for their lighthouse lamps and lantern glass was Winslow Lewis of Boston, Massachusetts.

In the early 19th Century, the most common lighting apparatus used in lighthouses was a series of oil lamps and parabolic reflectors grouped together on a frame or chandelier to produce a light that could be seen for many miles in clear weather. Winslow Lewis was an enterprising American sea captain who had patented a modified version of such an illumination system that was in widespread use in Britain and France at the time. Lewis had sold his patent to the United States government who then contracted him to install his Lewis lamps in every lighthouse in the United States.[32]

Using an Argand lamp as the illumination source, Lewis added a dished reflector behind the lamp to amplify the light and a magnifying lens in front of it to focus the beam. The Argand lamp was the invention of Swiss engineer Aimé Argand. Fueled by highly-prized sperm-oil, this lamp used a hollow wick which increased the oxygen flow to the flame resulting in a very bright, nearly smoke-free light. The Argand lamp was widely used not only in private homes, but also in lighthouses where the bright, smoke-free source of illumination was highly valued.[33]

As early as 1783, an array of parabolic reflectors paired with Argand lamps was first used with great success in the ancient

Cordouan lighthouse in France. In Scotland, the famous lighthouse builder Robert Stevenson (grandfather of the author of <u>Treasure Island</u>, Robert Louis Stevenson) developed a similar system that was eventually adopted throughout the British Isles and used in a number of lighthouses in Canada. The effectiveness of this apparatus was due to the very bright, smokeless flame from the Argand lamps, and the carefully crafted copper reflectors lined with highly polished silver. This reflecting arrangement was known as a catoptric light (from the Greek *katoptrikos*, meaning mirror).[34]

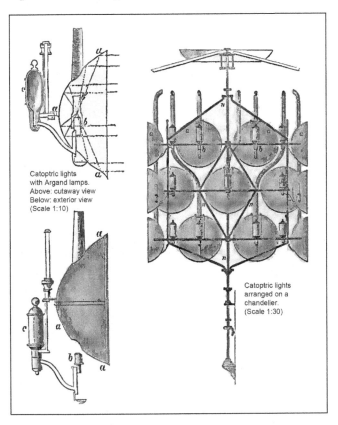

Catoptric lights with Argand lamps. Above: cutaway view Below: exterior view (Scale 1:10)

Catoptric lights arranged on a chandelier. (Scale 1:30)

(20) Details of catoptric lights and lighthouse chandelier. Illustrator unknown.
Key: a) parabolic reflector b) Argand lamp with glass chimney c) cylinder containing sperm oil n) chandelier frame.
Lewis lamps would have been a crude version of these lights. In addition, each Lewis lamp would have had a thick glass lens positioned in front of the reflector.
[From Stevenson, *On the Theory and Construction of Lighthouses*, 1857]

In 1810, Winslow Lewis was the first person to demonstrate this effective catoptric system of lighthouse illumination to the United States government. Lewis had modified the European design by substituting low-quality wicks in the lamps and very thin copper with minimal silvering in the reflectors. His reflectors were not true parabolas and this, combined with the largely ineffective "magnifier" made of thick green glass that he placed in front of each lamp resulted in a system that produced only a fraction of the amount of light compared with that of the British and French versions. Nevertheless, the Lewis lamps were still considerably brighter than the simple oil lamps then in use in American lighthouses. In addition, Lewis' lamps burned only half as much fuel as the old lamps to create a much brighter light. This was the key factor that led the U.S. Treasury Department to buy Lewis' patent and award him the contract for upgrading all U.S. lighthouses with his apparatus.[35]

The relative merits of the high-quality, extra bright British catoptric lights compared to the inferior American ones were probably not widely known in the early 19th Century. What the False Ducks Island lighthouse commissioners purchased from Winslow Lewis was a proven technology that was readily available. In addition, it was a technology that fit their budget.

Lewis was paid $703.70 (approximately £145).[36] For that sum the commissioners received all of the necessary lighting apparatus including ten lamps and reflectors, and 160 panes of glass for use in the lantern as summarized in the Lewis' statement of account in figure 21.

The fabrication of the lantern itself, however, was contracted for separately. For this, the commissioners turned to a blacksmith in Brownville, New York, William Hardy:

> For the construction of the frame and roof of the lantern, it was necessary to make a separate contract, and as we could not until after some time spent in inquiry, discover and determine upon the most suitable plan and dimensions for that important part of the structure, it was not until

the 30ᵗʰ day of August, that we could close an agreement respecting it with a mechanic resident at Brownville, in the State of New York. This person contracted for the sum of one hundred and sixty eight pounds, fifteen shillings, to make and set up the frame and roof of the lantern, furnishing at the same time the materials — and to complete the whole on the first day of November.

The COMMISSIONERS for building a Light House on the FALSE DUCKS' Island in Lake Ontario,
Bought of Winslow Lewis.

1828 November 5.	2 casks and 1 box, containing 10 lamps, 10. 16 inch reflectors, 10 heaters, stove and funnel, and frame or chandelier for the lamps,·················· 2 pieces iron, 1 the spindle on which the chandelier and stove is placed, the other to lay across the top of the lantern for the end of the spindle to play in—1 Tin box, containing hand lantern and lamp, torch, oil-feeder, 6 wick-formers scissor, 2 files, 6 gross wicks,	$ 560	00
	6 gross lamp wicks, at $1 50, ····	9	00
	1 box containing 100 lamp glasses at 18 cents, ··················	18	00
	3 boxes containing 160 lights 14 ᴍ 12 double thick glass, at 72 cents,··	116	20
	Box for tube glasses, ·············	00	50
	$	703	70

Received payment in full of the above account, having signed triplicate receipts.

WINSLOW LEWIS.

Boston, Massachusetts,
18th December, 1828.

(21) Statement of Account, Winslow Lewis, Boston Massachusetts, 18ᵗʰ December, 1828. The commissioners responsible for the False Ducks Island lighthouse originally ordered only ten lights and reflectors but later ordered another five sets. The "160 lights 14x12" refers to the 160 panes of glass for the lantern, including some extras as spares. [From "Report of the Commissioners appointed to Superintend the erection of a Light House on the False Ducks' Island", 1828]

The form of the Lantern was to be octagonal with a copper dome or roof—the whole of the frame work for the windows was to be made of wrought iron, sufficiently stout with a copper door opening towards Point Traverse, and one range of copper sheets instead of glass along the lower part of the sash on each face of the Octagon.[37]

It appears that the contract for the lantern had not been sent out to public tender as had the construction of the tower. Instead, the Brownville blacksmith, situated in this small village outside of Watertown, New York was approached directly by the commissioners to undertake this project. It is not known how the commissioners happened to choose Hardy. Perhaps he was recommended by the Winslow Lewis, or it may have been that during their inspection of the Galloo Island lighthouse, the commissioners were informed that it was William Hardy who had constructed the lantern for that lighthouse.

The design that Hardy was required to execute specified a lantern which conformed closely to those in use at other lighthouses of the day. The octagonal plan maximized the platform space available at the top of the round tower while allowing for relative ease of construction. With the exception of the side facing toward Timber Island, each side of the octagon contained a grid of 14-inch x 12-inch iron glazing bars designed to hold the small panes of double-thick glass ordered from Winslow Lewis. These were the identical panes used in the Galloo Island lighthouse.[38] The lantern was to be topped with a domed roof made of copper.[39]

The appearance of this lantern would have been somewhat different from the polygonal lighthouse lanterns that came into use towards the end of 19th Century (and are still commonly seen today). These "modern" lanterns often have ten sides or twelve sides, with each side having only a single large pane of plate glass instead of many smaller panes. In addition, the roof of the later lanterns is usually peaked instead of domed.

Curiously, the specification for the False Ducks Island lighthouse lantern makes no mention of a chimney or vent in the roof of the lantern. This would have been needed to allow the smoke and excess heat from the lamps to escape.

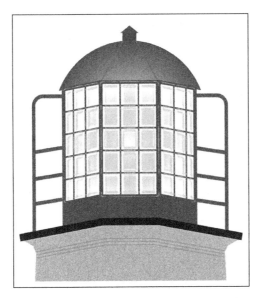

(22) Drawing of typical early 19ᵗʰ Century domed lantern. Drawn by Marc Seguin, 2015. The early lighthouse lanterns were usually octagonal, each side fitted with multiple panes of glass and the whole structure topped off with a domed roof. [Author's collection]

Like the stone tower, the construction of the lantern met with some delays:

> The contractor of the blacksmith work was disappointed in obtaining, at the proper time, his supply of iron at the furnace from which it had been ordered; and thus, he too, failed in fulfilling the conditions of his agreement within the stipulated period. Instead of erecting the frame work and roof of the lantern before the first day of November, he did not succeed in getting the roof in its position until the beginning of the present month[December]; and he was obliged by the state of the weather and the prevalence of boisterous winds at so late a period in the season, to defer the completion of the work until the ensuing spring.[40]

By December, 1828 the lighthouse was nearly finished. However, as December marked the end of the shipping season and the beginning of the winter freeze-up, the False Ducks Island lighthouse would not go into operation until the following year. With the lantern atop the tower's platform, the domed roof would have been some 72 feet above the lighthouse's base; making this an architectural marvel as both the tallest lighthouse on the Great Lakes and the tallest building between Montreal's Notre Dame Basilica and the Michigan Territorial capitol building in Detroit.[41]

Before concluding their report with a discussion of the possible sources of revenue for the maintenance of the lighthouse and repayment of the money granted by the legislature, the commissioners found it necessary to comment on some additional expenditures that they thought were necessary for the proper operation of the False Ducks Island lighthouse:

> We have now to offer a few remarks on the purchases made at Boston for fitting up the lantern. It will be seen on reference to the invoice of the apparatus for lighting, that the chandelier or frame for the lights has been prepared for the reception of *fifteen* lamps; though ten *only* have been imported. It is our opinion that fifteen lamps with reflectors are required in order to render the light house distinctly visible from every point on the horizon, embracing the entire scope on the lake from the vicinity of Point Petre to the gap between Point Pleasant and Amherst Island.
>
> In order to finish the light house in a proper manner, we have calculated that further disbursements will be necessary under the following heads:
>
> Painting, glazing the lantern, putting up lamps, &c &c. - £25.
>
> Completing the number of Lamps to fifteen with tube glasses, wicks, &c. and all expenses for transportation, duty, &c. oil buts, &c. - £85.[42]

(23) False Ducks Island lighthouse, 1924. Photographer unknown.
The original lantern had been replaced with a "modern" lantern consisting of fewer, larger panes of glass and a peaked roof. This modern lantern can still be seen at the Prince Edward County Mariners Park Museum. The people in the doorway of the tower are probably the lightkeeper and his children.
[Courtesy of Library and Archives Canada, RG12-Vol.1511-21754R]

Moreover, they also identified one of the major oversights of the original legislation; the lack of a house for the lightkeeper. Given the remote location of False Ducks Island, it would be essential that the keeper have a house on the island as well as a boat to be able to fetch supplies on the mainland:

> Besides the light house itself, it is necessary to build a convenient and comfortable dwelling house for the keeper and his family, and to provide him a good boat, which, as well as his house, should be kept in repair at the public expense. We recommend that the house should be constructed of stone, in a durable and substantial manner; and of opinion, that if built on the plan of those provided for the keepers of light houses in the United States, it would cost from four to five hundred pounds.
>
> In order, therefore, to finish the light house and furnish it, and to provide a boat and a comfortable habitation for the keeper, (who in that solitary place should, at least be made comfortable,) an additional appropriation of from six to seven hundred pounds will be required.[43]

The commissioners also stated that it would be useful to have a fog bell installed at the lighthouse since "... a bell rung at stated intervals by the keeper, may warn the mariner of the vicinity of the light house and enable him to ascertain and correctly shape his course."[44] Although it would be several decades before a fog horn was installed on the island, this is one of the earliest known references to any type of fog signaling device anywhere on the Great Lakes.

The commissioners also discussed the possibility of installing coloured glass in the lantern in order to distinguish the False Ducks Island light from the one on Galloo Island, only fifteen nautical miles away. Later in the 19th Century, characteristics such as flashing lights and coloured lights would be commonplace in lighthouses. However, this is among the earliest known references to establishing different characteristics for lights on the Great Lakes.

In concluding their report, the commissioners stated that:

> Upon the completion of the work according to the plan hitherto acted on by us with the additions we have suggested, the province will possess, on the False Ducks, a good and sufficient light house built in conformity to the injunctions of the statute, and according to our view of the intentions of Parliament.[45]

The next year, in March 1829, acting on the recommendations of the lighthouse commissioners, the provincial legislature voted additional funds for the completion of the False Ducks Island lighthouse:

> An act to provide for the completing the light house
> on the False-Ducks island and for the keeping and
> maintaining the same during the present year.
> Passed March 20, 1829
> Whereas a further sum of money is found to be necessary for the completing and furnishing the light house upon the False-Ducks island, in lake Ontario; may... there be granted to your Majesty the sum of seven hundred and fifty pounds; which sum of seven hundred and fifty pounds shall be applied in aid of the monies heretofore granted for erecting and furnishing the said light house, and providing all necessary equipments and appendages to the same...
> And whereas it is necessary to make provision for the support of the said light house during the present year, be it therefore enacted by the authority aforesaid, That it shall an may be lawful for the collector of the port of Kingston to advance... sums of money as may be necessary for maintaining the light in the said light house during the present year, and for bearing the charge of a keeper of the said light house, and all expenses necessarily attending the same, which monies so advanced shall be allowed him in his account with the government.[46]

In April, tenders were let for the construction of the keeper's house.[47] There is no record of who the successful bidder was, but it is likely that Thomas Rogers was retained as the architect for the stone dwelling.

With the construction of a keeper's dwelling well in hand, the commissioners then had to concern themselves with hiring a lightkeeper. On this subject, they commented that:

> The Island is a bleak and lonely spot which cannot be subjected to daily visitation like a light house in the immediate vicinity of a port. The keeper should be particularly respectable and trusty, for to him is confided the careful and regular lighting of the lamps — the custody of the oil &c., and on his judgment it must chiefly depend at what periods to commence and discontinue the lighting up of the lantern in each season....
>
> The keepers should be required to render a quarterly account to the nearest collector or other proper superintendant, in which they should state the number of lamps lighted each night, the number of wicks, tube glasses, buff skins, and the quantity of oil on hand at the commencement of the quarter, together with the quantity they may receive in the course of the quarter. They should also keep a journal in which they should note, each day, whatever may occur with respect to the subjects under their charge. In addition... he should be permitted to use the wood growing on the Island as fuel, and even to cultivate if he chose, the whole Island, which probably does not contain more than a hundred acres. Besides this, we recommend that Timber Island, which lies about three miles to the North west of the light house, should be held in reserve as a sort of appendage to it, for the purpose of supplying fuel, with which it now abounds, for the future use of the keeper.[48]

(24) False Ducks Island lighthouse, 1908. Photographer unknown.
Oil storehouse at left and the 2nd lightkeeper's dwelling to the right (the first dwelling burned down in 1904). One of the two men in the photograph is probably the lightkeeper, Dorland Dulmage, and the woman at the far right is probably his wife, Jennie Rose Dulmage.
[Courtesy of Library and Archives Canada, PA-172453]

Soon thereafter, forty-three year old Joseph Swetman was engaged as the first lightkeeper of the False Ducks Island lighthouse at an annual salary of £100.[49] Joseph relocated from Amherst Island to the False Ducks with his wife Sarah White along with their three daughters and two sons. A third son would be born within the year.[50] Three decades later, when his father retired in 1863, the middle son, Frederick, would take over as keeper of the False Ducks Island light.[51]

With the lighthouse finished, the lightkeeper hired and a house built for him and his family, the False Ducks Island lighthouse was ready to be placed into active service in the summer of 1829. Throughout the day on Saturday July 25, Joseph Swetman would have been putting the finishing touches on the lantern and lamps; ensuring that each pane of glass was clean, inside and out, filling each lamp with sperm-oil, trimming each lamp wick, and polishing each lens and reflector until they were all gleaming.

In the early evening that Saturday, the keeper would have slowly climbed the eighty or so stone steps that spiraled up inside the massive cylindrical tower. At the top of the stairs, in the brick-vaulted watch-room where he would have stocked extra lamps and wicks, spare panes of glass, and a few small barrels of oil, Joseph would have ascended a short ladder leading directly into the lantern.[52] The centre of the lantern was dominated by the enormous chandelier with its fifteen Lewis lamps; five facing north-east, five south-east, and five south-west. The panoramic view from a height of more than sixty feet would have been breathtaking. As twilight approached, Joseph would have just been able to catch a glimpse of Main Duck Island off to the east, Wolfe Island near Kingston to the north-east, and Amherst Island and the Upper Gap off to the north. Away to the west the huge peninsula of Prince Edward County stretched to the horizon.

The lightkeeper would have then gone about his business of methodically lighting each of the fifteen lamps. When he was finished, an intensely bright arc of light would have spread across the eastern end of Lake Ontario from the Canadian shore for the very first time.

The July 29, 1829, edition of Kingston's *Upper Canada Herald* reported the following:

> We learn from Mr. Macaulay, one of the Commissioners, who returned from the False Ducks yesterday, that the Light House is completed; and for the information of Mariners we beg to state that it has been lighted up since Saturday last. There are fifteen Lamps and reflectors shewing in every direction except towards Timber Island.[53]

The Canadian shore of eastern Lake Ontario had its first lighthouse. Over the next eighty years, a continuous chain of lake lights would be built from Kingston to Presqu'ile to help ships find their way safely through these dangerous waters.

CHAPTER 4

A Chain of Stone

Much has been done in the matter of building lighthouses.
("The British Whig," 1834)

The opening of the Welland and Oswego canals in the late 1820's coincided with pleas from ship owners and ship captains attempting to convince Canadian authorities of the need for additional lighthouses on Lake Ontario. In addition, immigration was increasing the population of Upper Canada at a steady rate into the 1830's, and more ships were being built to handle the increasing trade on the Great Lakes. This activity prompted the Legislative Assembly of the province to acknowledge:

> From the great increase of population and the consequent increase of trade and commerce upon Lakes Erie and Ontario, that Light Houses should be erected in other parts of these Lakes, as it has frequently happened in stormy weather and dark nights that much property, and even lives, were lost for the want of proper lights to direct them.[1]

While the False Ducks Island lighthouse continued to be an important aid to navigation for mariners sailing from York or Oswego to Kingston, there was still a long stretch of treacherous waters from Cobourg, past Presqu'ile and along the south shore of Prince Edward County that remained unlit. Between 1832 and 1840, the pace of lighthouse construction along the north shore of Lake Ontario quickened. By the time this latest lighthouse building phase was at an end, there was a veritable chain of stone lighthouses stretching from Kingston to Presqu'ile. This "chain of stone" helped to keep goods and people moving by guiding ships safely through the hazardous waters around the Prince Edward peninsula.

Point Petre Lighthouse (1833)

Within two years of the False Ducks Island lighthouse going into active service, mariners on Lake Ontario were once again petitioning the government for the construction of more lighthouses at the eastern end of the lake. In 1831, the Upper Canada Legislature received a petition for a second lighthouse in Prince Edward County.

The petition was submitted by Captain Joseph Whitney of Prescott on behalf of twelve ship captains, all of them masters of schooners or steamboats, and all of whom would have had experience navigating the hazardous waters of eastern Lake Ontario. Whitney himself had been master of the schooner *Julia* for more than ten years and then captain of the steamboat *Queenston* for four years. In 1831, he had just been appointed captain of the newly built *Great Britain*, then the largest steamboat on the Great Lakes.[2] His experience would have made him well aware of the dangerous Prince Edward coast and the difficult approach to Kingston, and the importance of additional lighthouses in this area for the safety of vessels.

A committee of the Legislative Assembly, convened to consider the mariners' petition, was chaired by William Chisholm. Chisholm was an influential landowner and the elected member for Halton who, a few years earlier, had been one of the commissioners for the Burlington Bay Canal.[3]

In December, 1831, the committee submitted their report to the Legislature:

REPORT
Of the Select Committee on the Petition of
Captain Whitney and others, on the subject
of a Light House on Long Point
To the Honorable the House of Assembly

The Select Committee to whom was referred the Petition of Captain Whitney, of the Steam Boat *Great Britain*, and twelve others, Masters of Vessels on Lake Ontario, on the benefit to be derived from a Light House on Long Point, situate sixty miles from Kingston, on the North side of Lake Ontario — Beg leave to Report as follows:

Your Committee, in order to gain the necessary information respecting the benefit to be derived from a Light House on Long Point, otherwise called Salmon or Wicket Point, have had before them Captains Whitney, Mosier, John McIntosh, Tase, Charles McIntosh, Boyle, Zealand, Kerr, Kendrick, Ross, Smith, and Kent, who all perfectly coincide in opinion that the navigation of Lake Ontario would derive a very great and important advantage from a Light House on Long Point, as it is the most prominent place on the North side of the Lake, and where Vessels, either in going up or down, make for in order to shape their course for the head or lower end of the Lake; and for the want of a Light House upon it, lives and property are frequently exposed to risk and danger; and they all particularly recommend a revolving light to be adopted, that it may be distinguished from the one on the False Ducks, as when head winds prevail, should both lights be of the same description, the one, in some instances, (from their contiguity to each other), might be taken for the other.

Your Committee have no doubt of the importance and advantage to the navigation of Lake Ontario to be derived from a Light House on Long Point, other wise called Salmon or Wicket Point, and they think the sum of — pounds would defray the charge of its erection, and the necessary lamps; and they recommend that it be provided for agreeable to the prayer of the petition: that Commissioners be appointed to fix upon the proper site, and Contract for, and superintend its erection.

December 30th, 1831.[4]

Among the captains called to testify before the Committee were Charles Macintosh, the primary witness for the False Ducks Island lighthouse committee two years earlier, along with his older brother John, who was also an experienced schooner captain.[5] In addition, there was Captain John Mosier, a twenty-year veteran of the Lakes who formerly commanded the schooners *Mary Ann* and *Lady Maitland* and then became master and owner of the steamboat *Niagara*,[6] as well as Edward Zealand of Hamilton with fifteen years of sailing experience on the Lakes. In addition, Joseph Whitney himself appeared as one of the witnesses. The legislative committee could not hope for a more experienced group of mariners.

The references made in the Committee's report to "Long Point" are somewhat ambiguous. Many early maps mark the whole southern portion of Prince Edward County, from Point Traverse and Prince Edward Point in the east to Point Petre and Salmon Point in the west, as Long Point. The report specifically refers to Long Point as also being called Wicked Point or Salmon Point. Other sources limit the term Long Point to the area in the immediate vicinity of Point Petre. The *Atlas of Canada* shows that only the area at the extreme south-easterly end of Prince Edward County, between Gravelly Bay and Point Traverse, is today called Long Point.[7] None of these places should be confused with Long Point on the north shore of Lake Erie where another lighthouse was being built at the same time.

Perhaps the Committee's ambiguity about the location for the lighthouse was intentional as there may have been some disagreement among the ship captains as to precisely which place would be best for an aid to navigation. In order to ensure that the new lighthouse would be situated in the most advantageous location, the Parliament of Upper Canada passed an act in January, 1832, authorizing the construction of a lighthouse to be located somewhere between Nicholson Island (which is some distance west of Salmon Point) and The Ducks where the False Ducks Island lighthouse stood:

> AN ACT for granting to His Majesty a sum of Money to defray the expense of erecting a Light-House between Nicholson's Island and the Ducks, and for appointing Commissioners to superintend the erection thereof
>
> Passed 28th January, 1832.
>
> WHERAS it would tend greatly to the safety and convenience of the Navigation of Lake Ontario, if a Light-House were erected between Nicholson's Island and the Ducks, in the County of Prince Edward, on the said Lake.—Be it therefore enacted...
>
> That it shall and may be lawful immediately after the passing of this Act for the Commissioners hereinafter named to erect a good and sufficient Light House, upon the most eligible situation between Nicholson's Island and the Ducks, in the county of Prince Edward, in the Midland District, as they shall judge the most proper; and also to provide the necessary apparatus for Lighting the same.
>
> II. And be it further enacted by the authority aforesaid, That John Macaulay, Esquire; Simeon Washburn, Esquire, James McKenzie, Esquire; John Marks, Esquire; and Louther Pinnington McPherson, Esquire, in the Midland district, be Commissioners for the purposes of this Act.
>
> III. And be it further enacted by the authority aforesaid, That from and out of the Rates and Dues now raised, levied and collected, or which may be hereafter raised, levied

and collected, and remaining in the hands of the Receiver General unappropriated, there be granted to His Majesty the sum of One Thousand Pounds, to enable His Majesty to defray the expense of erecting the said Light-House and furnishing the same....[8]

Certainly there were a number of suitable locations to build a lighthouse along the 30-mile stretch of shoreline between Nicholson Island and False Ducks Island. Nicholson Island itself was a prominent feature off the western-most point of Prince Edward County and situated just beyond the north-eastern terminus of the mostly-submerged Scotch Bonnet shoal. Further east there was Salmon Point (also known as Wicked Point), Point Petre and Gull Point, all of which were located near dangerous shoals. The newly appointed commissioners would have to make a difficult decision about which of these locations was the best site for the new lighthouse.

Undoubtedly because of their experience with the construction of the False Ducks Island lighthouse, both John Macaulay and Captain James McKenzie were re-appointed as commissioners. They were joined by three other commissioners, two of whom — Simeon Washburn and Lowther P. Macpherson — were Prince Edward County residents.

Simeon Washburn was the son of Hallowell merchant Ebenezer Washburn. He had studied law in York and had became a successful lawyer. In 1830, he had tried to win a seat in the Legislative Assembly as member for York County, but was defeated by William Lyon Mackenzie. After Mackenzie's expulsion from the Assembly, Washburn ran against him again in a by-election in 1832, and again was defeated by the popular reformer. As the government's preferred candidate, Washburn's appointment as lighthouse commissioner may have been one of his rewards for trying to unseat Mackenzie who was disliked by many conservative government officials and members of the Family Compact. Washburn later became the chairman of the Prince Edward district school board and was eventually appointed as a member of the Legislative Council.[9]

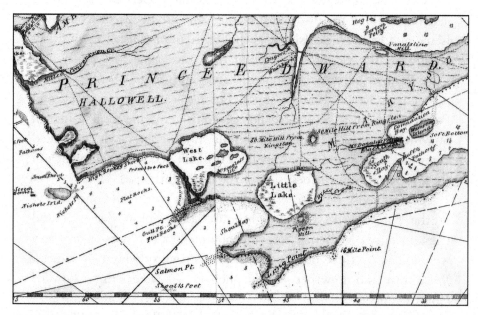

(25) Prince Edward County's south shore. From Augustus Ford's *Chart of Lake Ontario,* 1836 (detail).

To the left, Nicholson Island is marked as "Nichols Island". At lower centre, Salmon Point is shown, East Lake is marked as "Little Lake" and Point Petre is marked as "Long Point". Gull Bar is marked as "16 Mile Point". At upper centre, Picton is marked as "Washburn" and Glenora is marked as "Vanalstine Mill".

[Courtesy of Library and Archives Canada, NMC11314]

Lowther P. MacPherson, was a Scot who had settled at Kingston before moving to Hallowell in Prince Edward County to practice law. He is usually remembered as the sickly cousin of John A. MacDonald. The eighteen-year-old Macdonald took over cousin Lowther's law practice in Prince Edward County from 1833 until 1835, and later became Attorney-General of the Province of Canada before becoming the Dominion of Canada's first prime minister in 1867.[10]

The fifth commissioner, John Marks was a resident of Kingston and secretary to Commodore Barrie, the ranking naval officer on the Great Lakes. He was also a business associate of John Macaulay's, being a fellow shareholder in the Cataraqui Bridge Company. Marks later went into provincial politics and sat as a member of the Assembly in the last Parliament of Upper Canada (1836 to 1840) before Upper and Lower Canada were joined to form the United Province of Canada in 1841.[11]

In May, 1832, three of the commissioners, Macaulay, Marks and Macpherson, together with the architect of the False Ducks Island lighthouse, Thomas Rogers, set out to make a detailed examination of the southern shoreline of Prince Edward County. Their purpose was to find the best location for the proposed lighthouse. After examining several potential sites, they were disappointed at being unable to agree on the best location. In their report to the legislature, the commissioners summarized their subsequent decision-making process:

16 November 1832
The undersigned Commissioners...
Humbly Report:
That three of their number proceeded personally to examine the coast lying between Nicholson's Island and the Ducks, in order to ascertain the proper site for the building they were directed to construct. Subsequently, on conferring with the other two Commissioners on this subject, it was found that the Board were not unanimous in their opinions. One Commissioner was in favour of Gull or Gravel Point [Gull Bar], five or six miles east of Point Peters [Point Petre], in the County of Prince Edward; and another Commissioner

considered Salmon Point, lying about seven miles west of Point Peters, as the most eligible site. The remaining three Commissioners, among whom was the late Captain James McKenzie... gave a preference to Point Peters, (commonly known among mariners as Long Point) in which preference they were confirmed on inquiring into the opinions of such Masters of Steamers and other vessels as they had an opportunity of consulting. It was then determined by the voice of the majority that the Light House should be built on Point Peters; and advertisements having been issued requiring tenders for the construction of the tower, the contract was, on the sixth day of June, given to Messrs. Matthews and Scott, who undertook for the sum of three hundred and ninety-eight pounds to complete the mason's and carpenter's work by the fifteenth day of September last. A contract was also made with Mr. Thomas Masson, blacksmith, for the lantern, which was to be completed on the first day of October, for the sum of one hundred and sixty-four pounds and ten shillings; and the chandelier, lamps, reflectors and glass, were ordered from Boston, at which city it appeared that those articles could be most advantageously obtained. The whole work was placed under the superintendence of Mr. Thomas Rogers.

John Macaulay, John Mark, L.P. Macpherson [12]

Ultimately, the commissioners based their decision on the recommendations of the ship captains who had experience sailing these waters. An examination of nautical charts of the area show that Point Petre[13] was a good choice. (See figures 25 and 57) Extensive shoals extend for some distance into the lake from this point as part of the submarine Point Petre Ridge. This is also the most southerly point of the Prince Edward peninsula, making it a natural landfall that mariners used to set their course either towards the False Ducks and onward to Kingston, or towards Presqu'ile and onward to Cobourg, York and Niagara.

The commissioners proceeded to hire local land surveyor William Conger to mark off a six acre lighthouse reserve at Point Petre. There was some uncertainty about whether or not local resident Benjamin Gerow had clear title to the land at the point which he had acquired from the Canada Land Company. In the end, Gerow was paid nine pounds ten shillings for his interest in the parcel, and the Canada Land Company was paid three pounds.[14]

As with the False Ducks Island lighthouse, Kingston architect Thomas Rogers was engaged to design the Point Petre lighthouse and to oversee the construction project. Robert Matthews, Rogers' long-time associate, won the contract to do the mason-work in partnership with William Scott, one of the other masons who had worked on the False Ducks Island lighthouse. In May, 1832, Rogers drew up plans for the new lighthouse and published the detailed building specifications:

PUBLIC NOTICE.
Light-house on Point Peters [Point Petre],
commonly called Long Point.

The Commissioners appointed by Statute for the erection of a Light-house, between Nicholson's Island and the Ducks, in the County of Prince Edward, hereby give notice, that they will receive tenders until Wednesday the 6th day of June next, for the construction of a Stone Tower for the said Light on Point Peter, in the township of Hallowell, according to the design (which may be seen on application to the subscriber) and to the following

SPECIFICATIONS

The Tower is to be built sixty feet high from the ground line to the bottom side of the projecting courses, under the landing of the Lantern Gallery. The said ground line is to be fixed on by the Commissioners appointed for carrying on the said work, or by some other person whom they may appoint for that purpose. The said Tower is to be circular, and at the ground floor line seventeen feet in diameter, from outside to outside. The well hole for the stairs, &c. to be ten feet two inches in diameter: the walls at the ground floor line to be three feet six inches thick, and two feet thick at the top. The wall, on the inside, is to be carried up plumb and fair from the ground floor line to the springing of the brick arch at the top: the outside face of the building to have a regular batter of one foot six inches all round, from the ground line to the projecting courses at the top, and every part is to be carried up straight and fair, and all is to be neatly hammer dressed. Put over the door, an 18 inch hammer dressed arch. Put in six windows in the whole height of the tower, of two lights each, 9 by 7 glass....

To build and turn a foot brick arch, substantially filled in behind. Leave a trap door way through the said arch, two feet square in the clear, and put in the proper place: also, put a cut stone landing or floor on the top....

After the tower is built, it is to be well pointed on the outside face, with good cement made up for that purpose, and it is to be made up with such materials and in such a manner as the Commissioners, or such person as they may appoint, shall direct; in short, every part of the building is to be made water tight and of lasting materials....

An outside scaffold is to be erected the whole height of the tower, and left for the use of the person who may be employed to set up the lantern; and after the lantern has been set up. the scaffold is to be removed, and the whole of the pointing completed by the Contractors....
The work must be completed on 15th September next.
THOMAS ROGERS, Superintendant
25th May, 1832 [15]

Although no copies of the original plans of the Point Petre lighthouse have been found, architectural drawings of the lighthouse based on the detailed specifications have been reproduced in figure 26.

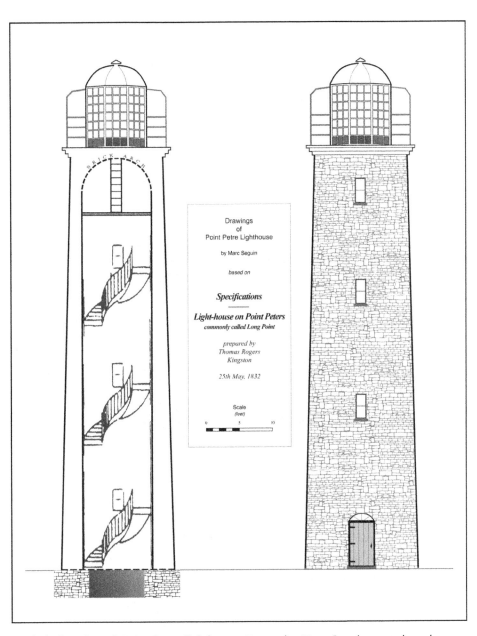

Drawings
of
Point Petre Lighthouse

by Marc Seguin

based on

Specifications
———
Light-house on Point Peters
commonly called Long Point

prepared by
Thomas Rogers
Kingston

25th May, 1832

Scale
(feet)
0   5   10

(26) Elevation of Point Petre lighthouse. Drawn by Marc Seguin, 2012, based on specifications prepared by Thomas Rogers, architect, May 1832.
[Author's collection]

Instead of sourcing the lantern in the United States as had been done for the False Ducks Island lighthouse, the fabrication of the lantern was contracted to a Kingston blacksmith, Thomas Masson. Masson would later become one of the founding members of the Kingston Mechanic's Institute together with fellow lighthouse associates John Macaulay and Robert Matthews.[16]

The lamps, reflectors and other fixtures for the light were ordered, as before, from Winslow Lewis of Boston, Massachusetts.

Work on the tower proceeded quickly. Under the direction of the masons Robert Matthews and William Scott, ground at Point Petre was excavated to a depth of about two and a half feet, and a solid stone foundation was laid. Good progress was made on the tower through the spring of 1832. Then tragedy struck.

A cholera epidemic, which had swept through Europe and Britain, had arrived in Canada. It is thought that emigrants from Ireland who had taken passage to Canada on board the brig *Carricks*, carried the disease with them when they landed at Quebec on June 3, 1832.[17] The disease spread quickly. There were fifteen cases reported at Quebec as of June 9, and ninety-one cases at Montreal three days later.[18] Kingston, being the largest port on Lake Ontario at the time, would have been one of the first stopping points for many Upper Canada-bound immigrants who had disembarked at Quebec or Montreal. A Kingston newspaper reported that the disease had reached there by June 20:

> Our most fearful anticipations have been outdone, and we have to announce the appearance of the disease in this town, within two weeks of its first breaking out on the continent, and in less than a week after its near approach had so much increased the apprehensions of our town. — We know not what a day may bring forth, and therefore, leave the future to the realities which God in his Providence will disclose....
>
> The Cholera is indeed among us, and is running with unretarded steps along the great thoroughfare from Quebec up the St. Lawrence.[19]

(27) Immigrants in the hold of a steamer on the St. Lawrence River. Woodblock engraving, *Emigrants on the St. Lawrence*, by Gustave Dore, 1870.
Although this engraving dates from 1870, transportation and health conditions had not changed much for most immigrants since the cholera epidemic of 1832 swept across Upper Canada.
[From Ainsworth, *All Round the World*, 1871]

In 1832, little was known of the disease or how it was spread, and there was no known cure. The symptoms of nausea and severe gastro-intestinal distress were well documented, and mortality rates of close to 60% were often recorded.[20] It would not be until 1854, however, that it was first postulated that cholera might be a water-borne disease transmitted by fecal contamination of drinking water. Later in the 19th Century the bacterium *Vibrio cholerae* was confirmed at the cause.[21] In the 1830's, however, people were desperate for anything that might prevent or cure the disease, and numerous, ineffective mixtures and potions were proposed. One such recipe was published at the height of the epidemic in Prince Edward County's Hallowell *Free Press*:

> One pennyworth of cinnamon to be boiled in a pint
> of water, on a slow fire, so as that there will be one pint

when cold and strained — mix carefully in a bottle with one ounce of calcined magnesia, half a teaspoonful of grated ginger, and the like quantity of powdered lump sugar, shake very well, & take a wine-glass full each day about twelve o'clock. This will prove a most effectual preservative against Cholera, more especially in persons of temperate habits.[22]

By the end of June 1832, the epidemic had taken 39 lives at Kingston. By the middle of July, the official death toll had climbed to 48, but no new cases of the disease had been reported since July 11.[23] Just as the epidemic was on the decline in Kingston, one of the lighthouse commissioners, Captain James McKenzie, contracted the disease and died in August. The sad news of his death was printed in the *Upper Canada Herald*:

It will be perceived that Captain James McKenzie, a gentleman universally known and respected in Upper Canada, died of Cholera on Monday last. He was attacked with the disease in its most violent form on Sunday, and altho' efficient medical aid was promptly procured, every exertion for his recovery proved fruitless.

Died - Of cholera, at his lodgings at Kingston, on Monday the 27th inst., aged 50 years, James McKenzie, Esquire, a Master in the Royal Navy....

In the year 1816, he ... assisted in fitting up the *Frontenac*, the first steamboat used on the waters of Upper Canada, which he commanded till she was worn out - since he has commanded the *Alciope* on this Lake, and at the time of his death was engaged in the construction of two other steamboats, one at the Head of the Lake, and one at Lake Simcoe; and he was on most occasions consulted respecting the construction and management of steamboats, so that he may be justly called the father of steam navigation in Upper Canada.

In his manners he was mild and unassuming. His memory will be long cherished in the recollection of his numerous friends and acquaintances in this town as well as in other parts of the province, and his death may be considered a great loss to society and to the country.[24]

Both of the principal masons for the Point Petre lighthouse were also infected with cholera. William Scott died. Robert Matthews was more fortunate and survived his encounter with the disease. After some weeks, he had recovered and returned to Prince Edward County to complete the stonework on the tower.

As a result of the delays caused by the epidemic, the main structure of the lighthouse was not completed until some six weeks after the original target date. Its completion was delayed further when, just as Thomas Masson had secured the lantern in its place on top of the tower, a sudden, violent storm blew out many of the lantern's glass panes. As a result, Thomas Rogers and Alexander Ross, a member of the building crew, worked feverishly over the course of the following twelve days to replace many of the more than 100 panes of glass in the lantern.[25]

By November 8, 1832 the whole structure was complete and the light had been successfully tested. The commissioners proudly remarked that:

> This Light House is a neat structure, and less costly than the building at the False Duck's Island. The Commissioners have indeed great satisfaction in speaking favourably of the work of the Contractors, who are most respectable persons, and have performed their engagements in a very creditable manner. The tour is build in the most substantial manner, and cannot fail to endure for ages. It is pointed out-side instead of being rough-cast like that at the False Ducks, and has less batter [less taper from bottom to top] than the last mentioned one....
>
> The tower is sixty-one feet and six inches above the floor or ground line. The lantern is precisely of the same dimensions as that at the False Ducks; but as there is not so wide a range over the water at Point Peters as at that

Island, fewer lamps were considered necessary. At the False Ducks there are fifteen lamps used, while at Point Peters eleven only have been set up. There will of course be a corresponding reduction in the annual consumption of oil at the latter place.[26]

Although the two lighthouses were almost identical in size and shape, the Point Petre lighthouse had been less costly to build than the False Ducks Island lighthouse. Of the £1,000 allocated to the Point Petre project, only £856 was spent. At the False Ducks, cost overruns of more than ten percent resulted in a final cost of more than £1,110. While some of the cost difference can be attributed to the fact that the False Ducks light used fifteen lamps and reflectors compared to the eleven at Point Petre, most of the cost difference lay in the amount paid to the masons, which at £546 for the False Ducks tower was some £150 more than at Point Petre. This significant difference was most likely due to the extra expenses that the masons incurred at False Ducks Island in transporting most of the building materials and the workmen to the remote island location.

On November 14, John Macaulay sent a letter to Jacques Bâby, the Inspector-General of Upper Canada, stating:

> That the Light-house on Point Peters is completed, and that the lamps, reflectors, and other furniture, are in their places and ready for use. All that is now required is to appoint a keeper, provide oil, and build a dwelling-house, which the Act did not authorise....[27]

With no oil for the lamps, no keeper to light the lamps and no house for a lightkeeper to live in, it would appear that the commissioners had not planned very well for the final stage of actually putting the Point Petre lighthouse into active service!

Macaulay's reasoning on the subject of the oil may be valid:

Every thing is now in preparation at the building for lighting it up, except the oil, which the Commissioners did not purchase, because until very recently, they were not certain that the building would be completed so as to be used (if thought proper) before the close of the navigation.[28]

The Inspector-General forwarded Macaulay's request for oil, staff and housing to Lieutenant Governor Sir John Colborne, with an urgent appeal for additional funds:

I beg to submit, that as the use of this Light-house is so much wished for, particularly at this season of the year, that until some provision be made, I may be authorised to direct the necessary expenses to maintain the same, to be defrayed from the receipts of duties arising on Imports, and on Inn and Shop-keeper's licences... until suitable provision should be made.[29]

It would appear that either the Lieutenant-Governor did not make any monies available for these extra expenses, or it was decided that it was already too late in the year to make a difference, as the navigation season on Lake Ontario usually did not extend much beyond the first week of December. Regardless, the lighthouse was not officially activated until the spring of 1833.

An amount of £125 was eventually allocated for a dwelling for the first keeper, Owen Richards.[30] Richards was a founding officer of the Township of Hallowell and had been the colonel of the 2nd Battalion of Prince Edward Militia since the regiment had been formed a decade earlier. Colonel Richards' appointment as lightkeeper at the age of sixty-five was probably a political favour. He kept the light at Point Petre for ten years after which, at the age of 75, he found it too difficult to perform his duties and was appointed as keeper of the Queen's Wharf lighthouse in Toronto.[31] In 1843, William Anson Palen replaced Richards as the Point Petre lightkeeper.[32]

(28) Point Petre lighthouse, c. 1910. Photograph by Marsden Kemp.
A steam-powered fog horn was added to the light station in 1890. The fog-alarm building behind the lighthouse was built at that time to house the steam engine. [Courtesy of Archives of Ontario]

Nine Mile Point Lighthouse (1833)

Barely two months after the completion of the work on the Point Petre lighthouse, the Upper Canada legislature read a petition from "Robert Hamilton, and eight others, masters and owners of vessels navigating Lake Ontario, praying that a Light House may be erected on the Nine Mile Point, near Kingston. Jan. 19, 1833".[33]

As far back as 1803, a lighthouse had been planned for Nine Mile Point. While the Mississauga Point lighthouse at Niagara and the Gibraltar Point lighthouse at York had been constructed, it is not clear why the tower at Nine Mile Point was not built as directed by the original legislation. Now, thirty years later, realizing the importance of lighthouses to the vital shipping trade, the legislature was willing to revisit this subject.

Robert Hamilton, who brought the petition before the legislators, was a prominent Queenston resident and influential ship owner. Before the improvement of the Welland Canal in the 1830's diverted much of the carrying trade away from the Niagara River, his company controlled the Canadian portion of the trade around Niagara Falls between Queenston and Chippewa. In addition, he financed the construction of the Lake Ontario steamboats *Queenston* and *Alciope*, as well as the *Queen Adelaide* on Lake Erie.[34]

Two weeks after its introduction to the Assembly, the petition was discussed by a legislative committee which immediately recommended the allocation of £750 for the construction of the lighthouse. Fourteen days later, on February 13, 1833, the Legislative Assembly passed a bill for the construction of the Nine Mile Point Lighthouse. The Act was quickly approved by the Upper House, the Legislative Council, and by the Lieutenant-Governor's advisors in the Executive Council before is was given Royal Assent by Lieutenant-Governor Sir John Colborne. The speed by which the Upper Canada parliament passed this legislation was an indication of the perceived importance of this lighthouse for the safety of the vital shipping trade into and out of Kingston harbour. It took a mere 28 days from the reading of the original petition, through the committee process and having the legislation passed and proclaimed into law:

AN ACT
granting a Sum of Money to defray the expense of
erecting a Light-House
on Nine Mile Point, at the entrance of the
Harbour of Kingston.
(Passed 13th February, 1833)

Whereas it is necessary, for the security of vessels navigating Lake Ontario, that a Light House should be erected on a Point called Nine Mile Point, at the entrance of the Harbour of Kingston, in the Midland District: We beseech Your Majesty that it may be enacted: And be it enacted, by the King's Most Excellent Majesty, by and with the advice and consent of the Legislative Council and Assembly of the Province of Upper Canada...

That there be granted to His Majesty, from and out of the rates and duties levied and collected, and in the hands of the Receiver General unappropriated, the sum of Seven Hundred and Fifty Pounds, to be applied towards the erection and completion of a Light-House on a Point called Nine Mile Point, at the entrance of the Harbour of Kingston, in the Midland District.

And be it further enacted by the aforsaid authority, That John Macaulay, John Marks, and Hugh Christopher Thomson, Esquires, be Commissioners to contract for, and superintend the erection and completion of the said Light-House.[35]

Again, John Macaulay was appointed as lighthouse commissioner along with the navy's representative, John Marks. They were joined this time by fellow Kingston resident, Hugh Thomson who was the owner and editor of a Kingston newspaper, the *Upper Canada Herald*, as well as being one of the elected members of the Legislative Assembly representing Frontenac County. Both Thomson and Macaulay, concurrent with their lighthouse commissions, were also members of the board of commissioners looking into the establishment of a provincial penitentiary at Kingston.[36]

The lighthouse commissioners' first task was to procure a plot of land at Nine Mile Point. The point is on the western tip of what is today known as Simcoe Island. During the French Regime, the governor of New France, Le Comte de Frontenac, had granted the island, then known as Belle Isle, to one of his lieutenants, Monsieur Du Foret, after which time the island was usually known as Isle du Foret, Ile Foret, or Forest Island.[37] The island was later known as both Simcoe Island and Gage Island. In 1951, the name Simcoe Island was officially adopted.[38]

Given that the point is only about six statute miles [9.6 kms] from Kingston, it seems odd that it is called Nine Mile Point. One possible explanation is that, during the French Regime, it had been determined that the distance from Fort Frontenac, at the mouth of the Cataraqui River, to the tip of Ile du Foret was a distance of *trois ligne ancienne* or three old French leagues. This French league was roughly equivalent to just over two English miles. The British, it seems, never did the conversion from the *ligne ancienne* to the English league which is equal to three statute miles, not two. The original Upper Canada lighthouse legislation passed in 1803 itself was mistaken when it stated "...Isle Forest, situated about three leagues [9 statute miles] from the town of Kingston,"[39] when in fact is was only two English leagues (6 miles) from Kingston. The mistake was never corrected and the name Nine Mile Point stuck.

In 1833, the owner of most of the land on Simcoe Island, the Honourable Charles Grant, Baron de Longeuil — who also owned Wolfe Island[40] — donated five acres at the island's western point to allow the government to build a lighthouse. In their report of November 22, 1833, the commissioners noted Grant's generosity:

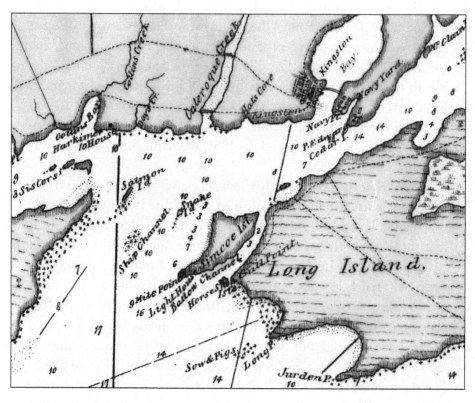

(29) The approaches to Kingston. From Augustus Ford's *Chart of Lake Ontario*, 1836 (detail).

Simcoe Island and Nine Mile Point are clearly shown. To the left, the Lower Gap is marked as "Ship Channel" and the Brother Islands are marked as "3 Sisters". To the right, Wolfe Island is marked as "Long Island", Point Henry is marked as "P. Edward", and Portsmouth (Hatters Bay) is marked as "Hats Cove".
[Courtesy of Library and Archives Canada, NMC11314]

The site for the Light-House having been fixed by the Legislature, it was found that it belonged to the Honourable Charles W. Grant and others, who were about disposing of the whole of Gage Island or Isle Foret, of which it forms a part, to an individual resident at Kingston.... Mr. Grant immediately, and without any hesitation, offered the Commissioners five acres on the Point, so laid off as to be most convenient for their purposes, and declined all compensation for it — an instance of liberality which the Commissioners felt themselves bound particularly to notice.[41]

As speedy as the legislation was passed to authorize the building of the lighthouse, the actual construction progress was similarly quick. Specifications for a forty-foot tall tower were drawn up by Thomas Rogers who had been hired as superintendant, and tenders were let in May, 1833. Robert Matthews, hired to build the tower, completed his task by November 1. The Lewis lamps and lantern glass had been purchased from Boston in September, and Thomas Masson had finished building and installing the lantern by November 11. Within six months of its commencement, the Nine Mile Point lighthouse was ready to be placed into service.

The commissioners further reported that:

The Light-House on Nine mile Point is similar, in respect to form and construction to the buildings at the False Ducks and Point Peters. It contains eleven lamps and reflectors like the latter, but is twenty feet lower. Being not more than twenty miles from the False Ducks, its light will be always distinctly visible even from that Island, which was more than the accommodation and safety of vessels absolutely required. A less elevation than forty feet was not thought advisable: indeed the Commissioners would have felt inclined to have raised the tower fifty feet above the surface of the lake, had the amount of the appropriation warranted them in so doing....

In the construction of the lantern, the Commissioners have to commend the skill of Mr. Thomas Masson, the Contractor; and to remark that they have added to it, with the advice of Mr. Rogers, the Superintendant, a gutter and spouts which they consider a great improvement.[42]

(30) Nine Mile Point lighthouse, c. 1896. Photographer unknown.
Note the original domed lantern. The new steam fog plant used to power the foghorn is on the left and the old fog bell in its wood-framed tower is at centre. [Courtesy of Queen's University Archives, V108.1 3-4]

As with the two earlier lighthouses, there had been no provision made for a lightkeeper's dwelling in the original legislation. As a result, the first keeper, Thomas Sparham, had to wait four years before the government provided him a residence close to the Nine Mile Point lighthouse in 1837.[43] There is no record of where Sparham lived until then.

—————⟶ ∾∿∘◦❍◇❍◦∘∿∾ ⟵—————

By the end of 1833 then, three key lighthouses had been constructed in eastern Lake Ontario to guide mariners most of the way around the anvil-like peninsula of Prince Edward County. Lighthouses at False Ducks Island, Point Petre, and Nine Mile Point allowed ships to sail these waters with greater safety and convenience than ever before. However, the lighting characteristics, and even the existence of these lighthouses, was not completely without controversy. The Nine Mile Point commissioners had hinted of that in their original report:

> Many persons are of opinion that if the Tower at Nine mile Point had been built upwards of sixty feet in height, the light at the False Ducks might have been dispensed with. At present the three Light Houses at Nine mile Point, the False Ducks, and Point Peters, contain stationary lights of a white colour, and are all alike. It may become, in time, advisable to make some distinction between them by means of red lights and revolving machinery, to prevent mistakes by negligent, or incautious, or inexperienced mariners.[44]

Perhaps the commissioners' comments had been influenced by a letter written that October by a steamboat passenger from Prince Edward County and printed in the *Kingston Spectator* :

> To the Editor of the Spectator.
> Sir, - Perhaps it may be a future benefit to Captains and masters of vessels to state a few particulars through your paper in reference to the Light Houses on Point Peters [Point Petre] and the False Ducks, etc., these two lights give the same appearance, there is only one building on Nine Mile point (Simcoe Island) intended to give a similar light.

The fish lights which are numerous on the shores and bars of the lake, give the same appearance, so that it baffles the skill of mariners to distinguish them especially in hazy weather; now to show the difficulty sailors have in this case, and the necessity that the middle light [at False Ducks Island] ought to be a revolving one, cannot better be illustrated than by stating the difficulty we had in a foggy night, not seeing Point Peters light, and our being obliged to call at the Duck's light house in "the dead of the night" to enquire what light this is: our Captain and hands saying it must be Point Peters light; a distinguishing light on the False Ducks would obviate all objections respecting the Light Houses and remove the difficulty of sameness in that particular with regard to the fish lights; for it can hardly be conceived that Point Peters light can be taken for the one building on Simcoe Island, having a revolving light between them....

Now suppose a vessel crossing the lake from the American side for South Bay or the upper gap, the False Ducks light not being seen but the one as Point Peters, how is the mariner to be satisfied he cannot mistake this light for the False Ducks, they being about twenty miles distant from each other, whereas in a distinguishing light, there could be no such mistake. A thing so obvious need not to be enlarged on, would it not be preferable to dispense with the lights altogether, than not be able to distinguish them. To render them efficient and useful must be to make them so distinguishable that there remains no doubt to the mariner about it.

The above is respectfully submitted to those who have the care of such matters.

Your obed't Servant, A LANDSMAN.

Hillier, October 24th, 1833.[45]

Two years later, with the three lighthouses still exhibiting a fixed white light, the same complaint was still being made:

To the manifold advantages arising from the navigation of the inland seas of North America, may be ascribed the present state of prosperity, limited as it is, which the Upper Province of Canada enjoys, and consequently it must be universally felt that every improvement suggested for the encouragement of this trade, should be forwarded with all the energies which the population are capable of exerting.....

While on this subject we have to observe, that many complaints have reached us of the uniformity of the lights on the British side of Lake Ontario, which must necessarily, in dark or foggy weather, occasion much doubt in the mind of the navigator, and have a tendency to lead to very fatal consequences. The light on Nine Mile Point we would more particularly allude to, as being one which first deserves the attention of the Legislature. The dangerous situation of this point of land is too well known to require description; but the many fatal and ruinous accidents which it occasions call for some immediate remedy. It has been suggested to us, that if a revolving light was substituted, in place of the one now used, it would have the effect of removing, in a great measure, the dangerous character of the Nine Mile Point. The cost of an alteration of this kind, would be but trifling; say about £50 to £100 - but the consideration of even a greater sum should not be entertained for a moment, when life and property are so much involved in the question.

We hope soon to see the day, when matters calculated to advance the internal improvement of the country, such as the one we have now touched on, will occupy more the attention of our legislators, and take the place of the useless and acrimonious discussions on comparatively trifling subjects, which have hitherto too much characterised the proceedings of our domestic Parliament.[46]

In 1831, the original petition of the twelve ship captains for the Point Petre lighthouse had recommended that it be fitted with a revolving light, "... that it may be distinguished from the one on the False Ducks."[47] After considering all three lighthouses to determine which one should have a different lighting characteristic, on March 4, 1837, the legislature passed a bill authorizing, "... the further sum of One Hundred Pounds, for the purpose of changing the construction of the light on False Ducks Island, so as to make it a revolving light."[48] However, this revolving apparatus was never installed in the lantern of the False Ducks Island lighthouse, and six more years would pass before the Board of Works had a revolving light installed, not at the False Ducks, but at Point Petre, in 1843.[49] The following notice was published at the beginning of the navigation season, in May 1844:

> Point Peter, or Long Point
> Light House.
> On Lake Ontario
> Notice is hereby given that the light hitherto established on Long Point, Lake Ontario, [Point Petre] as a fixed one, has been altered, and now shows as a revolving light, for the purpose of its being easily distinguished from the other Lights at Presqu'isle and the False Ducks. Its period of revolution is about two minutes.
> THOMAS A. BEGLY
> Secretary, Board of Works, Kingston
> May 1st, 1844[50]

Presqu'ile Point Lighthouse (1840)

While the debate was going on over which of the first three lighthouses should get a new lighting system, the Provincial Parliament passed an act in 1837 authorizing the construction of a fourth lighthouse in eastern Lake Ontario waters.[51] This new lighthouse was to be located on Presqu'ile Point, at the entrance to Presqu'ile Bay to the west of the Prince Edward peninsula.

Unlike the previous lighthouses that were authorized and built relatively quickly, several years of petitioning and political wrangling preceded the Legislature's approval of the Presqu'ile Point lighthouse, and several more years followed before its construction was completed.

In 1797, when the capital of the Newcastle District was laid out on the Presqu'ile peninsula, Presqu'ile Bay had been viewed as a potentially important commercial harbour. Even though the district seat was later moved to Cobourg, the bay was still an important harbour of refuge, if for no other reason than it was the only natural harbour between York and South Bay, on the eastern side of Prince Edward County. Writers in the 1820's described its importance:

> The District of Newcastle is rapidly increasing in population, & its lands, in point of fertility, are inferior to none in the Province, but it is, unfortunately, destitute of good harbours. The only one indeed, deserving the name, is Presque isle, but that is situated at the lower extremity of the District, and of no use whatever to the whole line of coast extending from thence to York, a distance of one hundred miles. [*Kingston Chronicle,* 1820] [52]

> Presque isle or Newcastle harbour is in the township of Cramahe, more than half way from York to Kingston. It is protected from winds, and almost encircled by a peninsula, which projects in a curve into the lake. The basin of water thus embayed is of sufficient depth, and the shore is convenient for a landing place. But the entrance into the harbour, being not very direct and plain, requires considerable care. [*Statistical Account of Upper Canada,* 1822][53]

As a harbour of refuge, Presqu'ile Bay provided shelter for numerous ships including the steamboat *Cobourg* that sheltered in the bay for two days in October 1834 while a gale raged on Lake Ontario:

Severe Gale - Wednesday night last was one of the stormiest ever experienced on the Lake, and in consequence the several steamboats on their trip during the gale have been more or less thrown out of their regular course for the present. Great apprehensions were entertained for the safety of the *Cobourg*, that should have made her appearance here on Tuesday. She however arrived safe and sound yesterday, (Friday) having remained in shelter for two days at Presque Isle.[54]

(30.1) The steamboat *Great Britain*. Sketch by W.J. Thomson, 1893.
Built in 1830 with two steam engines, the *Great Britain* was the most powerful ship on the Great Lakes, a title she held for several years. She was plagued with mechanical failures due largely to the use of brittle cast iron engine components. Like most steamboats of the time, the *Great Britain* was designed to carry both passengers and cargo.
[From *Robertson's Landmarks of Toronto*, 1896]

Had it not been for the shelter afforded by the Presqu'ile peninsula, the *Cobourg* might have suffered the fate of the steamboat *Great Britain*, under the command of Captain Whitney, which, after setting out from Kingston on her way up the lake, was badly damaged in the same gale:

The *Great Britain* went out from our harbour [Kingston harbour] on Wednesday evening, and succeeded in breasting the gale till within six miles of the Ducks, when she was compelled to put about. On her way back, near Kingston, the crank of one of her engines broke, and before the steam could be blowed off, so much mischief was done, that the engine is rendered perfectly useless. In consequence of this accident, this noble vessel will, we regret to be informed, have to be laid up for the season.[55]

Later that same year, Dr. Edward Barker, owner and editor of the Kingston newspaper the *British Whig*, printed an extensive account of his steamboat excursion to Toronto in which he made a strong case for establishing a lighthouse on the Presqu'ile peninsula:

THE EDITOR'S TRIP TO TORONTO
(Part 3)

Our conclusion last Tuesday left us safely ensconced and fast asleep in one of the berths on board the *St. George*, then on her passage from Kingston to Toronto, gallantly buffeting a south-west wind and a heavy head sea....

The next morning, our surprise was somewhat excited by the howling and whistling of the wind, which blew half a hurricane, coupled with the almost motionless condition of the vessel: this riddle was solved by ascending the deck, when there lay the steamboat, snug at anchor, under the lee of the land in Presque Isle harbor. During the night it seems the gale increased in fury, and the Captain willing to avoid the wear and tear of the vessel, by prosecuting the voyage in such heavy weather, wisely took advantage of the only harbor in the whole route, and turned in....

Having a quantity of goods on board destined for Cobourg and Port Hope, Captain Harper knew that with the wind & swell as they then were, it would be impossible to approach either of those places, and therefore stopped at Presque Isle under the hope of the gale subsiding.

It is a most singular circumstance, that while other places of far inferior attractions should have been made choice of for the sites of large towns, that Presque Isle should at the present day be almost wholly unknownd, or known only to the masters of the various sailing craft navigating this lake. Presque Isle is not only the sole harbor between Kingston and Toronto, but it is actually the very best in Upper Canada. A late writer thus describes it.

"Presque Isle harbor possesses more natural advantages than perhaps any other in Canada. The depth of the water is so great, and the area of the basin so extensive, that it is capable of affording safe anchorage to all the vessels which are ever likely to navigate Lake Ontario for commercial purposes...."

Presque Isle has two harbors, an outer and an inner one, with a bar between, on which there are usually 11 or 12 feet water. In the outer harbor, the entrance to which is partially closed by Nicholson's Island, vessels can lay with any wind except a south wind; while in the inner harbor, they are completely land-locked and safe from every danger, which is more than can be said of any other harbor on the lake. Thirty or forty years ago, the admirable situation of this place was better appreciated than it appears to be now-a-days, for a town was laid out on Presque Isle Head, called Newcastle, and a Court House built.... had it been properly patronized by men of property, and a canal dug to connect the waters of the lake with those of the Bay of Quinte, Newcastle would ere this have become a town second to none in the province.

A canal from the Carrying Place at the head of the Bay of Quinte into some part of Lake Ontario has long been a desirable object, and has taken up the attention of several successive Governors of this Province.... We shall not take up the reader's time in painting the benefits which would accrue to the whole of the province, were some such canal carried into effect, since they must be cognizant to every person who has thought once upon the subject, but shall pass to the consideration of another topic connected with the lake navigation.

Considering the comparative infant state of the Upper Province, much has been done in the matter of building lighthouses on the shores of Lake Ontario. There are four between Kingston and Toronto: one on the Nine Mile Point, in the entrance to Kingston harbor from the southward and westward; one on the False Ducks; one on Point Peter, between the Ducks and Presque Isle harbor; and the fourth on Point Peninsula [Gibraltar Point] in Toronto Harbor. The whole of these lights are in excellent positions and well attended to, but two more are imperatively necessary to make the northern shore of the lake safely navigable. A light house on Nicholson's Island, or on Presque Isle Head has been long spoken of; it would be useful in either place, but particularly so on Presque Isle Head, as it might be so placed as to prove of the greatest benefit in running for that excellent harbor in the night; a harbor which we repeatedly exclaim, has been most unaccountably overlooked, although the only natural one, between the "Ducks" and Toronto....

(Part 4)

Until the evening of Friday did the *St. George* continue at her anchorage in Presque Isle Harbor. During this period, several schooners made their appearance in the same place of shelter; among others, the *Union*, Capt. Patterson, which strange to tell, had been obliged to bear up for Presque Isle, no less than three several times, in endeavoring to make the roadstead of Darlington, where she was engaged to take her cargo. Could anything with advantage be added to what we said in favor of this harbor, last Tuesday, this simple fact might be so appended; for had not Presque Isle stood in the way, this schooner must each time have bore away for the Lower Gap....

Towards evening, the wind abating and the swell subsiding, the Captain ordered the kettle to be put on, and when the water was made hot, up came the anchor and out to sea went the boat; with the prospect of sufficient moonlight to touch at the ports of Cobourg and Port Hope.[56]

In 1835, the first of many petitions was sent to the provincial legislature asking for the construction of a lighthouse on Presqu'ile Bay. This petition contained an astounding two hundred twenty-four signatures. On Thursday, February 5, 1835, the petition was tabled in the Legislative Assembly:

Pursuant to the order of the day.... The Petition of John Steel and two hundred and twenty three others, inhabitants of the District of Newcastle, praying that a Light house may be erected at the harbour of Presqu'isle in said District.[57]

Never before had the legislature received a petition for the construction of a lighthouse with such an extensive list of names. Those who signed the petition would have included not only owners and masters of ships who would benefit directly from the presence of a lighthouse, but also merchants and others throughout the Newcastle District who understood that the prosperity of the district, and of the province as a whole, relied on the shipping trade, so it was essential to provide the means to keep ships safe. John Steele himself, in addition to being a magistrate and roads commissioner, was a prominent shopkeeper in the town of Colborne, fifteen kilometers west of Presqu'ile Bay.[58]

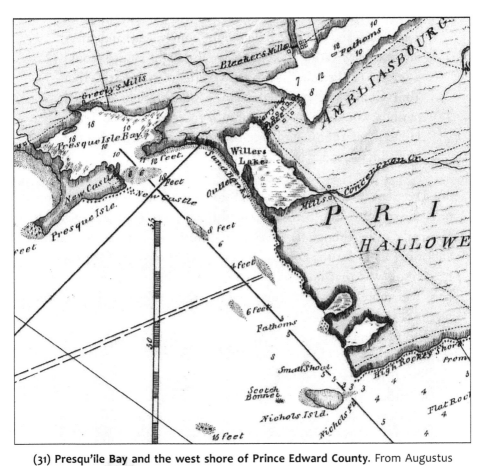

(31) Presqu'ile Bay and the west shore of Prince Edward County. From Augustus Ford's Chart of Lake Ontario, 1836 (detail).
Trenton is marked as "Bleekers Mills". The Bay of Quinte is shown but not marked. Wellers Bay is marked as "Willers Lake". Scotch Bonnet Island is shown at bottom centre next to Nicholson Island which is marked as "Nichols Island".
[Courtesy of Library and Archives Canada, NMC11314]

Steele's petition was sent to a Select Committee for review:

> The Committee to whom was referred the Petition of John Steele, Esquire, and others, beg leave respectfully to report,
>
> That they conceive it would tend to the advantage of commerce, and conduce much to the convenience and safety of vessels navigating Lake Ontario, if a Light House should be erected at Presque Isle, in the District of Newcastle. That Your Committee consider that the sum of eight hundred pounds would be a sufficient sum to erect the said Light House, and Your Committee therefore recommend that the said sum of money be granted for that purpose.[59]

The report was then referred to the Committee of Supply on February 28. The petition was also reviewed by the Legislative Council. Even though the Select Committee had recommended allocating £800 for the construction of a lighthouse at Presqu'ile, the final result was that no monies were voted. The reason for this may have had more to do with party politics than it had to do with the merits of the petition itself.

The General Election of October, 1834, had brought a Reform majority into the Legislative Assembly of Upper Canada. Even though the liberal reformers controlled the Lower House, the Upper House of the Parliament, the Legislative Council, remained, as it always had, firmly in control of the conservative-minded members of the Family Compact. The Legislative Council had been established in 1791 when the Constitutional Act created the Province of Upper Canada. It consisted of men who were appointed for life, and it was intended as a colonial version of the British House of Lords. All bills passed by the Legislative Assembly had to be approved by the Legislative Council before being sent to the Lieutenant-Governor for review by his pseudo-cabinet, the Executive Council, before being given royal assent. With a Reform majority in the Legislative Assembly, and a conservative majority in both the Legislative Council and Executive Council, many bills did not get passed, including a number of lighthouse bills.

The following year, another attempt was made to have the government vote funds to build a lighthouse at Presqu'ile. Another petition was submitted to the Legislative Assembly, this time by James Wilson, the Reform member of the Assembly from Prince Edward County. The petition was referred to the House committee on Canals and Internal Improvements, of which Wilson himself was chairman. Not surprisingly, the committee recommended to the Legislative Assembly that the lighthouse be built:

> To the Honourable the Commons' House of Assembly.
>
> The committee to which was referred the petition of James Wilson, Esquire, praying for the erection of a Light House on Presqu Isle Point, in the township of Murray Beg leave to Report:
>
> That your committee having bestowed upon the subject of the petition due consideration, are of the opinion that the erection of a Light House as prayed for would be the means of conferring a signal benefit upon the shipping interests of the Lake in facilitating the ingress and egress to and from an excellent harbour, at present dangerous of access by night, to which vessels are often driven by stress of weather, independent of the regular trade to that port, which, by the Collector's returns appears to be greatly on the advance, and under all the circumstances of the case humbly beg leave to submit to your Honourable House the expediency and propriety of granting to His Majesty a sum of money sufficient for the erection and completion of a suitable Light House on Presque Isle Point, aforesaid, on such site as may be selected by commissioners to be appointed by your Honourable House for the purpose.
>
> All which is respectfully submitted.
> JAMES WILSON,
> Chairman.
> Committee Room, House of Assembly,
> 23rd March, 1836 [60]

That same day, on the floor of the Assembly, Wilson himself made the motion "...That the sum of one thousand pounds be granted to His Majesty, for the erection of a Light House at Presque Isle, in the township of Murray."[61] The motion was passed, allowing a draft bill to be prepared which, by April 13, had gone through the mandatory three readings in the Assembly and was then passed. The bill was then sent to the Upper House, the Legislative Council for, what would normally be quick approval.

Two days later, the Upper House reviewed the bill and referred it to a Select Committee. The committee, chaired by wealthy Toronto landowner and former naval officer John Elmsley, reported on April 16:

> That upon obtaining the evidence of intelligent Ship-masters, who have navigated Lake Ontario for several years past... it appears to your Committee that the Light-house required for the Harbor of Presqu'isle would be erected and furnished for a sum far smaller than that provided for the purpose by the bill. The Light could only be of service to vessels entering or leaving the Harbor.
>
> Vessels passing up or down the Lake would rather be embarrassed than benefitted by a large light on Presquile, unless it was constructed on the revolving principle, or was of a different colour to those on the False Ducks or on Long Point, or to that erecting on Gull island, either of which principles would involve an expense which the necessity by no means warrant.
>
> Your Committee therefore, for these reasons, cannot recommend your Honorable House to concur in this Bill.[62]

Over the previous eight years, dozens of lighthouse construction bills had been presented by the Assembly to the Legislative Council. This was one of the only ones that had been outright vetoed by the Upper House. Perhaps the legislative councilors truly believed that £1,000 was too high a demand, although the Council had approved spending that exact amount a year earlier on a lighthouse on Gull Island near Cobourg. Perhaps it was true that, as Elmsley stated, the light would be of little or no benefit to most mariners who had no reason to enter the harbour at Presqu'ile, although numerous writers at the time stated otherwise.

The most likely reason for the bill being rejected by the Upper House was that it had started with James Wilson, approved by James Wilson's committee, and generally pushed forward by James Wilson. As a Reformer, not only was Wilson opposed to many of the policies of the conservative Family Compact, but he was also not a member of the official established church supported by the Family Compact, the Church of England. Instead, as a Methodist, he would have been viewed as an "outsider" by the members of the Family Compact,[63] a position which, by 1836, was an increasingly confrontational in the months before the outbreak of armed rebellion in Upper Canada.

It appears that the bill was killed by the conservative, Church-of-England-dominated Legislative Council purely for partisan reasons.

That Autumn, a General Election was called and a conservative majority sympathetic to the Family Compact was elected to the House of Assembly. Within weeks of the opening of the 13th Parliament of Upper Canada, another petition was presented to the Legislature asking for a lighthouse on the Presqu'ile Peninsula. This time, the petition was presented by conservative Bernard McMahon, customs collector for the District of Newcastle, along with 127 other residents of Presqu'ile and vicinity. The petition was tabled by the conservative member from Northumberland, Benjamin Ruttan, who was also speaker of the Assembly.[64]

The petition was tabled on January 4, read on January 6, and immediately referred to a Select Committee of the Legislative Assembly.[65] Simultaneously, the petition was presented to the Legislative Council for consideration. Less than seven weeks later, on February 21, 1837 the Legislative Assembly passed the bill authorizing the construction of a lighthouse at Presqu'ile Point. The resolution that was passed was for the construction of not just one lighthouse, but for five lighthouses in the Great Lakes region, for which a total of £3,500 was allocated, including £1,000 for the Presqu'ile Point lighthouse. This time, a conservative supporter had presented the petition via a conservative member of the Assembly. The bill was drawn up by a conservative-dominated committee, passed by a conservative majority in the Assembly and approved by the conservative Upper House.

After three attempts at petitioning the legislature over the course of three years of unprecedented political partisanship, a lighthouse for Presqu'ile Point was finally approved by the Legislative Council, given royal assent by the Lieutenant-Governor, and passed into law on March 4, 1837:

AN ACT granting to His Majesty
a sum of Money for
the erection of certain Light-houses, within the
Province, and for other purposes therein mentioned.

(Passed 4th March, 1837)

WHEREAS it is necessary for the safety and convenience of Navigation in this Province, to provide for the erection of Light-houses in certain places in this Province, may it therefore please Your Majesty that it may be enacted, And be it enacted by the King's most Excellent Majesty, by and with the advice and consent of the Legislative council and Assembly of Upper Canada...

That from and out of the Rates and Duties now raised, levied and collected, and remaining in the hands of the Receiver General, unappropriated, there be granted to His Majesty the sum of Three Thousand Five Hundred Pounds, to enable His Majesty to defray the expense of erecting Light-houses, and furnishing the same, in the following places, and for the following sums respectively, that is to say: — At Presqu'isle Point, in the Newcastle District, the sum of One Thousand Pounds — At Oakville, in the District of Gore, Five Hundred Pounds — At Port Colborne, in

the Niagara District, the sum of Five Hundred Pounds —
At Port Burwell, in the London district, the sum of Five
Hundred Pounds — At the mouth of the Thames, on
Lake Saint Clair, in the Western District, the sum of One
Thousand Pounds....[66]

These would be the last lighthouses whose construction was
authorized by the Parliament of Upper Canada. Barely six weeks
after the bill was passed, Lieutenant-Governor Sir Francis Bond Head
prorogued Parliament and set in motion the last of a series of events
which would result in the Upper Canada Rebellion of 1837-38, which
in turn led the British government to institute a number of reforms
including the union of Upper and Lower Canada. After 1841, the
newly formed Public Works Department would have responsibility for
lighthouse affairs for the new United Province of Canada stretching
from the Gulf of St. Lawrence to Lake Superior.

As soon as the Presqu'ile Point lighthouse bill was passed, three
commissioners were duly selected to oversee the construction of the
new lighthouse. They were Thomas Reid, Donald Campbell and
Bernard McMahon the local customs collector who had presented the
successful petition to Parliament.[67] Like all lighthouse commissioners
before them, all three of these men were well connected with the
conservatives who then dominated both houses of the provincial
legislature.

The lighthouse commissioners proceeded with their duties and
immediately engaged the services of the man who would come to
design one of the most elegantly styled lighthouses on Lake Ontario:
Nichol Hugh Baird.

N.H. Baird had emigrated Scotland in 1827. As son of a Scottish
canal builder, he had followed in his father's footsteps and gained
practical experience building canals in Scotland and in Russia. When
Baird arrived in Canada, he was quickly hired as Clerk of Works for
the Rideau Canal which was then being cut between Kingston and
Bytown (later Ottawa). After the completion of the Rideau Canal, he
was hired to survey a new route for the Welland Canal and then went

on to the Newcastle District where he surveyed routes for the proposed Trent Canal and Murray Canal.[68] As a result of these latter duties, Baird's work would have been well known throughout the Newcastle District, in which Presqu'ile Bay was located. He was also one of the few experienced engineers available who was qualified for this work. While he had no experience building lighthouses, there were very few qualified engineers in Canada at the time and his skills would have been seen as quite valuable.

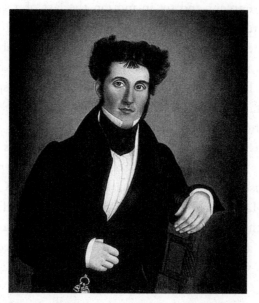

(32) Portrait of lighthouse designer and engineer, Nichol Hugh Baird. Oil on canvas by Nelson Cook, 1833.
In addition to designing the Presqu'ile Point lighthouse, Baird also surveyed some early routes for the proposed Murray Canal and built the first bridge across the Trent River at Trenton.
[Courtesy of Library and Archives Canada, MIKAN3012111]

In the commissioners' report to the legislature, they described the first steps taken toward the construction of the Presqu'ile Point lighthouse:

REPORT OF COMMISSIONERS
FOR
ERECTING PRESQU'ISLE LIGHT-HOUSE

The Commissioners for superintending the erection of a Light-house at Presqu'isle Point, respectfully report:

That considering it advisable for the public interest — for the more efficient prosecution of the work in its details — for reporting on the most eligible site — furnishing the necessary plans, specifications, &c. as well as for the general superintendence of the work — they engaged the services of N.H. Baird, Esquire, Civil Engineer, and on the 29th July, 1837, in company with that gentleman, inspected the ground along the point, and on his recommendation, which met the concurrence of your Commissioners, the south-easterly point of the Peninsula, commonly known as Gibson's Point, at the entrance to Presqu'isle Harbour, was fixed upon as in all respects the site best suited for the Light-house, in which opinion they find themselves generally borne out by the Captains of vessels navigating Lake Ontario.[69]

The commissioners called for tenders as Baird drew up the detailed specifications and plans for the lighthouse:

To experienced contractors,
FOR THE ERECTION OF A LIGHT-HOUSE AT PRESQUE ISLE POINT, LAKE ONTARIO.

SEALED TENDERS will be received for the execution of the above work till the first day of September next, at the Office of B. McMahon, Esq., Presque Isle Harbour, for the due performance of which good and sufficient security will be required.

Plans and Specifications of the Work may be seen after the 12th day of August, at the said Office, where any necessary information may be had, or on application to N.H. Baird, Esq., Civil Engineer, Cobourg....

Presque Isle, 29th July, 1837.[70]

Baird's notebooks contain the first rough sketches and handwritten specifications for the lighthouse which was to be an octagonal masonry tower, 62 feet tall, on top of which was to be placed a cast iron lantern, eleven feet tall, painted blue. The interior was to have six wooden landings connected by a series of wooden stairs. The entire work was to be completed by September 1, 1838. His complete specification for the lighthouse is transcribed in Appendix 3.

Baird's design, with its octagonal plan and gothic-arched windows was, architecturally, a significant departure from Thomas Rogers' simpler, Doric column-style lighthouses. The multi-lateral style proposed for the Presqu'ile Point lighthouse had not been seen since the construction of the Great Lakes' first lighthouses at Niagara and Gibraltar Point, both of which were six-sided. While this style of lighthouse would later be reproduced in wood and in concrete, this was one of the last octagonal lighthouses built of stone in Canada.

Baird's experience with stone as a building material is evident in his meticulous specifications for the fitting and dressing of the masonry for the Presqu'ile Point lighthouse. His work on the limestone locks of the Rideau Canal likely gave him experience dealing with stone and with stone masons.

The tenders were received and the contract for the entire lighthouse, including the mason work, the carpentry and the construction of the lantern, was awarded to John McLeod. This may have been the same John McLeod of Kingston who had been one of the masons employed on the construction of the False Ducks Island lighthouse nine years earlier.

Even though McLeod had been able to get the commissioners to extend the deadline for the completion of the lighthouse by an extra two months to November 1, 1838, it was reported in the spring of 1839 that the lighthouse was still not nearly finished.[71] The masonry tower had been completed, but the lantern had yet to be built and installed and Baird had found a number of deficiencies in the work:

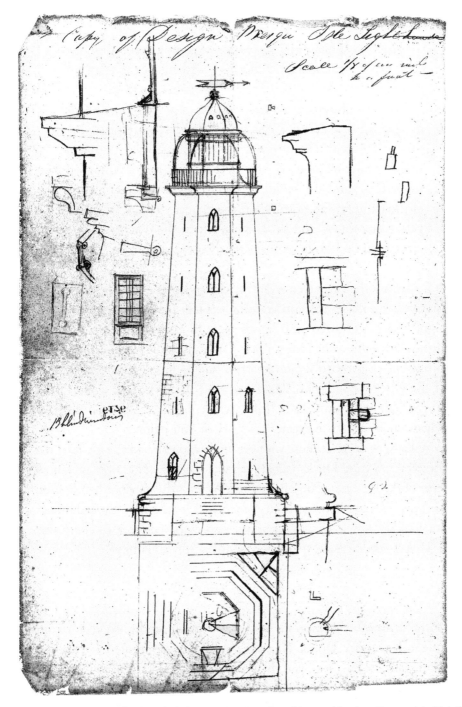

(33) Drawing of Presqu'ile Point lighthouse, August, 1837. "Copy of Design, Presqu Isle Light", from N.H. Baird's notebooks.

Many of the design elements sketched by Baird were used in the lighthouse, making this one of the most ornate lighthouses on the Great Lakes.

[Courtesy of Archives of Ontario, Baird Papers]

The work has not progressed to completion so rapidly as your Commissioners could have wished — the term for completion of Contract being 1st November, 1838.

By the Engineer's report, there still remains to be completed, "the railing to the stairs — two coats of plastering — glazing the sashes — replacing the main door with one in terms of specification — some re-pointing, and levelling off properly around the building, together with the completion of the clearing and burning off the quantity of land required per agreement — and the lantern, which the Contractor has pledged himself to have immediately completed."[72]

It was another eighteen months; the summer of 1840, before the lantern was in place, the construction deficiencies had been corrected, a lightkeeper was hired, the lamps were lit and the Presqu'ile Point lighthouse finally went into service.[73] The chain of lights, all the way around Prince Edward County from Nine Mile Point near Kingston, to False Ducks Island, past Point Petre and along the lake to Presqu'ile Point, albeit with only four links, was complete. Ships could now navigate these waters in greater safety than ever before.

William Swetman, whose younger brother Joseph had already been the lightkeeper on False Ducks Island for more than a decade, was appointed keeper of the Presqu'ile Point lighthouse. As with the previous lighthouses, a keeper's dwelling had not been constructed by the time the lighthouse went into service. It was to be another six years before a dwelling was provided at government expense for Swetman and his family.[74]

———————

The tower on Presqu'ile Point was the last lighthouse to go into service under Upper Canada's system of appointed lighthouse commissioners. As a result of the reforms instituted after the Rebellion of 1837-38, Upper and Lower Canada were joined together as the United Province of Canada and the responsibility for the construction, maintenance and administration of lighthouses in Canada West (formerly Upper Canada) was effectively transferred in 1841 to a newly formed Board of Works:

(34) Presqu'ile Point lighthouse, 1927. Photograph by John Boyd.
While the original lantern designed by N.H. Baird is still in place, the masonry tower had been covered with wooden shingles in 1894, thereby obscuring the distinctive Gothic-arched windows. The fog-alarm building in the foreground was built in 1907. [Courtesy of Library and Archives Canada, PA-087846]

An Act to repeal certain Ordinances therein mentioned
and to establish
a Board of Works in this Province
17th August, 1841
Whereas it is expedient to... establish a Board of Works in and for this Province; Be it therefore enacted...

That there shall be in and for this Province, a Board of Works for the superintendence, management and control of public works therein; which said board of works shall consist of such and so many persons not exceeding five in number...

and the said Board, shall have such powers, authority and capacities as are provided by this Act....

And be it enacted, that it shall be the duty of the said Board to examine and report upon all matters which may be referred to it by the Governor, Lieutenant Governor, or person administering the Government... to obtain all such evidence and information, plans, estimates, drawings, or specifications, and to cause such surveys, visits, and examinations to be made, and generally to do all such things as may be necessary to enable it to make such report in the manner best adapted to advance the public good....

And be it enacted, that the said board may suggest... any public works or improvements therein, which it may appear to the Board, could be undertake with advantage to the Province....

And be it enacted, that the said Board shall... employ for the accomplishment of the objects for which it is constituted, such and so many engineers, Surveyors, Architects, Clerks, Draughtsmen, Superintendents, and other persons as may be necessary....[75]

For the next decade and a half, the Board of Works would endeavour to augment, improve and extend the "Chain of Stone"; the first segment of the network of lighthouses that was slowly developing to provide safety and convenience for all shipping in eastern Lake Ontario.

Within a month of the Board being constituted, the new Legislature of the Province of Canada allocated to it an operating budget of £659,600 to cover a long list of public works, including roads, bridges, canals and harbours, as well as a number of lighthouses:

An Act to appropriate certain sums of Money for Public
Improvement
in this Province, and for other purposes therein mentioned
18th September, 1841

Whereas it will conduce to the prosperity and
advancement of this Province, that the Public works
hereinafter mentioned, be undertaken and completed
with the least possible delay, May it therefore please Your
Majesty that it may be enacted... that for the construction
and completion of the Public Works of this Province,
there be granted... six hundred and fifty-nine thousand six
hundred pounds, Sterling, which said sum shall be applied
and expended under the charge and superintendence of the
Board of Works of this Province...

For constructing or improving Harbours and Light
Houses on Lakes Ontario and Erie, and roads leading
thereto, seventy-four thousand pounds, Sterling....

And be it enacted that from and after the passing of this
Act, all directors or Commissioners appointed by or under
the authority of any of the Laws now in force, authorizing
the construction or carrying on of any of the said works
and improvements shall be superseded, and their respective
offices shall cease and... shall be transferred to... the Board
of Works....[76]

A Board of Works had been first formed in Lower Canada in 1839
and was one of the first government departments that operated in a
manner similar to today's federal public service. Instead of relying
solely on concerned citizens or individual members of the legislature
to propose the construction of various works such as canals, roads or
lighthouses, the Board of Works was authorized to hire engineers and
other experts to prepare plans so that the Board could make reasonable
representations to the legislature for the construction of these public
works. In addition, a part-time salaried chairman and a full-time
salaried secretary were employed to keep track of all monies allocated

and expended, thus replacing many of the duties previously performed by *ad hoc* lighthouse commissioners.[77]

After Confederation in 1867, the Board of Works would become the Public Works Department of the new Dominion of Canada. This department would retain responsibility for the construction of roads, bridges, harbours, canals and public buildings. However, after 1868, the newly created Marine and Fisheries Department would be responsible for the construction and maintenance of lighthouses.[78]

PART II – THE LIGHTHOUSES

CHAPTER 5

Harbour Lights

For the guidance of Vessels entering.
("Upper Canada Land Petitions," 1850.)

While the provincial government was occupied with building lighthouses along the shores of the open lake to keep ships safer while carrying their cargoes and passengers through the dangerous waters of eastern Lake Ontario, commercial interests in a number of port towns came to realize that there could be direct economic benefits gained by building lighthouses in their own harbours. These harbour lights could help ship captains locate a harbour at night with greater ease, and then guide them safely to the town's wharves. In the Canadian waters of eastern Lake Ontario, the first true harbour lighthouses to be built were located at Kingston and Belleville, in the region's busiest ports, and also at Presqu'ile, then the only harbour of refuge between Prince Edward County and Toronto.

Kingston Harbour Lighthouse (1846)

As the major trans-shipment port for goods transported up and down the St. Lawrence River, Kingston was long-considered the most important port on Lake Ontario. Gourlay described the harbour in 1822:

> The harbour is on the east side of the town, and is formed by a bay stretching up northerly by the front of the town.... The west shore of the bay is bold and suitable for wharves, of which there are already as many as ten, where vessels of any burthen may lie in safety, and load and unload with convenience and ease.
>
> As to commercial business [Kingston] is the third town in the Canadas, being inferior to none but Quebec and Montreal.
>
> From its situation, it is the natural depot of those articles of commerce, which are transported over the lake in vessels, and up and down the river in boats. Here they meet and deposit, and exchange their cargoes.
>
> As a harbour, certainly, and perhaps in other points of relation to navigation and commerce, Kingston unites more advantages than any other place, on either the Canada or New York side of the lake.[1]

Twenty-five years later, Sir Richard Bonnycastle commented on the prosperity that newly incorporated City of Kingston had achieved by 1846:

> There are ten daily first-class steamers running to and from Kingston, and about thirty smaller steamers and propellers, with a fleet of two hundred schooners and sailing barges.... This rising city, now containing near twelve thousand inhabitants....
>
> Kingston is, in fact the key of the Great Lakes, the St. Lawrence and the Rideau Canal being their outlets for commerce....[2]

(35) View of Kingston Harbour, 1842. Detail of sketch by W.H. Bartlett.
On the left, next to the building, the smokestacks of a steamboat (probably the William IV) can be seen docked at the wharf. To the right of the steamboat can be seen the Cataraqui Bridge and a sloop sailing out of the harbour. In the background on the right is the Royal Navy dockyard below the fortifications of Point Henry. [Author's collection]

While the Nine Mile Point lighthouse on nearby Simcoe Island had been doing double-duty as both a lake light and an outer harbour light for the port of Kingston for more than a decade, there was no lighthouse in the inner harbour to guide ships to the city's wharves. An editorial in Kingston's *Chronicle and Gazette* in 1840 had suggested that the newly formed Kingston Marine Railway Company could build a long pier to protect the harbour from southerly gales, along with a lighthouse:

> We would now wish to draw the attention of that very enterprising Company to a public improvement, which we think worthy of their consideration, and which we think they might effectually aid in completing — and thereby confer a lasting benefit not only on the shipping and commercial interests of Kingston, but on that of the

Province of Canada at large — as this is the only Great Inland trans-shipment Port above Montreal. We refer to the erection of a pier or breakwater, to extend from Mississaugua Point to sufficient distance into the channel, so as effectually to protect our harbour from the tempestuous southerly and southwesterly gales which frequently do considerable damage to our shipping and wharves. On the end of this Pier a lighthouse might be erected, which would be quite visible from Nine Mile Point lighthouse, adding much not only to the beauty, but more essential requisite of safety to the harbour.[3]

Even though the official history of the Canadian Coast Guard, written by Thomas Appleton, lists a lighthouse at Kingston in 1844,[4] it is unlikely that a lighthouse was in existence at that time. The Board of Works' report for that year indicates that there were no aids to navigation there, although they recommended the construction of a "... coloured light in Kingston Harbour."[5] It was two years later, in the summer of 1846, that the possibility of a lighthouse in Kingston harbour was first mentioned when the *Kingston Herald* criticized the city government for supporting the construction of a public lighthouse on the privately owned marine railway wharf:

> The Corporation [of the City of Kingston] have agreed... to erect a Light House on the Marine Railway Wharf. It seems odd to us that the Town should put up a building on private property. Besides, we have been informed that the best site for a light house for this harbour is the shoal which lies off the Marine Railway. To build one there would cost more, but it would be on and improve public property.[6]

Despite the newspaper's criticism, the city proceeded with the construction of the lighthouse and contracted local builder Sidney Scobell to do the work. Scobell completed the lighthouse by

April, 1847, and Kingston resident G. Clark, was hired as the first lightkeeper.[7]

The following spring, the city undertook to increase the size of the lighthouse, an improvement that was met by further criticism:

> The readers of the *British Whig* for some years past have been accustomed to see, during the month of March, some account of the preparations making to carry on the Forwarding Trade, that main stay of Kingston's prosperity, during the coming season of navigation....
>
> The Marine Railway and Ship Yard - This place of very extensive business is now solely tenanted by Mr. S. D. Fowler, formerly Messrs. Fowler & Hood. Two large steamboats are on the Large Railway, and several smaller vessels on the Small Railway.
>
> We must not forget to mention, that the new Light House, built by the Corporation [of the City of Kingston] at the extremity of the Railway Wharf, is now being raised twenty or thirty feet higher. Even with this addition to its height, the Kingston Light House will prove but a very sorry affair. How much better would it be to apply to the Home Authorities, for permission to erect a wooden tenement on the top of the Martello Tower, on the Shoal, a tenement that could readily be demolished, in case of the Tower being needed for war purposes.[9]

An early map of the City Kingston clearly marks the location of this lighthouse.

The *Admiralty List of the Lights,* published by the Hydrographic Office of the British Admiralty almost twenty years later, in 1864, lists a white, square wood tower located in the "S.E. part of Town" that, so it states, went into service in 1844.[10] The date of 1844 is likely a mistake that was later repeated in Appleton's book.

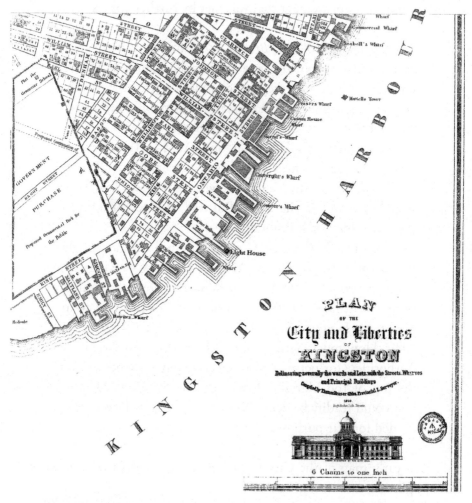

(36) *Plan of the City and Liberties of Kingston,* 1850 (detail). Drawn by Thomas Fraser Gibbs. Lithographed by Hugh Scobie.
The Kingston harbour lighthouse is clearly marked at the end of the marine railway wharf.
[Courtesy of Library and Archives Canada]

More significantly, the Admiralty List noted that the lighthouse was "not lighted"; which probably meant that it was no longer in service as of 1864. It had likely been discontinued before 1857 when Dr. Edward Hodder, Commodore of the newly formed Royal Canadian Yacht Club in Toronto, published his very detailed cruising guide, *The Harbours and Ports of Lake Ontario*. In it, Hodder comments on all manner of buoys, markers, lights and lighthouses near Kingston,[11] but he makes no mention of any lighthouse in Kingston harbour, so this aid to navigation may have already been removed after less than a decade of service.

(37) Kingston Harbour and City Hall, 1862. Sketch by G.H. Andrews from *The Illustrated London News*, Jan. 18, 1862.
This view of the city is from the perspective of a person on a boat or timber raft in the harbour. Throughout the 19th Century, Kingston was one of the most important harbours on the Great Lakes. Vessels in the harbour include a schooner at right, a steamboat to the left of the Martello tower, and another schooner beyond with at least one square-rigged sailing ship, and a number of boats and timber rafts. A light was shown from the cupola of Kingston City Hall as an aid to navigation. It was kept by the city but paid for by the Government of Canada's Marine and Fisheries Department. [Author's collection]

Nevertheless, the city still saw the value of a lighted aid to navigation in the main harbour. In 1866, the *Daily News* reported that the large clock tower of the Kingston City Hall was kept illuminated after dark to help guide ships to the wharves. While this was not a purpose-built aid to navigation, it was well appreciated by ship captains entering the harbour at night.[12]

Belleville Harbour Lights (1835 & 1851)

Where the Moira River empties into the Bay of Quinte, the village of Meyer's Creek grew quickly after the first European settlers arrived there in 1787. Later renamed Belleville, the town was incorporated in 1834, by which time it had become one of the most prosperous settlements in the Bay of Quinte area.[13]

The lumber trade was of great importance to early Belleville and a number of sawmills had been established at the mouth of the river where logs were cut into deals and boards and loaded onto schooners and steamboats for export to the United States and Great Britain. One mill owner realized the competitive advantage he might gain by providing a light to guide ships to his wharf after dark, and in 1835, Billa Flint Jr. hoisted a lamp atop his warehouse for just such a purpose:

> It is now twenty days since Billa Flint Jr. commenced building a large commodious warehouse a the foot of his wharf, and on Wednesday night last for the first time, a light was suspended from the steeple of the same as a beacon to guide the boats navigating the Bay. — This building was raised by 17 men in 17 hours without any other refreshments but Coffee and hot cakes. — So much for the cause of Temperance.[14]

At age 22, Billa Flint had been one of the founding members of the first temperance society in Upper Canada,[15] hence the reference to "coffee and hot cakes" as refreshments instead of the more common beer and whisky. He later went on to elected office, first as mayor of Belleville and then as member of the Legislative Assembly for Hastings County. In 1867, he was appointed to the Canadian Senate. In addition to being a sawmill owner and lumber merchant, Flint was a promoter of railway lines, canals (including the Murray Canal) and steamboat companies, and he undoubtedly understood the importance of harbour lights to the shipping trade.

Perhaps taking their lead from this Belleville businessman — seeing the utility of his wharf light — town councilors decided in 1850 that having a proper lighthouse in their harbour would be a benefit to the commercial prosperity of the entire region. The town was already benefitting indirectly from the four lake lights that were then making it safer for ships to navigate around the Prince Edward peninsula and into the Bay of Quinte. Belleville mayor, R.F Davy, sent a petition to the Governor-General at Quebec asking that a shoal on the bay shore at the mouth of the Moira River be transferred from the Crown to the town for the purpose of building a lighthouse:

> To His Excellency The Right Honorable James Earl of Elgin and Kincardine, Governor General of British North America, &c. &c. &c.
>
> The memorial of the Town Council of the town of Belleville Humbly sheweth
>
> That the entrance to the Harbour of Belleville is difficult to access to strangers; owing to the narrowness of the channel, the shoals on each side, and the want of a Beacon
>
> That on the West side of Pinnacle Street, and south of Water lots E F G, granted to the Town, is a point or Shoal, pointed out on the accompanying rough sketch where a beacon could be erected, for the guidance of Vessels entering — and your memorialists humbly pray that Your Excellency will be graciously pleased, to grant the said Shoal to the Town Council, with a view of a Light house being placed thereon....
>
> 4th June 1850 (signed by Mayor R. F. Davy)[16]

The town's petition was immediately forwarded to the Commissioner of Crown Lands who recommended that the shoal be granted to the town. The Governor-General's Executive Council approved the recommendation on August 20, 1850.[17] and the grant received Royal Assent.

On the shoal at the end of Belleville's Pinnacle Street, a pier was constructed as a foundation for a thirty foot tall octagonal wood-framed lighthouse[18] that was in service by 1851. A dock was also built to connect the pier to the wharves on the east side of the Moira River.

Unlike most other lighthouses in the province, the Belleville harbour light was not funded by the province. Instead, its construction, maintenance and operating costs were paid by the Town of Belleville itself. In that respect, it was similar to the lighthouse built in Kingston harbour five years earlier, and to other privately owned lighthouses that would be built later at Portsmouth, Bath and Garden Island.

By 1871, commercial shipping into and out of Belleville harbour amounted to more than one thousand shipments annually, totaling in excess of 150,000 tons of cargo — a number surpassed at Canadian Great Lakes ports only by Kingston and Toronto.[19] A port guide to Lake Ontario published that year; *Atkin's Pocket Compass of the Harbors, Ports, Lighthouses and Buoys of Lake Ontario and River St. Lawrence*, gives a detailed description of Belleville harbour and its lighthouse:

> Belleville is situated in the township of Thurlow at the mouth of the river Moira, and on the shores of the Bay of Quinte. It covers an area of 1,200 acres, and for beauty of situation cannot be surpassed. The lumber trade has been a source of prosperity to Belleville; for some years past, the number of saw logs brought down the Moira have averaged from 150,000 to 200,000 a year. The greatest part are manufactured at the different mills, some of which are the largest, West of the Ottawa. The two largest of those of

Messrs. Flint & Yeomans, which is situated at the foot of Water street, and that of Messrs. H.B. Rathbun & Son, on the island at the mouth of the river. The capacity of both is about equal. In each there are from 90 to 100 saws, chiefly in gangs, capable of manufacturing from 75,000 to 100,000 feet of lumber every 24 hours.

Another mill on the south line of the Bay, is owned by Messrs. Page & Co. It was erected in 1864, and its capacity has since been largely increased. It manufactures about 50,000 feet per day.

East Channel — The channel leading into Belleville harbour is defined by buoys painted red, on the East side, and buoys painted white, on the West side. The depth of water in the channel is about 10 feet....

Lighthouse — The Belleville lighthouse is erected on the outer dock, on the East side of the harbour, and is constructed of wood, with a tin dome. The height is 30 feet above the level of the water, and shows a white stationary light, which can be seen a distance of 9 to 12 miles in fine weather.[20]

However important this lighthouse may have been to the town and to the captains sailing their ships into the harbour, neither the Canadian nor the British Admiralty light lists ever included this Belleville harbour light as an official aid to navigation.

Presqu'ile Range Lights (1851)

The same year that the Belleville harbour lighthouse went into service, a unique pair of lighthouses was built thirty kilometers to the west in Presqu'ile Bay.

While the Presqu'ile Point lighthouse at the entrance to the bay was effective at guiding ships toward the general vicinity of this harbour of refuge, ship captains had difficulty navigating the winding

(38) Belleville Harbour, 1874. From *Bird's Eye View of Belleville* (detail).
The lighthouse built in 1851 can be seen at centre right at the end of the Grand Junction Railway pier. To the left of the lighthouse are two schooners at the town wharves and another schooner is docked at Rathbun's lumber mill on Victoria Island (now Victoria Park). Entering the harbour are a steam ferry and a tugboat towing a schooner. Leaving the harbour are a tugboat, a small open boat with three fishermen, and a large steamboat flying American colours.
[Courtesy of Hastings County Historical Society]

entrance to Presqu'ile Bay. Additional lighthouses were required to enable vessels to follow the safe channel until they arrived at a sheltered anchorage inside the bay.

The main navigational hazard was the broad "Middle Ground" shoal that forced mariners to sail well past the Presqu'ile Point lighthouse before coming about to access the deepest channel into the bay. Gourlay identified this shortcoming in 1822 when he wrote that, "... the entrance into the harbour, being not very direct and plain, requires considerable care."[21] Later, Commodore Hodder would report that, "... the channel which leads into this fine harbour now becomes difficult, owing to the shoals which surround it being entirely destitute of buoys or beacons to mark them".[22]

In 1844, the Board of Works made a recommendation for lighting the entrance to Presqu'ile Bay:

> At Presqu'isle, a small colored Light on the end of Salt Point is very much required to enable vessels to take that Harbour in dark nights; and a Buoy on the North East end of the Bar outside, together with a small landing wharf within the Harbour, are absolutely necessary.[23]

Again in 1847, the Board, by then renamed the Department of Public Works, reiterated its earlier recommendation and made further suggestions:

> Presqu'Isle Harbor
>
> The late Board of Works recommended the expenditure of £300, for the construction of a Landing Pier at the head of the Bay; no appropriation was however made.
>
> The Commissioners recommend this improvement to the favorable consideration of His Excellency, and also a further expenditure of £200, for placing Range Lights and Buoys, so as to enable vessels, at all times, to enter the Bay with safety; this being the only Harbor of Refuge between Kingston and Windsor [Whitby, Ontario].[24]

It was another four years before the Legislature approved the recommended funds. In 1851, an official notice from the Department of Public Works notified mariners about the unique pair of aids to navigation that were erected in Presqu'ile Bay:

> Notice is hereby given that the Commissioners of this Department have caused the following named Lights etc. to be placed to mark the entrance to Presqu'Isle Harbor viz.:

Two leading Lights, one on Salt Point, and the other near to an old Barn on the opposite hill....

Vessels entering the Harbor should run for the main north shore, eastward of the large Light House and of the Black Buoy, until they get into nine or ten feet of water, then shape their course N.W. until the leading lights come in range, then keeping the lights in range, in a W.S.W. course until they have passed the first leading Light, when anchorage ground will be found.

By order, THOMAS A. BEGLY, Secretary.

Department of Public Works,

Toronto, April 23, 1851.[25]

These "leading lights", also referred to as "range lights", were one of the first lighthouses of their kind to be built in Canadian waters. In *Patterson's Illustrated Nautical Dictionary* of 1891, Captain Howard Patterson defines range lights as, "...two lights placed on shore in such situations that when they are in line with one another, as seen from a vessel, the latter may know that she is in the channel."[26]

As early as 1788, the State of Massachusetts had erected a pair of range lights on Plum Island off the town of Newburyport to guide ships into the Merrimack River.[27] Since that time, range lights had been built wherever ships had to navigate through narrow channels. The Presqu'ile Range lights were likely the first to be used as such in Canadian waters.

The front range light was usually painted a different colour or showed a light of a different colour than the rear range light. The lighthouse on Salt Point was the front range light. Nine hundred meters behind it situated on higher ground was its partner, the rear range light. This tandem arrangement allowed the two lighthouses to line up with the centre of the navigable channel so that masters of vessels entering Presqu'ile Bay needed only to sail directly toward the aligned towers to know that they were in the deepest water.. This was called "sailing on a range". Then, when they were within about sixty meters of the front light, they could safely veer off into the deep waters of Presqu'ile Bay.

This is described by Commodore Hodder in *The Harbours and Ports of Lake Ontario*:

> Twenty-four miles E. 1/4 N. of Cobourg is the west or bluff point of Presqu' Isle, well wooded, and with 90 feet water within a short distance of the shore.
>
> LIGHTHOUSE. Five miles N. E. by E. of this point will bring you abreast of the [Presqu'ile Point] lighthouse, which is 67 feet high, and upon which there is a very good fixed bright light, that can be seen in fine weather from 12 to 15 miles.
>
> Immediately under the lighthouse, to the southward, there is shoal water with boulders; but by keeping half a mile from the shore, this danger is easily avoided.
>
> CHANNEL. The channel which leads into this fine harbour now becomes difficult, owing to the shoals which surround it being entirely destitute of buoys or beacons to mark them.
>
> When making this harbour in the day time, steer to within 1/2 or 3/4 of a mile S. by E. of the lighthouse ; thence N. by E. for a very large and solitary *Pine Tree,* which stands on the main land, some distance from the shore; (this object is so conspicuous as to render a mistake impossible); continue this course for a mile and a quarter, or until the range lights (in the harbour) are brought into line ; then alter your course, and steer S. W. directly for the easternmost of the two lights.
>
> HARBOUR LIGHTS, At night, as the pine tree cannot so well be seen, steer N. by E. until the range lights are seen in line ; then change your course, steering directly for them, (that is S.W.) keeping within fifty yards N. of the point on which this range light is built, (or even nearer,) as there is from 18 to 22 feet water directly under it. Having passed this point, anchor in the little bay between the two range lights.[28]

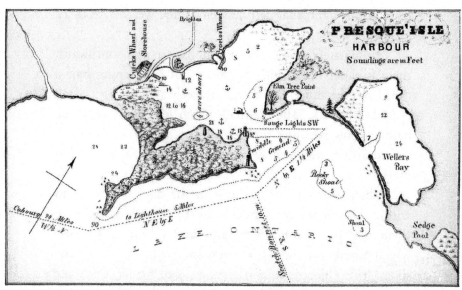

(39) "Sketch of Presqu'isle Harbour" (Presqu'ile Bay). Edward Hodder, 1857.
The presence of the "Middle Ground" shoal made access to the bay very difficult. The two range lights as well as the Presqu'ile Point lighthouse are marked.
[From Hodder, *The Harbours and Ports of Lake Ontario*, 1857]

The lighthouse on Salt Point, together with its tandem range light, had been constructed by Thomas Lee, James Newman and James Smith according to the following specification:

> Specification of Range Lights Towers to be built at Presque Isle Harbour C.W. [Canada West]
>
> The Towers to be Eighteen feet high to the lantern, twelve feet wide at base and four feet at platform which is to be eight feet square of double boards or plank and covered with felt & zinc with a proper scuttle to enter the lantern, & hand rail round the edge. The towers to be well framed with sufficient girts, studs, joist & Braces. To be covered first with common pine boards and sheeted over with well matched grooved & tongued inch pine boards. To have one window of four lights, one Double batten door mounted with T hinges, lock & latch. Two floors of 1½ inch matched grooved & tongued pine plank on each tower.
>
> To have an Iron lantern fitted on top of platform with lamp frame, Lamps, reflectors etc. complete.
>
> The lanterns to be glazed & painted if necessary. The outside of towers to receive two coats of paint. All the materials will be furnished by the Department Public Works.[29]

As range lights, these lighthouses not only served a new purpose, but they were also built in a new style. These were wood-framed lighthouses built in the shape of a pyramid with a flat top that was used as the platform for the lantern and gallery. The Presqu'ile Bay lighthouses were the first known example of the pyramidal style of tower that would eventually outnumber all other lighthouse styles seen on Canadian shores.

In between the front range light and the rear range light, the first keeper, William Swetman Jr., son of the keeper of the Presqu'ile Point lighthouse, built himself a small house. Except for 1873 when all of the lights on the Presqu'ile peninsula were the responsibility of a single keeper,[30] the keeping of the Presqu'ile Range lights was always a separate job from the keeping of the main light on Presqu'ile Point.

SALT LIGHT. (PRESQUILE LIGHT IN DISTANCE)

(40) Presqu'ile Front Range. Photographer unknown, c. 1908.
The front range light was also known as the Salt Point lighthouse. Its partner, the Presqu'ile Rear Range light was situated on the mainland off to the right of this photograph. The tower in the background is the Presqu'ile Point lighthouse.
[Postcard in author's collection]

As a testament to the usefulness of range lights, they would eventually be constructed all along the St. Lawrence River as well as in numerous other passages and harbours across Canada, including twelve others in the eastern Lake Ontario region: at Wellers Bay, Trenton, Portsmouth, Barriefield and four more in Presqu'ile Bay.

PART II – THE LIGHTHOUSES

CHAPTER 6

Strengthening the Chain

The importance of adding to the safety of the Lake Navigation
(Calvin, Cook & Co., 1845)

In the middle of the 19th Century, the population around the lower Great Lakes was approaching 4 million.[1] By 1870, it would surpass 6.5 million.[2] Roads were still in a crude state and long-haul railways such as the Great Western and Grand Trunk were just beginning to offer some competition to ships for the transportation of freight and passengers. Shipping on the Great Lakes continued to grow to keep pace with high demand brought on by such rapid population increases. By 1850, there were more than 600 ships on the Lakes[3] carrying more than seven million dollars worth of goods annually.[4] Within ten years, the number of ships would more than double to include 329 steamships and 1,163 sailing ships[5] which, by 1870, were carrying almost forty million dollars worth of goods; three-quarters of which was shipped directly across the lakes between Canada and the United States.[6]

Navigation of the St. Lawrence River had been improved by 1843 with the completion of six canals comprising twenty-nine locks, all with a minimum depth of nine feet (2.7 meters) of water over the lock sills.[7] The St. Lawrence canals were large enough for steamboats and sailing ships which could carry much larger loads than the old Durham boats and bateaux which they quickly replaced. Sailing downstream to Montreal, steamboats would run the rapids with their cargoes of flour, potash, staves, cornmeal, beans, peas and wheat.[8] Using the canals on their return trips, they would be loaded with sugar, liquor, tea, wine, salt, fruit and spices.[9] Kingston remained as the Great Lakes' busiest trans-shipment port with more than 1,200 ships from all across the Great Lakes calling there every year.[10]

(41) Long Sault rapids and the Cornwall Canal in the 1850's. Sketch by John Andrew. This scene shows two steamboats running the rapids on the St. Lawrence River en route to Montreal, and one steamboat in the canal, up-bound for Kingston. [From *Hunter's Panoramic Guide*, 1857]

In order to support this continued growth in shipping, the chain of four lake lights stretching around the Prince Edward peninsula from Presqu'ile Bay to Kingston harbour was strengthened in the fifteen year period from 1856 to 1871 with the addition of five more lighthouses on the shores of eastern Lake Ontario.

Scotch Bonnet Island Lighthouse (1856)

The first of these new links was built in 1856 within sight of Presqu'ile Point — on Scotch Bonnet Island. This island, together with Scotch Bonnet Shoal and nearby Nicholson Island, are the highest points of the submerged Scotch Bonnet Ridge that runs from Huyck's Point, at the south-western corner of Prince Edward County, for several nautical miles underwater toward the centre of Lake Ontario. For more than twenty years, there had been numerous demands and recommendations for a lighthouse in the vicinity of these dangerous shoals.

Within weeks of the Nine Mile Point lighthouse having been put into service in November, 1833, the *Kingston Chronicle and Gazette* had already published an editorial on the need for more lighthouses, including one on Nicholson Island:

> Light Houses - Our attention having been frequently directed to the necessity of an addition to the number of Light houses erected on the borders of Lake Ontario, we think the present the proper time to offer a few remarks upon the subject.... The entrance into Presque Isle Harbour being at all times difficult when the wind blows fresh, and at night nearly impracticable; and Nicholson's Island affording excellent anchorage and protection against most winds if there were a Light House on this island, vessels could in all weathers make it, and either anchor there, or enter Presque Isle Harbour as might be considered most desirable. It has been stated to us, that during the last trip of the *William the Fourth* steamer, she found it absolutely necessary either to come to anchor under Nicholson's Island, or to return to the Ducks. The weather was so thick at night, that she passed the island, and only ascertained it by the sounding [with a lead-line]. She was then abreast of the Scotch Bonnet — from which a dangerous shoal extends outward several miles. The boat was obliged to put back - there being a heavy swell from the South West at the time - and feel her

way to the island, which was discovered by the weather clearing up a little. Mr. Speaker and several members of the Assembly were on board at the time. After making the Island she rode perfectly safe during the gale.

The expense of erecting these light houses should not enter into the consideration of the Legislature, when it is considered what a vast amount of merchandise and property of every description is afloat upon the Lake during the season of navigation. And for three or four months, thousands of lives are depending on the safe arrival of the steamboats. We trust that these observations will, in some measure, tend to render the risk of travellers across Lake Ontario, much less than it is at present.[11]

(42) Sketch of the steamboat *William IV*. Artist unknown.
When she was launched at Gananoque on the St. Lawrence River in 1831, the *William IV* was one of the fastest steamboats on the Great Lakes. With her 100 HP engine, she could reach speeds of up to 14 knots (26 km/hr). She was easily distinguished from other steamboats of her time by her four smokestacks.
[From Croil, Steam Navigation, 1898]

The editorial mentioned one of the newest steamboats then on Lake Ontario, the *William IV*. Even with its one hundred horsepower engine, the steamboat had a very difficult time trying to round the Prince Edward peninsula, confirming that it was not just sailing ships that had to contend with dangerous conditions when that part of Lake Ontario was whipped up by a gale. More lighthouses would be a benefit to all ships; schooners and steamboats alike.

A broad, extended bay was formed by Nicholson Island on the south, the Presqu'ile peninsula on the north, and Prince Edward County on the east, and this bay was often used by mariners as the outer harbour or roadstead of Presqu'ile Bay which was then the only protected harbour on the north shore of Lake Ontario between South Bay and Toronto.

As if taking their lead from the newspaper editorial, just a few months after the completion of the Nine Mile Point lighthouse, Captain Charles McIntosh and a group of twenty-five ship owners and masters of vessels had presented another lighthouse petition to the provincial legislature. A legislative committee reported on the petition in January 1834:

> The Committee to whom was referred the petition
> of Charles McIntosh, and others—
> Beg leave to Report:
> That from all the information obtained by your Committee, it appears highly desirable for the safety and convenience of steam boats and other vessels navigating Lake Ontario, that two Light-houses should be built, the one on Nicholson's Island, and the other on Green point, between Port Hope and Cobourg. These Light-houses are considered necessary by all masters or owners of all steam boats and other vessels on Lake Ontario. The expense of the one on Nicholson's Island is estimated to cost about £750....

Your Committee therefore recommend, that the sum of £750 should be granted to build a Light-house on Nicholson's Island....
All which is respectfully submitted,
G.S. BOULTON, Chairman
Committee Room,
28th January, 1834.[12]

There is no evidence that Captain McIntosh's petition got any further than the committee stage. The fourth session of the 11th Parliament ended in March and Parliament was dissolved later that year resulting in no further action being taken on the petition. This was the fate of many petitions for lighthouses proposed to be constructed on the shores of eastern Lake Ontario.

A decade later, in 1844, the Province of Canada's Board of Works recommended that a lighthouse be built on Scotch Bonnet Island:

A [Light] House and second class Light upon the Scotch-bonnet Island, near Nicholson Island...
There is a shoal running to a long distance, to the South of it, upon which the breakers shew themselves in heavy weather; the establishment of the Light would add much to the safety of the navigation of that part of the Lake. It should be colored.[13]

Seven years later the possibility of building the Scotch Bonnet Island lighthouse was still being discussed when the sailing ship *Christiana* was wrecked and several lives were lost as reported in the Kingston *Daily News* in October 1851:

Wreck of the *Christiana* — The "Picton Sun" furnishes the following particulars of the wreck of the three-masted schooner *Christiana*, off Wellington: -

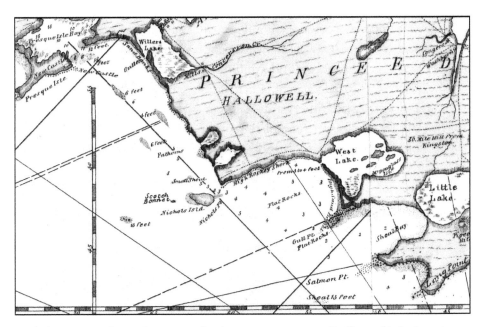

(43) Location of Scotch Bonnet Island. From Augustus Ford's *Chart of Lake Ontario*, 1836 (detail).
Nicholson Island is marked as "Nichols Isld" and Point Petre is marked as "Long Point".
[Courtesy of Library and Archives Canada, NMC11314]

"It is our melancholy duty to chronicle the loss of the brig *Christiana*, of Port Sarnia, the late Wm. Lang Master, laden with Oak Timber and Pot Ash; which vessel was capsized in the gale of Friday morning 27ᵗʰ ult. in the neighborhood of the small island known as "Gull Island," or the "Scotch Bonnet," on Lake Ontario, with the loss of all on board, including the owner, the late Mr. Cross of Port Sarnia, who for the first time was making a trip to Quebec. It is supposed that the crew consisted of William and John Lang (brothers) master and mate, with eight seamen. From the appearance of this ill-fated vessel on Friday morning, it was thought by some persons who were watching her that she was disabled, and in a very short time afterwards she went over....

The decks were completely swept, with the exception of a few barrels of pot ash and a stick of timber on the lee side. Examination was then made as to the probable cause of the disaster, which turned out to arise from the steering chains becoming foul and choked when she attempted to go about. Every measure has been taken to secure the remains of the vessel and cargo, notwithstanding. A steam tug boat is now in the neighborhood, and it is expected the wreck will be taken in tow to Kingston so soon as the wind lulls a little.[14]

It is possible that if there had been a lighthouse on Scotch Bonnet Island at that time, the captain of the *Christiana* would have steered well clear of the island and the ship and her crew may have been spared.

Two years later, there was still no word that the government had any intention to build a lighthouse on Scotch Bonnet Island. In 1853, an editorial appeared in *The Daily British Whig*, complaining about the situation:

Lights are... elsewhere wanted, the present condition of Egg Island, vulgarly known as the Scotch Bonnet, sufficiently testifies. Standing directly in the track of steamers plying between Toronto and Kingston, and being only one and a half miles out from St. Nicholas Island [Nicholson Island], Egg Island is in thick weather, or at night, a source not only of much uneasiness to masters of steam and sailing vessels, but of positive danger, a wide berth to islands of that kind being oftentimes impossible, in a fog and the more especially so when, in addition to the thickness of the weather, there may be a breeze upon the Lake and not only a breeze but a current, at least sufficiently strong to drag a vessel out of her course. Egg Island is a kind of millstone or half way house, which instead of being at the side, stands in the middle of the way, undiscoverable to travellers unless the moon shines out.[15]

It would be another year still before the Board of Works' own recommendation of a decade earlier was finally acted upon. In June, 1854, The Commissioners of Public Works reported to the Legislative Assembly that:

> In Lake Ontario, a Light House is being built on the "Scotch Bonnet" or "Egg Island," a small low island lying S.E. off Presqu'isle, and in the direct line of the Mail and other vessels running down the Lake from Cobourg, &c.[16]

Unfortunately, the lighthouse was not finished in time to help prevent the wreck of the schooner *Norfolk* and the loss of all hands in November of that year. The *Norfolk* was a small two-masted schooner of 130 tons that had been launched just that spring. She hailed from Port Dover on Lake Erie and was loaded with staves when she was driven onto Scotch Bonnet Island by a gale. The doomed mariners may have been able to discern the outline of the partially completed tower on the island just as they struck the reef, but by then they would have been helpless to do anything but to try to save themselves. There were reports that the captain was killed when hit in the head by the fore-boom, one crewman was caught in the rigging and was strangled, and the other three crewmen drowned.[17]

Two weeks later, the steamboat *Ontario*, bound Montreal for Cobourg and Toronto with a cargo of sugar was driven ashore at nearby Nicholson Island by a south-westerly gale. This accident might have been averted if the Scotch Bonnet Island lighthouse had been in operation. Fortunately, no one aboard the *Ontario* was harmed and much of her cargo was saved. The ship was eventually towed off the island and later rebuilt as a schooner.[18]

Sadly, these tragedies did not seem to hasten the completion of the lighthouse. In 1855, the Commissioners of Public Works reported that it would be another year before the lighthouse could be put into service: "The important light on the 'Scotch Bonnet,' in Lake Ontario will be brought into use as early as the lighting apparatus can be taken to the place and fitted up, next spring."[19]

According to *The Harbours and Ports of Lake Ontario*, it was the end of the summer of 1856 before the lighthouse finally went into service :

> The Board of Works have just completed an excellent lighthouse on Egg Island, or the Scotch Bonnet, which is one mile S. S. W. of Nicholas Island [Nicholson Island]. It was lighted for the first time in September, 1856. A bright fixed light, bearing S. E. of Presqu' Isle Light. Can be seen 13 miles.[20]

No explanation was given for the delay of almost one year between the date that the brick-lined masonry tower[21] was completed, and when the lamps of the lighthouse were first lit. The lighting apparatus had been purchased from C. Garth of Montreal for £467,[22] and there may have been a delay in having it delivered to the island. Construction delays at such a remote site would not have been uncommon. It would have been difficult at the best of times to land men and materiel on the island located more than two nautical miles from the mainland. Since Scotch Bonnet Island is little more than an exposed reef with no protected landing place for any boats loaded with bricks, building stones, men and equipment, it would only have been possible to land on the island when the waters of Lake Ontario were relatively calm.

The delay may have been due to the difficulty in finding a keeper for the lighthouse. For the first time since the False ducks Island lighthouse was established almost thirty years earlier, the government had the foresight to include the lightkeeper's dwelling as part of the original construction project for the lighthouse. The island being so small, the dwelling was attached directly to the stone tower itself. Even though a sturdy stone house was ready to be occupied, the idea of living on such a tiny rock some two miles from the mainland, especially in the winter, would likely have made most prospective lightkeepers reject such a prospect out of hand. It would require a special person who would have the fortitude to reside in such a difficult and remote location for long periods of time, and those who did take on the job did not last long.

(44) Scotch Bonnet Island lighthouse with attached keeper's dwelling, c. 1939.
Photographer unknown.
The island was a tiny sliver of exposed rock covered with a small amount of vegetation.
[Courtesy of Library and Archives Canada, PA-211516]

The first lightkeeper at Scotch Bonnet Island was John Giroux (or Gerow)[23] who kept the light for only two seasons. He was followed by Samuel Wilson in 1859. It may have been Wilson who recommended that a more suitable location for the keeper's house was required. In 1861, the Public Works Department purchased four acres of land on nearby Nicholson Island where a second keeper's dwelling was to be built, "... the present house [on Scotch Bonnet Island] being unfit to be occupied, except during the summer months."[24]

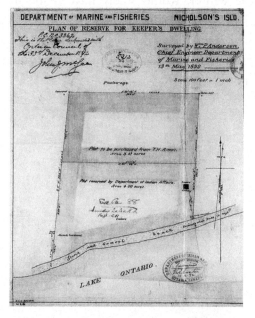

(45) Plan of a portion of Nicholson Island to be reserved for the Scotch Bonnet Island lightkeeper's dwelling. Surveyed and drawn by W.P. Anderson, 1892.
The stone dwelling attached directly to the Scotch Bonnet Island lighthouse was largely uninhabitable from late fall through to early spring, so a second keeper's dwelling was constructed on Nicholson Island in 1861. However, it was not until 1892 that the Department of Marine and Fisheries gained title to the land from the First Nations peoples when the land was sold to them by the Department of Indian Affairs. [Courtesy of Library and Archives Canada, RG2, Order-in-Council 1892-3362]

Even with a second lightkeeper's dwelling on Nicholson Island, every evening the keeper would have to row his boat more than a mile in the open lake to reach Scotch Bonnet Island. He would then light the lamps of the lighthouse and spend the night on the desolate rock watching the light. In the morning before rowing back to his regular home, he would extinguish the lamps, trim the wicks, refill the lamp oil, clean the lantern glass and perform any other maintenance duties that might be required. If there were signs of fog or an approaching storm, the keeper would have to keep the light burning longer to ensure that the lighthouse was always an effective aid to navigation.

In total, there were ten different keepers at Scotch Bonnet Island over the course of some sixty years; a higher turnover rate for lightkeepers than at any other lighthouse in eastern Lake Ontario.

1st Snake Island Shoal Lighthouse (1858)

Two years later, in 1858, the Board of Works commenced construction on what would be the last stone lighthouse built on Lake Ontario.

More than a decade earlier, in 1844, the Board had recommended that a pier and lighthouse be built just off of Snake Island near Kingston to mark a dangerous shoal where several ships had been stranded or wrecked. Unfortunately for Calvin, Cook and Company, the owners of the schooner *William Penn,* that recommendation had not been followed. In the summer of 1845, the schooner belonging to the Garden Island-based lumber merchants had struck a rock in the channel near Snake Island. Captain John McIntyre, commander of the Royal Naval dockyard at Kingston, had to dispatch one of his ships to render assistance to the *William Penn.* The company directors sent the following letter to Captain McIntyre in August of that year:

> Dear Sir: - We beg to return to you our sincere thanks for the prompt and efficient service rendered to the schooner *William Penn,* when she grounded yesterday, on the small "shoal," a Rock lying between Long [Wolfe] and Snake Islands; and at the same time, as large schooner owners, we cannot but avail ourselves of this opportunity of expressing to you the correct views you entertain of the importance of adding to the safety of the Lake Navigation

by recommending the building and placing of additional lighthouses and buoys; and in none is this more necessarily required than one on the shoal or rock mentioned above. Many schooners have been grounded and some have been wrecked upon it, and this too within a few miles of Kingston, the foot of Lake Navigation.

Wishing you that prosperity and success which your meritorious and enlightened conduct entitle you to,

We are, Dear Sir, Yours very respectfully,

Calvin, Cook & Co.[25]

The following year, the Merchant Seamen's Society made a request to the Board of Works "... to cause a crib to be sunk on the shore at Snake Island, and a permanent Beacon to be erected thereon."[26] Despite numerous such appeals, petitions and recommendations, the shoal water around Snake Island remained unmarked. Another eight years passed before further urgent requests were made for a lighthouse at Snake Island.

In 1854, Thomas Maxwell, owner of the Provincial Tug Line which had the government contract to tow vessels up and down the St. Lawrence River, wrote to Thomas Begley, secretary to the Board of Works:

> The writer has been frequently asked to address you respecting a light at Snake Island, this I am of opinion is much needed; in the absence of a light I would suggest in its place a beacon.[27]

In 1855, the Board of Works again recommended the construction of a lighthouse at Snake Island:

> The necessity for the establishment of a light on Snake Island, off the entrance to Kingston Bay, is daily becoming more apparent. Several disasters have occurred from want of it, and it is proposed, therefore, to recommend in the estimates a sum for the erection of such Lighthouse.[28]

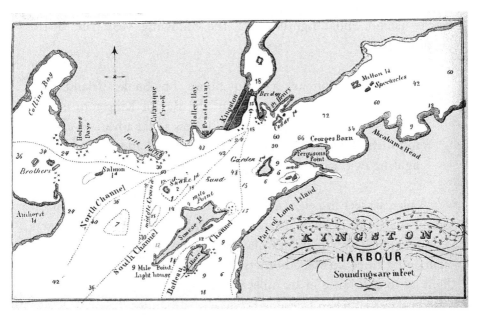

(46) Sketch of Kingston Harbour showing the location of Snake Island (detail).
Edward Hodder, 1857. Snake Island is separated from Simcoe Island by the South
Channel. This was the most direct route between Kingston harbour and other ports
on Lake Ontario. The Lower Gap is marked as "North Channel". Amherst Island is at
the far left. Wolfe Island is at the far right. At the top, Hatters Bay is where the town
of Portsmouth was located.
[From Hodder, *The Harbours and Ports of Lake Ontario*, 1857]

The "disasters" alluded to by the Commissioners of Public Works undoubtedly included the stranding of the schooners *Weather* and *William Cayley* in 1841, the grounding of the schooners *William Penn* in 1845, *Ann Jane Brown* in 1848 and *Mansfield* in 1854, as well as the grounding of the steamer *Europa* in 1855.[29]

On that last recommendation of the Board of Works, the legislature finally appropriated £3,000 for the construction of the Snake Island Shoal lighthouse.[30] The following year, the Board reported that:

> The erection of a light house on Snake Island, Lake Ontario, at the entrance of the Bay of Kingston, is progressing very satisfactorily, and is now so far advanced as to justify the belief, that it will be completed and ready for lighting by the first of June next.[31]

A pier, six feet in height above the water, had been built on a shoal on the south side of Snake Island. The lighthouse topping the pier was a square stone tower, painted white, twenty-nine feet tall with a lantern containing three kerosene burners and three reflectors showing a red light up to a distance of six miles in clear weather. The stone keeper's dwelling was attached to the lighthouse in a manner that would have been similar to the arrangement on Scotch Bonnet Island.[32] The Snake Island Shoal lighthouse went into service in August, 1858.

Although no pictures or plans of this lighthouse have been found, it may have been similar in appearance to the square stone lighthouse that had been built a decade earlier at Goderich on Lake Huron, the only other square stone lighthouse known to have been built by the Province of Canada.

As to the effectiveness of this lighthouse at warning ships of the nearby underwater hazards, it is difficult to ascertain. We do know, however, that the lighthouse did not prevent numerous groundings which occurred after the lighthouse was completed in 1858, including the schooners *Atlantic* (1862), *Frank Crawford* (1863), and *Canada* (1864), as well as dozens of others over the following decades.[33]

(47) Concept drawing of the 1ˢᵗ Snake Island Shoal lighthouse, constructed in 1858.
Marc Seguin, 2015.
This drawing is based on the details given in the Admiralty's List of Lights combined with images of a similar lighthouse erected at Goderich, Ontario in 1847.
[Author's collection]

Despite these occurrences, there were likely thousands of ships which did benefit from this lighthouse. It can be safely estimated that at least one-quarter of all ships calling at Kingston would have passed by the lighthouse on the shoal off of Snake Island. That would amount to some 250 ships inbound and 250 ships outbound every year.[34] From 1858 when the Snake Island Shoal lighthouse was built, to 1900 when it was replaced by a new lighthouse further out in the channel, a total of more than 20,000 ships would have passed the lighthouse over the course of 42 years. Considering the several dozen ships that were stranded during that time period as compared to the many thousands that passed through that channel, it can be concluded that the Snake Island Shoal lighthouse was quite effective at guiding ships safely to and from Kingston harbour, and that the lighthouse contributed to the growth and prosperity, not only of the port of Kingston, but of the entire province.

While this chain of lighthouses would be strengthened over the decades by the construction of other towers, this was the last lake light to be built of stone along the Canadian shores of Lake Ontario. After 1860, masonry lighthouses were no longer being built anywhere in Canada. Wood-framed construction for lighthouses would predominate all across the country for the next fifty years.

Pleasant Point Lighthouse (1866)

While the busy East-West shipping routes across Lake Ontario were vital for the overseas import-export trade via the Kingston-St. Lawrence River-Montreal corridor, the north-south routes across the lake connecting American ports with Canadian ports were also important and at least as heavily travelled. Once they had successfully navigated the treacherous waters around the Ducks, ships destined for Picton, Deseronto, Belleville, Trenton and other ports in the Bay of Quinte had to find the entrance to the bay at the Upper Gap. In order to facilitate this and to, "... give confidence to Masters of Vessels",[35] another link was added to the chain of lake lights in eastern Lake Ontario when a lighthouse was built at Pleasant Point in 1866.

By then, more than 100,000 tons of cargo annually were being carried into and out of the Bay of Quinte aboard some 800 ships, most of which would have sailed by Pleasant Point as they passed through the Upper Gap.[36] Building a lighthouse at that location was seen by many as essential.

When Thomas Maxwell had written to the Board of Works in May, 1854, about the necessity for a lighthouse near Snake Island, he had also emphasized the need for a lighthouse at the Upper Gap:

> The entrance to the Bay [of Quinte] of the Upper Gap would be rendered quite safe by having a pier and light on Indian point [also called Point Pleasant, Pleasant Point or

Fifth Town Point], there are a great many Vessels trading between the Bay and Oswego, and on entering the Gap of a dark stormy night, is difficult and dangerous; this light would give confidence to Masters of Vessels and enable them to enter; when without it, they are obliged to stand out and face the storm all night.[37]

The Commissioners of Public Works heeded this advice and later that year recommended to the Legislature of the Province of Canada that a lighthouse be built to mark the Upper Gap.[38] However, no monies were voted by the legislature for the construction of the lighthouse until 1857 when the tiny sum of £750 was allocated for the construction of no fewer than five lighthouses which had been proposed for the Bay of Quinte and surrounding area, including Pleasant Point:

> Resolved, That a sum not exceeding Seven hundred and fifty pounds, currency, be granted to Her Majesty, toward five new Light Houses in Bay of Quinté, for the year 1857.[39]

No further details are provided, and there is no indication of exactly where the five towers were to be built. It is difficult to understand the thinking of the legislators when they voted such a small amount of money for the construction of five lighthouses; an average of only £150 per lighthouse, which would have been the equivalent of $600 in 1850's dollars.[40] Most of the lighthouses previously constructed in eastern Lake Ontario had cost in excess of £1,000; the equivalent of almost $4,000. Perhaps this was the reason that masonry towers were no longer being built and wood-framed lighthouses were proliferating across Canada: the cost of building a wood-framed lighthouse was considerably less than a stone one. Nevertheless, £150 was simply not enough to cover the cost of building even a wood-framed tower.

In September, 1857, a tender was let for the construction of three of the five proposed lighthouses:

LIGHT HOUSES, BAY OF QUINTE
TO CONTRACTORS

The Commissioners of Public Works having selected five Sites recommended for erecting LIGHT HOUSES with the view of affording greater facilities for the Safe Navigation of the Bay of Quinte and the easterly entrances thereto, will at the present time receive Tenders for Three of the number, to be built at the following places:

1. The Northern Brother Island — Lower Gap.
2. The Upper Gap [Pleasant Point] — Entry from Lake Ontario.
3. The Belleville Shoal — Entrance of River Moira.

Plans and Specifications can be seen at the Office of the Collector of Customs, at Kingston, and at the Department of Public Works, Toronto, on or after the 7th day of September....

> T.A. Begly, Secretary
> Department of Public Works
> Toronto, 1st Sept. 1857 [41]

It appeared as though the construction of these three lighthouses was assured as funds had been voted by Parliament and specific sites had been chosen. In addition, the assistant-engineer of the Public Works Department, Frederick P. Rubidge, had surveyed a site for the Pleasant Point lighthouse,[42] and more than $100 of the allocated money had already been spent.[43]

In spite of all of these preparations, there was no work done to build any lighthouses in or near the Bay of Quinte at that time, and four years would pass before mention was made again of any of these lighthouses.

In 1861, a petition was received by the Legislature on that subject:

Of Thomas McIntosh and others, Masters and Owners of Vessels trading from the Port of Belleville to the United States; praying that a Light House may be constructed at the

Upper Gap, situated at the Southwestern extremity of the County of Prince Edward.[44]

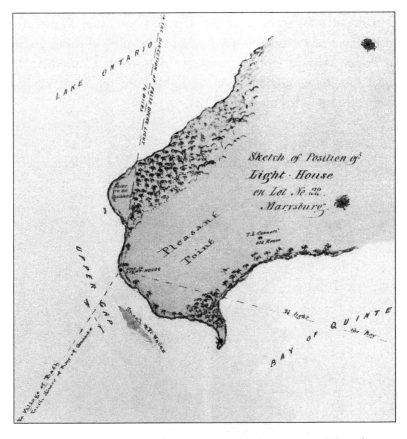

(48) Sketch showing location of Pleasant Point Lighthouse. From "Plan of Proposed Light-House at the Upper Gap, Bay of Quinte" (detail), drawn by F.P. Rubidge, 1864.
Note: North is at the bottom.
[Courtesy of Library and Archives Canada, RG11M77803-38]

The petition was introduced to the Assembly in April 1861 by the Conservative member for Prince Edward, Willet C. Dorland. The petition's mention of the Upper Gap being in the south-western part of Prince Edward County rather than at its true location in the north-eastern part of the County may have been a simple clerical error. Nevertheless, the petition was not acted upon as the 6th Parliament was soon dissolved and a General Election was held the following month.

The 7th Parliament of the Province of Canada was convened later in 1861, but it was short-lived, and another General Election was held in May 1863. As a result, it is not until 1864 that any further mention was made of a lighthouse at the Upper Gap when Walter Ross, former Mayor of Picton and newly-elected member of the Legislature from Prince Edward County, wrote to the provincial premier, John A. Macdonald, enquiring about a lighthouse for Pleasant Point. Macdonald responded on August 12:

> My dear Ross,
>
> I have called the attention of the Board of Works to the necessity of erecting a Lighthouse at Point Pleasant, but have not received an answer yet.[45]

(49) Prince Edward County political rivals. Walter Ross, left (1875) and James McCuaig, right (1879). Photographs by William Topley.

Ross was the four-term mayor of Picton before he was elected to the legislature of the Province of Canada in 1863. After Confederation in 1867, he ran against McCuaig in three successive elections and defeated him in every one. After Ross retired from politics in 1878, McCuaig was finally elected to the House of Commons for a single term, being ousted by the voters in 1882 over the Murray Canal issue. Coincidentally, both were Picton business men with an interest in shipping, and at different times they each owned the steamer *Alexandria*.

[Courtesy of Library and Archives Canada, Topley Series]

The answer that Macdonald eventually received from the Board must have been a positive one. By September, 1864, plans for a timber-framed octagonal lighthouse at the Upper Gap had been drawn and tenders were let for its construction.[46] Further details are provided in Frederick Rubidge's report of June 13, 1865:

LIGHT-HOUSE, UPPER GAP, BAY OF QUINTE

The site proposed in 1857 by the undersigned for this much-required light, was visited again in the month of August last [1864], under Departmental instructions, and the choice of the previously chosen spot was confirmed, after consulting with the Inspector of Light-houses and parties resident in the neighborhood. The entrance to the Upper Gap from Lake Ontario, in dark and stormy weather, is attended with much uncertainty and danger — many vessels having been wrecked in making the entrance from the lake.

As the sum appropriated for this and other lights in the vicinity was limited, a tower of wooden frame-work, based on a crib foundation, the light on which will be about fifty feet above water level, has been projected; and a plan and specifications were, in September last, put before the public in the Kingston papers by advertisement.

Only two tenders were received, both of which, probably from the late period of the year, were found too high to be accepted; it was consequently proposed by the Engineer to erect the tower under the supervision of the Departmental Inspector of Lights, who resides in this vicinity. The cost of which tower and foundation, not however, including the lantern and lighting apparatus, was estimated at $1,564.[47]

(50) Plan of Proposed Light-House at the Upper Gap (Pleasant Point) Bay of Quinte. Drawn by F.P. Rubidge, 1864. This is one of the few complete sets of plans still in existence for a Lake Ontario lighthouse. [Courtesy of Library and Archives Canada, RG11M77803-38]

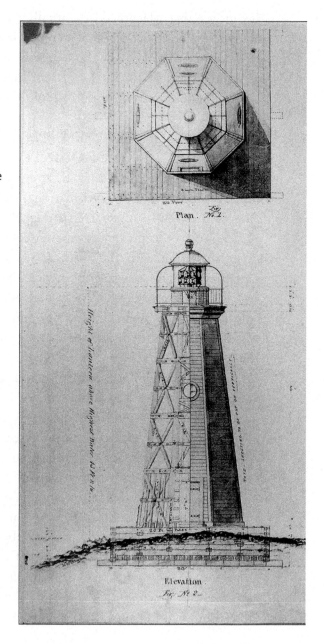

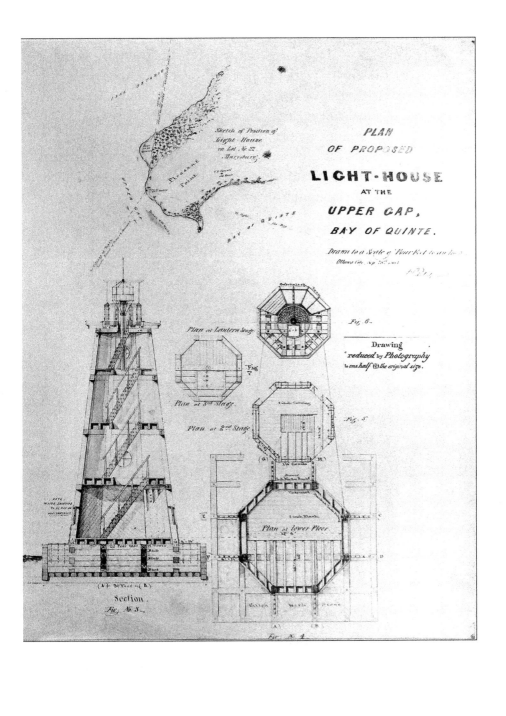

Sketch of Position of Light-House on Lot No. 22 Marysburg.

PLAN
OF PROPOSED
LIGHT-HOUSE
AT THE
UPPER GAP,
BAY OF QUINTE.

Drawn to a Scale of Four Feet to an Inch

Fig. 6.

Drawing reduced by Photography to one half (½) the original size.

Plan at Lantern Stage
Fig. 7

Plan at 3rd Stage

Plan at 2nd Stage

Fig. 5

Plan at Lower Floor

Section.
Fig. No. 3.

Fig. No. 4.

On the recommendation of the Department's assistant engineer, the construction of the Pleasant Point lighthouse would be handled entirely by the Public Works Department with no involvement of a private contractor. This was done, supposedly, as a cost-saving measure. However, the final cost of erecting the tower at the Upper Gap would be $2,819.42, nearly double the engineer's original estimate. In addition, there was the extra cost of the lantern and lighting apparatus as well as miscellaneous expenses all of which totaled $4,344.12; more than the whole amount originally voted by Parliament in 1857 for the construction of a total of five lighthouses.[48]

(51) Pleasant Point lighthouse, c.1950. Photographer unknown.
This lighthouse was known by many other names including Upper Gap, Indian Point, and Point Pleasant.
[Courtesy of Prince Edward County Mariners Park Museum, Willis Metcalfe collection]

The *Report of the Commissioners of Public Works* for 1867 noted the Pleasant Point lighthouse was put into service in 1866 with nine coal-oil lamps and nine reflectors in an iron lantern atop an octagonal tower measuring fifty-two feet from base to vane.[49] The reference to "coal-oil lamps" is the first indication that eastern Lake Ontario lighthouses were no longer burning sperm-oil in their lamps. Coal oil, also known as kerosene, had been discovered by a Nova Scotia geologist and physician, Dr. Abraham Gesner, some twenty years earlier.[50] From bituminous substances such as naturally-occurring tar and coal, Gesner was able to distill a flammable liquid that burned up to seven times brighter than sperm-oil and was one-third the cost.[51] Gesner patented his product in the United States and started the Asphalt Mining and Kerosene Gas Company in 1853. By 1859, kerosene was being produced on a commercial scale in Petrolia, Ontario,[52] and quickly became the preferred illuminant used in lighthouses.

(52) Portrait of John Prinyer, first lightkeeper of the Pleasant Point Lighthouse. From a photograph by O.C. Hubbs.
[From Belden, *Illustrated Historical Atlas of the Counties of Hastings and Prince Edward,* 1878.]

In 1866, Premier Macdonald received a number of letters from correspondents hoping to be hired as the lightkeeper for the Pleasant Point lighthouse.[53] That position was filled by local resident, John Prinyer, from nearby Prinyer's cove, a staunch conservative who was a political supporter of the premier.[54] During his 30-year tenure as lightkeeper, Prinyer was also a councilor and reeve of Marysburgh township and warden of Prince Edward County. In addition, he held positions as Justice of the Peace and Dominion Customs Officer.

The Pleasant Point lighthouse was the last lighthouse built under the authority of the Board of Works of the Province of Canada. On July 1, 1867, with the confederation of Nova Scotia, New Brunswick, Canada East and Canada West, the government of the new Dominion of Canada took over responsibility of all public works including lighthouses, and in 1868, the construction, maintenance and staffing of all lighthouse came under the authority of new branch of the public administration, the Department of Marine and Fisheries.

1ˢᵗ Pigeon Island Lighthouse (1870)

Within two years of its establishment, the Department of Marine and Fisheries added another link in the "chain of lights" when a new style of lighthouse was built on Pigeon Island in Lake Ontario in 1870. This tiny exposed reef south-west of Wolfe Island was a hazard to navigation as it was on the direct shipping route between Oswego and Kingston, and numerous vessels had been wrecked or grounded there over the decades.

During a typical late-season storm in 1846, the brigantine *General Brock* had been wrecked on Pigeon Island and her crew stranded for several days before being rescued by the Royal Navy. The *Grenville Gazette* reported the incident:

> A storm commenced on Wednesday evening last [Nov. 27], and continued with slight intermission, until Saturday morning. We much fear that it has proved disastrous to a number of vessels which on Tuesday and Wednesday

left this port, upward bound, as well as coming down. The brigt. *General Brock*, struck on Pigeon Island reef on Wednesday night, and we believe has become a total wreck. Capt. Pearson and the crew were taken off the island, - on which after some difficulty they had effected a landing - by *H.M.S. Mohawk*, which was despatched by Capt. Fowell to their assistance.[55]

In 1853, the schooner *Royal Susan*, bound Buffalo to Kingston, went aground on the island.[56] In 1862, the *Governor*, bound Toledo for Kingston with 10,000 bushels of wheat in her hold was severely damaged when she was wrecked there. She was eventually towed off and repaired at the marine railway in Portsmouth.[57] The following year, the propeller *Young America* was reported ashore on Pigeon Island with a cargo of wheat and flour,[58] and three years later, in 1866, the schooner *Annexation*, bound Belleville to Oswego, went aground there with a loss reported at $2,300.[59]

These and many other accidents occurred at Pigeon Island and, as shipping increased on the Great Lakes, it became more important to establish an aid to navigation at this location to augment he existing chain of lights in eastern Lake Ontario.

In his annual report for 1870, the Minister of Marine and Fisheries remarked that:

> A new lighthouse with keeper's dwelling attached, was erected lately on Pigeon Island, near Wolfe Island, in Lake Ontario. It shews a white revolving light, is elevated 46 feet above the level of the water, and can be seen a distance from 12 to 16 miles in clear weather. It was lighted for the first time on the 1st of November, 1870. The importance of this light can scarcely be over-estimated in guiding the mail and other steamers and lake craft into Kingston, and to the entrance of the River St. Lawrence. Reports have reached the Department of the satisfaction which its establishment has given to the shipping trading in that locality.[60]

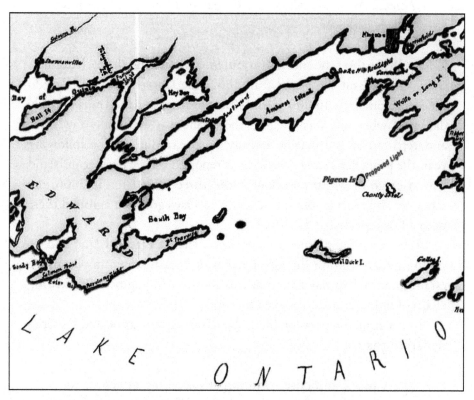

(53) Sketch showing the location of the proposed Pigeon Island Lighthouse, 1870 (detail). Order-in-Council 1870-1247.
Kingston is shown at top right, below which is marked "Snake Is. Red Light". At bottom left, Salmon Point is marked and Point Petre is marked as "Revolving Light".
[Courtesy of Library and Archives Canada, RG2, Orders-in-Council]

The new style of lighthouse constructed on Pigeon Island is often referred to as the "schoolhouse style". Two of these lighthouses were built at the same time that year; one on Pigeon Island and the other on Telegraph Island in the Bay of Quinte. These two lighthouses were built on the identical plan by the same builder, Roderick Cameron of Lancaster, Ontario.[61] However, because of their very different situations, they were used for different purposes. The Pigeon Island light was designed as a lake light with twin reflecting lamps and a revolving white light projecting up to fifteen miles over the lake. The Telegraph Island light was fitted with a less powerful fixed harbour light with a single reflecting lamp with a range of twelve miles.

These were among the first lighthouses built under the authority of the Dominion of Canada.

Further details about the Pigeon Island lighthouse were provided in the Marine and Fisheries report of the following year:

> The new revolving Light on Pigeon Island, Lake Ontario, alluded to in my last report was lighted up for the first time on the 1st November, 1870, and cost $2,405.73. the amount voted by Parliament was $2,000. This Light was originally intended to be a fixed Light, but in order to meet the wishes of the trade and to distinguish it from the other fixed Lights in the Lake, it was made a revolving Light, which involved the additional expense of machinery. It has been found to be a very useful Light, as it is seen a distance of sixteen or seventeen miles. It is a revolving white Light, on the catoptric principle. with two circular burner lamps and two 18-inch reflectors. Mr. James Eccles was appointed keeper on the 1st November, 1870, at a salary of $300 per annum.[62]

(54) Pigeon Island lighthouse, 1907. Photographer unknown.
This lighthouse and an identical one on Telegraph Island in the Bay of Quinte were
built in a unique "schoolhouse" style by Roderick Cameron in 1870.
[Courtesy of Library and Archives Canada, PA-172530]

The report went on to comment on a serious incident that occurred
only ten months after James Eccles' appointment:

> By some want of management of the lamps on the
> part of the keeper, they took fire on the night of the 4th
> September last, and had to be extinguished for a few nights
> until new ones could be procured. An investigation was
> made by the Department into the matter, when it was found
> that the keeper had gone to the mainland to transact some
> business and left the Light in charge of his son and another
> person, who probably did not understand the management
> of the lamps. Another keeper will probably be appointed
> before the commencement of navigation as the present one
> does not wish to hold the appointment.[63]

Not only had the lamps gone out, but the steamboat *Spartan*, with a full compliment of passengers and cargo, ran aground on Pigeon Island as a result of this. The incident was reported in detail by the Kingston *Daily News*:

September 6, 1871. — Ashore — The Royal Mail Line steamer *Spartan*, from Oswego to Kingston, went ashore at Pigeon Island during the night. Messrs. Calvin & Breck's steamer *William* went to her assistance this morning, having in tow with her the schooner *Gazelle* to receive the *Spartan's* cargo if it was found necessary to lighten her.

The steamer *Spartan* — The steamer *William* and schooner *Gazelle* returned from the steamer *Spartan*, ashore on Pigeon Island, this (Wednesday) afternoon, and arrived at the wharf about three o'clock, bringing with them the passengers and their luggage. There were about one hundred and fifty passengers on board the *Spartan* when she struck. The following are the particulars of the catastrophe obtained from the passengers and purser of the *Spartan*:- The latter reports that the weather last night was rather hazy and a fresh breeze prevailed when the *Spartan* neared Pigeon Island, and no light was visible except a small glimmer, which appeared to be a long distance from the vessel, and was only seen at intervals. The vessel, which was in charge of both the captain and mate at the time, was running at full speed, which was slackened upon finding that the water commencing to shoal; not sufficiently soon, however, to prevent the vessel striking with a heavy shock. The purser further states that subsequent inquiries showed that the lamp at the lighthouse had exploded, and the keeper, being unable to replace it immediately, had substituted a candle, the deceptive light of which was the cause of the accident. Several of the passengers who were on deck at the time of the vessel striking, however, gave a different version of the occurrence, and stated that the light on the island was plainly visible, and that the vessel appeared to be steered right on to the shore with unaccountable carelessness. One gentleman remarked that he had watched the light for some time before the vessel struck, and wondered at the vessel continuing a course so plainly wrong. However, it is probable that the captain of the *Spartan* will be able to give a satisfactory account for the accident.

When the *William* neared the stranded vessel she found it was impossible to get alongside, consequently the *Gazelle* took on board the passengers and their luggage, and was towed with them on board into port. The *William* with the *Hercules* will at once return to the *Spartan*, towing the *Gazelle*, which last will take out the *Spartan*'s cargo in order to lighten her. The *Spartan* is only insured against fire. When the passengers arrived they were too late to take the afternoon trains, and the majority of them claimed their hotel expenses from the company for the night. This the manager here refused to allow, and the dissatisfaction shown among the passengers was great, and made itself evident by remarks by no means complimentary to the steamboat company.

THE STEAMER SPARTAN.

(55) The steamer *Spartan*. Sketch by W.J. Thomson, 1895.
In September 1871, the *Spartan* ran aground off of Pigeon Island. The lamps in the new lighthouse had malfunctioned and since lightkeeper James Eccles was not present, his son had substituted a candle for the lamps and reflectors normally used. None of the fifty passengers was injured, but Eccles lost his job over the incident. [From *Robertson's Landmarks of Toronto*, 1896]

Mr. James Eccles, lighthouse-keeper of Pigeon Island, states that the lamps had never worked properly, and last night the reflectors were destroyed, but the light was kept burning and was visible at a long distance. The land was plainly to be seen from the *Spartan*'s decks, and it is difficult to account for the captain steering directly towards it. It is usual to give the island a wide berth. The *Spartan* is badly damaged, and will be got off with difficulty.[64]

September 7, 1871. — The Steamer *Spartan* — The following explanation of the accident to the steamer *Spartan* has been furnished on the part of the Inland Navigation Company:- We are glad to learn that the steamer *Spartan* arrived into port this morning, having sustained no damage. She leaves tomorrow (Friday) at the usual hour for Toronto and Hamilton. The accident was caused by the light on Pigeon Island having exploded. The lighthouse keeper had a small light placed in it, which deceived the captain, he supposing the usual light to be lit, and it showed so dim that he had given it a good berth. This is the second time this season that the light on Pigeon Island has exploded, and we hope it will be looked after by the proper authorities. It would be much better when such accidents do occur for the lighthouse keeper to make a large fire on the beach in front of his lighthouse than to try and make a lighthouse out of a hand lamp.

The Steamer *Spartan* - The schooner *Gazelle* arrived at the wharf at one o'clock this morning, having on board the cargo of the *Spartan*, which vessel also arrived about an hour afterwards. Captain Dix, of the *Gazelle* attributes the accident to the *Spartan* entirely to the insufficiency of the light on Pigeon Island. He states that last night while off the island the light, owing to its small size and the prevalence of a mist, appeared to be at such a far off distance, that, although he was intimately acquainted with the position of the island, he should have been deceived by it, and considers the captain and mate of the steamer to be entirely blameless for the occurrence of the accident. It is also reported in connection with the light on Pigeon Island that the lighthouse keeper had repeatedly reported the defect in its working. It is a revolving light, and when the lamp is in order, it emits a very brilliant light. Upon the night of the accident the small size of the light was rendered less conspicuous by the revolutions of the lamp, and the deception was greater. The *Spartan* is said to have received but little damage, and will at once resume her regular trips.[65]

Fortunately, no lives were lost in the accident. James Eccles, however, lost his job over the incident and he was replaced as keeper of the Pigeon Island lighthouse by William Davis who settled on the island with his wife and ten children. Sadly though, two years later both Eccles and Davis were drowned along with four others after a day of fishing at Pigeon Island:

Sad Drowning - On Tuesday last, between 12 and 1 o'clock, a boat, with 6 men in it, left Pigeon Island, where they had been fishing, to come to Kingston. While about half way between Pigeon Island and Nine Mile Point the boat suddenly disappeared, and the occupants were seen no more. The names of the persons, so far as we could learn, were James Eccles, William Davis, and Louis Cadotte, with three Americans, whose names are not known. The boat was found bottom up at Nine Mile, and was a total wreck. It is supposed that she foundered during the severe gale of Tuesday, and the men were thrown overboard by the pitching. The heavy sea running prevented her righting again, and in consequence the men were drowned.[66]

After the death of William Davis, his widow, Mary, was appointed as the temporary keeper of the lighthouse; a position she held for more than ten years. After her retirement in 1884, other members of the Davis family continued to keep the Pigeon Island light for several decades.

Salmon Point Lighthouse (1871)

With the completion of the Pigeon Island lighthouse in 1870, it appeared that all of the gaps in the chain of lake lights around the Prince Edward peninsula had been filled with strong links. With eight lighthouses now guiding ships through these dangerous waters of eastern Lake Ontario, the Marine and Fisheries Department had no plans to build any more lake lights between Kingston harbour and Presqu'ile Point.

Tragedy and political manoeuvering intervened, however, and these plans were quickly altered. The tragedy involved the wreck of the schooner *Jessie* and the loss of her entire crew.

Built at St. Catharines in 1855 by Maltese-born shipwright Louis Shickluna, the *Jessie*'s home port was Port Stanley on Lake Erie. At the time of her construction she had been praised as "one of the finest vessels" on the lake:

> This magnificent schooner is now loaded at the Freight Warehouse of the Mad River and Lake Erie railroad and is one of the finest vessels that we have ever seen. She was built by Lewis Shickluna, of St. Catharines, who finished her from keel to truck. She is 122 feet keel, 25 foot beam, 10 feet 6 inch depth of hold.... She has on board 15,000 bu. of corn - a very large load - and only draws 9 feet of water. This vessel will realize the most sanguine expectations of her enterprising builder....[67]

(56) The Shickluna shipyard, 1863. Photographer unknown.
At centre, the schooner *C.G. Alvord*, is undergoing repairs. The schooner *Jessie*, built by Shickluna in 1855, would have looked similar to the *Alvord*.
[Courtesy of Toronto Marine Historical Society]

By 1870, the *Jessie* had been sailing the lower lakes for 15 years and had reached middle-age for a schooner. Eight years earlier, she had undergone extensive repairs and refitting, and was still a sound vessel.[68]

In October, the *Jessie's* captain, John Shevlin of Belleville, Ontario, brought the schooner through the Welland canal and sailed to Toronto where she was loaded with 13,000 bushes of wheat before setting sail for Kingston. Some twelve hours out of Toronto, the *Jessie* would have been rounding the Prince Edward peninsula when, on the evening of Sunday, October 30, a gale began to blow out of the south-east. The crew may have been able to see the low white flashes of breakers crashing over the reef that extends for some distance from Salmon Point, also known as Wicked Point. Unable to make much headway, Captain Shevlin would have had to decide whether to risk lowering all sails and set his anchors or to run for shelter. As he was on a lee shore, he would have known that if he tried to ride out the storm in the open lake his ship would be in danger: if his anchors dragged or if the anchor chains broke his ship would be cast upon the shore and wrecked. Alternatively, he could try to reverse his course and run with the wind to seek shelter behind Nicholson Island, some two or three hours away. Instead, Shevlin decided to seek refuge in nearby Little Sandy Bay (now called Athol Bay) that had a large opening and offered relatively calm waters in the lee of Salmon Point.

Most ships trying to enter the bay would have bottomed out on the sandbar guarding its mouth. The *Jessie*, however was drawing less than nine feet of water with a load that was less than her maximum capacity, and although she may have touched the sandy bottom as she entered, she reached the calmer water without incident.

This respite from the storm would only be temporary. By the early hours of the next morning, the gale had veered to the southwest turning Athol Bay from a harbour of refuge to a cauldron of destruction. The gale was now blowing directly into the bay. Under such severe conditions and unable to tack within the restrictive confines of the bay, the captain ordered all anchors to be set in an attempt to prevent his ship from being blown onto the shore and surely wrecked. The sandy bottom of the bay, however, gave no purchase for the anchors and the *Jessie* was soon breaking up in the shallows with huge waves crashing over her decks.

Newspapers in ports all around Lake Ontario carried news of the *Jessie's* fate. *The Intelligencer* of Belleville printed the following melancholy account on November 4, 1870:

THE LATE GALE: WRECK OF THE SCHOONER *JESSIE*. ALL HANDS LOST — Accounts from all parts of the country show that the loss of shipping and loss of life has been very great.

The *Jessie* is owned by Mr. W.H. Poole Esq., and sailed by John Shevlin of Belleville. We have not yet learned the names of the crew, but fear they are all lost. The following are the particulars by telegraph up to the latest moment: —

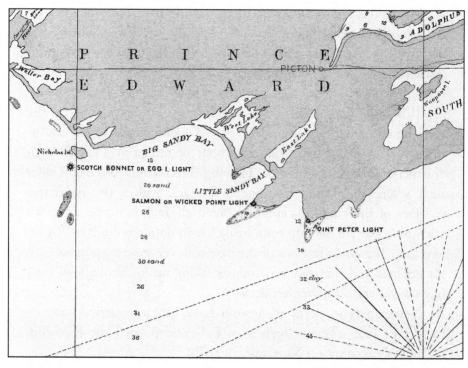

(57) Chart of Lake Ontario showing the location of Salmon Point. *Survey of the Northern and Northwestern Lakes – Lake Ontario (detail), by the U.S. Corps of Engineers, 1877.*

Athol Bay is shown as "Little Sandy Bay", where the schooner Jessie was trapped by a storm in 1870 and all hands were lost.

[Courtesy of NOAA's Office of Coast Survey Historical Map & Chart Collection http://historicalcharts.noaa.gov, LC00061_00_1877_LS]

Picton, Oct. 31. — Another fearful [storm] set in last night from the south-east shifting to south-west about 12 o'clock, and has continued to blow a gale until this p.m. The steamer *Bay of Quinte* only came as far as here on her trip to Kingston, and returned to Belleville this p.m.

A large white vessel, name unknown, dragged anchor and went ashore on the north side of Salmon Point. She is a total wreck. All hands are lost. Nothing has come ashore to give any clue to her name. Eight men could be counted in her rigging this morning. Two of the crew tried to swim ashore; but did not reach it — one of them fought desperately with the waves for 20 minutes. The six remaining men dropped off. None of the bodies have come ashore yet. Several attempts were made to launch boats and save the crew, but there was such a tremendous sea running that it was impossible to get near the wreck.

LATER ABOUT THE DISASTER AT SALMON POINT — Picton, Nov. 1 — The schooner reported ashore on the north side of Salmon Point is the *Jessie*, of Port Stanley, loaded with wheat. She is going to pieces, and the wheat is coming ashore.... One man can be seen hanging in the rigging.

The only additional particulars we have been able to obtain respecting the wreck of the *Jessie*, of Port Stanley, at Salmon Point are that the man seen hanging in the rigging yesterday was not visible this morning, having fallen off during the night. There is no doubt that all hands are lost. Among those belonging to the crew from Belleville were John Shevlin, Captain, and Harry Dupont, mate. It is feared that others of the crew were from this port, but their names have not transpired. Efforts were made yesterday and to day to recover the bodies by dragging, but without avail. No bodies have been washed ashore yet.... The vessel is completely broken up, and the shore for two miles strewn with the wreck.[69]

(57.1) Ship foundering. "Vessel in the Trough of the Sea", engraved by Linton. The 19th Century engraving depicts a scene that onlookers at Salmon Point may have witnessed when the schooner *Jessie* was breaking up in the shallows of Athol Bay (Little Sandy Bay) in 1871.
[From *Patterson's Illustrated Nautical Dictionary*, 1891.]

Many years later, Amos McDonald, who later became lightkeeper at Salmon Point, gave the following recollection of the wreck of the *Jessie*:

> She came into Little Sandy Bay, near the point, in the afternoon. She was a fore-an-after schooner, loaded deep with 13,000 bushels of grain for the foot of the lake. Those who saw her wondered how she got into the bay without striking on the "bar", but she just cleared it by chance.
>
> What she was ever doing there we never knew. There was a wharf and storehouse in the bay, and barley used to be shipped out of it, but she was fully loaded and did not go to the wharf. Instead she hauled down her jibs and came to anchor, with her lower sails standing.
>
> The wind had been light, from the south, south east and perhaps she decided to wait for a shift so as to let her clear Point Petre. No one ever came ashore from her alive. God only knows what happened.

Next day the wind did shift and came roaring in from the southwest. In all my years afterwards, tending the light, I never saw such a gale. It piled up seas like houses.

The schooner tried to get out but failed. Probably she never got away from her anchors. She drove right in on the Point, and the seas burst over her as though she had been a reef. She was quite close in, so close we could have talked to her crew from the shore, had it not been for that raving wind.

We saw four men and a woman clinging to the mainboom, the highest part above water. They waved to us again and again for help. The brave farmers and fishermen launched their sturdy boats and tried time and again to get out to the wreck. They would only get to where the storm wave met the backwash from the shore, and then the pyramids of white water would toss their boats and throw then over backwards, and they would all be spilled back on the beach.

One man on board decided to try to swim ashore. He was young, tall and powerful. He made careful preparations for his battle. He was so close that I could see the colour of his hair as he prepared for the plunge.

I can see him yet, as in a nightmare. He climbed up on the rail and noted carefully the eddies the bursting seas made around the schooner like a whirlpool. Then, watching his chance he ran along the rail and jumped clear. I watched him come up, and saw him rise from the water and shake his hair.

He was a strong swimmer, and he struck out parallel with the beach, so as to take the best chance with the undertow. Hundreds were watching him, encouraging him, and running along the beach to where they thought he could make a landing.

Twice he came in so close that he could stand up upon the bar with the seas as only as high as his waist. Twice he was swept out again by the undertow, before those on shore could grasp him.

By this time the surf was full of tossing planks and whirling timbers, torn from the wreck. Every time he made a try for the shore the backwash would hurl a piece of wreckage at him.

He was for hours fighting for his life. At last weakened by his struggle, he failed to dodge a piece of the vessel's rail, launched at him by an enormous sea. It struck him on the head, and he disappeared, sucked lakeward by the undertow.

We found his body afterwards; and he was the only one, living or dead, who came ashore from the schooner *Jessie* of Port Stanley".[70]

Those lost on the *Jessie* included two men from Belleville, four from Barriefield (near Kingston) and three other unfortunate souls:

John Shevlin, Captain, Belleville
Daniel Ryan, 1st Mate, Barriefield
Harry Dupont, 2nd Mate, Belleville
Michael Burke, seaman, Barriefield
Charles Stephens, seaman, Barriefield
Thomas Patrick, seaman, Barriefield
Martin Ryan, St. Catharines
Scottie, Quebec
Unknown man, shipped at Welland Canal

The *Jessie* was one of dozens of ships wrecked or damaged during that Autumn storm in 1870. Kingston's *Daily News* described it as "... the roughest experienced this year...",[71] and listed seven ships that were casualties of the gale:

Schooner *W.W. Grant,* ashore with 5,000 bushels of barley
Schooner *John Williams,* sunk in Kingston harbour with 4,000 bushels of wheat
Propeller *Belle P. Cross,* lost two barges at Nine Mile Point
Steamer *Rochester,* damaged paddlebox

Schooner *Emperor* and another, vessel ashore at Presqu'ile

Tug *Sara H.* grounded on rocks at Point Frederick

Schooner *Nellie Brown,* capsized with 200 barrels of salt and 525 bushels of oats.[72]

The official Canadian government "Wreck Register" for 1870 listed an additional nine vessels, as having been damaged on October 31, 1870. Among them was the *Jessie*:

Barquantine *Admiral*, stranded at Oswego

Propeller *Bruno*, sprung a leak in heavy weather on Lake Huron and later sunk

Barquantine *F. Campbell*, lost sails

Schooner *Jessie*, drove ashore at Salmon Point — 9 lives lost

Schooner *Maggie*, ran against another vessel at Cobourg

Schooner *Marie Annetta*, lost sails on Lake Ontario

Schooner *Jessie Macdonald*, driven onto the wharf at Wellington

Schooner *Octavia*, driven onto the wharf at Colborne

Barge *W.G. Keith*, stranded at Long Point Lake Erie — 1 life lost.[73]

In his annual report, Senator Peter Mitchell, Minister of Marine and Fisheries, lamented that:

> The weather during the fall of 1870 was much more boisterous and stormy than usual, and I much regret to state that the loss of life and property on the seaboard in connection with the Mercantile Marine of the Dominion has, during the last few months, been heavy, as a reference to the Return of Wrecks and Casualties in the Appendix of the Report will show. There are, no doubt, many vessels belonging to Canada which are now missing, of which no official intimation has as yet reached this Department, so that the Wreck Register accompanying the report cannot be considered as an account of all the casualties which have occurred on our coasts. It only contains a notice of the wrecks and casualties, information of which have reached this office. The storms which prevailed on the seaboard appear also to

have reached the great lakes which separate Canada from the United States, as will be seen by the list of disasters on our inland waters in the accompanying appendix, and in the case of one of the wrecks which occurred in Lake Ontario, the whole crew, composed of nine persons, were drowned immediately after the vessel stranded and went to pieces.[74]

This last comment, of course, is in reference to the wreck of the *Jessie* at Salmon Point.

Response to the tragedy was swift. Within weeks, editorials appeared in Kingston and Picton newspapers, all of them calling for the establishment of a life-boat station at Salmon Point, or a rescue tugboat service in addition to a harbour of refuge at nearby East Lake or West Lake:

> The late disastrous wreck of the schooner *Jessie*, near Picton, which resulted not only in the loss of the vessel and cargo, but also the life of the entire crew, four of whom belonged to Kingston, has given rise to serious suggestions, both from parties interested in shipping and the press of this vicinity, for the immediate establishment of a life boat service on the most exposed and dangerous points along the coast of Prince Edward. The *Picton Times*, in referring to this subject, says:- "Either life boats or powerful tugs, built especially for the purpose, might be despatched to look out for vessels helpless and drifting upon certain destruction." After speaking of the many instances of which this mode of assistance has been instrumental in saving innumerable lives on the coasts of Ireland and England during heavy gales, it goes on to state:- "The expense of fitting up such boats would, no doubt, be considerable, and probably too great for private resources, but why should it not be assumed by the Government?... For purposes of defence against warlike aggression, money is spent without stint. Why then against appalling calamities such as will again

and again occur, as surely as the sun will rise tomorrow, should not provision for rescue be made without reference to expenditure?" [Nov. 17, 1870][75]

A Dangerous Locality - Thirty precious lives, and nine vessels, valued, with their cargoes, at $175,000, have, during the past 10 years, been lost near Salmon Point, on Lake Ontario. A survey was made some years since by the Government engineers, who estimated that for $10,000 a perfect harbour of refuge could be made by dredging out the entrance at this spot to the west of the lake, yet nothing has been done, not even a life-boat provided. The nine men composing the crew of the *Jessie* could easily have been saved had the means been available. [Nov. 23, 1870][76]

The minister of Marine and Fisheries added his recommendation for the establishment of a life-boat station:

As I am of opinion that there are some dangerous places, both on the seaboard and on our great inland Lakes, where life boats should be stationed for the purpose of saving life during heavy storms or gales such as have occasioned so much loss of life on our coasts during the last few months, I would recommend that a sum of money should be placed in the estimates, to be laid before Parliament at its next session to enable this Department to supply this want, and station life boats and other life-saving apparatus at certain points where they appear to be much needed.[77]

Walter Ross, the Liberal Member of Parliament for Prince Edward County, thought the government should go further and erect a lighthouse at Salmon Point. In March, 1871, barely five months after the loss of all hands on the *Jessie*, he enquired in the House of Commons:

... whether it is the intention of the Government to place in the Estimates a sum for the erection of a lighthouse or a fog whistle at Salmon Point, in the County of Prince Edward?

Hon. Dr. Tupper said the attention of the Government had been drawn to the subject and the matter was under the consideration of the Government.[78]

Considering that Prince Edward County was a Liberal riding and that Sir John A. MacDonald's Conservative government was not inclined to spend money in such a riding, Ross must have been surprised when Parliament resolved only five weeks later, "... that a sum not exceeding One thousand dollars be granted to Her Majesty, towards a Lighthouse on Salmon Point, Lake Ontario, for the [fiscal] year ending 30th June, 1872."[79]

The contract for the construction of the new lighthouse was hastily awarded to Roderick Cameron, who had just finished building the lighthouses at Pigeon Island and Telegraph Island, and the lighting apparatus for the Salmon Point lighthouse was purchased from E. Chanteloup of Montreal.[80]

(58) Salmon Point lighthouse constructed in 1871. Photographer unknown.
This "pepperbox" design, used earlier in the Presqu'ile Range lights, would become the most common form for lighthouses all across Canada.
[Courtesy of Library and Archives Canada, PA-172455]

Details are given in the annual report of the Department of Marine and Fisheries:

> A substantial new lighthouse, with keeper's dwelling combined, was recently erected at Salmon Point, in the County of Prince Edward, on Lake Ontario, as wrecks have occasionally occurred there, some of which were attended with loss of life. It is a square wooden tower and the light is a powerful red one on the catoptric principle, and has been seen a distance of upwards of fourteen miles. There are two No. 1 circular burner lamps with 20-inch reflectors, and three mammoth burner flat-wick lamps with 18-inch reflectors, and the light was lit for the first time on the 23rd of October, 1871. Mr. Lewis Hudgins was appointed keeper, at a salary of $300 per annum, which includes remuneration for his services in connection with the lifeboat stationed there under his charge. The total cost of construction of this lighthouse, keeper's dwelling and equipment, was $1,913.71.[81]

Walter Ross may have been surprised further, and undoubtedly pleased that, before the end of October 1871, the anniversary of the loss of the *Jessie* and her crew, not only had the lighthouse been built, but a new lifeboat, the first on Canada's Great Lakes, was stationed at Salmon Point as reported by the Minister of Marine and Fisheries:

> ... expended between the 1st July and the 31st December, 1871... $315 for a new metallic life-boat which has been placed at Salmon Point, Prince Edward County, Ontario, near which place a vessel was wrecked sometime ago and all hands drowned.[82]

Lifeboats and surfboats manufactured by the Francis' Metallic Life-Boat Company of New York were in common use along many seacoasts at that time. These specialized boats were built with a corrugated, galvanized iron hull containing water-tight compartments.

The metal bottom was protected from damage by a false keel made of wood.[83] It was one of these boats that was purchased for the new Salmon Point lifesaving station.

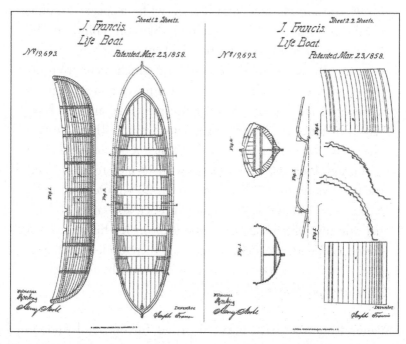

(59) Francis' Metallic Life Boat, 1858. Photo-lithograph by H. Peters.
In 1845, Joseph Francis developed a process of using a large press to form a sheet of galvanized metal into one-half of a boat hull. Two identical halves were riveted together along the keel to create a durable metallic boat that was well suited to lifesaving service. One of these metallic lifeboats was stationed at the Salmon Point lighthouse beginning in 1871.
[Courtesy of United States Patent Office, Letters Patent No. 19,693]

Other than a passing mention some forty years earlier when the Point Petre lighthouse commissioners had briefly considered Salmon Point as a location to build a lighthouse, there is no record of any other discussion, newspaper editorial, citizens' petition, staff recommendation or official request for the construction of the Salmon Point lighthouse before the wreck of the *Jessie* on Salmon Point. The speed at which the government reacted to the tragedy, not only by establishing a life boat station, but by building a lighthouse and putting it into service within a year of the loss of the *Jessie* and her crew, was quite remarkable. Such swift action by the government to have a lighthouse built had not been seen since the construction of the Nine Mile Point lighthouse almost forty years earlier.

It may never be known whether or not this was a sincere reaction by the government to the loss of lives at Salmon Point in 1870, or if it was just political manoeuvering: a convenient way of currying favour among Prince Edward County voters who, along with the rest of the Canadian electorate, would soon be going to the polls to vote in the Dominion of Canada's second general election.

It would appear that by spending some $2,200 on a minor lake light and life boat station, the government was gambling that this pre-election spending would help them at the polls and, at the same time, allow them to avoid the much greater expense that would have been incurred to perform some major marine engineering work to create a badly needed harbour of refuge along Prince Edward County's exposed southern shore.

On all counts, the government's gamble failed. Liberal Walter Ross was re-elected in Prince Edward County. The Conservative government led by Sir John A. MacDonald had only enough seats to form a minority government which was ousted by a non-confidence vote a year later. The Liberals formed the new government in 1873 and quickly called a general election which they won with a respectable majority in the House of Commons. Furthermore, the lifeboat station at Salmon Point was eventually moved further east to Poplar Point, and the harbour of refuge, when it was established a few years later, was not near the site of the demise of the *Jessie* and her crew as had been originally suggested, rather it was further up the shore at Wellers Bay, more than twenty nautical miles away.

Regardless of the government's motivations, the Salmon Point lighthouse stood as a warning beacon for forty-two years, marking the dangerous waters around "Wicked Point". Although it is no longer an active aid to navigation, the lighthouse still stands today as a memorial to the nine mariners who lost their lives there in 1870.

PART II – THE LIGHTHOUSES

CHAPTER 7

More Harbours... More Lights

Good anchorage and shelter can be obtained.
(Edward M. Hodder. 1857)

F ollowing the Confederation of Canada in 1867, much of the
focus of the government's transportation policy had slowly
begun to shift away from shipping, and more attention was being
given to the development of inter-provincial and trans-continental
railways. Nevertheless, shipping on the Great Lakes was still a key
component of the government's inland transportation policy and
more than $300,000 was being voted every year for the construction
and maintenance of canals, harbours and lighthouses in the region.[1]
With more than 3,000 vessels on the Great Lakes,[2] shipping was still
a key factor contributing to the prosperity of the developing country.
In addition, Canada's Canal Commission, established in 1870 to
report on improving inland waterways, recommended spending
some $19,000,000 on canals.[3] If these recommendations were to be
implemented, existing harbours would have to be improved and new
harbours would have to be established. It was these harbours that were
the essential ports for both outbound agricultural products, lumber,

and other natural resources, as well as for inbound manufactured goods, luxury items like sugar and tea, and necessities including salt and coal.

As the main forwarding terminal for the Great Lakes, Kingston continued to be the most important port on Lake Ontario. In addition, other ports scattered along the Bay of Quinte and the north-eastern shores of the lake, including Portsmouth, Bath, Picton, Deseronto, Northport, Belleville, Trenton, Brighton, Consecon, and Wellington, also prospered. Between 1870 and 1881, seven new lighthouses were built at a number of bays and harbours in the region. While these harbour lights were never as grand as those built as lake lights on the shores of Lake Ontario itself, they served many of the same purposes; giving ship captains a needed point of navigational reference during a storm or at night, and acting as a welcoming guide to a safe anchorage.

Telegraph Island Lighthouse (1870)

With some 800 ships sailing up and down the Bay of Quinte every year, the government had been convinced of the necessity of building the Pleasant Point lighthouse in 1866 to guide ships to the bay's entrance at the Upper Gap. The town of Belleville, three-quarters of the way up the bay, had built its own lighthouse more than a decade earlier to take advantage of the growing shipping trade. However, at the most dangerous point of this Inside Passage, there were no aids to navigation. At Telegraph Narrows, between Deseronto and Belleville, the Bay of Quinte is pinched into a narrow, winding passage less than five hundred meters across which, combined with shoal water and a rocky bottom, made navigation at that point treacherous.

On the night of November 4, 1867 a fierce gale struck eastern Lake Ontario. While ships caught out in the open waters of the lake did not fair well in the storm, those in the relatively sheltered Bay of Quinte were also affected. The schooner *Mayflower* was driven ashore eight miles below Belleville, and the schooner *Mary Ann* was wrecked on Telegraph Island:

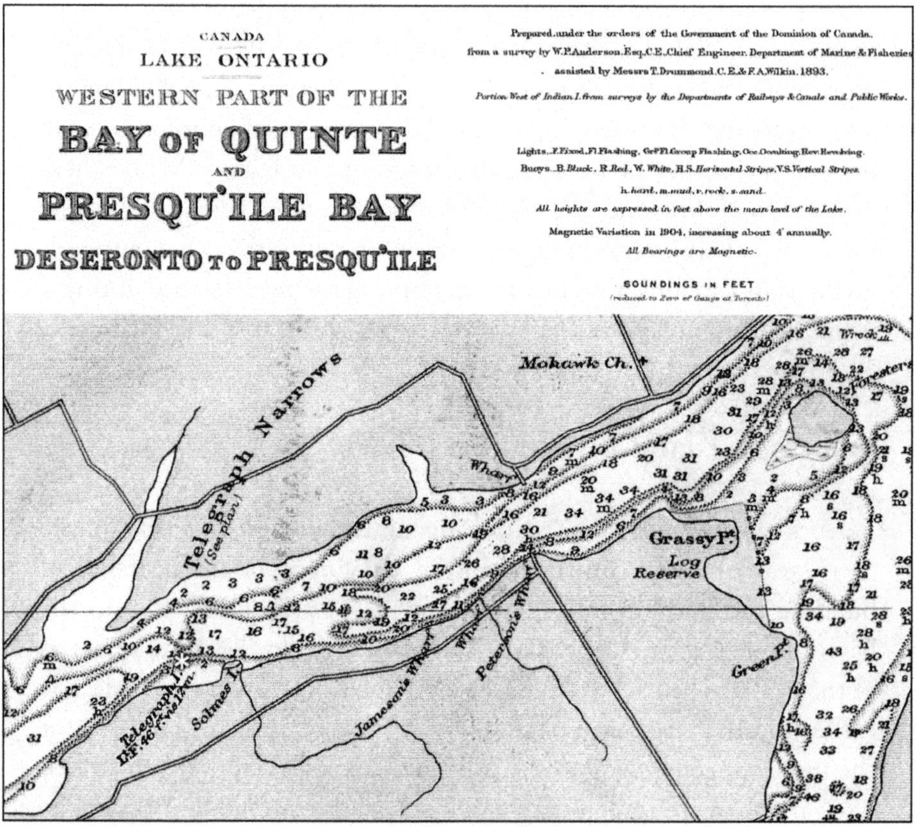

(60) Telegraph Narrows on the Bay of Quinte. From a survey by W.P. Anderson, 1893. Detail of *Lake Ontario, Western Part of the Bay of Quinte and Presqu'ile Bay*, published by the British Admiralty, 1900, updated 1904.

This chart shows Hastings County at the top and Prince Edward County at the bottom with the Bay of Quinte separating them.

[Courtesy of Library and Archives Canada, R11630-2427-2-E]

Belleville, Nov. 5th - The schooner *Mary Ann*, of Belleville, was driven ashore by the gale on Sunday night on Telegraph Island in the Bay of Quinte, about fifteen miles east of this place. She was light, and is badly on.[4]

Other ships had undoubtedly been grounded or wrecked at this location in the past, and ship captains and owners had likely expressed their concerns about the navigational hazards at these narrows. Engineers from the Public Works Department had conducted a preliminary survey of the Bay of Quinte in the summer of 1867, as part of a project to determine the feasibility of digging the oft-proposed Murray Canal to complete the Inside Passage by connecting the western end of the Bay of Quinte with Lake Ontario. Their report, which was published in December 1867, confirmed what ship captains already knew:

It appears that at certain places in the Bay of Quinté, the channel is comparatively shoal.... At Telegraph Island, 4 miles above Mill Point [Deseronto], the bottom is of rock, and there was for a short distance only 13 to 13 ½ feet water in the channel at the time the soundings were taken.

It was further ascertained, that at several points and headlands along the bay, shoals extend outwards, contracting the width of the channel, and render its line somewhat tortuous.....

To add to the difficulty of navigation, the channel at this point is narrow and makes a considerable bend, and, with a strong westerly wind, there is such a current that vessels are sometimes obliged to come to an anchor, being unable to beat up against it: at times the current is in a contrary direction.[5]

While it would be many years before the question of the Murray Canal was finally settled, the House of Commons' Select Committee on the Maritime and Fluvial Fisheries and Sea and Inland Navigation of the Dominion recommended in 1868 that a "beacon light" be located at Telegraph Island and that similar lights be placed at Steam Mill Point (Deseronto) and at Picton. Although there are no details about what exactly they meant by a "beacon light", the Committee does mention beacon lights separately from lighthouses, so it is possible that a beacon light was a type of lighted buoy or simple lighted mast.[6] However, the beacon lights were never erected.

The best solution to the navigational hazards at Telegraph Narrows would have been to dredge the channel and mark it with a number of floating buoys. Buoys by themselves would have been a relatively inexpensive solution. The expense of dredging, however, would have been considerable. For example, just five years later, the Department of Public Works reported that it cost more than $10,000 to dredge a small portion of Belleville's harbour in 1873:

> A shoal to the south-east of the [Belleville] Lighthouse proved a great hindrance to the entrance of sailing vessels, from their inability to pass over it with their centre-boards down....
>
> Dredging was commenced on the 9th of May, 1873.... The western arm of the harbor was relieved from boulders, and from several large flat stones embedded in clay; a work of much labor and difficulty.
>
> The eastern arm was cleared of the deposit found there, which consisted of gravel and bark, and several large boulders.
>
> To the south of the harbor a channel 20 feet wide [6 meters] was cut, for a length of 275 feet [84 meters], to connect with the main channel of the river....
>
> The sum of $10,000 was expended on this work but the improvement is yet far from complete.[7]

To dredge Telegraph Narrows could have cost two or three times that amount. As a less expensive alternative, the government decided to build a lighthouse on Telegraph Island to mark the dangerous passage.

In 1870, the Minister of Marine and Fisheries announced the completion of the Telegraph Island lighthouse in his annual report to Parliament:

> A very good minor light was recently established on Telegraph Island in the Bay of Quinte, Lake Ontario. The lighthouse and keeper's dwelling are combined. The light is a fixed white light, one shewing a distance of 12 miles, and is elevated 46 feet above the level of the water. It was lighted for the first time on the 12ᵗʰ November, 1870. Numerous applications and recommendations in favour of the establishment of this light had been made to this Department, and there is no doubt it will prove very useful to the local traffic of the Bay and the Belleville trade.[8]

Technically, the Telegraph Island lighthouse was not a harbour light, for there was no harbour at that location. However, as a passage light, it was equipped with lighting apparatus similar to that used in many harbour lighthouses. The Marine and Fisheries report for 1871 provides additional details about the lighthouse:

> ... cost for construction and equipment $1,991.35. The amount voted by Parliament for this work was $2,000. Mr. John Mason was appointed keeper at a salary of $200 per annum. This Light has given great satisfaction to the masters of steamers and others trading in the Bay of Quinté.[9]

This lighthouse was built by Roderick Cameron and was constructed at the same time and in the same style as the Pigeon Island lighthouse in Lake Ontario; the Telegraph Island light went into service only twelve days later. Both of these wood-framed lighthouses were built in the "schoolhouse" style, with the glass and lamps for the lantern provided by two Montreal firms, C. Garth & Co., and E. Chanteloup.[10] The schoolhouse style was characterized by a slender, square tower affixed to the gable-end of a storey-and-a-half house. The combined lighthouse and keeper's dwelling resembled a small church with a steeple, or a schoolhouse with a bell tower. This style was rare for a lighthouse in Canada, the only other example being built in Nova Scotia that same year at Pugwash harbour.[11] This type of lighthouse was much more common in the United States where brick or stone lighthouses of this style had been built on the New York side of Lake Ontario at Sodus, Stony Point and on Horse Island, as well as at various locations on the American side of lakes Erie and Huron.[12]

Telegraph Island Light, Bay of Quinte, Canada

(61) Telegraph Island lighthouse, c. 1910. Photographer unknown.
This photograph was taken from Telegraph Narrows with the Prince Edward County shore in the background. To the left of the lighthouse is a woman standing on the boardwalk that leads to the island's boathouse.
[Postcard in author's collection]

A review of his business activities shows that Roderick Cameron was an industrious contractor from Lancaster in Eastern Ontario's Glengarry County. The lighthouses on Pigeon Island and Telegraph Island were the first of more than a dozen lighthouses that Cameron would build from the lower St. Lawrence River in Quebec to the Long Point cut on Lake Erie over the next twelve years, including the

Salmon Point lighthouse in 1871 and the Calf Pasture Shoal range light (2nd Presqu'ile Range Rear) in 1879.

In November, 1870, John Mason was hired as the first lightkeeper on Telegraph Island where lived with his wife and two children.[13] Some later writers indicate that Mason died sometime in the 1880's, and his wife took over as lightkeeper. Other writers state that John Mason's daughter-in-law filled the position after his death. If a Mrs. Mason was ever the keeper of the Telegraph Island light, there is no official record of it. Government documents from 1895 record that John Mason was still the lightkeeper at Telegraph Island with an annual salary of $199.96.[14] After 1895, George Rowe held the position until 1912.[15]

Wellers Bay Range Lights (1876)

Six years after the construction of the Telegraph Island lighthouse, the following "Notice to Mariners" was published:

NOTICE TO MARINERS

No. 12 of 1876

WELLER'S BAY RANGE LIGHTS

Notice is hereby given that two Lights, erected by the Government of Canada, near the west end of the Quinté Carrying Place, in the County of Prince Edward, and Province of Ontario, to guide vessels through the entrance to Weller's Bay, will be put in operation on the 8th August next,

Lat. 44° 2' 0" N.

Long. 77° 40' 40" W.

The lights are fixed Catoptric Lights; the front one Red, elevated 29 feet above high water mark, and the back one White, elevated 43 ½ feet above high water mark.

The towers are of open frame work, painted white. The front tower, distant 150 feet from high water mark is 27 feet high from base to vane; the back tower 480 feet behind the other and in range with the channel, is 37 feet high from base to vane.

WM. SMITH,
Deputy Minister of Marine and Fisheries
Department of Marine and Fisheries,
Ottawa, 25th July, 1876 [16]

These were the Wellers Bay Range lights.

The first steamboats and schooners had begun visiting Wellers Bay as early as 1856, but it would take twenty years of public pressure to have the bay made into a useable harbour of refuge by having lighthouses built to guide ships into its sheltered waters.

Wellers Bay is one of six bays that formed over the course of millennia along Lake Ontario's north-eastern shore where tons of glacially deposited sand formed sandbars and sand spits wherever currents and waves encountered fixed rocky headlands. Eventually, extensive barrier beaches of sand dunes were created which were slowly covered with grasses, shrubs and trees.[17] Behind these dunes were located the six sheltered bays named Presqu'ile Bay, Wellers Bay, North Bay, Pleasant Bay, West Lake, and East Lake.

Prior to the 1850's, only one of these bays, Presqu'ile Bay, had an entrance large enough to admit schooners and steamboats. Even though the opening to Presqu'ile Bay appeared to be more than 1,500 meters across, it was difficult to enter the bay as the navigable channel was less than 150 meters in width and the approach was intricate. It was for this reason that the Presqu'ile Range lights had been constructed there in 1851.

By the 1830's, a small outlet in the barrier beach guarding Wellers Bay was being used by lumbermen to float timber to The Carrying Place where it was hauled across the 2.5 kilometer isthmus separating that bay from the Bay of Quinte.[18] Then, in the 1850's, for the first time since ships began sailing the waters of Lake Ontario, a combination of ice and storms opened a substantial breach in the sand spit between Lake Ontario and Wellers Bay. Soon afterward, ships were taking advantage of the sheltered waters of the bay as a refuge during storms as well as to transport passengers and cargo to and from the town of Consecon, situated at the far end of the bay.

Newspapers carried numerous reports of the advantages of Wellers Bay. The *Cobourg Sun* of Tuesday, July 1, 1856 reported:

> On Saturday the steamer *Chief Justice Robinson*, Capt. Young, entered Weller's Bay, through the breach which has been lately made in the sand ridge where but a short time since a good Carriage Road was to be found.
>
> The bay is a most beautiful one, with room enough, and sufficiently deep to float all the vessels on Lake Ontario. And by a small expenditure of money in sinking a few cribs at the entrance, a safe Harbor, easy of access, can be formed, which will eclipse Presqu' Isle.

(62) Steamboat *Chief Justice Robinson*. Sketch by W.J. Thomson, 1893.
"*The Chief*" was the first large vessel to sail into Wellers Bay after a substantial breach in the sand spit between the bay and Lake Ontario had been made by a winter storm in 1856.
[From Robertson, *Robertson's Landmarks of Toronto*, Vol. 2. 1896]

At the eastern extremity of the bay is the village of Consecon, a smart and thriving place, with the right kind of inhabitants of both sexes, for a more spirited class of businessmen it would be hard to find in any of its surroundings. They appear determined, even at a large expenditure of both time and money, to possess themselves of the advantages of a steamboat communication with other places. Government should, and undoubtedly will give them assistance, for where nature forms a harbour that admits without difficulty, such a craft as the *Chief Justice Robinson*, art need do but little. I think Capt. Young will find it his interest to make it one of his regular calling places.[19]

On July 3, the *Daily News* of Kingston also reported on the momentous occasion and included additional details:

Steamer at Consecon - On Saturday last, on her way up to Cobourg, the steamer *Chief Justice*, Capt. Young, passed through the outlet connecting Lake Ontario with Weller's Bay, and steamed up to the village of Consecon. The Steamer was drawing nine feet water at the time, and as she is a steamer that draws more water than perhaps any other on the lake, the feasibility of occasional steamboat connection with Consecon seems pretty well established. Capt. Young deserves great credit for being the first who made the attempt to enter Weller's Bay with a steamboat. He intends to call there as often as circumstances render it advisable. The *Chief* will call again on her way over to the 4th of July celebration at Oswego. There is an excellent shelter for vessels at Consecon, and if the difficulties which were always apprehended in entering the harbor prove illusive, a large business will be done with that port, and the spirited village be immeasurably benefitted. At all events the citizens of Consecon should remember Capt. Young as the pioneer navigator of Weller's Bay with steam craft. We learn that the enthusiasm which prevailed in that village on Saturday last was truly astonishing.[20]

Before the government had a chance to consider the possibility of improving access to Wellers Bay for use as a harbour of refuge, one of Lake Ontario's feared November gales struck. The late season storm of 1856 resulted in at least three schooners being wrecked or grounded in the vicinity of Wellers Bay: the *Charlotte* of Genesee, New York; the *Montgomery* of Chicago, Illinois carrying wheat from Kenosha, Wisconsin to Oswego, New York, and the *Ann Jane Brown* of Port Hope, Ontario.[21]

A Port Hope newspaper report of November 8, 1856, provided details about the wreck of the *Ann Jane Brown*:

THE LATE GALE ON LAKE ONTARIO
The *Ann Jane Brown* Ashore
The Captain and First Mate Drowned
Other Casualties

The *Ann Jane Brown*, hailing from this port went ashore at Presque Isle during the severe gale on Tuesday night last, the unfortunate event, we regret to add, was attended with loss of life. Mr. Thomas Slight, the captain and Mr. George Campbell, the first mate, met with a watery grave.

It appears, as we gather the particulars, although they are not as full as we could wish, that some time after the vessel struck, Mr. Slight and Mr. Campbell jumped overboard, with a hope of swimming to shore, they were both expert swimmers, but all their efforts to reach land were unsuccessful.

After buffetting with the waves for a short period the poor fellows sunk to rise no more.

Mr. Slight was for many years a resident of this town, we have known him from boyhood and believe him to have been a straight forward honest man - a good seaman - and a good citizen.

Mr. Campbell we did not know. We understand he leaves a wife and one child, the rest of the crew remained on board and were saved. The vessel was loaded with wheat owned by Mr. Burnham of this town, being fully insured, we learn that there are strong hopes of saving the vessel, it appears it is a sand bar that she struck and the injuries received are not very great.

Mr. W. Bletcher, one of the owners was telegraphed yesterday morning, and went down by railway to see what could be done.

The *Ann Jane Brown* left this port on Tuesday afternoon, about 4 o'clock, at that time the wind was blowing very violently - she was heavily laden. There are two more vessels ashore at Presque Isle, one is named *Charlotte* of Greece, the name on the other we could not ascertain.

————

Since writing the above, we have heard another rumor that the Captain and Mate did not jump overboard, but were washed over by the waves. We are inclined to believe this, from what we know of Captain Slight we believe he would be the last man to leave the vessel, until all hopes of saving her were at an end.[22]

Even though there were a total of three lighthouses at Presqu'ile Bay — the Presqu'ile main light on the point, and the two range lights inside the bay — all of which were within a few nautical miles west of the entrance to Wellers Bay, none of the captains had been able to manoeuvre their ships to gain access to the narrow, winding channel into Presqu'ile Bay, nor had they been able to locate the unmarked entrance to Wellers Bay where calm waters awaited. Even the newly established Scotch Bonnet Island lighthouse, activated just that September and only eight nautical miles to the south, could not guide the mariners to safety that night.

In order to make Presqu'ile Bay, a captain would have to sail his ship north-easterly, past the main lighthouse on Presqu'ile Point, almost all the way across the entire mouth of the bay, constantly glancing back over his left shoulder until he could make out the two range lights inside the bay. As soon as the range lights came in line, he would then have to tack hard to port and hope that his ship would respond quickly enough before running aground on the far shore. Once the tack was made, he could then sail directly in range with the two lights and then veer off into the deeper water once inside the bay. In a heavy westerly or south-westerly gale, this would be a difficult manoeuvre for steamboats and almost impossible for schooners and other sailing ships.

Within months of the loss of life on the *Ann Jane Brown*, no fewer than eight petitions representing "underwriters, forwarders, masters of vessels and others" from ports all around Lake Ontario including Kingston, Trenton, Picton, Consecon, Oakville, and St. Catharines were sent to the Legislative Council of the Province of Canada, "... praying that Weller's Bay may be examined by some competent person in order to ascertain its eligibility as a Harbour of Refuge".[23]

A separate petition from interests in the City of Hamilton, at the far western end of Lake Ontario, was sent directly to the Governor-General asking that the bay be developed as a harbour of refuge:

A PETITION TO SIR EDMUND HEAD, GOVERNOR GENERAL OF BRITISH NORTH AMERICA by :-

Underwriters, Forwarders, Masters of Vessels and others interested in the navigation of Lake Ontario, Humbly Shewith

That owing to the want of a safe harbour on the north shore of Lake Ontario many vessels every year are driven on shore and wrecked, on the shore of the County of Prince Edward.

That owing to the difficulty of entering the Harbour of Presque Isle many schooners have driven on shore in the attempt to enter with west or south-west winds.

That an opening 1,000 rods wide [5,000 meters] with a channel 150 feet wide [45 meters] and 14 feet deep has within the past two or three years been opened through the beach from Lake Ontario into Wellers Bay has sufficient depth of water and is large enough to contain all the vessels on Lake Ontario.

That the entrance of the said channel is easy with any wind, and if properly marked out and generally known, would be the means of saving many vessels from loss, as it affords a complete harbour, land locked on all sides which is so much desired in navigating the lakes in stormy weather.

That the schooner *Montgomery* laden with 11,000 bushels of wheat and the *Ann Jane Brown* of Port Hope of equal size, also three others of less tonnage were driven ashore within three or four miles of the said entrance last Autumn, all of which might have been saved had the master been aware of the safe harbour so near them.

Your Petitioners therefore humbly pray your excellency will be pleased to cause the said entrance and Harbour to be examined by some competent person with a view of ascertaining its eligibility as a Harbor of Refuge, and also that your excellency will take such steps to have the entrance marked out and protected as to your excellency shall seem proper....

Hamilton, February 1857

[SIGNED BY NINETEEN PETITIONERS][24]

The editor of Kingston's *Daily News* was of the opinion that the government would take immediate action:

There can be no doubt that the Government will entertain the prayer of the petitioner, and immediately take proper steps to erect a Harbor of Refuge to our fresh water seamen that will serve to encourage them in their arduous and dangerous calling. In fact, it is the duty of Government to render every aid in facilitating and advancing the interests of marine investments, which contributes so largely to the revenue of the Province and the convenience of the people; and we feel confident the object will be acceded to without any circumlocution or useless delays.[25]

Indeed, the Commissioners of Public Works immediately dispatched an Engineer to Wellers Bay to conduct an on-site technical assessment. However, the engineer quickly pronounced the scheme of creating a harbour of refuge there "most unadvisable":

> ... the Engineer of the Department examined the locality, and reports that the greater part of the beach, which originally faced the south side of the bay consisting of sand, and separating the bay from the open lake, has been swept away, during the past year, so that the opening is now from three-fourths to one mile in width [1,600 meters]; consequently, it can afford little or no shelter, in any wind with which a vessel could make the bay, and that during any blow from south to west, no vessel, once in, could come out of it. He states further the impracticability, at any moderate expense, of securing permanently the immediate entrance to the bay, and the existence of two formidable rocky shoals lying in the direct line by which it could be approached, presents, in his judgment, great objection to any expenditure on its improvement. He reports, finally, that one-fifth of the expense that would effect anything of service toward making a harbor at this place (if it could be made at all) would effect the necessary improvement of the entrance to the fine harbour of Presqu'Isle, which is well sheltered and land-locked.
>
> Any outlay upon Wellers Bay, under these circumstances, would appear to the undersigned to be most unadvisable.[26]

Instead, the Department's engineer recommended that £6,000 be spent to improve the harbour at Presqu'ile.[27]

The following spring, the *Daily News* printed another article about "Weller's Bay and Its Advantages":

Weller's Bay, situated on the north-western part of the Prince Edward District, is about six miles long [9.7 kilometers], by two to four miles in width [6.4 kilometers], and from twelve to fifteen feet in depth; the bottom is mostly clay or of a sandy character, is separated from Lake Ontario by a sand beach or bar from five to twenty-five rods in width [125 meters]; near the centre of this sand beach an outlet has formed within the last three or four years of nearly a quarter of a mile in width [400 meters], and from ten to fifteen feet in depth, and is continuing to wear deeper still. The Bay is easy to enter with almost any wind, and being land-locked is a complete shelter from any storm.

At the south-east corner of the Bay is the thriving little Town of Consecon, where wharves and storehouses are in course of erection, and will shortly be completed and ready for use. The Steamer *Chief Justice Robinson* and several schooners have shipped considerable produce and general freight from here to Oswego, Cape Vincent, and Toronto.

It is a subject of astonishment to the enterprising neighbors of Prince Edward, that the people of that district, who stand so preeminently high for talent, enterprise and wealth should so long remain inactive on a subject of such vital importance to their prosperity, viz: improving a good natural harbor on the Western coast, and a front door to the commerce of the Lakes, with all its conveniences and vast advantages.

With the exception of Weller's Bay, there is not a place where a vessel can lay to load with any degree of safety on the whole coast of the district from the north-west end to South Bay, a distance of sixty or seventy miles [112 kilometers], and in consequence the shipping of produce from the coast has been attended with so much danger and loss that the business has been but trifling to what it might be under more favorable circumstances.

Good people of Prince Edward, turn your eyes to the west, and see a spacious harbor formed for your use, and not only that, but a natural outlet cut out without cost; consider your great natural privileges, and immediately improve upon them; you want the outlet pierced, a harbor light, the mouth once disposed, and you may have your daily steamers to Toronto, Rochester, or where you like, and directly commence a business that must prove of the greatest consequence and profit to you and your district.

You have as yet received but a very small share of Public money for Public improvements in comparison with other Districts of the province; you may therefore with justice claim from the Government that assistance that your noble harbor demands.[28]

The "very small share of Public money" that came into Prince Edward County for public works projects was due in large part to the fact that the County consistently elected Liberal members to the Conservative-dominated legislature of the Province of Canada. As a result, "political plums" like funds for the development of new harbours and the construction of lighthouses were often very slow to be granted, and it appeared that the expectations of ship owners, captains and newspaper editors for a harbour of refuge at Weller's Bay would never be met.

In February, 1858, the *Daily News* reported that the channel into Wellers Bay was getting wider and deeper:

A resident near Consecon informs us that the channel between Weller's Bay and the Lake has increased to fully half a mile in width [800 meters], and is from 12 to 14 feet deep throughout. This fine bay which three years ago was only an inland pond has thus become, solely by the action of the waves, the best and most easily accessible harbor of refuge on the North Shore of Lake Ontario - no offence to Presqu' Isle. (*Colborne Transcript*).[29]

This was good news for those hoping for some government action on improving the harbour. Still, the government did nothing and two years later, in July, 1860, the *Daily News* took up the cause once again when they printed a poignant letter to the editor:

> To the editor of the Daily News.
> Sir, -
> Allow me through the medium of your columns to notice a neglect on the part of our Government in never having taken any steps to improve what nature has already commenced, namely, the formation of an outlet to Weller's Bay, through Weller's Beach, thereby making material for the best, safest, and most accessible harbor on Lake Ontario: the width of said outlet being half a mile [800 meters], and the depth sufficient to admit the largest vessels sailing on the lake - being fifteen feet at lowest water, and continually deepening from the action of the water.
>
> It is universally acknowledged by all captains trading through said outlet, together with those who have been obliged to run in for safety, that it is easily accessible in any wind, the breach running north and south, and the prevailing winds being from the West, Northwest, and Southwest.
>
> The matter has been agitated before, and the question laid before Government, but they have neglected their promise in not sending commissioners. They may probably have been influenced by a report that there is a ridge of rocks in front of said breach - a report that is utterly untrue. It is hoped that these remarks will reach the proper authorities, and urge them to do a duty to the community at large, and more especially to mariners.
>
> What is immediately wanted is a survey and buoys.
>
> Last year not less than 50,000 [bushels] grain, besides other produce, passed through said outlet for foreign ports; and from the present appearance of crops there will not be less than 100,000 bushels, which must go through that

channel this year. There were upwards of 25 vessels ran in for shelter last fall.

When we take into consideration the amount of benefit to be derived from the expenditure of a small amount, we feel confident that no further hint will be necessary to move the proper parties into action. Why not send on commissioners at once? Yours truly, Consecon, 23d July, 1860[30]

The following year, another petition to the Governor-General — this one from interested parties in Cobourg — asked for specific improvements at Wellers Bay including the building of piers at the entrance and, for the first time, the construction of a lighthouse to mark the channel:

> To His Excellency Sir Edmund Walker Head, Baronet Governor General of British North America, etc, etc, etc.
>
> The Petition of the Undersigned Underwriters, Forwarders, Masters of Vessels and other Inhabitants of the Town of Cobourg and Vicinity interested in the Navigation of Lake Ontario
>
> Humbly Sheweth
>
> That owing to the want of a Harbour of Refuge on the North Shore of Lake Ontario many Vessels are every year wrecked on the shores of the County of Prince Edward
>
> That the Channel leading into Wellers Bay near the Harbour of Presq'Isle on Lake Ontario has now been open for Seven years
>
> That at the lowest period of the water in Lake Ontario last year, the depth of water in the Channel was not less than Fourteen feet and that it is of sufficient width to allow a vessel to beat out or into the Bay
>
> That Wellers Bay is naturally one of the finest Harbours on Lake Ontario and by improving its entrance could easily be made the best Harbour of Refuge on the Lakes

That in contradistinction to the Harbour of Presq'Isle, the Channel leading into Wellers Bay is straight and during Westerly gales which are those generally compelling Vessels on Lake Ontario to seek shelter on this part of the Coast, it can be entered by Sailing directly before the Wind whereas to get into Presq'Isle Harbour in Westerly gales a Vessel must beat to Windward through a very narrow and crooked Channel, a feat which eight out of ten cannot accomplish and they are consequently obliged to come to anchor in an exposed and dangerous Roadstead

That all that is required to make Wellers Bay a Harbour of Refuge is the building of two piers, one on each side of the Channel and one Light House, and this could be done at a very moderate expense and would be the means of saving an amount of Life and property that cannot easily be computed, but owing to the want of which serious accidents occur in this neighbourhood every year

That besides the many previous disasters that have occurred in the Vicinity in consequence of the absence of the necessary piers and Light House now prayed for, your petitioners would respectfully refer to the loss of the Schooners *Montgomery, Ann Jane Brown, Welland* and others and all of these Vessels (two of them no later than last Autumn) went ashore close to this Channel in endeavouring to enter Presqu'Isle Harbour and the consequent loss of Life and property would have been avoided had this Channel been properly lighted and made known

That the Village of Consecon situated at the head of Wellers Bay has been growing in Commercial importance ever since the opening of this Channel until its Exports reached last year One hundred and twenty thousand Bushels of Grain, besides considerable quantities of Flour and Fish, and it is now the most natural Outlet for the produce of this part of the Country

That the Report of there being a Shoal off this Channel as marked in some Charts of Lake Ontario is incorrect and can be proved to be so on proper examination

That your Petitioners would pray that a competent person be sent by your Excellency to minutely examine and Report upon the correctness of the foregoing statements.

Your Petitioners feel convinced that your Excellency is fully sensible of the importance of protecting the vast Shipping Interests of the Canadian Lakes and believing this they humbly pray your Excellency to have the necessary Lights and piers erected and built for the purpose of marking out this Channel and making Wellers Bay a Harbour of Refuge....

[SIGNED BY TWENTY-FOUR PETITIONERS] [31]

In response to this latest petition, the Board of Works sent another engineer to conduct another survey of Wellers Bay. Mr. F.A. Wise made his assessment in October, 1861 and the details of his findings were published in the Board's report of that year:

WELLER'S BAY

To carry out the instructions of the Honorable the Commissioner of Public Works in reference to this Harbour, it became necessary to have an accurate survey made of the offing and the entrance to it, in order to ascertain the extent of the shoals, banks, depth of water in, and direction of the channel leading into it, so that by comparing their present state with that shewn by former surveys, a safe opinion might be arrived at, as to whether there was much tendency in the channel and bars to shifting or altering their direction and depth.

The results of the survey are very satisfactory, as they shew that the state of the entrance, in all essential particulars, is in no way less favorable than at the period of the former survey [of 1857]. In fact the only perceptible difference is that there is rather a better depth of water in the channel now than formerly.

The sheet of water named Weller's Bay, is divided by a spit of sand and island into an inner and outer bay. The former averaging about 1 ½ miles wide [2.4 kilometers] by about 2 ½ miles [4 kilometers] deep, at the bottom of which is situated the village of Consecon; the outer bay, from which is the entrance leading to lake Ontario, is about two miles deep [3.2 kilometers long] and one mile wide [1.6 kilometers]. For two thirds of the area, the water is from 15 to 20 feet in depth, with a good clay bottom.

The breadth of Weller's Bay from land to land at the entrance is about 4,800 feet [1,450 meters], in the centre of which is the channel to the bay, 450 feet [135 meters] wide in the narrowest part, and about 1,300 feet [400 meters] in length. Through this channel there is a depth of water sufficient for any vessel navigating the lake.

A sand bank extends from this channel, on each side, across the mouth of the bay. — On this bank, immediately at the sides of the channel, the water is from 7 feet to 8 feet 6 inches in depth, which diminishes gradually as it approaches the shore, near which it is about two feet deep.

At each end of the entrance channel, both in the lake and in the harbour, the water deepens quickly to 20 and 24 feet.

In strong west and south-west winds, there is a heavy surf on this bank.

To establish the entrance channel beyond all question, it would be necessary to erect piers on each side, of about 1500 feet [450 meters] in length, with a light-house on one of the ends next the lake; and from the piers to the shore, on each side, a breakwater would be required — all of which would involve a very heavy expenditure, not warranted by the trade; but the bay presents so many inducements to vessels to shelter in, from the direct and deep channel leading into it, and the fine width of water and good anchorage inside, it seems to me highly desirable the channel should be buoyed out clearly, for which four buoys would be ample. Then with two range lights, erected upon cribs to be sunk for that purpose — or probably one light on a crib, the other on the main land — the entrance would be safely made at all times.

I believe the department has at its command some screw buoy moorings, which would answer very well in this position. In this case the principal outlay would be on the cribs and light-houses, neither of which need be of an expensive character. The approximate estimate for these is £750.[32]

Even though the engineer recommended against the petitioners' request for a lighthouse at the proposed harbour entrance, he did recommend the construction of a pair of lighthouses as range lights to guide ships through the channel. The following year's report of the Commissioner of Public Works refers to Wise's survey and adds:

> Upon comparing this survey with the Admiralty Chart, the Chief Engineer noticed a shoal on the latter, off the entrance to the Bay and lying outside the field of Mr. Wise's survey, on which was marked only three feet of water, and suggested that it should be ascertained by further examination whether there was any shoal there, or not.
>
> The shoal represented on the Admiralty Chart lies directly in the track of vessels entering the Bay, and would, without any doubt, if really there, prove a serious obstacle to the navigation.
>
> With these facts in view, no chart could be accepted as correct until further soundings were undertaken to determine this question.

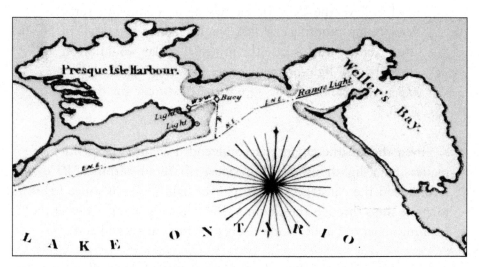

(63) Proposed harbour of refuge, Wellers Bay. Detail from "Sketch of the Coast from Colborne to Nicholas Point" (Huycks Point), shewing the accessible position of Wellers Bay, in contrast with the dangerous and intricate entrance to Presque Isle Harbour (Presqu'ile Bay), during Gales from the N.NW, W.SW and S. Also the necessity of Lighting the Channel to Wellers Bay that it may become a Harbour of Refuge." Inset from the map, "Chart Shewing the Entrance to Presque'Isle Harbour and the Channel into Wellers Bay". Prepared by F.A. Wise, Department of Public Works, 1861.

F.A. Wise was one of several engineers who surveyed Wellers Bay and vicinity to determine whether or not the bay could be developed for use as a harbour of refuge. [Courtesy of Library and Archives Canada, RG11M-923004]

An Engineer from this office [Mr. Rowan] was, accordingly, sent there for this purpose, but, owing to the lateness of the season and the roughness of the weather, he found it impossible to make a proper survey. Still, after having sailed over the site of this shoal several times in every direction, in a vessel whose "centre board" was down, drawing 14 feet water, without touching bottom, he reports that "there is at least 12 feet of water on it, even at the present level of the Lake, which is some three feet lower than it has been for some time."

If may further be added that the published survey and sailing directions of Mr. J.N. Dumble for making this harbour, which is of recent date, show no trace of the shoal represented on the Admiralty Chart, and there is no record of any of the vessels trading at this port or seeking refuge in the adjacent harbor of Presqu'isle having touched upon it.[33]

In December 1862, the *Hastings Chronicle* published its own interpretation of the engineer's report:

We are happy to learn that Mr. Rowan, C.E., from the office of the Board of Works, Quebec, has returned, having made the inspection of the harbor of Weller's Bay, and is now enabled to report with certainty that there is no such obstruction to the entrance of Weller's Bay as is laid down on Bayfield's chart [the Admiralty Chart in question]. Mr. Rowan was fortunate in having good weather and in meeting with persons anxious to assist him in making a thorough search for this bed of rocks. The owners of vessels about there never knew anything of such rocks, and the inhabitants generally had never heard of them, until enlightened as to their whereabouts by the Board of Works. Now, at all events, they are proved to be entirely a myth — as no such obstruction is or ever was there. Bayfield's Chart, which is that made by order of the British Government for the Admiralty, is generally very accurate. In this instance, however, it is in error. (*Hastings Chronicle*)[34]

By the end of 1862, then, the way seemed to be clear for the improvement of the entrance to Wellers Bay and for the construction of one or more lighthouses. However, before Parliament could act on this last report, the minority Conservative government was brought down by a vote of non-confidence and a General Election the next year would further distract the attention of the legislators. The election was held in August, 1863 and the Conservatives won a majority. The only mention of Wellers Bay during the next Parliament was in conjunction with renewed discussions about the Murray Canal. After the many petitions that had been signed, the surveys that had been conducted, the reports that had been presented, the recommendations that had been made, and the editorials that had been written, suddenly the official record goes silent and, for more than a decade, there was no more discussion in Parliament on the subject of lighthouses or a harbour of refuge at Wellers Bay.

(64) "At anchor off Consecon". Pen and ink sketch by Lt. Henry E. Baines R.A., August 1863, from his manuscript notebook, "A Month's Leave or The Cruise of the *Breeze*". Consecon became a port of call for many ships after 1856 when a channel was opened up between Wellers Bay and Lake Ontario. The sloop *Breeze* (shown at centre) was Commodore Hodder's yacht in which he toured Lake Ontario in the summer of 1863 accompanied by Lieutenant Baines and some of his fellow officers of the Royal Artillery. To the left is the spire of the Methodist church (now the United Church), and to the right is the steeple of the Church of England (now the Consecon library). [Courtesy of Library and Archives Canada]

Unofficially, however, there continued to be communications between concerned business interests in Prince Edward County and government officials. In November, 1871, prominent Consecon resident Joseph Pierson, wrote to Prime Minister Sir John A. Macdonald concerning Wellers Bay. Macdonald replied a few days later:

Private — Ottawa, Dec. 4, 1871
My dear Sir

I have your letter of the 30th ultimo.

The subject of appointing a Custom House officer for Consecon, & put it on the same footing as Wellington, is now under consideration. I think that Consecon is of sufficient importance to have this done for its increasing trade, & I shall endeavour to have the matter settled before the opening of navigation

I wish you would furnish me with the statistics that you speak of respecting the Harbour at Wellers Bay & of the number of vessels that have taken refuge in it for the last few years, and the probable cost of improving the entrance into the Harbour.

On your furnishing me with these stats I will bring the matter before the Department of Public Works.

With respect to a Light at the mouth of the Harbour, will you please inform me whether there will be any difficulty in procuring, at a cheap rate, a fitting site.

I shall be glad to hear from you on these points a an early day.

Yours faithfully
JOHN A. MACDONALD.[35]

In spite of such correspondence, there was no action taken on making Wellers Bay a harbour of refuge. It is difficult to say whether or not the source of this inaction was due to the fact that monies were allocated to other, more pressing projects instead, or more because Prince Edward County fell out of political favour with the government of the day. Certainly, other lighthouses were built in and around Prince Edward County during this decade of inaction: there was the Pleasant Point lighthouse built at the Upper Gap in 1866, the Telegraph Island lighthouse built in 1870, and the Salmon Point lighthouse built in 1871. Perhaps it is only coincidental that for the fifteen years during which former Picton mayor Walter Ross was the elected Liberal representative for Prince Edward County, the subject of a lighthouse on Wellers Bay as part of a harbour of refuge never came up. It was only after the Liberals were brought to power and Walter Ross was again re-elected in 1874 that a lighthouse on Wellers Bay once again came under consideration in the House of Commons. It is also possible that by 1875, the long-planned Murray Canal was being talked about again, and Wellers Bay was being considered seriously as the canal's western terminus.

The Parliamentary estimates for 1875 listed an amount of $2,500 for a, "New light at entrance of Weller's Bay, Prince Edward County."[36] This seemed to indicate that one lighthouse would be built on the sand spit as a solitary harbour light as requested by the petition of 1861, instead of building a pair of range lights on or near the mainland as recommended by the Board of Works engineer in 1862. However, in March, 1876, the following tender notice for two lighthouses was published:

> Light Houses - Tenders are asked for by the Department of Marine and Fisheries, at Ottawa, for the construction of two light houses at Weller's Bay, near Consecon. When erected they will be of great advantage to sailors on that dangerous coast.[37]

It appears that the tender notices were not widely distributed and many potential bidders were not aware of the proposed work. Three weeks after the notices were first published, the editor of the *British Whig*, complained about this situation:

> PENNY WISDOM — It is rumored that the Government intends to have two light houses off the Prince

Edward shore during the coming Spring. The navigators of Kingston will be glad to hear it, for it is a dangerous and much frequented shore, but regretfully rumor is not a very current one, and there is no official confirmation of it here. Some contractors last week called at the *Whig* to enquire whether tenders had been invited for such a work, but though our sources of information are pretty general, we were at a loss to answer. It is stated, however, by the Belleville *Ontario* that blank proposals for light-house work were with astounding profligacy left at the post offices at Picton and Trenton, and thereupon our contemporary remarks:—

"The Government ought to know that neither at Trenton nor at Picton are there to be found contractors competent to handle jobs of the character of Light Houses, to compete with the contractors of this place [Belleville] (or Kingston). There could have been no improper design in the matter, but there certainly was lacking the application of common sense...."

Not one contractor in Kingston, we are bound to say, knew of the work on the market, and the officers of the Government by restricting the competition have squandered the price of a two hundred advertisement....[38]

The tender for the construction of the Wellers Bay Range lights was awarded to carpenters Messrs. Love and Harper[39] who, assuming the editor of the *British Whig* was right, must have been from either Trenton or Picton. Love and Harper were paid a total of $1,260.00 for the work. Once completed, each of the lighthouses was equipped with a single lamp supplied by the Montreal firm of E. Chanteloup, at a cost of $92.00 apiece.[40]

The official "Notice to Mariners" announced that the Wellers Bay Range lights were to be lit on August 8, 1876. In his report that year on the inspection of the lighthouses above Montreal, Darius Smith, the superintendant of lights, wrote:

[July 13, 1876]

WELLER'S BAY

We brought the lantern and lighting apparatus for the two lights at this place for which they were both ready. The one nearest the water is 22 feet high, covered in, and painted white all the way down. The other farther back is 35 feet high, and made with open trellis work, and is painted red. I found the material and workmanship good.[41]

While these towers would have been square in plan with a tapering, pyramidal form similar to the Presqu'ile range lights, there were a number of discrepancies between the "Notice to Mariners" and the superintendent's report, among which were the exact height of the towers, whether or not one of them was an open framework or "covered in", and what colours they were painted.

(65) Wellers Bay range lights, 1878. Artist unknown.
The open framework rear range tower is on the left and the front range tower is on the right, next to the lightkeeper's dwelling where the unofficial assistant-keeper, Edward Silverson, lived until 1889. In the background, a steamboat is towing a schooner-barge in Wellers Bay, beyond which the line of trees marks the sand spit separating the bay from Lake Ontario.
[Detail of sketch from Belden, *Illustrated Historical Atlas of the Counties of Hastings and Prince Edward*, 1878.]

Where both the "Notice to Mariners" and the Superintendant's report agreed was on the fact that the rear range light was an open framework structure. This is corroborated by an illustration appearing in Belden's Atlas of 1878 (figure 65). This was a significant new approach to lighthouse construction since all lighthouses up to this time had been fully enclosed structures. This open-frame construction, or "trellis" work, indicated the beginning of a change in lighthouse design. A tower constructed without siding would require less material and presumably would be somewhat less expensive to build than a fully enclosed tower, yet it would be just as functional. This simplification of lighthouse design would be used in other light towers constructed in eastern Lake Ontario, and it would become very common later in the 20th Century when open framework steel skeleton towers were used to replace many traditional lighthouses.

In August 1876, the lamps of the two range lights were lit by the newly appointed lightkeeper, Reuben Young, on whose land the lighthouses were situated. His appointment to the position was confirmed by an Order-in-Council on August 16, 1876:

> On the recommendation of the Hon. the Minister of Marine and Fisheries, the Committee advise that Mr. Reuben Young of Weller's Bay, in the County of Prince Edward, in the Province of Ontario, aged __ years, be appointed Keeper of the two Lighthouses (range) recently erected at Weller's Bay aforesaid, at a salary of $150. per annum, such appointment to take effect from the date Mr. Young assumed charge of the Lights.[42]

Young was a prosperous farmer who owned 370 acres of land at the west end of the Portage Road in Prince Edward County. In addition to farming apples and other cash crops, he owned the local tannery, was a justice of the peace and had been the commanding officer of the 5th Battalion Prince Edward Militia. At 71 years of age, it is quite likely that Young did very little of the day-to-day work of keeping the lights himself. For thirteen years, his head tanner, Edward Silverson, performed the duties of the lightkeeper. In return for this extra service, Young allowed Silverson to live, rent-free, in the house that Young had built between the two lighthouses.[43]

Although it was not officially condoned, it was common practice for lightkeepers to hire an assistant. The job of keeping the light required many hours of work every day during the eight-month shipping season. The lightkeeper's primary duty was tending to the lamps all night long and during foul weather to ensure that they were always burning at their brightest. During the day, the keeper's other duties included refilling the lamps with fuel, trimming the wicks, polishing the lamps' reflectors, cleaning the lantern glass, and performing most of the other minor maintenance tasks required at the light station. The assistant, then, was usually indispensible if the lightkeeper wished to get any sleep between Spring thaw and Autumn freeze-up.

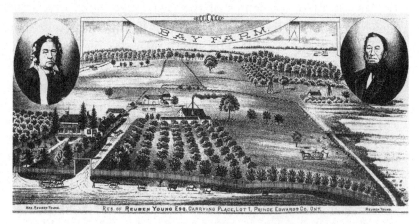

(66) Portraits of Reuben Young and his wife, Nancy Briant Young, with a view of their farm on Wellers Bay, 1878. Artist unknown
Below Mrs. Young's portrait can be seen the Young's residence facing The Carrying Place Road. The building with the smokestack is the Young's tannery where Edward Silverson worked as the head tanner. To the right can be seen the Wellers Bay range lights.
[From Belden, *Illustrated Historical Atlas of the Counties of Hastings and Prince Edward*, 1878.]

Often, the lightkeeper's assistant was a boy who lived in the neighbourhood. In some cases, the assistant was the keeper's spouse or son. Since there was no official provision for an assistant, he was paid out of the lightkeeper's own wages. When the keeper retired, the assistant often was given the keeper's job. However, in Edward Silverson's case, when Reuben Young retired in 1889 at the age of 84, Silverson was overlooked for the job and William Orser was appointed instead.[44] At the same time, the government purchased the house that Reuben Young had built so that Orser and his family could live near the range lights. In the process, however, Silverson not only lost the keeper's job, he lost his home.[45]

Finally, almost two decades after the barrier beach at Wellers Bay had been opened to Lake Ontario, there was some improvement to the harbour to "... the great advantage of sailors on that dangerous coast."[46] While the government did improve access to the bay by building the range lights, they stopped short of the more expensive improvements of building piers and breakwalls at the harbour entrance. Even without these additional improvements, the Wellers Bay Range lights made it easier and safer for ships to enter this badly needed harbour of refuge. Although there were never any plans to turn Wellers Bay into a commercial harbour, it had limited commercial use for some two decades. From Consecon, the only town on the bay, agricultural products such as salt fish, wheat, barley and apples were shipped as mentioned in a brief column in the *Trenton Courier*:

> CONSECON — Our little harbour has a gay appearance today. Four schooners laying too, some loading and some waiting to load the large quantity of grain in store here....
>
> The fishermen are catching large quantities of fish, some of which are salted down but the greater quantity is sent to Uncle Sam.
>
> Apple packers are busy in the country shipping apples. The crop falls short of last year, but is made up to a certain extent in price.[47]

By 1886, a second port was established on Wellers Bay, at Pine Point, where wharves were constructed and to where a spur line of the Central Ontario Railway was laid to facilitate the loading of iron ore from the Marmora iron mines onto ships bound for American ports.[48]

By 1896, iron ore shipments had stopped and agricultural shipments had dropped to a trickle. More importantly, the use of Wellers Bay as a harbour of refuge was continually being compromised by the shifting sands of the barrier beach at its entrance. Without the protection of piers and breakwaters, the location of the channel into the bay tended to shift over time. As a result, the rear range light had already been relocated in 1889 to mark the new channel:

NOTICE TO MARINERS

No. 18 of 1889

I. WELLER'S BAY BACK RANGE LIGHT.

The back range light tower at Weller's Bay has been moved 37 feet westwardly so as to bring the two lights in line with the extremity of the spit off Bald Head. In this position they show the best water over Weller's Bar, which lies about 3,300 feet [1,000 meters] outside of Bald Head Spit. Vessels entering should bring the lights in range bearing N.E. by E., and should find 10 feet of water on the bar on this line. Inside the bar they will have to open the lights to the westward to clear the spit, which is marked by a whitewashed tripod 16 feet high. Good water will be found on the line of range inside the spit until in line with Pine Point.

Department of Marine

Ottawa, 1st April, 1889.[49]

This natural process of shifting sands continued to alter the course of the channel and, three years later, yet another change in the location of the range lights was needed:

NOTICE TO MARINERS

No. 40 of 1892

CHANGE IN WELLER'S BAY LIGHTS.

The range lights at Weller's Bay, on the north shore of lake Ontario, in the County of Prince Edward, Ontario, have been moved, and the colours of the lights changed.

The front light tower now stands on the shore of the bay, at the south-west end of the Carrying Place road, 843 feet [257 meters] N. ½ W. from its previous position....

The light has been changed from fixed red to fixed white; it is elevated 26 feet above the level of the lake, and should be visible 10 miles in the line of range and to the eastward until cut off by Bald Head and to the westward until cut off by Presqu'Ile Point.

The back light tower has also been moved to a new site distant 508 feet [155 meters] N.E. ¾ E. (N. 46° E. true), from the front one. The light has been changed from fixed white to fixed red, and is elevated 37 feet above the lake level; it should be visible 7 miles in, and over a small arc on each side of, the line of range. Vessels approaching from the westward will not open this light until nearly reaching the alignment, as it is screened by trees.

The two light buildings are unchanged in character....[50]

As larger ships with deeper draughts carrying larger cargoes were then sailing eastern Lake Ontario waters, the ten-foot channel depth into Weller's Bay was not sufficient for many commercial vessels. Eventually, the bay was no longer used as either a commercial port or as a harbour of refuge, and in the early 20th Century, the Wellers Bay Range lights would be among the first lighthouses in the region to be de-activated.

Calf Pasture Shoal Range Light (1879)

Despite the establishment of range lights in Presqu'ile Bay in 1851, access to the harbour continued to be difficult because of the extensive Middle Ground shoal blocking most of the bay's entrance. This left only a narrow channel between the shoal and the far shore which could be navigated only with the help of the two range lights. As early as 1853, barely two years after the range lights had been erected, there had been complaints about where they were situated, and four additional lights were suggested by *The Daily British Whig:*

> Lake Ontario, containing water enough to float all the navies of the world, suppose they were combined into one, has even now hardly a harbour, if Kingston is not taken into account, capable of receiving a vessel drawing more than thirteen feet of water. But even these bad harbours are so indifferently lighted, that when most wanted they can with difficulty be reached. Take for example the harbour of Presqu'isle, which is designed for a harbour of refuge. With an insufficient depth of water for vessels of any size, and a mud bank or shoal [the Middle Ground shoal] obstructing direct entrance. Presqu'isle has only one attracting, we cannot say guiding, light upon the point, and two small lights to be used after the harbour is virtually entered, while there ought to be two leading lights, two lights that could be brought in line so as to show one on the main[land] opposite the point now lighted, these lights leading vessels clear of the middle bank or shoal, and affording them in the proper entrance channel no less than 20 feet of water, and the better to render the present interior lights more available than they are, two leading lights more to the northward of the proposed guiding lights opposite the point ought to be placed, for we defy any person not intimately acquainted with the harbour to enter safely.[51]

To improve access, the Board of Works added four buoys in 1857 to mark the winding channel.[52] The Presqu'ile harbour master, William Quick, was responsible for setting, retrieving and maintaining these buoys. Every Spring, immediately after the break-up of the ice in the bay, Quick would row out into Presqu'ile Bay and place the buoys to mark the channel, and every Autumn he would retrieve them before the winter ice formed on the bay once again. The buoys made it easier for ships to follow the narrow channel, however it did nothing to allow direct access into Presqu'ile Bay.

As difficult it was to enter and exit Presqu'ile Bay, its usefulness as a harbour of refuge was being further threatened by the deforestation of the Presqu'ile peninsula by squatters who had settled there over the years. Without the wind-break that the old-growth forest on the peninsula afforded, the waters of Presqu'ile Bay would provide little shelter for ships waiting out a storm.

In an effort to preserve Presqu'ile Bay as a harbour of refuge, Quick recommended in 1868 that the Government of Canada place a ban on the cutting of timber on the Presqu'ile peninsula:

> ... The squatters on Presqu'Isle point seem determined to destroy the remaining shelter which the bush upon the Isthmus and Peninsula still afford to the numerous vessels frequenting this Harbour either for refuge or for the purposes of trade....
>
> Presqu'Isle will soon become a low dangerous bank, affording no shelter from the wind, and this famous Harbour with its Light House its Beacon and its Buoys, will be useless as a refuge to the vessels on the Lake, and of service only to the miserable trade of the Port....
>
> I trust some determined means will at once be taken to check the growing evil complained of, for a very short period will elapse under the sweep of the axe and the ravages of Fire before damage may be done which half a century of [vigilant] and persevering protection and fostering care will hardly replace.[53]

Since the peninsula and the bay were under the jurisdiction of the Province of Ontario, the federal government had no power to act on Quick's recommendation. They did, however, take steps to have Presqu'ile Bay and the peninsula transferred from the province to the federal government. As a condition of the transfer, the Province of Ontario stipulated that the squatters be given ownership of the lots that they were occupying and that the federal Public Works Department spend $10,000 on the improvement of the harbour.[54]

The transfer was completed and Public Works took the opportunity to have a new channel cut through the Middle Ground shoal. Between 1872 and 1875, A.E Munson was contracted to dredge a channel through the shoal to a depth of 11 feet and a width of up to 67 meters. While this new channel provided a more direct entry into the Presqu'ile Bay after 1875, it remained unmarked until 1879 when a new rear range light was constructed on Calf Pasture Shoal to work in tandem with the original front range light on Salt Point.[55]

The new lighthouse was built in what was by then becoming the *de facto* standard style of a wood-framed pyramidal tower:

> An appropriation of $1,800 was made by Parliament at its last Session for the erection of a pier and lighthouse tower at Presqu'Isle Harbour, Northumberland County, and a contract was entered into with Mr. Roderick Cameron of Lancaster, to perform the work required for the sum of $1,695.... The lighthouse and pier have lately been completed, but owing to the lateness of the season, the new lights will not be shown till the opening of navigation. It is proposed to show a fixed red catoptric light, ranging with the old light on Salt Point, to indicate the entrance to Presqu'Isle Bay, through the new channel. The tower is square, built of wood, and is 22 feet high from the base of the pier to that of the lantern.[56]

This was the fourth lighthouse in the eastern Lake Ontario region that contractor, Roderick Cameron, had built. The others were at Salmon Point, Telegraph Island and Pigeon Island. This new lighthouse was built on top of a pier that was constructed on the shoal about 900 meters west of the Salt Point lighthouse. The Salt Point lighthouse would now act as the front range light for both the new channel in range with the new Calf Pasture Shoal light, and for the old channel in range with the original Presqu'ile rear range light.

G.B Simpson was retained as the keeper for all three range lights. In addition to his lightkeeping duties, Simpson was tasked with the maintenance of the channel buoys, the job previously done by Harbour Master Quick.[57]

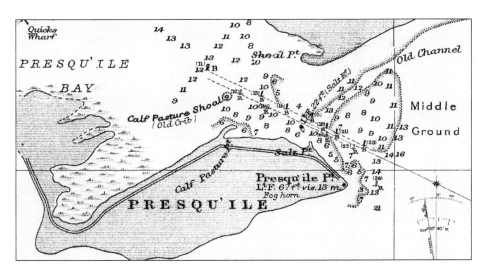

(67) Location of Calf Pasture Shoal in Presqu'ile Bay. Detail from *Chart of Western Part of the Bay of Quinte and Presqu'ile Bay*, surveyed by W.P. Anderson, 1893. Published by the British Admiralty, 1900, updated 1904.

This chart shows both the "Old Channel" along which the original range lights guided ships, and the new channel through the Middle Ground shoal. The Calf Pasture Shoal light was built to guide ships through this new channel in conjunction with the original Salt Point lighthouse.

[Courtesy of Library and Archives Canada, R11630-2427-2-E]

Like Wellers Bay, Presqu'ile Bay was largely a harbour of refuge but it also served as a minor commercial port for the town of Brighton with 93 ships entering the bay in 1878, explicitly for purpose of loading or unloading cargo.[58] Until the opening of the Murray Canal in 1890, the Presqu'ile Bay Range lights remained as essential aids to navigation to enable ships to enter the bay safely.

———— ∿◦◖◗◦◖◗◦∿ ————

With the construction of the Calf Pasture Shoal range light, a total of nine lake lights, seven harbour lights and one passage light now guided mariners around the treacherous Prince Edward peninsula between Presqu'ile Bay and Kingston harbour or into the Bay of Quinte. In 1878, Darius Smith, the Marine and Fisheries Department's Superintendant of Lights for the district from Montreal to Lake Superior, wrote a report of his annual lighthouse inspection tour which included the fifteen towers in the eastern Lake Ontario area that had been built by his department (the Belleville harbour lights were not under his jurisdiction, and the Kingston harbour lighthouse had already been discontinued). It was Smith's job to accompany the contracted lighthouse supply ship, *Celtic*, as she delivered supplies to each of the light stations between Lachine and Thunder Bay. The *Celtic* made the journey in twenty-nine days, stopping at 108 lighthouses. Remarkably, Smith visited the fifteen federally-owned lighthouses between Kingston and Presqu'ile in a single 48-hour period. His report to the Minister of Marine and Fisheries provides details about each of the lighthouses and lightkeepers he visited and serves as a apt summary of the state of the network of lighthouses in eastern Lake Ontario as of 1878:

Westbrook, 14th October, 1878.

Sir — In accordance with your instructions, I beg to forward herewith a detailed Report of my annual tour of supply and inspection to the lighthouses between Montreal and Fort William [Thunder Bay], on Lake Superior....

DARIUS SMITH

Superintendant of Lighthouses.

June 29th, 1878. — Received on board the steamship *Celtic*, at Montreal, 192 barrels of coal oil and other necessary stores for the supply of the lighthouses above Montreal, and on Saturday, 29th June, at 10 p.m. cast off from the wharf and proceeded up the Lachine Canal....

The steamer *Celtic* arrived at Kingston at 8 p.m. on the 3rd July, and remained until the 4th. Received on board 30 barrels of oil, and left on the morning of the 4th for

SNAKE ISLAND,

where we arrived at 2 p.m., and found everything in very good order. This is a white square stone building, with dwelling-house attached. It shows a fixed red catoptric light, 35 feet above the level of the lake. The lantern is 6 feet in diameter, and constructed of iron, and contains six No. 1 base-burner lamps, with three 16-inch and three 19-inch reflectors. Size of glass, 16½ x 14 inches.

The floor of the lantern requires to be re-leaded and the deck outside requires re-covering, as it leaks; weather vane requires repairs, as it will not work. Keeper instructed to send it to Kingston for repairs at once.

Nathaniel Orr is keeper, and has a family of ten, which consist of wife and nine children. [In 1888, Orr and his wife caught cold while rowing from the mainland to the Snake Island Shoal lighthouse. They contracted pneumonia and died in May, 1888. See *The British Whig,* Kingston, May 28, 1888, p. 2. Orr's son, William Breden Orr succeeded him as lightkeeper.]

NINE MILE POINT.

Arrived here at 3:30 p.m., July 4th, and inspected the Station and supplied oil and other stores. It is a white circular tower, 40 feet from base to vane in height, having an iron lantern 8 feet in diameter; it has seven mammoth flat-wick lamps, with 18-inch reflectors, and should be seen a distance of 15 miles. It shows a white fixed catoptric light.

Size of glass at the lantern is 12 x 14½ inches. This light is much obstructed by the smallness of the glass.

The top of the lantern requires painting. There is a bell tower [fog bell] attached to this Station, which is in very good order; the tower requires painting; weight of bell, 960 lbs.

The breakwater for the protection of the lighthouse is in a very poor condition and fast going to decay; 200 cords of stone are required for the breakwater. Mr. Dunlop, the keeper, was instructed to procure material to fence the property of the Government. Mr. Dunlop will do the work.

This Station is exceedingly well kept. The family number six.

PIGEON ISLAND

July 4th, 5:30 p.m., visited and inspected the lighthouse and premises, and supplied oil and other stores required.

This lighthouse is a white wooden building, with dwelling-house attached, and is 41 feet from base to vane in height. The lantern is constructed of iron, 4 feet in diameter, and contains two mammoth flat-wick lamps, with 20-inch reflectors. This light revolves in one minute and ten seconds, and is in good order.

The revolving apparatus works well and is kept clean.

I have examined the boat of this Station, and I consider she can be repaired at a small cost, the sills are old and worn out; a boat is absolutely necessary at this place on account of its isolation.

Mary Davis is the keeper, she has a family of ten young children. [Mary Davis was wife of the second lightkeeper, William Davis, who was drowned in November, 1873. See *The British Whig*, Kingston, Nov. 7, 1873, p. 3]

POINT PLEASANT

Arrived of this Station on 4th July, at 8:40 p.m., found everything in very good order and cleanly kept. This is an octagonal tower, painted white, and is 32 feet from base to vane. The lantern is of iron, 5 feet 6 inches in diameter, contains nine No. 1 base-burner lamps, with 16-inch reflectors. This light should be seen 15 miles.

The lighthouse is being underpinned with stone piers, it also requires painting. The repairs were in progress at the time of our visit, and were progressing very favourably.

John Prinyer is keeper, who has a family of three.

FALSE DUCKS.

We arrived at the False Ducks at 11:40 p.m., 4th July. This is a white stone circular tower, 62 feet high from base to vane, showing white fixed catoptric light, from an iron lantern 8 feet in diameter, having fifteen No. 1 base-burner lamps, with 15-inch reflectors, and can be seen 20 miles. Size of glass 12 x 14 smallness of which greatly obstructs the light.

The railing outside the lantern requires repairs, and an iron ladder is wanted to enable the keeper to get on the top of lantern; the stairs of the lighthouse require some repairs. Lighthouse wants whitewashing and painting.

Frederick Swetman is keeper, who keeps the Station in a very good order, he has a family of six.

LONG POINT, POINT PETER.

The steamer arrived here on the 5th July. This is a circular stone tower, 60 feet height from base to vane, and shows a revolving light every 40 seconds, and is of the catoptric order. The lantern is of iron 8 feet in diameter and contains ten No. 1 dual-burner lamps, with 10 x 14-inch reflectors, and should be seen 21 miles in clear weather. the size of the glass of the lantern is 12 x 14 inches, which is too small.

Mr. Buckingham [James Burlingham] is keeper, and everything is in very good order.

The vane of lantern requires repairs; the platform leading to the house is very much out of repair, and on dark nights is dangerous; the frame of the platform is rotten; 1500 feet of lumber will be required for repairs; keeper will do repairing.

SALMON POINT.

Arrived at Salmon Point on the 5th July, at 9 a.m., and landed supplies. this tower is of wood painted white; it shows a red fixed light of the catoptric order; the tower is 30 feet high from base to vane, and it has been supplied with a new lantern during the last closed season, which is a great improvement; the lantern is 8 feet in diameter, and contains three Silver No. 1 burner lamps, and two mammoth flat-wick lamps, with 18 inch reflectors; this light should be seen 12 miles in clear weather. Size of ruby glass, 20½ x 20 inches.

1000 feet of lumber required for a storehouse, the keeper will erect the building. A fence is required round the Government property, a wire one recommended, as it will not be so liable to be broken by the sea as a wooden one.

This is also a life-boat station. I inspected the boat, which is a metal one, and found it in good order, with all gear in its place and ready for use.

Peter Huff is keeper at this Station, and keeps everything in excellent order.

SCOTCH BONNET.

Arrived at this lighthouse on the 5th July; it is a white stone building, 54 feet height from base to vane; it shows a white fixed catoptric light, and can be seen 20 miles in clear weather; the lantern is of iron, 7 feet in diameter, and contains ten lamps, six mammoth flat-wick and four No. 1 base-burners with ten 14 inch reflectors. Size of glass 14½ x 18 inches.

This wants pointing and whitewashing; lantern requires repairs, as it leaks. A new boat is required at this Station; keeper states he can procure a suitable boat for $45, with centre board and sail. A new fog-horn is wanted, as the old one is worn out.

Robert Pye is keeper, who has a family of three; he keeps everything in very good order.

PRESQU'ISLE MAIN LIGHT

5th July the steamer arrived at this Station, at 4:15 p.m. This is a white octagonal stone tower, 63 feet high from base to vane. The diameter of the lantern is 9 feet; it is constructed of iron and has ten No. 1 base-burner lamps, with six 15-inch and four 12-inch reflectors, and shows a white fixed catoptric light, which should be seen at a distance of 15 miles; size of glass, 12 x 13 inches. The fence around the property is very old and decayed, and requires renewing. The lighthouse requires pointing and whitewashing; no other repairs are required.

Wm. H. Sherwood is keeper; who keeps the premises in very good order; his family consist of a wife and three children.

PRESQU'ISLE RANGE LIGHTS

Are four in number, two for the old channel and two to lead between the buoys by the new channel. They are all in charge of George B. Simpson, who keeps them in first-rate order. Three are square white towers, the corners of which are painted brown, constructed of wood. The size of the lanterns are 3 feet 3 inches, with one No. 1 base-burner lamp in each, with 15 inch reflectors. They require some repairs; the plaster has fallen off, and they require painting. I would recommend that they be ceiled with wood instead of being plastered.

The triangular gallows work which ranges with Salt Point, shows a very good light, and of great service to vessels coming in through the buoys. the keeper was instructed to have the buoys placed properly, as he had them placed wrongly.[59]

Curiously, Smith mentions four range lights in Presqu'ile Bay, not three. He speaks of the three "square white towers" which are likely the Salt Point lighthouse and the original 1851 rear range light, as well as the new Calf Pasture Shoal rear range light. In addition, however, in his brief but precise report, he speaks of a "triangular gallows work which ranges with Salt Point". This is in apparent contradiction to the report of the Minister of Marine of the same year. It remains unclear where this "triangular gallows work" was located.

Before sailing on to replenish the other lighthouses under his charge, Darius Smith completed his tour of the other lighthouses in eastern Lake Ontario waters:

WELLER'S BAY RANGE LIGHTS

Arrived here on the afternoon of the 5th July. These are two new lighthouses built for the purpose of guiding vessels into the Bay. They are 27 and 37 feet high, from base to vane, and show the front lighthouse a red fixed light, and the back one a fixed white. The lanterns are of galvanized iron, 4 feet square, and contain one mammoth flat-wick lamp, with 18-inch reflectors. Size of glass is 30 x 30 inches, The ruby glass in front lighthouse 19½ x 19 inches. Reuben Young, the keeper, has every thing in good order.

The land that is required around this Station is near six acres; two roads are necessary, one to the beach and the other from the front lighthouse to the back one, and from 30 feet in rear of each lighthouse at right angles from front road to the main public highway.

A new house has been built on this property during 1876 and 1877, 28 x 20 feet, well finished enclosed by a good board fence, with a garden of about three quarters of an acre. The house contains four rooms on the ground floor and three bed-rooms, there is also a good shed on the premises. I would recommend the land to be surveyed and the roads constructed....

TELEGRAPH ISLAND (BAY OF QUINTE.)
(John Mason, Keeper.)

This is a fixed white catoptric, containing two base-burner lamps and two 18-inch reflectors on cast-iron stands. There was no oil delivered, as the keeper had about 60 gallons on hand. The lighthouse is a white square wooden building, with dwelling attached. The lantern is 5 feet in diameter, and of wood. The light can be seen 10 miles. Size of glass, 21 x 41½ inches. The lighthouse is in good repair, and well kept, there are three of a family.[60]

Portsmouth Harbour Lighthouses (1880 & 1887)

At the eastern end of the Inside Passage, the Kingston area gained a new lighthouse when a harbour light was built on the pier at Portsmouth in 1880.

Commencing in the 1830's, numerous marine businesses had been attracted to the deep-water harbour at Hatter's Bay (later named Portsmouth) as described in the following newspaper accounts:

> We are glad to hear that the Messrs. Wm. Dickinson & Co. of this place have purchased Hatters Bay for the purpose of converting it into an extensive lumber establishment. They will commence immediately to erect piers and other buildings. The depth of water - the safety of the harbour - the enterprize and capital of the owners - its being on the mainland, and the only place in the immediate vicinity of Kingston where there is sufficient water for such a business, must give it a decided advantage. We understand it is also the intention of the proprietors to have several manufacturing establishments, such as Flour Mills, Distillery, Tannery, etc. May success attend their efforts. [1839][61]

> Messrs. Wm Dickinson & Co. have built a wharf at Hatter's Bay, extending from the shore 700 feet; there is 23 feet depth of water at the outer end of the pier. Hatter's Bay will be a very commodious and safe harbour. The enterprising owners are now preparing to do an extensive business at the opening of the navigation; they are purchasing all sorts of rafting materials, pine timber, &c.

They own five first class schooners, which are employed usually in the stave trade from Lake Erie, besides they have a number of vessels chartered. They are adding two new first class barges to their Montreal line. [1840][62]

Hatter's Bay, by some called Portsmouth, (a most improper appellation) is a village of some 500 inhabitants. It is hardly ten years old, having been erected since the establishment of the Kingston Penitentiary, which occupies the eastern side of the little bay or cove, which gives name to the locality. It has hitherto been a most prosperous and thriving village; and even now, in these most precious bad times, it holds its own with the best. The houses are nearly all built with stone, are large and even elegant; and though the streets are rough and as yet unformed, owing to the immediate vicinity of the working stone quarries, which supply all Canada with the finest and most durable blue lias lime-stone, yet they are being licked into shape and will vie its general appearance with the handsome houses. The inhabitants are enterprising and liberal. They have at vast labor and much expense, among themselves, built a large pier or breakwater, which defends the harbor from the lake swell....

The trade of Hatter's Bay is two-fold. Quarries and Shipyards. The former are in active operation; but the latter are at a comparative stand still. A vast many schooners are daily being loaded with the beautiful stone before alluded to, and despatched to all parts of the province....

Mr. Robert Fisher some few years ago built a small Steam Saw Mill, chiefly for the use of the city and its shipyards. This Mill he sold to an active and enterprising American, Mr. W. Lester of Syracuse.... Upwards of a million feet of boards for the New York Market are now piled near the mill, and at the time of our visit, three large vessels were loading at the wharf for Oswego.... The logs to

supply this vast sawing are brought from the River Trent....
these logs are brought down the whole length of the Bay of
Quinte, one hundred miles, with ease and facility.... [1849][63]

By the 1880's, there were some 180 dwellings in the village housing
a population of more than 1,700,[64] and companies like the Kingston
and Montreal Forwarding Company (K.&M.F. Co) were expanding
their operations into Portsmouth from nearby Kingston harbour to
trans-ship corn, wheat and manufactured goods between upper lakes-
based schooners and the company's steamers and barges.

Although the Public Works Department spent several thousands
of dollars improving the harbour facilities at Portsmouth, the Marine
and Fisheries Department never provided funds to build a lighthouse
on the Portsmouth pier. The lighthouse that was constructed there
in 1880 was a locally-funded aid to navigation, probably built and
operated by the village of Portsmouth. In June, 1880 the following
brief newspaper report was printed:

> New Light — A lighthouse has been built on the outer
> end of long pier, Portsmouth, that is, at the west side of the
> entrance to the harbour. A red light will be shown both
> up and down the lake. It will be finished and lighted on
> Wednesday, the 9th inst.[65]

It would appear that the lighthouse lasted less than seven years.
The *British Whig* reported in February, 1887 that another new
lighthouse was to be built on the long pier at Portsmouth,[66] but eight
months later, that lighthouse had been wrecked due to high winds.[67]
There is no record of whether or not it was replaced.

No documents have been found to indicate the size or shape of the
lighthouse, nor who the lightkeepers may have been.

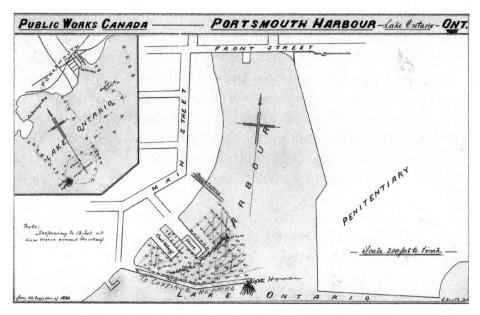

(68) Portsmouth Harbour. By E. Smith, from H.O. Gray's plan of 1880.
The lighthouse, erected by the Town of Portsmouth, is marked at the end of the pier
that was built by the Government of Canada's Public Works Department to protect
the harbour.
[Courtesy of Library and Archives Canada, NMC052150]

2nd Belleville Harbour Lighthouse (1881)

Just as the Town of Portsmouth was building and rebuilding its own lighthouses at municipal expense, Belleville's municipally-owned lighthouse was being replaced by one fully funded by the federal government.

In 1857, the provincial legislature had voted a small amount of money to build a number of lighthouses on the Bay of Quinte, including one in Belleville harbour.[68] However, Belleville harbour already had a lighthouse that had been constructed by the town in 1851. The provincially-funded lighthouse, like the others planned for the Bay of Quinte, was not built at that time.

Then, in 1879, the Belleville Harbour lighthouse caught fire and was destroyed.[69] Fire was always a risk in wood-framed lighthouses with their oil-burning lamps and open flames. After the destruction of their harbour light, Belleville Town Council had immediately petitioned the Dominion government for a new lighthouse.

Oddly enough, in 1880, before the new lighthouse was built, complaints were made about the poor quality of the light from the Belleville Harbour lighthouse. The June 4th edition of the Kingston newspaper, the *British Whig* reported that ... "Complaints are made that the Belleville light-house is a very poor one, and the light scarcely distinguishable."[70] What the newspaper failed to report was the fact that the this lighthouse was no longer standing; it had burned down a year earlier. Town Council may have had a temporary light set up — perhaps similar to Billa Flint's original wharf light placed on a mast — in the hopes that ships could still be guided into the harbour. It may have been this temporary light that was said to be of poor quality. Such a light would have been very dim compared to that of a proper lighthouse, and this is what the *British Whig* may have been reporting on.

In October, the newspaper published a brief announcement that, "A lighthouse will be erected in the Belleville harbour. The gov't will bear the expense for it."[71]

With a Conservative government in power and three Conservative members, John White, James Brown and Mackenzie Bowell, representing

Hastings County (of which Belleville was the largest town and county seat), it is no surprise that the Belleville Harbour lighthouse, previously built and staffed at the expense of the municipality, was fully funded this time by the federal government. By 1881, the new lighthouse was in place.[72]

Instead of being built a the end of the railway pier where the old lighthouse had been located, the new Belleville light was built on a crib constructed on a shoal in the middle of the harbour as described in the report of the Department of Marine and Fisheries:

> A lighthouse in Belleville Harbour, Bay of Quinté, to replace that formerly maintained by the City Corporation which was destroyed by fire in 1879. The light is fixed white, from a small dioptric apparatus, and shows around the whole horizon. It is elevated 38 feet above water mark, and should be seen 11 miles in clear weather. The tower is a square wooden one, 36 feet high, and stands upon an octagonal pier built upon the south-east edge of the shoal at the entrance of the harbour. The sum of $388.67 was expended on this lighthouse during the past fiscal year, and the further cost will be shown in the accounts of the present year.[73]

The lighthouse was constructed by Belleville building contractors Northcott and Alford,[74] and the lantern supplied by E. Chanteloup of Montreal.[75] These same contractors were also responsible for the construction of the federal building in downtown Belleville that was built the following year to accommodate the Post Office and Customs House.[76]

The mention of a "small dioptric apparatus" in the lighthouse is significant. This refers to the use of a refracting lens instead of the more common catoptric light which used a parabolic reflector as the means of enhancing the illuminating power of the lamp. The lamp itself was a type referred to as an "anchor light", and it was supplied by Chance Bros. & Co. of Birmingham, England. A typical anchor light was a large, weather-proof, hand-held lantern that was hoisted aloft aboard ships at anchor.

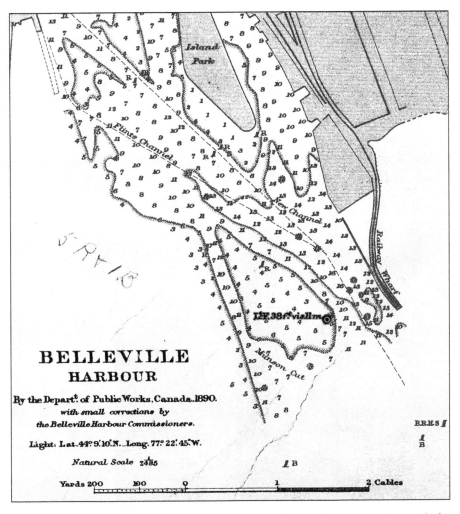

BELLEVILLE

HARBOUR

By the Depart.^t of Public Works, Canada, 1890.

with small corrections by
the Belleville Harbour Commissioners.

Light. Lat. 44° 9.10.N. Long. 77° 22.45.W.

Natural Scale 2485

Yards 200   100   0   1   2 Cables

(69) Chart of Belleville Harbour, 1890. Department of Public Works Canada. Detail of inset from *Chart of Western Part of the Bay of Quinte and Presqu'ile Bay*, surveyed by W.P. Anderson, 1893. Published by the British Admiralty, 1900, updated 1904.
The 2nd Belleville Harbour lighthouse, built in 1881, is marked as "Lt.F. 38ft. vis. 11m" (Light, fixed, elevated 38 feet above the water, visible 11 miles in clear weather). "Flint's Channel" leads to Flint's wharf were Billa Flint had placed a private navigational light in 1835. The "New Channel" leads to Lazier's Wharf where 2 beacons (daymarks) are indicated on the original plan. The "Island Park" is now Victoria Park.
[Courtesy of Library and Archives Canada, R11630-2427-2-E]

Dioptric lights had been perfected by the French engineer Augustin Fresnel in the 1820's when he had crafted large beehive-shaped cut-glass lenses, inside of which lamps could be placed to produce a light much brighter than that from the parabolic reflectors used in a catoptric light.[77] Due to its superior illuminating characteristics, Fresnel lenses were quickly adopted by lighthouse authorities in France and Britain. However, due to the greater expense of manufacturing the precisely cut and ground glass lenses, no lighthouses on the Canadian side of the Great Lakes had used a Fresnel lens until 1858, when six lighthouses built on Lake Huron had been fitted with them.[78]

(70) Anchor light of the type used in the 2ⁿᵈ Belleville Harbour lighthouse. Photographer unknown.
This glass plate negative is marked "DLD Chance Type 2.11 Anchor Lantern", and was probably photographed at the Dominion Lighthouse Depot at Prescott, Ontario. [Courtesy of Marine Museum of the Great Lakes, Kingston]

Even though the anchor light in the Belleville harbour lighthouse was not a large, complex, cut-glass Fresnel lens like those used on the seacoasts of Europe, it was the first dioptric light to be installed in a

Canadian lighthouse on Lake Ontario. This marked the beginning of a change in lighting technology. By the early years of the 20th Century, the old system of catoptric lights, introduced with the Lewis lamp in 1828, would be phased out and the brighter dioptric lenses of various sizes would be installed in all lighthouses in eastern Lake Ontario.

By Order-in-Council, John Covert of Belleville was appointed lightkeeper of the new Belleville Harbour lighthouse in June, 1881:

(71) 2nd Belleville Harbour Lighthouse, c.1910. Photographer unknown.
A man and his dog stand on the octagonal pier built in 1881 to support the pyramidal style lighthouse.
[Courtesy of Bay of Quinte Yacht Club, Belleville, Ontario]

On the recommendation of the Honorable the Acting Minister of Marine and Fisheries, the Committee advise that Mr. John Covert of Belleville, aged 50 years, be appointed Keeper of the new Light House recently erected in Belleville Harbour at a salary of Two hundred dollars ($200) per annum, such appointment to date from the 1st June 1881....[79]

It is not known whether or not Covert was provided with a dwelling at government expense as was the practice at most other lighthouses. The government did, however, supply the boat which the lightkeeper rowed out to the lighthouse in the middle of the harbour every evening to light the lamps and watch the light.[80]

Prince Edward Point Lighthouse (1881)

Fifty kilometers southeast of Belleville, at the eastern end of Prince Edward County's Long Point, another harbour light was constructed in 1881.

Long Point forms the southern shore of an expansive bay which was known in the 19th Century as Prince Edward's Bay or South Bay.[81] The lighthouse built at the eastern extremity of Long Point was originally called the South Bay Point lighthouse. Now known locally as the Point Traverse lighthouse, its official name is the Prince Edward Point lighthouse, named after the small cape on which it stands.

The protected waters of Prince Edward Bay were well known by mariners as a safe anchorage during storms blowing from the west or south-west. There was also a small area between the end of the point and False Ducks Island that could be used as shelter during a storm as described by Dr. Hodder in his *Harbours and Ports of Lake Ontario:*

Should a gale be coming up from the W. or S.W., good anchorage and shelter can be obtained inside South Bay Point: to make it, keep to the eastward of the Outer Drake Island [Timber Island], and to the north of the Inner Drake (the False Ducks) and anchor off the N.E. point, or run alongside a small wharf which will be found there.[82]

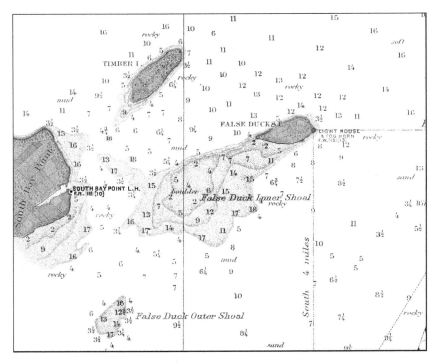

(72) Chart of Lake Ontario showing the location of Prince Edward Point (South Bay Point). Detail of *Coast Chart No. 1 - Lake Ontario, Survey of the Northern and Northwestern Lakes,* U.S. Corps of Engineers, 1904.

The tiny indentation at the end of what is marked as "South Bay Point" is Long Point Harbour. The Prince Edward Point lighthouse was built on the south side of this harbour in 1881. The lighthouse is marked "F.R. 11 ½ [10]" (Fixed Red light, visible 11 ½ miles or 10 nautical miles in clear weather). Offshore depths are in fathoms. Near-shore depths are in feet.

[Courtesy of NOAA's Office of Coast Survey Historical Map & Chart Collection http:// historicalcharts.noaa.gov LS106-01-1904]

The small wharf mentioned by Hodder was located inside the narrow Long Point Harbour, adjacent to Prince Edward Point, which had long been used by local commercial fishermen. In 1879, there were thirty small boats together with three ships officially registered as fishing in the vicinity of this harbour. Undoubtedly, many other, unregistered fishing boats also sheltered in Long Point Harbour. Eventually, a small seasonal fishing village sprang up there. Government records for 1879 show that a single year's catch in the area amounted to 185,000 pounds of whitefish, worth some $11,500. This represented more than fifteen percent of the total catch for the Canadian side of eastern Lake Ontario.[83]

This combination of safe anchorage for passing ships as well as its importance as a commercial fishing station may have been enough justification to have a lighthouse built to mark the harbour entrance. Like most lighthouses before it, the impetus behind the construction of the Prince Edward Point lighthouse was a petition sent to Parliament, as reported by *The British Whig* in February 1880:

> South Bay Point - The Dominion Gov't has made an appropriation of $1,200 for a lighthouse on South Bay Point [Prince Edward Point]. The grant is made in response to a petition which was numerously signed by vessel and steamboat captains. The light will be very serviceable.[84]

It was likely due to the efforts of Prince Edward County Conservative Member of Parliament, James McCuaig, that government funds for the construction of the lighthouse were voted as part of the $40,000 lighthouse construction supply bill of 1879.[85] McCuaig had been elected to replace the Liberal, Walter Ross, in the sweeping Conservative victory of the general election held in 1878.

Progress on construction of the lighthouse was slow. It was almost two years before the contract was awarded. The reports of the Department of Marine and Fisheries provide few clues as to the reason for the delays:

At the last Session of Parliament appropriations were made for the construction of new Lighthouses at Byng Inlet, Georgian Bay, Parry Sound; at Leamington, in the County of Essex; and at South Bay Point, Prince Edward County, but contracts have not as yet been let for the carrying out of these works. [1879][86]

A contract has been let for the construction of the lighthouse at South Bay Point, Prince Edward County, referred to in last year's Report, but the work has not yet been completed. [1880][87]

A plot of land at Prince Edward Point had been purchased for $300.00 from Z. Palmatier who owned 480 acres at the end of Long Point.[88] The construction contract was awarded to J.W. Fegan to build the lighthouse for $400.00. The lantern and catoptric lights were purchased from E. Chanteloup of Montreal for $642.00.[89] The lighthouse was finally placed into service in 1881:

> A lighthouse upon the extremity of South Bay Point or Point Traverse, on Lake Ontario, in the County of Prince Edward. This light is a fixed red catoptric, elevated 36 feet above water mark, and should be visible 10 miles from all points seaward. The building consists of a square wooden tower, 36 feet height, with keeper's dwelling attached. The sum of $1,349.57 was expended in the construction of this lighthouse during the past fiscal year, and further expenditure will appear in the accounts of the present year.[90]

With its square pyramidal form and attached keeper's dwelling, the Prince Edward Point lighthouse was the second of its kind in eastern Lake Ontario as it was identical in design to the Salmon Point lighthouse constructed ten years earlier. This new lighthouse, however, served a very different purpose. Instead of being a lake light like the Salmon Point lighthouse, it was a lesser harbour light, designed to guide fishermen and others into the sheltered harbour and to warn ships of the dangerous shoals less than one nautical mile offshore. Its lantern showed a red light to distinguish it from the nearby False Ducks Island light.

(73) Prince Edward Point lighthouse, constructed 1881. Hand-coloured photograph. Photographer unknown.
This lighthouse was originally known as the South Bay Point lighthouse and is most commonly referred to today as the Point Traverse lighthouse. It was virtually identical to the Salmon Point lighthouse built in 1871, and to the slightly smaller Centre Brother Island lighthouse built in 1890.
[Photo courtesy of Aubrey Johnson, author's collection]

Member of Parliament, James McCuaig, commented on the usefulness of the lighthouse in an interview on the subject:

Mr. J.S. McCuaig, M.P., Gives His Views On Several Vital Questions Agitating Marine Circles — Mr. J.S. McCuaig, M.P. minister for Prince Edward County, was in the city today, and about noon was met by a *Whig* reporter, who, knowing the interest he takes in marine matters, interviewed him respecting various subjects of importance to mariners....

Among other matters discussed was that relative to lighthouses. Mr. McCuaig avers that the small light at South Bay Point has saved many vessels from running ashore.[91]

By the time the South Bay Point lighthouse was completed, the Parliament of Canada had authorized the construction of the long-planned Murray Canal. This waterway would connect the waters of the Bay of Quinte to Lake Ontario through Presqu'ile Bay, thus completing the last leg of a safe Inside Passage and prompting the construction of numerous new lighthouses over the following decades.

CHAPTER 8

The Inside Passage Completed

Escape the boisterous sea.

("Reports of the Commissioners of Internal Navigation," 1825)

The isthmus connecting Prince Edward County to the rest of the Ontario mainland is a neck of land barely 2.5 kilometers wide at its narrowest point between the Bay of Quinte to the east and Wellers Bay to the west. Just north of this narrow point, the isthmus widens to 7.5 kilometers between the Bay of Quinte and Presqu'ile Bay. Until 1890, this was the only significant obstacle to a continuous "Inside Passage", some sixty-five nautical miles of relatively calm, sheltered waters stretching from Kingston harbour, westward along the North Channel past Amherst Island and through the winding Bay of Quinte to Presqu'ile Bay or Wellers Bay on Lake Ontario. Once completed, this Inside Passage would allow mariners to avoid the well known dangers of an open lake voyage around the Prince Edward peninsula.

The shortest of the routes across the isthmus; between the Bay of Quinte and Wellers Bay, is known as "The Carrying Place" and was likely used for centuries by First Nations peoples as a portage route. In the late 18th Century, one of the area's early settlers, Asa Weller, established a commercial freight business along this route transporting logs and bateaux laden with goods on a wooden railway pulled by oxen.[1]

In 1796, the idea of digging a canal at The Carrying Place to complete the Inside Passage was expressed by Upper Canada's first lieutenant-governor, John Graves Simcoe. The proposed canal was sometimes referred to as the Simcoe Canal, but more commonly called the Murray Canal after Murray Township in which the government had reserved 3,000 acres of land for canal purposes:

> In the year 1796, it was resolved by His Excellency, the Lieutenant governor, in Council, "that 3000 acres of land in front of the Township of Murray, be reserved for the purpose of facilitating the cutting of a Canal between the Bay of Quinté and Newcastle (or Presqu'Isle,) or for such other public benefit, as it may be appropriated to."[2]

Surveyor-General Smyth's map of Upper Canada published in 1800 also clearly marks the canal reserve. (See figure 15)

Since then, the establishment of the Murray Canal to create a complete, navigable Inside Passage had been proposed, debated, studied, discussed, shelved and resurrected many times over many decades. Various routes had been surveyed on at least four separate occasions by different engineers, and numerous formal reports had been presented to successive governments of Upper Canada, the Province of Canada, and the Dominion of Canada. For almost one hundred years, the construction of the Murray Canal was deferred by successive legislatures. Decade after decade, residents of Northumberland County and Prince Edward County, along with their elected representatives, continued to lobby the government for the construction of the canal.

The first serious proposal to build the Murray Canal had been made in 1825 by John Macaulay's "Commission of Internal Navigation". In their report, the commissioners stated that:

> The advantages of a navigable communication between the head of the bay of Quinty [Bay of Quinte], and Presqu'ile

harbour, are great and numerous.... With the aid of a canal across the Isthmus in Murray, vessels encountering adverse winds off Long Point in their way downwards [eastbound], might enter Presqu'ile harbour, and running through the bay of Quinty, effect their passage without much delay or inconvenience. Vessels proceeding upwards [westbound] might, in like manner, expedite their passage....

It is as it respects Steam-boats, however, that the canal in Murray demands attention; for by Steam-boats, the greater part of the trade will eventually be carried on. A vessel of this description proceeding down the lake, and encountering a heavy easterly gale, as frequently happens near Long Point, might run through the canal into the bay of Quinty, and effect her passage in narrow waters regardless of the storm without. In the same manner during the occurrence of westerly gales, a Steam-boat from Prescott or Kingston, by passing up the bay of Quinty, might escape the boisterous sea, which at such times prevails off Long Point....[3]

The Commission proposed constructing a seven-meter-wide canal deep enough to allow the passage of steamboats and schooners drawing up to nine feet of water. They estimated that such a canal would cost £16,621.[4] By comparison, the Welland Canal, construction of which had been started by a private company the year before, would be slightly narrower and have a depth of eight feet.[5]

Eight years later, civil engineer N.H. Baird, an experienced canal engineer who later designed the Presqu'ile Point lighthouse, was contracted by the government of Upper Canada to conduct a detailed survey of the route of the proposed Murray Canal. In 1833, Baird surveyed two routes starting from Twelve O'clock Point on the Bay of Quinte: one along the Canal Reserve to Presqu'ile Bay, and a shorter one to Wellers Bay. Baird's recommendation to the Lieutenant-Governor of Upper Canada was for an eight-foot deep canal along the Wellers Bay route which would include one lock and cost £42,845.[6]

Other surveys were done in 1845 and in 1867, examining variations of these two routes. In each case, detailed plans and estimates for the construction of the canal suffered the same fate as Baird's recommendation: they were discussed and debated, then deferred.

From 1835 to 1879, no fewer than thirty petitions from groups of private citizens as well as from municipalities, in total containing several thousand signatures, were submitted to both houses of the various Canadian parliaments. This petition to the Legislative Assembly of Upper Canada in 1836, was typical:

> Of Reuben White and 223 others, of the Newcastle, Prince Edward and Midland districts, representing: that a canal uniting the waters of Lake Ontario with the head of the bay of Quinte would be a work of the greatest utility, at all times affording a safe and convenient channel for the transport of merchandize and military stores, and a less dangerous navigation for our vessels than that of the open lake; that it would enhance the wealth and prosperity of the Province; that the advantages derived would much more than compensate for the expense; that the advancement of the Province is mainly attributed to the construction of canals, which will long remain sources of opulence and honor to the Province. Petitioners respectfully direct the attention of the House to the object, and pray for the means of effecting the same.[7]

Despite such petitions, either the funds for digging the canal were not available or, more likely, the political will to have the canal built was not strong enough. There is no doubt that from the 1850's onward, much of the attention of the legislators, not to mention a large portion of the available public funds, were diverted to a new and fast-growing transportation method: railways. Dozens of small commercial railways as well as larger railroad systems such as the Northern, Great Western and the Grand Trunk railways were given substantial government grants, loans and loan guarantees. By 1867, financial contributions from the province to support railways amounted to more than $33,000,000, representing almost one-quarter of the total construction costs for some 3,500 kilometers of track.[8]

Whatever money was left over in the annual transportation infrastructure budgets of the Public Works Department was often divided between cutting and resurfacing roads, and maintaining and upgrading the existing canals, especially the St. Lawrence canals and the Welland Canal, as their improvement was considered vital in the face of competition from New York's Erie Canal which continually diverted a substantial amount of freight from the Great Lakes to New York City.

After decades of many frustrated attempts at having the government fund the Murray Canal, a group composed of private individuals and municipalities in the region of the proposed canal determined to form a private company in order to construct the canal and run it for profit from the tolls that would be collected. In this manner, they were following the model used by William Hamilton Merritt in 1824 when he started a private venture to build the first Welland Canal. In 1854, the Ontario and Bay of Quinté Canal Company was granted a charter by the Legislature of the Province of Canada:

> An Act to incorporate the Ontario and Bay of Quinté Canal Company.
>
> Whereas the construction of a Canal across the peninsula separating the Bay of Quinté, from the Lake Ontario at Presqu'Isle, would greatly tend to the advantage of the Province, and it is expedient to incorporate a Joint Stock company to construct such Canal: Be it therefore enacted by the Queen's Most Excellent Majesty...
>
> The said Company, their Agents or Servants, shall have full powers under this Act to lay out, construct, make and finish a Canal at their own costs and charges, from any point at the head of the Bay of Quinté, to any point in Presqu'Isle Harbor....
>
> The Honorable Robert Charles Wilkins, James L. Biggar, Francis McAnanny, William Butler, Stephen

Young, William Hamilton Ponton, John O'Hare, James Cumming, and James Ross, together with the heads of such Municipalities representing corporations which shall within six months after the passing of this Act become Shareholders of the Stock in the said Company to the amount of Five Thousand Pounds, shall be and are hereby constituted and appointed the first Directors of the said company...

The said Company to entitle themselves to the benefit and advantages to them granted by this Act, shall and they are hereby required to make and complete the said canal, railway, towing paths, and other erections required for the navigation thereof, within five years from the passing of this Act, so as to be navigable for ships, steamers, schooners, boats, barges and rafts, otherwise this Act, and every matter and thing herein contained, shall cease and be utterly null and void, to all intents and purposes whatsoever...[9]

It appears that the company failed to attract sufficient investors. No work had been done on constructing the Murray Canal by the time the company's charter expired in 1860, and little was heard of the company again.

The commercial importance of the Murray Canal was not lost on the business interests at Canada's commercial centre, Montreal. In 1865, the Board of Trade of the City of Montreal published a report entitled "Improvement of Inland Navigation" in which they stated...

It was long ago proposed to connect Lake Ontario with the Western extremity of the Bay of Quinté, by a short Canal....

When it is remembered that the stretch between Presqu'isle Harbor and Kingston is the most hazardous on Lake Ontario, the advantages to be derived from such a cut-off will be evident, especially in the fall, when stormy weather is most prevalent. Had that little Canal existed last year, a number of marine disasters might have been avoided.[10]

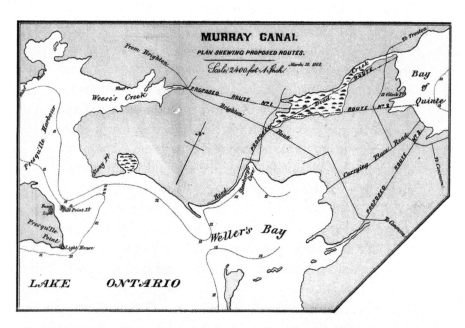

(74) Map showing three of the proposed routes for the Murray Canal, 1868. Inset from *Map Shewing Position of Proposed Murray Canal*, lithographed by Copp Clark & Company, Toronto.

Between 1796 and 1882, numerous routes were surveyed and proposed for the Murray Canal. In the end, a fourth route, a straight cut from 12 O'clock Point on the Bay of Quinte to the mouth of Weese's Creek on Presqu'ile Bay, was adopted.

[Courtesy Library and Archives Canada, NMC21724]

The "marine disasters" referred to by the Board of Trade likely included the wreck of the schooners *Cataraqui, James Coleman*, and *J.C. Wheeler*, all of which were total losses on Lake Ontario in the waters around Prince Edward County during severe weather in the autumn of 1864.[11] In all, between 1798 and 1889, the loss of no fewer than seventeen ships and fifty-five lives on Lake Ontario can be attributed directly to the fact that the Murray Canal was not in place to allow mariners to avoid the dangerous open lake.[12] Nevertheless, government after government refused to commit funds for the construction of the canal.

Some proposals for the canal had included not only safety and commercial reasons for building the canal, but also military reasons. In February 1862, with the American Civil War raging to the south, and a large, well-equipped Union Army never far from Canada's borders, a special commission, composed of officers of the British Army and the Royal Navy along with a civil engineer, was charged with examining the defences of Canada. In September, they made a number of recommendations concerning the Bay of Quinte and the Murray Canal:

> ... that the naval establishments on Lake Ontario should be removed from Kingston to some point on the Bay of Quinté. At this place also the vessels should be laid up for the winter....
>
> The inlet at Presqu'ile at the head of the Bay of Quinté, from which it is divided by a narrow neck of land, is a good harbour. A canal has been projected across the isthmus; this, Your Commissioners consider, would be of very great importance in a naval point of view, as it would afford a safe direct communication between the proposed dockyard and the upper part of the lake....
>
> Belleville, on the River Moira, down which some of the best timber in the province is rafted, having ironworks in the immediate neighbourhood, and in direct communication by rail with the Rideau Canal, would seem

to be an excellent site, if it is found from the necessary survey that the depth of water is, as there is reason to believe, sufficient.

The establishments, if placed here, could not be shelled from the lake; they could only be attacked by an enemy undertaking the larger operations of war, and effecting a disembarcation on the mainland, or on the peninsula of Prince Edward. This would be attended with great hazard, and would hardly be attempted unless the invader had the complete mastery of the lake.[13]

Surely with the support of the military, the Murray Canal would be constructed immediately, citing military expediency, as was the justification for the Rideau Canal four decades earlier. However, in spite of the defence commission's recommendations, there was still no action taken on digging the Murray Canal.

In 1869, the Canadian House of Commons directed that the matter be referred to the "Select Committee on Maritime and River Fisheries, Ocean and Inland Navigation, and the Inspection of Fish". The committee was composed of twenty-five members of the legislature, including Walter Ross, member for Prince Edward, and Joseph Keeler, member for Northumberland.[14] The committee's report to the House echoed many of the statements presented in previous reports:

That if the proposed Canal was open to vessels, about eighty miles of the most dangerous navigation of Lake Ontario would be avoided, that it would also afford a Western outlet to the very extensive trade of the Bay of Quinte, more than one hundred miles shorter that the present route, besides transferring the growing and important Towns of Picton, Napanee, Belleville and Trenton to the great water highway between the St. Lawrence ports in the east and the Lake ports in the west.

That it is a work urgently required for commercial purposes, and would be of the utmost importance as a military work in case of hostilities with the United States.

That the delay in the construction of this work is an act of injustice to the locality inasmuch as the lands were sold upon the understanding that such a work would be built at the time the lands in the neighbourhood were first settled.

And in consideration of these premises the Committee do earnestly recommend the construction of this Canal at the earliest moment the state of the finances will permit, believing that it has the oldest and strongest claim of any work in the Dominion; and being a work only two miles [3 kilometers] in length and of very easy construction.[15]

The Committee's report led to a Royal Commission being embodied in 1870 to look into the entire Canadian canal system, "... with the object of obtaining such reliable information as may furnish the data on which to base a plan for the improvement of the Canal System of the Dominion, of a comprehensive character, and such as will enable Canada to compete with success for the transit trade of the Great West [west of Lake Superior]...."[16]

Among the six men appointed to the Canal Commission were noted engineer C.S. Gzowski of Toronto, prominent lumber merchant D.D. Calvin of Garden Island and shipping magnate Hugh Allan of Montreal. After thoroughly examining the canals of Canada, the commissioners presented their final report to Parliament in 1871. While they recommended that more than $19,000,000 be spent on improving Canada's canals, none of it was slated for the Murray Canal, about which they commented only that:

The Murray Canal is entirely a work of local importance, and is not required by the general trade of the Dominion. In this view, while so many works of general importance are calling for execution, the Commissioners recommend that for the present the consideration of this Canal be deferred.[17]

This official "stamp of deferral", then, seemed to end any prospect of having the Murray Canal built. For the next seven years there were no petitions, no committees, no surveys, no debates and no reports of any kind concerning the Murray Canal. One more feeble petition from residents of Brighton presented to the House of Commons in April 1879, fared an identical fate to all previous petitions: no action was taken.[18]

Barely seven months later, sensational newspaper headlines of "A Terrible Catastrophe" and "The Great Disaster" concerning an accident that occurred on Lake Ontario in November 1879, brought the need for the Murray Canal once again to the attention of politicians and the public.

(75) "Fearful Loss of Life".
Headlines like this one from the Belleville newspaper *The Daily Ontario*, were instrumental in reopening the debate for the construction of the Murray Canal. [The Daily Ontario. Nov. 20, 1879].

On Wednesday, November 19, the following newspaper story appeared in Belleville's *Daily Ontario*:

FEARFUL LOSS OF LIFE
A Tow Broken Up on Lake Ontario.
THIRTY-ONE PERSONS DROWNED.

The steam tug *Seymour* of Ogdensburg, left Cape Vincent Monday noon with a tow consisting of three dredges, two derricks, and seven scows, owned by Eccles & Arnold, of Buffalo. They had fine weather until after passing the Galloup Island [Galloo Island], off Sackett's Harbor, when a gale of wind from the north-east with a heavy snow storm set in. The tug and tow got within five or six miles of Oswego, when they lost their lights. The tug then turned around and endeavored to hold the fleet until day light, but the fleet broke away and was lost, with all hands excepting six, who were rescued by the tug. Thirty-one persons, including three women and one girl, were drowned. The fleet is a total loss.[19]

News of ships foundering on Lake Ontario were commonplace in the 19th Century. Even the occasional report of loss of life due to a shipwreck was not uncommon. However, news of the loss of thirty-one persons together with the total loss of a large number of vessels, all in a single accident, was indeed shocking. Over the following two days, many conflicting reports were sent by telegraph and printed in newspapers all around the lake. Depending on the source, the number of vessels involved varied from nine to eighteen, and the number of lives lost fluctuated between six and thirty-two.

It appears that the steam tug *Seymour* was towing an enormous procession of thirteen dredges, derricks and scows to Buffalo, New York from Montreal where they had been employed on the Lachine Canal. Even though the *Seymour* was assisted by four other tugboats, many experienced mariners thought that this was an extremely unwieldy collection to be towing across Lake Ontario, especially at a time of the year that was known for severe storms. When a powerful gale struck the lake just as the fleet was between Galloo Island and Oswego, most of the vessels were separated and they lost sight of one another in the ensuing snowstorm.

After all reports of the incident became known, it appears the loss of life was not as great as had originally been stated in the newspapers' sensational headlines. The *Daily Ontario* reported more on the story:

> LATER... Exaggerated reports of the disaster have no doubt been circulated, which the latest information does not justify....
>
> LATEST. Sackets Harbour, N.Y., Nov. 19 — When the gale struck the lost fleet, all tugs were cut loose from the tow except the *Seymour* and sought to save themselves. The scows soon parted from the rest of the fleet. The tug *Thayer* sunk and it is supposed all the crew were lost. The tug *Becker* was abandoned in a sinking condition, but in getting her along-side of the dredge *Gordon*, stove a hole in the latter which quickly filled her with water, and both crews were lost, except Thos. Smith and two Swedes. These clung to the cabin of the dredge and were picked up at daylight by the *Seymour*.
>
> THE VERY LATEST. Ogdensburg, Nov. 19 — From last information to this a.m. it is believed the only persons lost on board the tow of tug *Seymour* were Capt. Logan, his brother Wm. Arnold part owner and the cook and her husband, of dredge *No. 3*. They would have been saved but for the tug *Becker* running into the dredge staving a hole in her. Nearly all the *Seymour's* tow have been found, and it is thought with the assistance that has been sent out all will be picked up except dredge *No. 3* and tugs *Becker* and *Thayer* which foundered without any one on board. One of the dredges is in Sodus all right; one is off Sodus Point at anchor and will undoubtedly be picked up today.[20]

Instead of a total loss of the fleet along with thirty-one lives as had been initially reported, only three vessels sunk, although six people were drowned. Nonetheless, this was still a significant loss of lives and ships. This led the *Daily Ontario's* editor to pen an editorial about the dire need for the Murray Canal:

THE RECENT DISASTER ON LAKE ONTARIO.

Yesterday we gave the particulars of a terrible disaster on Lake Ontario. Later developments show that the loss of life was not so heavy as at first supposed, but six or eight persons were drowned. This catastrophe is another unanswerable argument in favor of the proposed Murray Canal.

Had such a means of communication between lake Ontario and the Bay of Quinte been in existence, the tug *Seymour* would not have ventured through the open lake with such an unwieldy tow. She could have crossed from Ogdensburg to Kingston in comparatively calm water, and without running out of her course. Once inside the islands, a stretch of nearly one hundred miles of sheltered sailing would be before her, and when arriving at Presqu'Isle the condition of the lake could be taken advantage of at leisure.

Two-thirds, or more, of the shipwrecks that occur on Lake Ontario take place between Point Petre and the Main Ducks. This reference holds good on both sides. Sailors dread the terrible sweep of wind and wave that beset them there, especially towards the close of navigation. Owing to frequent shallows sailing is treacherous and the motion of the water difficult to contend with.

The promoters of the Murray Canal should enforce this latest lesson upon the attention of mariners and ship-owners. There can be no doubt of the great importance of such a work, and the only wonder is that it has been so long neglected.[21]

The editor's claims of the proportion of wrecks in that part of Lake Ontario were significantly overstated as discussed in Chapter 1. As to whether or not the captain of the *Seymour* would have chosen to sail a safer route that would have taken him up to 25 nautical miles and several hours out of his way if the Murray Canal had existed at that time, will never be known. Nevertheless, this single incident seemed to be the catalyst that re-ignited the debate over the Murray Canal and finally ended with the canal being built.

The newspaper editor's point seems to have been understood by many with an interest in the Murray Canal for, within a few months, thousands of citizens in more than a dozen communities along the north shore of Lake Ontario had once again signed petitions demanding that the government take action on the issue. In February and March, 1880, more than forty separate petitions were read in the House of Commons and in the Senate.

During the budget debates that April, two of the local Members of Parliament spoke on the subject. Joseph Keeler, the member for Northumberland, addressed the House by saying:

> I think that during the present Session, I have presented no less than twenty-five petitions to this House in favour of that long neglected, but very necessary work — those petitions are from every city, county, township, town and village in the vicinity of the canal, and I earnestly call the attention of the Government to their prayers. In addition to our old arguments and reasons for the Murray Canal, we have another in the recently developed and rapidly increasing iron ore trade of Hastings.... I have a telegram from Belleville in my hand, which says:
>
> "250 tons per day of iron ore and 150 tons of golden ore are now being shipped, and expect to double this amount next month. With Murray Canal we could largely increase these figures, and yet have plenty of iron ore for smelting works — vessels bringing back coal from Cleveland...."
>
> Another very strong argument, in favour of the construction of this canal, I find in a recent article in one of the Belleville papers, which is as follows:

"Another fact which shows the necessity for the cutting of a canal through the narrow isthmus which separates one of the best harbours of refuge on Lake Ontario, from the perfectly sheltered waters of the Bay of Quinte, is afforded in the wrecking of the schooner *David Andrews*, with a cargo of grain destined for Toronto. This event took place during a heavy gale on Sunday morning the 11th inst., and the result is the loss of a vessel valued at $4,000 and cargo worth about $7,500, or a total loss of $11,500. that no loss of life is to be added to the loss of property, is entirely owing to the efficient exertions of the Oswego life-saving crew, who appear to have discharged their duty ably and well. That this disaster would not have occurred, had the Murray Canal been built, is quite clear. In such case, the schooner, which was bound from Belleville to Toronto with 10,500 bushels of rye, would, instead of having to go eastward and coast around the whole of the peninsula of Prince Edward — the most dangerous coast on the whole lake during south or south-west winds — have proceeded to the head of the bay and through the canal, thus not only shortening her journey by 150 miles [136 nautical miles], but escaping the very dangers which proved her destruction. Thence she would have been enabled to proceed on her way to Toronto, as winds were westerly and north-westerly, and in all probability the vessel would have been enabled to complete her trip without detention."

That is only one of the many similar articles which I could read to show the necessity of proceeding with this canal."[22]

James McCuaig, the member for Prince Edward County, was next to speak on the subject:

Now, in regard to the Murray Canal. which I know will be of great benefit to that peninsula. There is 90 per cent of iron in the ore in that neighbourhood, and what we want is cheap transport. If we have not the coal to smelt this ore, we should have some means of getting the ore to a place where it can be smelted, and I think the canal will be a great help in that direction.[23]

Sir Charles Tupper, then Minister of Railways and Canals, responded to the comments of his two Conservative colleagues:

The Murray Canal is a work that could be completed at the smallest cost of almost any public work required to attain so large a result; and I only regret that the great obligations resting upon the Government — that there are so many other matters that cannot possibly admit of any postponement — which render it impossible to seriously look at the question, as to whether it would or would not be desirable to spend the small sum required to obtain this large result. The development of the adjacent mineral districts, the great advantage of facilitating transport, by obtaining 100 miles of barge navigation in exchange for a circuitous and dangerous navigation over a route where very many shipwrecks have occurred, would render it desirable, if in the power of the Government, to consider and ascertain at how small a cost that work could be done. I am afraid it will not be in the power of the Government to put in the Estimates the cost of these works.[24]

Even though none of the minister's $1,400,000 budget for canal improvements in 1881 was allocated to the digging of the Murray Canal, the following year's estimates included a small amount of government money for preliminary construction work on the proposed canal. During the budget debates of February 1881, the acting Minister of Railways and Canals, John Pope, commented that:

The estimated cost of the work is $700,000. This canal has been the subject of discussion at different times — in

1833, 1840, 1846, 1867, and during the past year. There is no doubt it is a very important work, and it is more important now than ever before. It has been represented by gentlemen of undoubted integrity that if this canal were built, iron smelting works would be started at that point and a large number of men employed. Under this pressure, and after the representation that was made by those gentlemen, the Government felt they could not any longer refrain from trying to open up this important section of the country, not only for the iron but the lumber trade as well.[25]

Eighty-five years after the canal had first been proposed by John Graves Simcoe, the House of Commons voted in March, 1881 an appropriation for the construction of the Murray Canal. Out of a total budget of more than $27 million for the 1881-82 fiscal year, the first $50,000 of an estimated $700,000 was finally allocated for the new canal.[26]

In the end, the funds voted by Parliament for the construction of the Murray Canal were not, however, to save ships, cargoes and lives, but instead to create jobs in the mining and lumbering sectors. By doing so, the government hoped to gain votes in the General Election that was to be held the following year.

In his annual report of 1881, the Minister of Railways and Canals announced the commencement of the project:

> The construction of a canal from the head of the Bay of Quinte, westward into Lake Ontario, having been authorized by Parliament, the location of the work is now in progress, and so soon as it is effected, the work of construction will be undertaken and pushed to completion without delay.[27]

One final survey of the proposed canal route was undertaken. This survey concluded that the best route would be along the original Canal Reserve to Presqu'ile Bay, even though the shortest route ran to Wellers

Bay. In spite of his best efforts to convince the government to run the canal along the shortest route — which would take it through his riding — Prince Edward County's Member of Parliament, James McCuaig lost out to his Conservative colleague from Northumberland County.

This was of such great concern to the residents of Prince Edward County that it became a local issue in the 1882 election campaign. One poster printed during the campaign proclaimed:

PRINCE EDWARD INSULTED!
The Murray Canal Goes to Presqu'ile!

The poster's author claimed that, "If we elect Mr. McCuaig we thus tell the government that we like to be spit upon."[28]

It appears that the voters of Prince Edward felt so slighted by the Conservative Government over the Murray Canal issue that McCuaig was not re-elected. Even though the Conservatives gained another majority government, the Liberal Party's candidate, Dr. John Platt, defeated McCuaig at the polls and took his seat in the House of Commons.

The route of the Murray Canal from the Bay of Quinte to Presqu'ile Bay having been confirmed, tenders were soon let for its construction. The firm of John D. Silcox of Welland, Ontario, together with N. Scanton Gere and H.J. Moury of Syracuse, New York, were the successful bidders. Silcox, Gere and Moury had done a considerable amount of dredging work during the enlargement of the Welland Canal a few years earlier and they were among the most experienced contractors for the job. However, in spite of having accepted the lowest bid, the government contract with Silcox & Co. was for $1,140,625,[29] almost sixty percent higher than the government engineer's latest estimate of $721,000.[30]

Mariners all around Lake Ontario welcomed the news of the beginning of construction of the Murray Canal. In August, 1882, the sod-turning ceremony was reported on the south side of the lake by the *Oswego Palladium* newspaper:

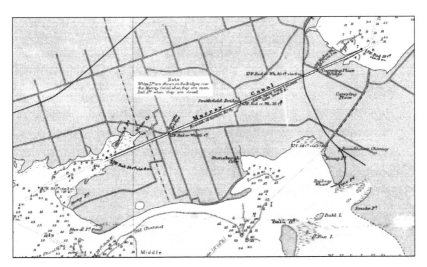

(75.1) Final route of the Murray Canal. From a survey by W.P. Anderson, 1893. Detail of *Lake Ontario, Western Part of the Bay of Quinte and Presqu'ile Bay*, published by the British Admiralty, 1900, updated 1904.

Even though the route across The Carrying Place from the Bay of Quinte to Wellers Bay was considerably shorter, the engineer who conducted the final survey recommended the first proposed route through the lands that had been reserved for canal purposes as far back as 1796. This resulted in a straight cut with no locks between the Bay of Quinte and Presqu'ile Bay.

[Courtesy of Library and Archives Canada, R11630-2427-2-E]

TRENTON, Aug. 31. - The turning of the first sod of the Murray canal was celebrated today by a grand picnic held on the farm of Mr. Charles Clendenning. Before 12 o'clock about 5,000 people had assembled on the grounds, and after dinner had been disposed of the ceremonies at once commenced.

Mr. Thomas Webb, reeve of Brighton, after reading an appropriate address, presented Mrs. Keeler, widow of the late Joseph Keeler, M. P., with a beautiful silver spade suitably engraved, with which the lady gracefully turned over the first sod, the bands meanwhile playing the National anthem.

The contract for the canal has been awarded to Messrs. Silcox and Mowry, who have already hired a large number of men who commenced work immediately after the ceremony. The canal commencing at a point known as Twelve o'clock Point on the shore of the Bay of Quinte, will be constructed in almost a straight line to Weeses creek, which empties into Presque Isle harbor. The entire length will be a fraction over five miles.

The width will be eighty feet at the bottom and 150 feet at the top, and the depth twenty feet [a depth of only 12 feet, the same as the Welland Canal, was actually specified]. The object of the canal is to connect the head waters of the Bay of Quinte with Lake Ontario, and thus ensure a perfectly safe passage for all the shipping going from the west to Kingston and Montreal, which instead of going down Lake Ontario to the St. Lawrence as formerly, will pass through the canal and down the Bay of Quinte, thus avoiding the dangerous storms which so frequently occur on Lake Ontario, besides reaching their destination a few hours sooner.[31]

With its completion projected for 1885, ship owners and ship captains were now looking forward to the day that the new Murray

Canal would be opened to allow their ships to sail eastern Lake Ontario waters in greater safety than ever before..

Deseronto Harbour Lighthouse (1885)

The government's decision to finally begin work on the Murray Canal in order to complete the important Inside Passage through the Bay of Quinte undoubtedly contributed to their decision to build several new lighthouses along the route in anticipation of the increase in shipping traffic. The first of these new lights was constructed at Deseronto.

In 1848, Hugo Burghardt Rathbun had built a sawmill at Mill Point on the Bay of Quinte, near where the Napanee River meets the bay. Over the next half-century, the H.B. Rathbun Company would expand at that location to include two sawmills, a flour mill, a shipyard and factories manufacturing window sashes, doors, blinds, shingles and railway rolling stock. The town that grew up at Mill Point, renamed Deseronto in 1881, was essentially a Rathbun company town. The Rathbun family would eventually have an interest in many other businesses including several railways, a terracotta works, and the Napanee Cement Works.[32] In addition, the company had its own fleet of steamboats that ran under the pennant of the Deseronto Navigation Company.

The products made at the Rathbun mills and factories were transported to their markets aboard both Rathbun ships and other ships. In 1884, more than 500 vessels carrying in excess of 40,000 tons of cargo arrived and departed Deseronto Harbour.[33] Those numbers alone would have been enough for the Rathbun Company to ask the government to fund the construction of a lighthouse at Deseronto. In addition, however, the Murray Canal was projected to be open to shipping within a year and traffic on the Bay of Quinte was expected to increase substantially.

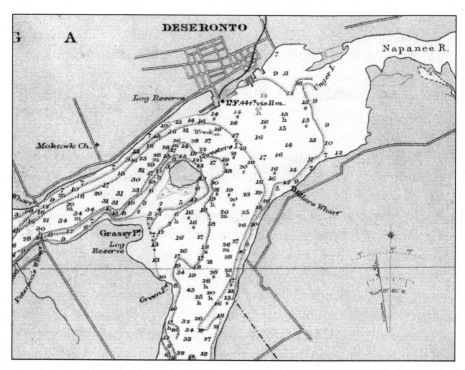

(76) Deseronto and the Bay of Quinte. From a survey by W.P. Anderson, 1893. Detail of *Lake Ontario, Western Part of the Bay of Quinte and Presqu'ile Bay*, published by the British Admiralty, 1900, updated 1904.

The Deseronto Harbour lighthouse is marked as "Lt. F. 44ft. vis 11m." (Light, Fixed, 44 ft. tall, visible 11 miles in clear weather). The Chapel Royal of the Mohawks of Tyendinaga, shown to the west of Deseronto, was also used as an aid to navigation for many years.

[Courtesy of Library and Archives Canada, R11630-2427-2-E]

In 1884, the Marine and Fisheries Department paid the Rathbun Company $437.49 to build a lighthouse on Rathbun Company property, to be staffed by Rathbun Company employees, and to be lit with gas provided by the Rathbun Company. This was a unique arrangement. The Deseronto Harbour lighthouse was one of the few government lighthouses on the Great Lakes that is known to have been built on private property and staffed by personnel employed by a private company. The Minister of Marine and Fisheries reported that:

A contract was... entered into with the Rathbun Company, of Deseronto, for the erection of a lighthouse at that place, for the sum of $437.49, and the lighthouse has been completed and the light will be shown on the opening of navigation next season.[34]

The official "Notice to Mariners" was published in 1885:

NOTICE TO MARINERS
No. 25 of 1885
DESERONTO LIGHT

Notice is hereby given that a Lighthouse, established by the Government of Canada, at Deseronto, on the Bay of Quinté, in the County of Hastings, Ontario, was put in operation on the opening of navigation this year

Lat. N. 44° 11' 15"

Long. W. 77° 2' 0"

The light is fixed white, elevated 44 feet above the level of the Bay, and should be visible 11 miles from all points of approach seaward. The illuminating apparatus is dioptric, of small size, and the illuminant is gas.

The building is a square wooden tower surrounded by a projecting gallery and surmounted by a hexagonal lantern, erected on the roof of the freight shed of the Bay of Quinté Railway, near the outer end of the Company's wharf at Deseronto. Both shed and tower are painted brown. The height of the lantern vane above the wharf is 46 feet.

The light will guide to Deseronto from the directions of Belleville, Picton and Napanee.

Wm. SMITH

Deputy Minister of Marine

Department of Marine,

Ottawa, 29th August, 1885.[35]

(77) Deseronto Harbour lighthouse, c.1915. Photographer unknown.
The lighthouse was unique because it was simply a gallery and lantern projecting from the roof of an existing building, in this case Rathbun's Bay of Quinte Railway freight shed. The ship docked at the steamboat wharf is likely the *CGS Grenville*, one of the lighthouse and buoy tenders of the Dominion Marine and Fisheries Department. [Courtesy of Deseronto Archives, DESNAVCO-06-05]

Unlike other lighthouses in the region, the Deseronto Harbour lighthouse was not a free-standing structure. Instead, it was a short tower projecting from the roof of a warehouse situated at the end of Rathbun's steamboat wharf. Otherwise, however, it possessed all of the other characteristics of a conventional lighthouse including a glassed-in lantern containing a lamp, and a dedicated lightkeeper. The construction of this lighthouse marked a shift in government thinking about lighthouses as free-standing, purpose-built structures, and this may have been the first time that another building had been used to support an official aid to navigation on the Great Lakes.

The use of gas as an illuminant also marked a change in lighthouse lighting technology that would later allow the Marine and Fisheries Department to automate many lighthouses. The gas used in the Deseronto harbour light was likely Pintsch gas; a distillate of naphtha that could be produced locally. The lighting apparatus itself was an anchor light, similar to the one used in the Belleville Harbour lighthouse, purchased from Chance Bros. & Co. for $83.06.[36]

As the Murray Canal was scheduled to open to ship traffic in 1885, the same year that the Deseronto Harbour lighthouse was activated, it appeared that the timing of the completion of the lighthouse could not have been better. However, as a result of numerous construction delays, the canal was still many years away from being completed.

———————

In July, 1885, Sir Richard Cartwright, Liberal Member of Parliament for Huron, asked the Conservative Government's Minister of Railways and Canals about the progress of the work on the Murray Canal:

> Sir RICHARD CARTWRIGHT. I should like to have full information about the position of work on the Murray canal. The work should have been in much more forward state than it is. The quantity of work to be done is comparatively small.... I should be glad to know what further information the hon. gentleman has on the subject.
>
> Mr. POPE. I have no further information on the subject. The contract was let on 4th August, 1882...[37]

The only other information forthcoming from the Minister was a brief comment contained in his annual report that, "The works have been steadily prosecuted and excavation has been carried on over the entire extent of the canal proper."[38]

In May of the following year, with the Murray Canal still not open for navigation, Sir Richard continued with the same line of questioning during the annual budget debates:

Sir RICHARD CARTWRIGHT. What time was it to be completed?

Mr. BOWELL [Conservative M.P. for Hastings North]. I think it was to be completed in three years.

Sir RICHARD CARTWRIGHT. What is the reason for the delay?

Mr. BOWELL. I think the work is of much greater magnitude than they supposed when they took it in hand. I am also under the impression that it is not being pushed as rapidly as contemplated — why I cannot say.

Sir RICHARD CARTWRIGHT. I would ask the Minister of Finance to be prepared to give us fuller information on concurrence as to the cause of delay, as I think it is not right that it should be delayed two or three years longer than the contract time.

Mr. BOWELL. I quite agree with you.[39]

(78) **View of the Murray Canal, showing the construction of the swing bridge pier, c. 1888.** Photographer unknown.
Three years after the original projected completion date of the canal, construction was still in progress.
[Courtesy of Library and Archives Canada, PA-181476]

Construction problems continued to delay the completion of the canal and, three years later, Sir Richard was still badgering the government on this point. Furthermore, by 1889, plans to deepen the St. Lawrence canals to fourteen feet were threatening to compromise the usefulness of the Murray Canal:

> Sir RICHARD CARTWRIGHT. It is seven years since it [the Murray Canal] was commenced, and it was promised to be built in two, or, in the outside, in three years, and the reason given for the delay was that there was difficulty experienced from time to time. That canal contract was let out in 1882, and certainly the time has been exceeded by several years. I think it has got a depth of only 10 feet....
>
> So that it cannot be used for vessels of the draught you propose to send down the St. Lawrence. It would be available only for vessels of small draught.
>
> Sir JOHN A. MACDONALD [Prime Minister]. Vessels of a smaller draught of course; vessels that would require to go by the Bay of Quinté by the County of Prince Edward into the open lake. It is calculated it would be extensively used by steamers and barges carrying ores across to the United States, which is expected to be a very large business.[40]

The contractors were able to dig the canal to a depth of just over twelve feet. After seven years of work, the first ships finally passed through the Murray Canal late in 1889. It was officially opened for navigation on April 14, 1890, as reported by a "Notice to Mariners":

NOTICE TO MARINERS.
No. 56 of 1891
MURRAY CANAL AND APPROACHES, INCLUDING
AIDS TO NAVIGATION.
Description of canal.

The Murray Canal is a straight cut (tangent) 6 ½ statute miles long between extremities of piers, 80 feet wide on the bottom, and 12 ½ feet deep below the ordinary low water level of Lake Ontario... joining the head of the Bay of Quinté with Presqu'Ile Bay in Lake Ontario.... At each end of the canal cribwork piers have been built out on both sides into the shallow water, and beyond them a dredged channel 200 feet wide has been continued until water of the same depth as that in the canal is reached....

The canal was opened for traffic on 14th April, 1890, and completed in August, 1890. Its approaches have been marked by a system of buoys and lighted beacons....[41]

The "lighted beacons" were small, open-framework light towers — one at each end of the canal, built and staffed by the Department of Railways and Canals. Details about these two towers are presented in the next chapter.

In spite of Sir Richard Cartwright's misgivings, the Murray Canal was an immediate success. The first ten weeks of operation saw 264 vessels use the canal.[42] The entire navigation season for 1890 saw a total of 101,504 tons of shipping and 12,589 passengers pass through the new waterway, while the following year saw a further fifty percent increase in tonnage and more than a thirty percent increase in passenger traffic. While those numbers represented only a fraction of the total tonnage that had passed through the well-used Welland Canal that year, they were comparable with traffic on the Rideau Canal between Kingston and Ottawa.[43]

With the opening of the Murray Canal, the Inside Passage was finally complete from Kingston harbour all the way through to Presqu'ile Bay. Six lighthouses already along this route, together with the new light towers at each end of the canal, helped to guide ships navigating this protected waterway. The number of ships sailing through the Bay of Quinte began to increase steadily, and this traffic was expected to continue to grow as ship captains took advantage of this safer, if not quicker, route to and from the St. Lawrence River. Over the course of the next two decades, as the number and size of ships sailing here increased, an additional fifteen lighthouses and light towers would be built along this waterway to further ensure the safety and convenience of navigation of the Inside Passage.

(79) Steamers in the Murray Canal, c. 1910. Photographer unknown.
The Murray Canal was officially opened to shipping on April 14, 1890. Over 100,000 tons of shipping passed through the canal that year along with more than 12,000 passengers aboard steamboats. In the foreground is the steamer *Varuna*, a wooden-hulled propeller built in 1880.
[Postcard from author's collection]

Centre Brother Island Lighthouse (1890)

Within five months of the opening of the Murray Canal in 1890, the first of these new lighthouses was constructed on Centre Brother Island.

The Three Brothers are tiny islands guarding the Lower Gap just opposite Collins Bay, twelve kilometers west of the wharves in Kingston harbour. A decade earlier, just as the government was deciding to proceed with the Murray Canal, Prince Edward Member of Parliament, James McCuaig, had asked that a lighthouse be built on one of these islands. As reported by the *British Whig* newspaper in 1881, "He advocated the placing of a light on one of the Brothers, as many vessels get ashore at that point. A light there would save hundreds of dollars."[44]

Six months later in the House of Commons, McCuaig pressed the Minister of Marine to have the lighthouse built:

> Mr. MCQUAIG. I called the attention of the hon. the Acting Minister of Marine to... the desirability of constructing a lighthouse, similar to the one recently placed at South Bay Point [Prince Edward Point], on the most northerly of the Islands in the Bay of Quinte known as the Brothers [at the Lower Gap]. The construction of this lighthouse is much needed in the interest of all vessels passing and repassing this narrow portion of the Bay of Quinte.[45]

Not only did McCuaig not get any satisfactory answers about this lighthouse, but he was voted out of office two months later after the government decided to dig the Murray Canal through Northumberland County instead of through McCuaig's own Prince Edward County.

Five years later, in 1887, a petition was sent to the Minister of Marine and Fisheries, George Foster, asking for a lighthouse on one of the Brother Islands:

> To the honorable minister of Marine & Fisheries
> The Petition of the undersigned Steamboat and vessel owners and masters and others interested in the navigation of Lake Ontario and the River St. Lawrence, respectfully shews, that a Light House is and has been for a long time past much needed, on Lake Ontario about nine miles West of Kingston near the lower gap at the entrance of the Bay of Quinte, on one of the Three Islands called The Brothers, there situated.
> There is a great deal of Shoal water in the vicinity and frequent accidents have happened in consequence. Your Petitioners therefore pray that a light house may be placed on one of the said Islands....[46]

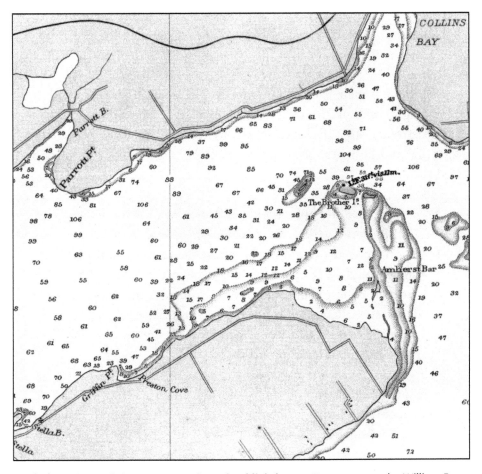

(80) Location of the Centre Brother Island lighthouse. From a survey by William P. Anderson, 1893. Detail of Lake Ontario, Eastern Part of the Bay of Quinte Kingston to Deseronto, published by the British Admiralty, 1898, updated 1901.

The Brother Islands are situated in the North Channel adjacent to the Lower Gap, between Collins Bay to the north and Amherst Island to the south. The lighthouse on Centre Brother Island is marked "Lt.F. 31ft. vis. 11m." (Light, fixed, 31 feet above the water, visible 11 miles in clear weather).

[Courtesy of Library and Archives Canada, R11630-1-2-E]

The Murray Canal was still under construction, but a number of the ship owners who signed the petition, including E.W. Rathbun of Deseronto and D.W. Allison of Ernestown, undoubtedly realized the potential of the new canal, so they lobbied further by writing to their Member of Parliament, Uriah Wilson, representing the riding of Lennox, urging him to bring the matter up with the Minister of Marine.[47]

Although there had been no money allocated in that year's budget for a lighthouse on Centre Brother Island, the political pressure had the desired result. In September, 1888, the Chief Engineer of the Marine and Fisheries Department, William P. Anderson, commented on the proposal:

> There is no appropriation in this year's list for a Light at this Point which has been asked for repeatedly. My report upon the matter has been to the effect that a small Light would be of benefit to the passenger steamers plying between Kingston and the Bay of Quinte, as the trade will doubtless be increased when the Murray Canal is open. As no one lives on the Island a small dwelling will be required: probable cost of building $2000.[48]

A small plot of land on the island was procured from the Indian Department, and the following year, the Marine and Fisheries Department announced that:

> Plans have been prepared and tenders will shortly be invited for the erection of a lighthouse on the north point of the Centre Brother Island, on the north Shore of Lake Ontario, in the County of Lenox. This light, it is expected, will be of great benefit to the constantly increasing traffic between Kingston and the Bay of Quinté and will also enable vessels to use the Inside Passage in heavy weather.[49]

In January, 1890, ten tenders were received for the construction of the Centre Brother Island lighthouse. The leading contenders for the contract were Roderick Cameron of Lancaster who had already built four lighthouses in the region, and J.W. Fegan of Milford who had built the lighthouse at Prince Edward Point a decade earlier. The tender amounts ranged from a high of $3,250 from Mr. George A. Cluff of Napanee, to a low of $1,085 from Mr. N.J. Leonard of Westbrook. In February, 1890, the contract was awarded to the lowest bidder, Leonard,[50] who completed the lighthouse by July of that year.[51]

The lantern for the Centre Brother Island lighthouse was built by the E. Chanteloup Company of Montreal and the lamp was ordered from Chance Bros. in England. Even though the lamp did not arrive on time, the Marine Department decided to place a temporary light in the new lighthouse so that they could put it into service as soon as possible.[52] The minister's report of 1890 announced the details:

> The lighthouse on the north point of the Centre Brother Island, on the north shore of Lake Ontario, in the County of Lennox, referred to in last year's report, was satisfactorily completed under contract by Mr. Nathaniel J. Leonard, of Westbrook, his contract price being $1,085.
>
> The light was put in operation for the first time on the 15th September, 1890.
>
> It is fixed white, elevated 31 feet above the level of the lake, and should be visible 10 miles from all points of approach. The illuminating apparatus is dioptric, of small size.
>
> The tower is a square wooden building, and, with kitchen attached, is painted white. The iron lantern surmounting it is red. The height from the base to the vane of the lantern is 31 feet.[53]

(81) Centre Brother Island lighthouse, c. 1910. Photographer unknown.
This lighthouse was a slightly smaller copy of the Salmon Point and Prince Edward Point lighthouses.
[Courtesy of Queen's University Archives, Kingston, V23-Reg-BrothersIsland]

The Centre Brother Island lighthouse became the third lighthouse on the shores of eastern Lake Ontario built with a pyramidal tower and an attached keeper's dwelling. It was virtually identical to the lighthouses at Salmon Point (1871) and Prince Edward Point (1881). However, instead of being fitted with a catoptric illuminator like its two sister towers, the apparatus in the Centre Brother Island lighthouse was of the dioptric type: an "anchor light lens" procured from England at a cost of $103.66.[54]

Amherst Island resident, Robert Filson, was hired as the first keeper of the Centre Brother Island lighthouse at a salary of $200.[55] It appears that Filson, who lived near the town of Stella, had quickly decided that he would prefer to be an "absentee" keeper, and he immediately hired an assistant named Richards who, with his family, resided on the island and performed all of the lightkeeping duties that Filson had been hired to do.[56]

During his annual inspection tour of lighthouses, Chief Engineer Anderson stopped at Centre Brother Island in June, 1891. In addition to inspecting the lighthouse, he was there to replace the temporary light with the Chance Bros. anchor lamp which had been received in Ottawa the previous October. Anderson's report to the Deputy Minister of Marine and Fisheries commented on the situation with the lightkeeper:

> Re: Centre Brother lighthouse site:
> I beg to report that I visited Kingston yesterday, fitted up in the lantern the illuminating apparatus sent out by Chance for that station, instructed the keeper in its use, and inspected the station generally....
> The lightkeeper is supplementing his income by fishing, but does not appear to be making a nuisance of it....
> I find that the keeper is farming out the light to a man named Richards, who is living at the station with his wife and young family, and has been there constantly since the light was put in operation. I believe the practice of having deputy keepers to be a bad one, although Mr. Richards seems to be a good, intelligent-looking man.[57]

The Deputy-Minister responded with his comments on the unofficial assistant keeper:

> Ask keeper about this & say this entirely against the regulations and that if he will not keep the light himself, some other person will be found do it. Also that he never mentioned this when at the Dept a short time ago.[58]

Filson replied by saying that the dwelling attached to the tower on Center Brother Island was too small for his family to live in. Since the town of Stella was a good two hours away by rowboat, Filson proposed that the Department build a two-room addition onto the lighthouse so that he could move to the island with his wife and children, and he went as far as having a contractor draw up plans and quote on the work. Anderson agreed that the original attached dwelling was not intended to be used by a family, and he commented that the $136 cost of the addition to the dwelling was reasonable:

> Re addition to lighthouse at Centre Brothers:
>
> It seems to me useless attempting to build any small towers without making full dwelling accomodation.
>
> The estimate herewith enclosed [$136.08] is very reasonable and the enclosed addition would make quite a comfortable house for the keeper....
>
> It was originally intended to entrust the keeping to a resident of the immediate locality who would not require to reside in the building. The man appointed resides 7 miles distant, I understand, and has a deputy with a family permanently resident in the lighthouse. If the building is to be used as a residence I consider the addition proposed necessary, and the offer is a very cheap one.[59]

Even though Deputy Minister William Smith agreed with Anderson, the Minister of Marine and Fisheries, Charles Tupper, refused the request saying:

> ... it is too expensive an outlay to make at present for this station.... I may here mention that it is against the rules of the Department to allow a lightkeeper to perform his duties by deputy, and unless the keeper can arrange to live at the lighthouse station himself some other person will have to be appointed lightkeeper who will personally attend to and perform the duties required....[60]

Filson reluctantly agreed to do the work of lightkeeper himself. Whether or not he moved his family to Centre Brother Island is unknown, but he stayed on as keeper for four years until he was replaced by Michael O'Rourke in 1894.[61]

Brighton Range Lights (1891)

At the other end of the Inside Passage, the Marine and Fisheries Department had come to the conclusion that buoys alone marking the circuitous channel through Presqu'ile Bay leading to the western end of the recently opened Murray Canal were insufficient to guide ships to and from the canal. Shortly after the canal was opened to shipping, the department's engineers had recommended that the winding channel through Presqu'ile Bay be marked with a combination of buoys and range lights. The Department's annual report for 1890 stated that:

> In consequence of the opening of the Murray Canal it has been necessary to place eight new spar buoys to indicate the channel in the approaches, and it is in contemplation during the coming winter to build three range-light towers on cribs in Presqu'Isle Bay, to guide through the dredged channel from the upper entrance of the Murray Canal to Presqu'Isle Point.
>
> It is expected that when these lights are established the range lights at Presqu'Isle [Salt Point and Presqu'ile rear range light] and the Calf Pasture Shoal light can be discontinued.[62]

In order to differentiate these new range lights from the old Presqu'ile Range lights, the new range lights were always referred to as the Brighton Range lights.

The report for 1891 announced that, "Three new range light buildings on piers were established in Presqu'Isle Bay, and were put in operation on the 10th of September last [1891]. They were erected under contract by Mr. Walter Alford, of Belleville, the contract price being $5,995."[63]

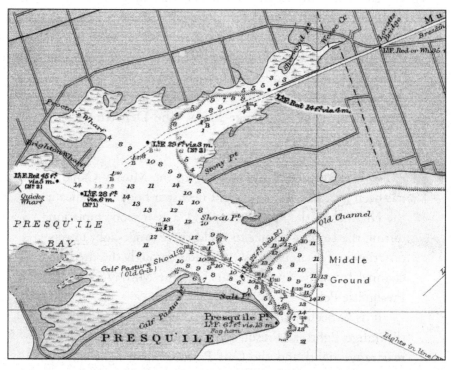

(82) Chart of Presqu'ile Bay showing the three Brighton Range lights. From a survey by W.P. Anderson, 1893. Detail of *Lake Ontario, Western Part of the Bay of Quinte and Presqu'ile Bay*, published by the British Admiralty, 1900, updated 1911.

The Brighton Range lights, established in 1891 to help guide ships to and from the Murray Canal, are marked as No.1 (moved from Calf Pasture Shoal), No. 2 between Quick's Wharf and Brighton Wharf, and No. 3 on the dredged channel leading to the canal. In addition, the Murray Canal West Pier light can be seen marked as "Lt.F. Red 14ft. vis.4m. (Light, Fixed Red, 14 feet above the water, visible 4 miles). The East and West Pier lights, were set on wooden towers erected by the Department of Railways and Canals in 1890 when the Murray Canal opened
[Courtesy of Library and Archives Canada, R11630-2426-0-E]

Alford was a well known local building contractor who had built post offices in Belleville and in Trenton, and had also erected the Belleville harbour lighthouse ten years earlier. He was contracted to build three piers — timber cribs filled with rocks — in Presqu'ile Bay. On two of the three piers, new lighthouses were to be erected. On the third pier, the lighthouse moved from Calf Pasture Shoal would be placed.

The official "Notice to Mariners", gave further details:

BRIGHTON RANGE LIGHTS

A range light, which will be known as Brighton Range Light, No. 3, established by the Government of Canada, was put in operation on the 10th instant.

The tower is a square wooden building painted white, and 30 feet height from its base to the vane on the lantern. It stands upon an octagonal cribwork pier sunk in 15 feet water in the axis of the canal and on the north side of the channel....

The light is fixed white, elevated 29 feet above the water and visible 3 miles down the canal and in the direction of No. 1 range light....

A range light which will be known as the Brighton Range Light No. 2, established under similar circumstances, stands... 1,440 feet from Brighton wharf.

The light is fixed red, elevated 45 feet above the water, and should be visible six miles down the canal in alignment with No. 3....

The tower is a square wooden building, painted white, 47 feet high and stands on a square cribwork pier sunk in Presqu'Ile Bay in 7 feet water.

A range light which will be known as Brighton Range Light No. 1, established at the same time, stands... 1,100 feet from Brighton wharf.

The light is fixed white, elevated 28 feet above the water, and should be visible six miles in alignment with No. 2, and also towards No. 3 light.

The tower is a square wood building, painted white, with iron lantern red, is 30 feet high and stands on an octagonal cribwork pier sunk in Presqu'Ile Bay in 14 feet water....

24th September, 1891.[64]

Hedley Simpson, who had become the keeper of the Presqu'ile Range lights after his father's death in 1888, was retained as the keeper of the new Brighton Range lights.[65]

The Narrows Shoal Lights (1892 & 1894)

The Marine Department engineers next turned their attention to the Bay of Quinte end of the Murray Canal, where there were shoals in the vicinity of the eastern approaches to the canal. With the increased traffic along the Inside Passage it was necessary that these shoals be adequately marked. By 1894, more than 11,000 passengers were being carried every year into and out of the Bay of Quinte through the canal on steamboats.[66] Canal statistics for the period 1891 through to the end of 1894, show that while the number of ships using the canal decreased from more than one thousand to less than seven hundred, the average registered tonnage of these ships almost doubled from 140 tons to 274 tons.[67] Ships of greater registered tonnage were larger ships, and larger ships generally required deeper water to navigate safely. These larger ships were more likely to "bottom out" on the shoals that dotted the bay at a number of locations. In addition, the safety of the ships' passengers was always a consideration of the Marine Department when determining the necessity of a lighthouse. This was especially the case with The Narrows Shoal (known as the Nigger Island Shoal until its name was officially changed in 1966 [68]), located between Belleville and Trenton, just nine kilometers from the eastern entrance to the Murray Canal.

Tom Rubidge, whose uncle, F.P. Rubidge, had designed the Pleasant Point lighthouse three decades earlier, was the Superintending

Engineer of the Trent Canal and the Murray Canal. He mentioned in his 1882 report on the improvements required to the Bay of Quinte that, for the purpose of safe navigation of steamboats, "... westward [from Telegraph Island] to the head of the bay, all that is now required to render the channel safe, and easy, is a light on Nigger Island [renamed Makatewis Island in 1966], 9 miles above Belleville, and a few buoys where it is tortuous or contracted." [69]

In 1892, the Marine and Fisheries Department established a temporary light on a nearby marshy point known as Potters Island:

> In consequence of the opening of the Murray Canal and the resultant increase of traffic, urgent demands were made for a light in the neighbourhood of Nigger Island [Makatewis Island], in the Bay of Quinté, at a point where the channel is narrow and intricate. It was not considered desirable to establish a permanent light at this point until a hydrographic survey of the bay should determine with exactness the proper location for such an aid to navigation, but partly as an experiment a temporary pole light has been established on the north point of Potters Island on the Prince Edward shore, opposite Nigger Island. The light, which is fixed white, shown from a tubular lantern hoisted to the top of a mast 20 feet high, was put in operation on the 22nd June last. It is elevated 22 feet above the water level and should be visible nine miles from all points of approach seawards.[70]

It is unclear from the chief engineer's report exactly what the "experiment" was meant to prove. He may have been testing the use of a weatherproof, hand-held lantern on an simple mast to determine how it might fare as an inexpensive alternative to the more common, and more expensive, enclosed lighthouse, or he may have been trying to gauge the effectiveness of a light in that vicinity by soliciting the opinions of mariners who frequented the Inside Passage.

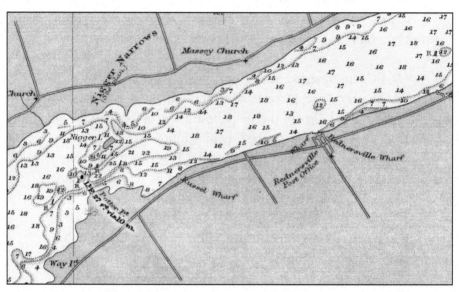

(83) Chart of The Narrows between Belleville and Trenton. From a survey by W.P. Anderson, 1893. Detail of *Lake Ontario, Western Part of the Bay of Quinte and Presqu'ile Bay*, published by the British Admiralty, 1900, updated 1911.

Potters Island is a marshy point marked on the chart as "Potter Pt." The Narrows Shoal lighthouse is shown as "Lt.F. 27ft. vis. 10m" (Light, Fixed, 27 feet above the water, visible 10 miles in clear weather). It was built on a pier just off of Makatewis Island (marked as Nigger I.) in 1894.

[Courtesy of Library and Archives Canada, R11630-2426-0-E]

The "Notice to Mariners" published in 1892, provides few clues about the purpose of the Potters Island light:

> A mast temporarily established by the Government of Canada on the outer point of Potters Island... was put in operation on the 22nd [of June]....
>
> The light is fixed white and is shown from a tubular lantern hoisted to the top of a mast 20 feet high....
>
> It is intended to guide to the narrow channel between Nigger Island [Makatewis Island] and the south shore from the Bay of Quinté Bridge [the swing bridge from Belleville to Rossmore] on the east, and from the east entrance of the Murray Canal on the west....
>
> 14th July, 1892.[71]

Frank Dempsey was paid ten dollars per month during the navigation season as keeper of the Potters Island light.[72]

In order to determine the best location for a light in the vicinity of Makatewis Island, and to provide a detailed navigational chart of the Bay of Quinte for use by the many ship captains then using the bay, Marine and Fisheries Chief Engineer William Anderson personally supervised a detailed hydrographic survey of the waterway in 1893. He summarized his activities in his annual report to the Minister:

> Hydrographic Survey of the Bay of Quinte
>
> The completion of the Murray Canal greatly increased the traffic, especially by steam vessels, through the Bay of Quinté, and it was found that the want of a chart of that bay, parts of which are very shallow, was a great detriment to navigation.
>
> In compliance with strong representations made by ship owners to the department, a hydrographic survey of the bay was undertaken, which has been carried out during the past season under my personal supervision. The triangulation of the bay was effected on the ice during February and

March, and the sounding was carried on between May and September, when the work was satisfactorily completed....

The whole of the Bay of Quinté has been surveyed from the Murray Canal to Centre Brother Island, and the charts to be published will include the work done by the American Government between Kingston and Centre Brother Island, in connection with the Murray Canal....

These charts are now being prepared by the permanent staff of the department, and it is to be hoped will be ready for publication by the opening of navigation....[73]

Following the completion of his hydrographic survey, Anderson announced that the Department would replace the light on Potter's Island with a permanent lighthouse to mark The Narrows Shoal:

During the past season a complete hydrographic survey of the Bay of Quinté has been made, and the results of this survey show that the temporary light established last year on Potter's Island was not in the best position for leading through the narrow and critical channel between Nigger Island [Makatewis Island] and Potter's Island. The Chief engineer having reported that a light at this point should be built on a pier on a shoal [The Narrows Shoal] south-west of Nigger Island, plans and specifications have been prepared and a contract has been entered into for the completion of the work by the opening of navigation next year. Mr. Wm. J. Gates of Kingston, who submitted the lowest tender, has been awarded the contract at $2,000.[74]

William Gates built the wood-framed pyramidal tower and it was put into service in the spring. The completion of The Narrows Shoal lighthouse and the de-activation of the Potters Island light was announced by the "Notice to Mariners" in June 1894:

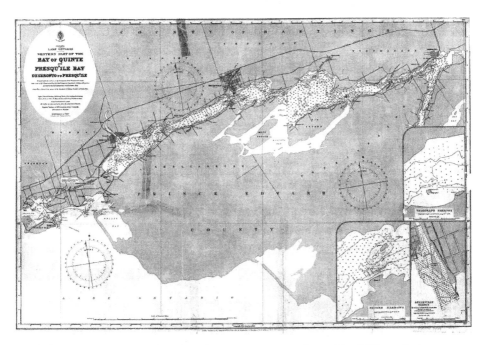

(84) Chart of the Bay of Quinte from a survey conducted by William Anderson, Thomas Drummond, and F.A Wilkin in 1893. *Lake Ontario, Western Part of the Bay of Quinte and Presqu'ile Bay.*

As a result of increased shipping traffic through the Bay of Quinte after the opening of the Murray Canal, William P. Anderson, Chief Engineer of the Marine and Fisheries Department, undertook to personally survey the bay from end to end. Initially trained as a surveyor, he also surveyed many of the islands in eastern Lake Ontario on which lighthouses were constructed. His survey of the Bay of Quinte was augmented by those done by the Department of Railways and Canals and by the U.S. Corps of Engineers. This chart of the eastern part of the Bay of Quinte was published by the British Admiralty in 1898. The chart of the western portion of the bay was published in 1900. Both charts were updated and reprinted throughout the early part of the 20th Century.

[Courtesy of Library and Archives Canada, R11630-2426-0-E]

NOTICE TO MARINERS
No. 21 of 1894
NIGGER ISLAND SHOAL LIGHT.
[Narrows Shoal Light]

A lighthouse established by the Government of Canada on a pier on Nigger Island Shoal [Narrows Shoal], in the Bay of Quinte, between the West riding of Hastings and the County of Prince Edward, Ontario, was put in operation on the 6th instant [June 6, 1894]....

The light is fixed white, elevated 27 feet above the level of the bay, and should be visible 10 miles from all points of approach. The illuminating apparatus is dioptric, of the 7th order.

The lighthouse is a square wooden tower, surmounted by a square wooden lantern, the whole painted white. It is 27 feet in height from the deck of the pier to the top of the lantern. It stands upon a cribwork pier sunk in 11 feet of water on the north side of the steamboat channel, and near the western extremity of the shoal running south-westwardly from Nigger Island [Makatewis Island] towards Potters Island....

DISCONTINUANCE OF POTTERS ISLAND LIGHT.

In consequence of the establishment of the light on Nigger Island shoal [Narrows shoal], as above described, the mast light temporarily maintained on the north point of Potters Island... is no longer required and has been discontinued....

Wm. Smith,
Ottawa, Canada, 1st June, 1894.[75]

The new lighthouse was a wood-framed pyramidal design, almost identical to a dozen other towers in the region, and its 7th Order dioptric apparatus was a small Fresnel lens similar to those used in anchor lights which had been installed in a number of other lighthouses.

(85) Narrows Shoal lighthouse, c.1903. Photographer unknown.
[From "Annual Report of the Department of Marine and Fisheries, 1903", *Sessional Papers of the Dominion of Canada*, Session 1904.]

Unlike other lighthouses in the region, no provision had been made for a lightkeeper's dwelling. The first lightkeeper, Carson Jeffery, would have lived on the mainland somewhere nearby where the Department built a boathouse where he stored the boat he would use to travel to and from The Narrows Shoal lighthouse.[76] For his services, Jeffery was paid a salary of $200.00 per year.[77]

Other Private Lights (c. 1900)

Not all harbour lights were built and maintained at the expense of the Canadian Government. Some, such as the wharf light atop Billa Flint's warehouse at Belleville, were strictly private affairs. Others, including the first Belleville Harbour lighthouse, the early lighthouse on the marine railway pier in Kingston harbour, and the Portsmouth Harbour lights, had all been established by local municipal councils who realized the importance of guiding ships safely to and from the wharves in their harbours.

In 1892, the Marine and Fisheries Department reported that there were twelve wharf lights at various harbours throughout the Province of Ontario that were maintained by municipalities or by private companies.[78] By 1899, there were more than twenty-three private lights scattered across the province that had either been built outright by towns or companies, or had been funded in part by the federal government but were staffed and maintained at local expense.[79] In addition, a number of private lights were built along the Inside Passage after the opening of the Murray Canal. These included a pair of private range lights erected at Trenton, private wharf lights shown at Bath harbour, and a private lighthouse on Garden Island.

Little is known about the private range lights at Trenton, except that they were replaced at government expense in 1905 (see Chapter 9).

At Bath, wharf lights had been in use for some time. In 1877, this deepwater port on the North Channel had been granted status as a customs outport under the jurisdiction of the port of Kingston, and a sub-collector of customs had been appointed.[80] A "Private Light" was marked on the 1904 edition of the U.S. Corps of Engineers' chart of Lake Ontario, but there is no indication of the type of structure that held the light.[81] By 1912, more than 80,000 tons of cargo were entering and clearing the port on an annual basis, and a number of private lights had been established there. A brief description of Bath is given in the Department of Marine and Fisheries' *Port Directory* for 1912:

> BATH HARBOUR, county of Lennox and Addington, Ontario, is in the north channel of Bay of Quinte, opposite Amherst island, in the eastern end of lake Ontario. The depth of water in the harbour is from 15 feet alongside the wharves to 40 feet off the town, where there is good anchorage. The wharves are: one 140 feet long with 17 feet of water, with coal shed, grain warehouse, ice-house and general freight shed; one 140 feet long and 85 feet front with 12 feet of water, with a flour mill upon it, coal shed and grain warehouse and

wharf with similar buildings. Lights are maintained on these wharves by the owners and steamboat companies.

The total tonnage entered and cleared at this port for the fiscal year 1912 was 87,994 tons.[82]

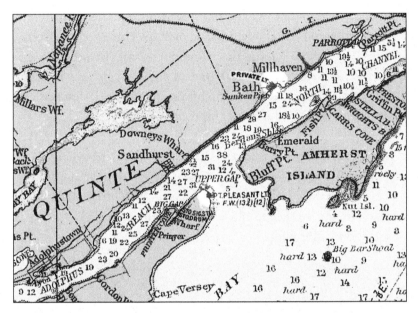

(86) Chart showing "Private Lt." at Bath. Detail from *Chart, Lake Ontario, by U.S. Lake Survey*, Corps of Engineers, 1904.

Although never recognized as official aids to navigation, private lights were often erected on wharves and warehouses at the expense of towns or private companies. This chart is an updated edition of the original U.S. Lake Survey chart published in 1877. [Courtesy of NOAA's Office of Coast Survey Historical Map & Chart Collection http:// historicalcharts.noaa.gov LS106-01-1904]

Twenty-five kilometers away, Garden Island, situated just off of Wolfe Island opposite Kingston, was the headquarters of D.D. Calvin's marine enterprises. Delano Dexter Calvin had started a lumbering business at Clayton, New York, before moving his operation to Garden Island in 1844. Calvin and several partners, had established a successful business rafting timber down the St. Lawrence River from Garden Island to Quebec City. The company also operated a steam tug service under government contract for towing barges to and from Montreal, a shipyard and a busy marine salvage operation. Later, Calvin was elected warden of Frontenac County, after which he was elected to represent the county in the Ontario legislature from 1877 until his death in 1884. Calvin had also been a member of the 1870 Canal Commission and became a major benefactor of Queen's University in Kingston.[83]

With all of Calvin's marine businesses headquartered on Garden Island, there would usually be dozens of ships going to and from the island's wharves throughout the shipping season. In order to guide ships safely to their berths, Calvin had his own private lighthouse built, a passing reference to which was made in a description of Garden Island by D.D. Calvin's grandson:

> Landing on the island — you stepped off the wharf on to the solid rock — you had on your right a double dwelling house (afterwards the store and Post Office) and, beyond that, to the west, the old sail loft with the firm's private lighthouse atop of it.[84]

(87) Calvin Company buildings on Garden Island, c.1900. Photographer unknown. The island, just 1.5 nautical miles from the wharves at Kingston, was the headquarters of the Calvin Company. The company engaged in the timber trade as well as shipbuilding and salvage operations. A private lighthouse on Garden Island was built atop the sail loft to help guide ships to the company's wharves. [From Calvin, *A Saga of the St. Lawrence*, 1945]

This lighthouse may have been similar to the Deseronto Harbour lighthouse atop the Rathbun Company warehouse; simply a lantern built onto the roof of an existing building.

2nd Snake Island Shoal Lighthouse (1900)

At nearby Snake Island shoal, the government decided, after almost four decades of complaints from mariners, to demolish the old stone lighthouse and replace it with one further out in the channel to better mark the shoal water. Even though shipping traffic into Kingston harbour was declining — from a high of 5,500 arrivals and departures of steamboats and sailing ships in 1885, down to 4,600 by 1900, Kingston was still the busiest Canadian port on Lake Ontario next to Toronto.[85] More importantly, ever since the establishment of the original lighthouse in 1858, ships continued to run aground on the shoals in the South Channel in the immediate vicinity of the lighthouse. This was not surprising as the average size of the ships coming into the harbour was ever increasing to the extent that, by 1900, the average ship had a registered tonnage of 288 tons, with at least sixty of them in excess of 400 tons, including the Calvin Company's schooner *Ceylon* at 908 tons, and the propeller *Rosedale,* owned by the St. Lawrence and Chicago Steam Navigation Company, at 977 tons.[86] All of these larger ships required deeper water in which to sail safely.

Tallying newspaper reports of ships grounded or ashore in the vicinity of Snake Island between 1858 and 1900, we find that there were more than forty such casualties, averaging at least one every year. This cost ship captains time and it cost ship owners money. Even if there was usually little damage to the ship, it could take several days to "lighter" the cargo — that is, to lighten the stranded ship by transferring a portion of the ship's cargo to smaller boats or lighters, until the ship could float free — or several days could pass before one of D.D. Calvin's tugboats from Garden Island, or another steamer was available to tow the stranded vessel off the rocks. Not only would this delay the ship, but it would often cost hundreds of dollars. The Kingston newspaper, the *British Whig*, reported the cost of one such occurrence in 1884:

(88) The steamer *Rosedale*, 1898. Photograph by William Traill.
At 246 feet long, with a registered tonnage of 977 tons, this steel-hulled ship was one of the largest ships sailing the Great Lakes at the end of the 19th Century. Larger ships like the *Rosedale* drew more water than smaller ships. As a result, new lighthouses were built to guide them towards the deeper shipping channels. [Courtesy of Toronto Marine Historical Society]

> The schr. *Halstead*, consigned to the Kingston & Montreal Forwarding Co., ran ashore on Snake Island last night. She is laden with grain. The tug *Wright* went to her assistance this morning. The K. & M.T. Co. charged the owners of the schr. *Halstead* $500 for services rendered in connection with taking her off the rocks opposite Snake Island.[87]

If the ship was also damaged or lost altogether, the costs could mount into the thousands of dollars.

Mariners had complained for years about the Snake Island Shoal lighthouse. Some thought it should be moved to a location closer to the centre of the South Channel, while others argued that it should be placed on the other side of the channel, on Simcoe Island's Four Mile Point. In 1886, Captain Dix of the schooner *White Oak* wrote:

> Snake Island shoals are not properly buoyed off.... There should be a lighthouse put on Four Mile Point as a guide to vessels entering the harbour on a dark night, as the deep

water is close to the shore. Snake Island light is too back on the shoal to be of any use on a dark night.[88]

It was not until 1898 that the Marine and Fisheries Department decided to build a new lighthouse further out in the South Channel. That winter, W.H. Noble, one of the Department's lighthouse construction foremen, took a work crew out onto the ice with the intention of taking advantage of the frozen channel to enable them to start construction on a pier that would hold the lighthouse. In the spring, Chief Engineer William Anderson reported on the crew's progress:

> Snake Island. — A steel casing for a concrete pier, to serve as a foundation for a lighthouse at a point nearer the channel than the existing lighthouse, which with its pier is in a very bad state of repair, was prepared last winter at a cost of $483.18, but the ice was not sufficiently strong to work upon, and the completion of this new aid was deferred until this winter. I conferred with Kingston mariners respecting aids in this locality and the pier is being placed, and additional buoys provided in accordance with their requirements.[89]

A "Notice to Mariners" for 1899 announced the pending change in the lighthouse's location:

NOTICE TO MARINERS
No. 39 of 1899
DOMINION OF CANADA — ONTARIO.

II. Proposed change in position of Snake Island shoal lighthouse
> A cylindrical steel and concrete pier has been built near the south end of the shoal surrounding Snake Island, at a distance of 850 feet S.E. by E. ¼ E. from the existing lighthouse on the shoal. It is intended to erect on this foundation a lighthouse during the present season to replace the old one which will be dismantled.[90]

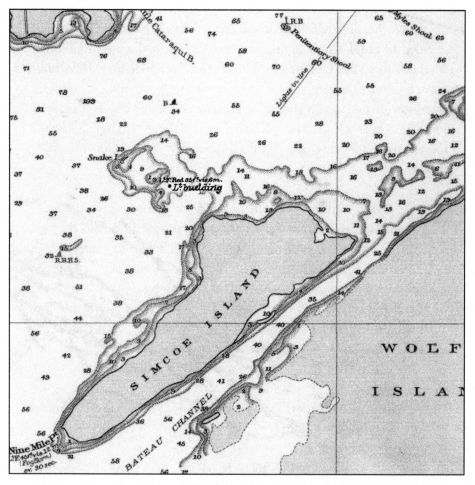

(89) Location of the 2ⁿᵈ Snake Island Shoal lighthouse. From a survey by William P. Anderson, 1893. Detail of *Lake Ontario, Eastern Part of the Bay of Quinte Kingston to Deseronto*, published by the British Admiralty, 1898, updated 1900.

The new lighthouse was to be built further out into the channel and placed on a steel pier filled with concrete. Construction of the pier was started in the winter of 1898. The tower was built the following winter. On this chart, the new lighthouse was still in the process of being constructed so it is marked "Lt. building". The 1st Snake Island Shoal lighthouse is marked "Lt.F.Red 35ft. vis.6m." (Light, Fixed Red, 35 feet above the water, visible 6 miles in clear weather).

[Courtesy of Library and Archives Canada, R11630-2414-4-E]

The following winter, Noble and his crew again ventured out onto the ice off of Snake Island and completed the lighthouse. The total cost was $1,309.07.[91] The official notice announcing the new aid to navigation was issued by the Deputy-Minister of Marine and Fisheries on March 22, 1900:

> The old lighthouse on Snake Island shoal at the eastern extremity of Lake Ontario, has been taken down and a new one has been built on the steel and concrete foundation described in part II of Notice to Mariners No. 39 of 1899, the new lighthouse being 850 feet S. 23º E. true from the old site....
>
> The new tower is an octagonal wooden building with sloping sides painted white, and surmounted by an octagonal iron lantern painted red. It is 39 feet high from its base on the pier to the ventilator on the lantern, and the top of the steel pier is 6 feet above the level of the water.
>
> The light will be put in operation on the opening of navigation, and will be fixed red, elevated 38 feet above the level of the lake, and should be visible 6 miles from all points of approach by water.
>
> The illuminating apparatus is dioptric of the 7th order.[92]

Instead of building a more common pyramidal wood-framed tower on a square plan, Chief Engineer Anderson had chosen to build a tapering tower on an octagonal plan. This was only the second octagonal wood-framed lighthouse to be constructed in eastern Lake Ontario. The first of this design, twenty-five kilometers away on Pleasant Point at the Upper Gap in Prince Edward County, had been constructed in 1866.

John Whitmarsh replaced William Orr as the keeper of the new Snake Island Shoal lighthouse. Unlike the first Snake Island Shoal lighthouse, the new lighthouse did not have a keeper's dwelling attached and there is no record of where Whitmarsh lived. The Whitmarsh family had been established on Wolfe Island since 1851,[93] so it is likely that the new keeper lived within rowing distance of the new lighthouse.

(90) 2ⁿᵈ Snake Island Shoal lighthouse, c.1918. Photographer unknown.
In 1918, the lighthouse was moved from Snake Island Shoal to Four Mile Point on
Simcoe Island. This photograph shows the lighthouse after it had been moved to its
new location on Simcoe Island.
[Courtesy of Library and Archives Canada, PA-172454]

The building of the second Snake Island Shoal lighthouse
represented the end of an era of more than seventy years of traditional
lighthouse construction in eastern Lake Ontario waters. Other fixed
aids to navigation would be built along the Inside Passage and on the
shores of the open lake and its bays, but the majority of these would

be simpler light towers; either open steel frameworks or simple masts with a weatherproof light on top replacing the conventional, enclosed lantern.

This was also the beginning of an era that would see many traditional lighthouses discontinued, demolished or replaced by these simpler, less expensive aids to navigation. The age of the classic, iconic lighthouse was not entirely over, but it was coming to a rapid close.

PART II – THE LIGHTHOUSES

CHAPTER 9

The End of an Era?

Discontinued... without further notice
("Notice to Mariners," 1913)

I n the seven decades since the construction of the first lighthouse
on False Ducks Island, fixed aids to navigation in eastern Lake
Ontario had evolved from conical, masonry structures with catoptric
lights burning sperm-oil, to octagonal and pyramidal wood-framed
towers using dioptric lenses with lamps burning kerosene, Pintsch
gas and acetylene. In spite of the differences in their designs and
lighting systems, they all shared characteristics that made them readily
distinguishable as lighthouses: they were tall towers, usually fully
enclosed, supporting a sizeable glass-enclosed lantern inside of which
was the lighting apparatus.

New building technologies that were adopted over time had altered
the form of the lighthouse, but the object of the lighthouse designer
and engineer never changed. Their intent remained to build a stable,
durable structure that would allow a bright light to be elevated to a
substantial height so that it could be seen at a significant distance over
open water, and to do this as inexpensively as possible.

As a result of newer construction methods in use and building materials that were available by the end of the 19th Century, the traditional lighthouse was being transformed into a simpler, open framework tower made of wood or iron or steel. Many of these structures did not even have a conventional lighthouse lantern. Instead, they were fitted with a weatherproof, hand-held lantern that was hoisted to the top of what would better be described as a light tower rather than a lighthouse.

Early examples of these simpler designs had already been seen in Belleville in 1835, Wellers Bay in 1876, and on Potters Island in 1892. As older lighthouses were replaced by these newer structures, and fewer new fixed aids to navigation were built, the era of the traditional, iconic lighthouse was coming to an end.

Murray Canal Pier Lights (1890 & 1899)

An open wooden framework tower had been used for the Wellers Bay rear range light in 1876, and this model was taken further by the Department of Railways and Canals when they established lights to mark each end of the Murray Canal in 1890, soon after the canal was opened.

While the Marine and Fisheries Department was responsible for building lighthouses all across Canada, including the Brighton Range lights then under construction in Presqu'ile Bay, it was the Railways and Canals Department which controlled the Murray Canal and it was that department's responsibility to provide adequate aids to navigation along the canal proper. Accordingly, the four swing bridges over the canal (three road bridges and one railway bridge) were fitted with warning lights to indicate whether the bridge was opened or closed. After consulting with the Marine and Fisheries Chief Engineer William Anderson, the Department of Railways and Canals also erected light towers on the piers at each end of the Murray Canal to guide ships to the canal entrance.[1] These pier lights are described in the "Notice to Mariners" of 1891:

A fixed red light visible 4 miles from all points of approach by water, shown from a lenticular lantern, elevated 19 feet above the water, standing on a square pyramidal open frame 30 feet from the end of the north pier at the... entrance of the canal....

The frame is 12 feet high above the pier and is painted brown.

The light was first shown on 22nd August, 1890.[2]

The "lenticular lantern" would have been a lamp with a pressed glass lens similar to the anchor lights used in the lighthouses at Belleville and Deseronto. They are described as "copper pier lamps" which were purchased for fifteen dollars each.[3]

Figure 75.1 shows the location of the Murray Canal Pier lights at each end of the canal.

The first keepers of these lights were Fred Fitzgerald and M. McAuliff who were hired in August, 1890, to "attend" the East Pier light and West Pier light respectively. For their services, they were paid a wage of twenty-five cents per day. After only twenty-six days on the job, McAuliff was replaced by C.A. Harries who tended the West Pier light until the close of navigation that year.[4]

Unlike traditional lighthouses that were being built by the Marine and Fisheries Department up to that time, the Murray Canal Pier lights were neither enclosed towers nor did they have a platform at the top to hold a substantial lantern to contain the lighting apparatus. Instead, they were short, open framework structures using a hand-held lantern that would have been hoisted into place at the end of a halyard. Since they were very different from other fixed aids to navigation built before them, and since they were built by a department that had little experience in the field of lighthouse construction, it would be easy to dismiss these short towers as just an anomaly in design and not as a change in the form of lighthouses.

However, the Marine and Fisheries Department itself was always interested in adopting new technologies, designs and construction methods, especially if they were efficient, long-lasting and inexpensive.

The Wellers Bay rear range light with its wooden open framework construction had been an early example of this, and the Department would continue to adopt even simpler designs for light towers.

Five years later, the Superintending Engineer on the Murray Canal, Tom Rubidge, reported to the chief engineer of the Department of Railways and Canals that, "... new and more powerful range lights are required at each end of canal to indicate the dredged channel".[5] However, it was not until another four years had passed that the small open framework towers at each end of the canal were replaced. Rubidge, commented on the new structures in 1899: "The lighthouses erected on the east and west end of piers... are giving great satisfaction and complete the proper lighting of this canal."[6] William Anderson, Chief Engineer of the Marine and Fisheries Department, provided more details about the new lighthouses:

> Murray Canal — The Department of Railways and Canals have improved the character of the lights at the east and west entrances of the Murray Canal, adjoining the Bay of Quinte and Presqu'ile Bay. The former lights were fixed red lights shown from small lanterns standing on brown pyramidal open frames. The new lights are fixed white lights elevated 27 feet above the level of the water and visible five miles from all points of approach. The light buildings, which stand on the sites of the old frameworks, 30 feet from each end of the north pier of the canal, are inclosed hexagonal galvanized iron cabins, with cylindrical columns surmounted by the lenses rising from the apexes of the roofs. Each is 18 feet high, from the deck of the pier to the lens, and is painted white.[7]

These enclosed "cabins" surmounted by an open lantern were another variation of non-traditional lighthouse design. In addition to their design being unique, the galvanized, sheet iron cladding was also a unique material for use in lighthouse construction. The zinc coating on the sheet metal would slow the formation of rust and, presumably, this would last longer than traditional wooden siding. This material was not used on any other lighthouses in the eastern Lake Ontario region.

(91) 2ⁿᵈ Murray Canal East Pier Light, c. 1900. Photographer unknown. These galvanized iron towers replaced the earlier open framework wooden towers built by the Department of Railways and Canals to mark each end of the Murray Canal. [Courtesy of Library and Archives Canada, PA-172508]

Barriefield Common Range Lights (1892)

Range lights had shown their worth for the past forty years on Presqu'ile Bay and on Wellers Bay where they had proven to be effective at guiding ships through narrow channels. Based on that experience, the Marine and Fisheries Department decided to build range lights at Kingston to guide ever larger ships past dangerous shoals to Kingston's wharves. Instead of building enclosed pyramidal wood-framed towers similar to the earlier range lights, the Department chose to use a new and radically different building technology for the towers planned for Kingston: structural iron.

Structural iron had been used in bridges and other construction projects for more than a century. As early as 1788, the American political writer and inventor Thomas Paine had designed a wrought iron bridge that was erected in Yorkshire, England.[8] Cast iron plates had been used to build cylindrical lighthouses in Jamaica, Bermuda and Newfoundland in the 1840's and 1850's. The use of iron in various forms for various structures was well known by the end of the 19th Century. Always looking for ways to increase efficiency while reducing costs, the Department of Marine and Fisheries adopted this building material for the Barriefield Common Range lights.

Larger and larger ships with heavier loads and deeper draughts continued to call at Kingston, the main trans-shipment point for cargoes destined for Montreal and beyond. In December, 1890, a committee of Kingston City Council met to discuss the matter:

RANGE LIGHTS NEEDED — Yesterday a conference of the members of the wharves and harbour committee of the city council and prominent mariners was held in the council chamber, to discuss the necessity of the dominion government placing range lights in the harbour....

Ald. Fenwick asked for opinions whether range lights were desirable. Capt. Taylor, Jr., said lights would keep vessels off the Myles shoal.... Capt. T. Donnelly endorsed range lights. They were needed badly to make the harbor absolutely safe. Capt. Murray concurred and added that many shoals needed buoying.... Capts. Gaskin, Geoghegan, Saunders and Martin wanted range lights. The following committee was appointed to draft a position to the government showing the dangerous condition of the

Kingston harbor and what is necessary to remedy it: Messrs. Gaskin, T. Donnelly, T.F. Taylor, J. Murray, James Dix, and J. Geoghegan....[9]

A petition from the city was forwarded to Ottawa and, in his report of 1891 the Deputy-Minister of Marine noted that:

Urgent representations have been made to this Department for some years past of the necessity for improving the approaches to Kingston harbour, so as to accommodate the heavy draught vessels entering that port, especially late in the autumn, with cargoes of grain, and during the past season the Chief Engineer of the Department made a special examination and report of desirable improvements. As a part of the contemplated improvements it is proposed during the coming season to erect range lights on Barriefield Common, to lead into the freight wharves, clear of all shoals, and tenders will shortly be invited for the construction of skeleton iron towers for this purpose.[10]

The enlargement of the Welland Canal in 1882 had enabled larger ships from the upper lakes loaded with heavier cargoes of grain and drawing up to fourteen feet of water to enter Lake Ontario and sail as far as Kingston or Prescott, where their cargoes were offloaded onto smaller ships or barges for passage down the St. Lawrence River. In 1885, Government trade and navigation statistics showed that more than 5,500 steamboats and sailing vessels with an average registered tonnage of 207 tons had either arrived or departed Kingston harbour.[11] A decade later, even though the total number of ships had declined, the ships were, on average, larger. The 1895 statistics show that the number of cargo vessels had dropped by more than ten percent to some 4,900, but the average tonnage of those ships was almost fifteen percent greater at 232 tons, and a number of those ships had cargo capacities well is excess of 400 tons.[12]

These larger ships with larger cargoes had to contend with the shoals in Kingston harbour that had contributed to dozens of groundings. The Carruthers shoal had been dredged to a depth of thirteen feet back in 1876, and dredging of the Point Frederick shoal to fifteen feet had been finished in 1885. However, there was still a danger that any ships with deeper draughts straying outside of these channels would meet with difficulties[13]

In April, 1892, Chief Engineer William Anderson, travelled to Kingston to determine the best site for the new range lights on Barriefield Common.[14] The Common was part of the military reserve between Fort Henry and the village of Barriefield, just across the Cataraqui Bridge from Kingston. The range lights planned for that location would help to keep ships in the navigable channel to allow them to reach the wharves of Kingston harbour without incident.

In 1892, the Marine Department reported that:

> The range lights on Barriefield Common, to lead into Kingston Harbour, alluded to in last year's report, were duly erected and the lights put in operation for the first time on the 13th June last. The buildings are iron skeleton towers, triangular in plan, with oval slatted targets or beacons at their tops and sheds at their bases. The beacons are painted white, the iron framework red and the sheds brown. The lights are fixed white, shown from the locomotive headlight lanterns hoisted to the tops of the tripods, and should be visible 12 miles over a small arc on each side of the line of range....
>
> The two iron towers were provided by the Canadian Bridge Company, of Montreal, at a cost of $467.00. The headlight lanterns were furnished by Messrs. Robert Mitchell & Co. of Montreal, and cost $55 each. The towers were erected, the sheds built, and the works completed under the superintendence of Mr. W.H. Noble, foreman of works.
>
> The total expense in connection with the establishment of these lights was $1,190.67.[15]

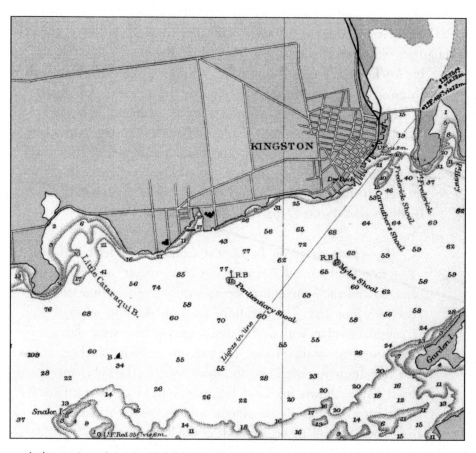

(92) Location of the Barriefield Common range lights. From a survey by William P. Anderson, 1893. Detail of *Lake Ontario, Eastern Part of the Bay of Quinte Kingston to Deseronto*, published by the British Admiralty, 1898, updated 1900.

The range lights (upper right) were needed to guide ships past a number of shoals in Kingston Harbour.

[Courtesy of Library and Archives Canada, R11630-2414-4-E]

Compared to the cost of the Wellers Bay Range lights, built sixteen years earlier, these new range lights were less expensive by $162. In addition, being made of iron, it is likely that they were expected to last considerably longer than the traditional wood-framed towers.

In 1892, the Marine Department also had plans to use similar iron towers from the same supplier to replace the wood-framed range lights on Bois Blanc (Bob-Lo) Island in the Detroit River.[16] This practice of replacing traditional lighthouses with structural iron or steel towers would be adopted on a very large scale by the mid-20th Century.

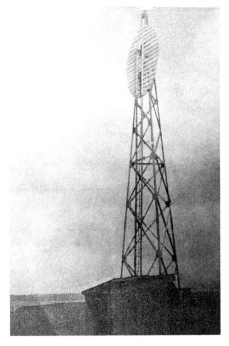

(93) Barriefield Common front range light, c.1918. Photographer unknown.
The front range light was on a tower 48 feet tall and the rear range light was on a tower 75 feet tall. These iron skeleton towers were a significant departure from the traditional enclosed, wood-frame lighthouses that had been in common use up to that point. Their construction marked a transition to simpler, more durable and less expensive structures as fixed aids to navigation.
[Courtesy of Library and Archives Canada, PA-172473]

The official "Notice to Mariners" was published in June 1892:

NOTICE TO MARINERS
No. 24 of 1892
I. BARRIEFIELD COMMON RANGE LIGHTS.

Two Range Lights, established by the Government of Canada on Barriefield Common, near the junction of the Great Cataraqui Creek and the St. Lawrence River, at the outlet of Lake Ontario, in the County of Frontenac and Province of Ontario, to guide between Four Mile Point [on Simcoe Island] and Kingston Harbour, were put in operation on the 13th instant.

The buildings are iron skeleton towers, triangular in plan, with oval, slatted targets or beacons at their tops, and sheds at their bases.

The beacons are white, the iron frameworks red, and the sheds brown.

The lights are fixed white, shown from locomotive headlight lanterns hoisted to the tops of the tripods, and visible 12 miles over a small arc on each side of the line of range....

The range leads inside of Carruthers and Point Frederick shoals....

23rd June, 1892.[17]

The "beacons" mentioned in the official notice are what are today referred to as daymarks. These slats were painted white and would be visible to mariners sailing into Kingston harbour during daylight hours.

While the Barriefield Common Range lights did not take on the traditional form of other lighthouses, they did, nevertheless, retain a number of features found in every lighthouse: they were tall towers; they had a light at the top, and they had a lightkeeper. Alexander Milligan was appointed lightkeeper of the Barriefield Common Range lights in April, 1892 with an annual salary of $150.00.[18]

The locomotive headlight lanterns with which the range lights were fitted, were on a cable and pulley system so that they could be hoisted up and down. Milligan would go out on the Common every evening, remove the lanterns from the shed at the base of the towers, light them, and then hoist them into place. In the morning, he would reverse the process and extinguish the lights. He would also be responsible for keeping the lenses of the lights clean, refilling the oil lamps, trimming the wicks, and generally keeping the station in serviceable order. In short, the keeper of the Barriefield Common Range lights did many of the same jobs that all lightkeepers were tasked with for, despite their unconventional design, these range lights still used the same lighting technology as was employed in all of the other lighthouses, lamps with open flames and lenses or reflectors to project the light.

(94) Lanterns used for the Barriefield Common range lights. Glass plate negative. Photographer unknown.
Each of these locomotive headlight-type lanterns was fitted with a single oil lamp and a parabolic reflector. Each evening the lightkeeper would light the lanterns and hoist them to the top of the towers. The lights were visible up to 12 miles.
[Courtesy Marine Museum of the Great Lakes Kingston, 1984.0028.0798]

There is no record as to whether or not Milligan was provided with a dwelling or where it might have been located.

Trenton Range Lights (1905)

This trend toward simpler, more utilitarian light towers — pole lights, open wooden framework towers, and structural iron towers — saw its ultimate expression in the range lights built at Trenton in 1905.

Like the other ports in the Bay of Quinte, Trenton benefitted from increased shipping on the bay after the opening of the Murray Canal. The entrance to Trenton harbour at the mouth of the Trent river had always been a difficult one, despite the dredging that had been done from 1878 to 1880, and the buoys that had been placed to mark the safe channel.[19]

For some time, private range lights had marked the channel from the Bay of Quinte to the harbour, but it was not until 1905 that the Marine and Fisheries Department committed to the establishment of government range lights to guide ships safely to the wharves at the mouth of the Trent River. (See figure 100.)

As simple as the iron skeleton towers on Barriefield Common were, the ones erected at Trenton harbour were even simpler still. They were wooden masts with lights hoisted to the top, similar to the "experimental" pole light set up on Potters Island a dozen years earlier.

In 1905 the official "Notice to Mariners" was published in the Canada Gazette:

NOTICE TO MARINERS
No. 104 of 1905
ONTARIO
(237) Lake Ontario — Bay of Quinte — Trenton —
Range lights

Range lights have been established by the Government of Canada at Trenton, Bay of Quinte, replacing the private range lights heretofore maintained in this locality....

The lights are fixed red lights, shown from anchor lens lanterns hoisted on white masts, and should be visible 2 miles. The masts have white diamond-shaped targets at their tops and small white sheds at their bases.

The front mast stands on the west side of the harbour, near the shore of the bay, and about 1/3 mile southward of the west end of the Trent river bridge. The mast is 20 feet high and the light is elevated 20 feet above the level of the lake.

The back mast stands 52º N. 70 ½ º W. from the front mast, and is 30 feet high. The light is elevated 42 feet above the level of the lake....

F. GOURDEAU
Deputy-Minister.
Department of Marine and Fisheries,
Ottawa, Canada, 27th October, 1905 [20]

Trenton, Ont. Harbour & Southern Outlet of the Trent Valley Canal

(95) Trenton Harbour, c. 1920. Photographer unknown.
Situated at the head of the Bay of Quinte and at the eastern end of the Murray Canal, Trenton was a busy port. Range lights were used to guide ships through the narrow approaches to the harbour. In 1905, government range lights (off to the left of this photograph), simple masts each with a lantern hoisted to the top, replaced the private lights.
[Postcard in author's collection]

The twin masts used as range lights at Trenton represented another step away from the traditional lighthouse form. These were certainly aids to navigation, however simple, and they certainly had lights on them. The only other feature that they shared with traditional lighthouses was that they still had a lightkeeper dedicated to maintaining the lights. William Fitzpatrick was appointed the first keeper of the Trenton Range lights with a salary of $125 per year.[21] The masts that held the lights would have been fitted with some type of rope and pulley mechanism, similar to that of a flagpole, to allow the keeper to raise the lit lamp at dusk and to lower it to be extinguished at dawn.

2nd Pigeon Island Lighthouse (1909)

With fixed aids to navigation evolving from traditional enclosed lighthouses to open framework towers and simple masts surmounted by a light, it is perhaps somewhat surprising that when it came to replacing the wood-framed lighthouse on Pigeon Island in 1909, the chief engineer of the Marine and Fisheries Department chose to build a hybrid structure: a combination of an open structural steel tower with a closed wooden watchroom and traditional lantern.

The original Pigeon Island lighthouse, a wooden, schoolhouse-style structure built less than forty years earlier, had not been able to withstand the harsh conditions on the tiny, exposed island in Lake Ontario. Chief Engineer Anderson of the Marine and Fisheries Department recommended in June, 1908, that the original lighthouse be replaced with a new tower.

By then, William P. Anderson had been on the staff of the department for almost thirty-five years, having been hired as a draftsman in 1874 at age 23. He had been educated at Bishop's College in Quebec, and worked for a short time as a surveyor in Manitoba. Within two years of joining the Department, Anderson had been promoted to assistant engineer, and in 1880, at age 30, he was appointed Chief Engineer of the Department of Marine and Fisheries. As chief engineer, Anderson was responsible for the design, construction and maintenance of all lighthouses in Canada. Over the course of his forty-five year career, he is credited with the design of some 300 lighthouses across the country, making him one of the world's most prolific lighthouse engineers. Before retiring from government service in 1919, Anderson also conducted hydrographic surveys for the British Admiralty, was a member of the Lighthouse Board of Canada and chaired the Geographic Board of Canada. In addition, he had an active military career, had seen active service during the Fenian Raid of 1870, and eventually attained the rank of lieutenant-colonel in the Canadian Militia.[22]

(96) Portrait of William P. Anderson, Chief Engineer, Marine and Fisheries Department. Photograph by William Topley, 1904
Anderson worked for the Marine and Fisheries Department from 1874 until his retirement in 1919. As chief engineer, he was responsible for the design, construction, maintenance, operation and staffing of all federally-owned lighthouses across Canada.
[Courtesy of Library and Archives Canada, MIKAN 3439031]

By Order-in-Council in 1908, Chief Engineer Anderson received approval to have the new tower and new keeper's dwelling on Pigeon Island built at an estimated cost of $4,800.[23] The practice of using Marine Department personnel to supervise day labourers for lighthouse construction was continued here, and an open steelwork tower was erected on the island under the supervision of the department's construction foreman M.J. Egan.

A second Order-in-Council that year authorized an additional expenditure of $6,911 for a new lighting apparatus and lantern. The light was to be converted from a series of catoptric reflectors to a single 4th Order Fresnel lens with a double-flashing mechanism.[24]

(97) Old and new lighthouses on Pigeon Island, 1908. Photographer unknown. The new steel framework tower can be seen rising up behind the original "schoolhouse" style lighthouse that had been built in 1870. The new lightkeeper's dwelling is next to the old lighthouse. The men by the new boathouse are likely part of the crew hired by the Marine and Fisheries Department to erect the new lighthouse. [Courtesy of Library and Archives Canada, PA-211513]

The following year in his annual report to the Minister of Marine and Fisheries, Anderson reported that the new lighthouse, keeper's dwelling and boathouse on Pigeon Island had been put into operation:

> The old combined lighthouse and dwelling was pulled down and replaced by a specially designed 4-section steel skeleton tower, and a separate dwelling. The new tower square in plan, with sloping sides, surmounted by an inclosed wooden watchroom, and has a spiral staircase, inclosed in cylindrical steel form, constructed from base of tower to watchroom floor. The new dwelling house is a neat

wooden building. A new boathouse was also built, as well as cribwork protection work. The steel tower was purchased from the Goold, Shapley & Muir Co., of Brantford, Ont., for $1,677, and the construction work was carried out by day's labour at a cost of $3,591. 84.[25]

This hybrid design was another innovation in lighthouse construction. The structural steel tower was ordered from the steel fabrication firm of Goold, Shapley and Muir based in Brantford, Ontario. Goold, Shapley and Muir had established a successful business manufacturing a variety of steel towers including small windmills sold to farmers across Canada who used them to drive pumps to water their livestock. The company also manufactured fire lookout towers for the forestry service[26] and it may have been this type of tower that caught the eye of William Anderson. This tall, galvanized steel tower with a cabin at the top appeared to be ideally suited for use as a lighthouse.

Anderson ordered a tower from Brantford and had it erected on Pigeon Island. The official "Notice to Mariners" announced that the lighthouse would be placed into service in November, 1909:

NOTICE TO MARINERS

No. 80 of 1909.

(Inland Notice No. 26.)

ONTARIO

(215) Lake Ontario — East end — Pigeon island —
New lighthouse — Change in character of light.

A new lighthouse tower has been erected on Pigeon island, Lake Ontario. It stands 80 feet S 67° W. from the old lighthouse. It is a steel skeleton structure, painted white, surmounted by a white wooden watchroom and a red circular metal lantern. In the middle of the tower there is a white cylindrical steel tube 5 feet in diameter inclosing the staircase, extending from the base of the tower to the watchroom. The height of the tower from its base to the vane on the lantern is 65 feet.

(98) Advertisement for the Goold, Shapley & Muir Company of Brantford, Ontario, 1899.
The company manufactured numerous steel products including farm windmills and fire lookout towers. In the early 20th Century, they supplied the Marine and Fisheries Department with the pre-fabricated structure for several lighthouses including the 2nd Pigeon Island lighthouse and the Portsmouth rear range tower.
[Author's collection]

The light will be a flashing white light, showing two bright flashes every 5 seconds....

The light will be elevated 65 feet above the level of the lake and should be visible 13 miles from all points of approach. The illuminating apparatus is dioptric of the fourth order, and the illuminant petroleum vapour, burned under an incandescent mantle.

The light will be in operation on or about 1st November, 1909, when the light shown from the old lighthouse will be discontinued, and the old lighthouse taken down.

A rectangular wooden dwelling, painted white, stands near the site of the old lighthouse....

G.J. DESBARATS,
Acting Deputy Minister
Department of Marine and Fisheries,
Ottawa Canada, 8th September, 1909.[27]

(99) 2nd **Pigeon Island lighthouse, c.1980.** Photographer unknown.
To the right of the lighthouse can be seen the outline of the foundation of the keeper's dwelling built in 1908.
[Courtesy Canadian Coast Guard, Fisheries and Oceans Canada]

The large, circular, steel lantern topping the lighthouse was another feature that was unique among lighthouses in eastern Lake Ontario where all other lighthouses had been fitted with polygonal cast iron or square wooden lanterns.

John Davis, who had been appointed lightkeeper on Pigeon Island in 1896, and who was the third generation of the Davis family to keep the Pigeon Island light, was retained as the lightkeeper for the new tower with its new light and new keeper's dwelling.

Onderdonk Point Lighthouse (1911)

Amidst the simplification of the design of light towers in the eastern Lake Ontario region, the Marine and Fisheries Department decided to build a lighthouse at the western end of the Inside Passage that was something of a compromise between the traditional lighthouse and the new form of light tower: This was the Onderdonk Point lighthouse.

Situated on the Prince Edward County shore of the Bay of Quinte, just over three kilometers from both the Murray Canal and Trenton harbour, the Onderdonk Point lighthouse was built to facilitate shipping traffic between these points. In conjunction with the lighthouses previously constructed at The Narrows Shoal and on Telegraph Island, this new lighthouse would add to the safety and convenience of navigation along the Inside Passage.

This was always a concern to the town of Belleville. Much of the town's economy depended on shipping through the Bay of Quinte and to and from the Murray Canal. Anything that would facilitate that trade, such as deeper channels to allow for the passage of larger ships, and more lighthouses to guide those ships, was always in the town's best interest. In February, 1909, it was reported that, "...the Belleville Board of Trade will ask the Government to deepen the Murray Canal to 14 feet; also to better light the Bay of Quinte, and dredge the channel in certain places.[28]

Debate over the deepening of the Murray Canal had begun in 1889, even before the canal had been fully completed, but no action had been taken. Dredging the approaches to the canal and other portions of the Bay of Quinte was an on-going activity, especially around Trenton. In spite of numerous attempts to dredge the so-called "Dark Channel", the direct line between the Murray Canal and Trenton harbour, the soft bottom of the Bay of Quinte at that point caused the channel to fill in quickly. A "Notice to Mariners" of 1909 mentioned this problem:

> The channel leading from Murray canal to Trenton west of Indian island, locally known as Dark channel, was dredged to 15 feet below low water level in 1907 and 1908, for a width of 90 feet, but the material is so soft that it runs into the channel from the sides completely filling it up so that in places depths not exceeding 6 feet are found.[29]

Consequently, the only safe route from the Murray Canal to Trenton for ships of deeper draught was to keep to the channel south of Indian Island and to approach Trenton harbour from the south-east. In order to guide ships along this route or onward toward Belleville, it was proposed that a lighthouse be erected on Onderdonk Point, on the south side of the Bay of Quinte opposite the mouth of the Trent River.

In November, 1910, the Dominion Marine Association, a trade association formed to discuss marine issues affecting Canadian shipping companies and to lobby the federal government on marine matters, had a meeting of their committee on aids to navigation and it was reported that:

> The developing trade in the Bay of Quinte was also the subject of special discussion, and the recommendations already made for additional lights and dredging, and for the early completion of works already undertaken in these waters, were strongly endorsed, and correspondence has been had with the proper authorities to give effect to these resolutions.[30]

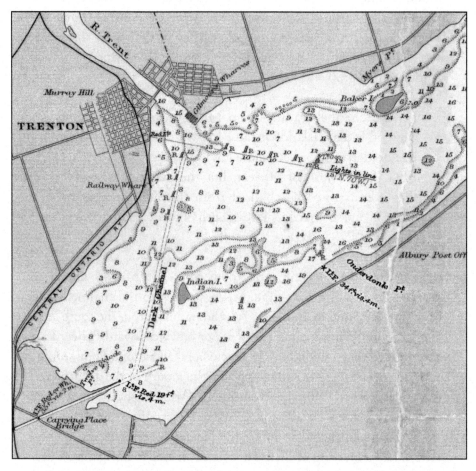

(100) Detail of chart of the Bay of Quinte showing the Onderdonk Point lighthouse, Trenton range lights (marked "Red Lts") and the Murray Canal East Pier light. From a survey by W.P. Anderson, 1893, *Chart, Lake Ontario, Western Part of the Bay of Quinte and Presqu'ile Bay*, published by the British Admiralty, 1900, updated 1912. This chart is based on Anderson's survey of 1893. When this updated chart was printed almost a decade later, it did not take into account the new, taller Murray Canal Pier light with its white light. Instead, it still shows the red light on the original, shorter tower. [Courtesy of Library and Archives Canada, R11630-2427-2-E]

One of the "works already undertaken" was a reference to the Onderdonk Point lighthouse on which the Marine and Fisheries Department had already begun work.

Marine Department construction foreman, T.H. Brewer, had been directed to hire a crew to build the wood-framed lighthouse on the shore of the Bay of Quinte. While it was a traditional lighthouse in the sense that it was a fully-enclosed tower with a conventional lighthouse lantern, the building was unconventional in its square plan and short height. The construction cost of the twenty foot tall tower amounted to $477.19. The lighting apparatus, including a 7th Order dioptric lens, was supplied separately for an extra charge.[31]

The official announcement of the new lighthouse was published in January 1911:

NOTICE TO MARINERS
No. 5 of 1911
(Inland Notice No. 2)
ONTARIO
(10) Lake Ontario — Bay of Quinte — Onderdonk
Point — Lighthouse Established

A lighthouse has been established by the Government of Canada at Onderdonk point, western end of the Bay of Quinte. The light will be put in operation on the opening of navigation in 1911....

The lighthouse stands on the south shore of the Bay of Quinte, 1 ½ miles eastward of Indian Island, and bears S. 37° E distant 2 1/10 miles from the west end of the draw span of the bridge over the Trent river at Trenton. It is an enclosed square wooden building, surmounted by a square wooden lantern, the whole painted white. The height of the lighthouse from its base to the top of the ventilator on the lantern is 20 feet.

The light is a fixed white light, elevated 34 feet above the water, and should be visible 4 miles from all points of approach by water. The illuminating apparatus is dioptric of the seventh order.[32]

The square form and straight walls of the Onderdonk Point lighthouse were typical of the simple harbour lighthouses that the department had been constructing at many other locations across Canada. In the Province of Ontario however, the Onderdonk Point lighthouse had the distinction of being the only lighthouse of its kind.

Mr. E. Bryant was appointed as the first lightkeeper, but was succeeded the following year by William Allison who held the position until the lighthouse was discontinued in 1941.[33]

(101) Onderdonk Point lighthouse, c.1925. Photographer unknown. This was among the smallest of the lighthouses built in the eastern Lake Ontario region. It helped to guide ships on the Bay of Quinte to and from the Murray Canal.
[Courtesy of Library and Archives Canada, PA-172497]

Portsmouth Range Lights (1912)

Chief Engineer William Anderson must have been impressed by the utility of the structural steel tower erected on Pigeon Island in 1909, for he ordered a number of similar towers from the Goold, Shapley and Muir Company to be used as lighthouses at other locations across Canada, including one for Little Cataraqui Bay just west of Kingston. A structural steel tower was erected there as the rear range light in 1911, just west of the village of Portsmouth. For the front range light at this location however, Anderson opted for a conventional wood-framed pyramidal style lighthouse. The result was a dissimilar pair of range lights that included a "modern" rear range tower combined with a traditional front range lighthouse. They were officially designated the Portsmouth Range lights.

Larger ships with deeper draughts approaching Kingston from the south-west could not sail through the South Channel past the Snake Island Shoal lighthouse. Instead, they were forced to sail north of the island and thread their way through a number of shoals as they approached Portsmouth, including Melville shoal, the Middle Ground, and Penitentiary shoal. The new range lights made this new route a safer one.

Again, the Marine and Fisheries Department employed day labourers to build the Portsmouth Range lights. The structural steel rear range tower was erected on the north side of Little Cataraqui Bay under the supervision of lighthouse foreman M.J. Egan who had previous experience in working with towers provided by the Goold, Shapley & Muir Company. The construction of the wood-framed pyramidal front range light, located on the south side of the bay on the shore of Lake Ontario, was supervised by foreman T.H. Brewer. Over the course of sixteen weeks[34] during the summer of 1911, these two lighthouses were constructed for a combined cost of $1,632.89[35]

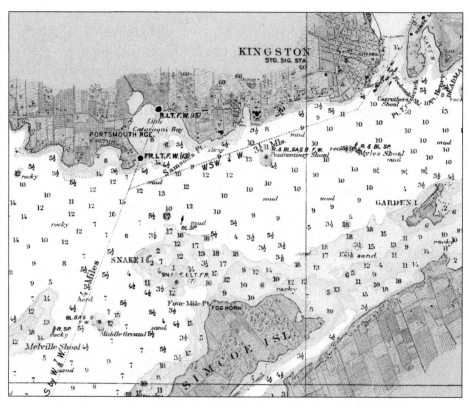

(102) Location of the Portsmouth Range lights. Detail of *Coast Chart No. 1 - Lake Ontario, Survey of the Northern and Northwestern Lakes,* U.S. Corps of Engineers, 1913.

Larger ships drawing more water needed a safer path into Kingston harbour. The Portsmouth Range lights on Little Cataraqui Bay, together with a number of acetylene buoys, helped to guide ships past the Melville and Middle Ground shoals and into Kingston's outer harbour where ships could range with the Barriefield Common Range lights to access the inner harbour.

[Courtesy of NOAA's Office of Coast Survey Historical Map & Chart Collection http:// historicalcharts.noaa.gov, LS21-09-1913]

The "Notice to Mariners" announced the activation of the new aids to navigation as of the opening of navigation in 1912:

NOTICE TO MARINERS
No. 19 of 1912
Lake Ontario, East End – Little Cataraqui
Bay – Range lights established near
Portsmouth

Date of establishment – Opening of navigation in 1912, without further notice.

(1) Front range light.

Position. – On east extremity of Carruthers point, west side of Little Cataraqui Bay....

Character. – Fixed white light.

Elevation. – 32 feet.

Visibility. – 11 miles in the line of range and down the channels towards Kingston.

Order. – Fourth dioptric.

Structure. – Enclosed tower, square in plan, with sloping sides, square lantern.

Material. – Wood.

Colour. – White

Height. – 33 feet, from its base to the top of the ventilator on the lantern.

(2) Back range light.

Position. – On north shore of Little Cataraqui Bay, 3550 feet... from the front light.

Character. – Fixed white light.

Elevation. – 61 feet.

Visibility. – 13 miles in the line of range.

Order. – Catoptric.

Structure. – Skeleton framed tower, square in plan, with sloping sides, surmounted by an enclosed watchroom and a square lantern.

Material. – Frame steel; watchroom and lantern, wood.

Colour. – Skeleton frame red; watchroom and lantern, white.
Height. – 64 feet, from its base to the top of the ventilator
on the lantern.

(103) Portsmouth front range light. (Inset: dioptric lens). Lighthouse photograph by
John B. Carruthers. Lens, photographer unknown.
The front range light was a traditional pyramidal style lighthouse built at Carruthers
point on the south side of Little Cataraqui Bay. The inset shows a 4th-order dioptric
lens of the type that was used in this lighthouse.
[Courtesy of Queen's University Archives, v138-5-20, and Marine Museum of the
Great Lakes Kingston, Glass Plate Neg. Coll.]

Sailing directions. – In coming down the lake vessels
may head for Ninemile point or Snake Island light until the
Portsmouth range lights are in one; the range kept in one
heads into the north channel between Seven Acre shoal and
the Middle ground with nowhere less than 4 fathoms [24 feet]
water; as soon as Snake Island is abeam the range may be left
and a course shaped to lead north of Penitentiary shoal.[36]

In addition to the two towers being dissimilar in style, they had
very different lighting systems. The more modern style rear range
tower contained and old-style catoptric light while the traditional front

range tower held a more modern dioptric apparatus. These lights were kept by E. Graham who was hired as the first keeper of Portsmouth Range lights at a salary of $230.[37]

(104) Portsmouth rear range light c.1923. (Inset: catoptric apparatus). Photographers unknown.
The rear range light was a structural steel tower with a watchroom at the top. The steel was provided by the Goold, Shapley & Muir Company of Brantford, Ontario. The lighthouse was situated on the north side of Little Cataraqui Bay and worked in conjunction with the front range light to guide ships through the Lower Gap. This lighthouse was originally fitted with a catoptric light (inset).
[Courtesy of Queen's University Archives, v138-5-20, and Marine Museum of the Great Lakes Kingston, Glass Plate Neg. Coll.]

The Portsmouth front range light was one of the last traditional lighthouses to be built in the eastern Lake Ontario region. Together with its modern, structural steel partner light, these range lights were symbolic of the transition that was taking place in the design and construction of lighthouses all across Canada; a transition that would eventually result in the demolition of many of the country's iconic lighthouses, and their replacement by less expensive and more utilitarian towers.

Automation and Demolition

The shipping trade on the Great Lakes remained strong into the early decades of the 20th Century in spite of the rapid rise and success of railroads. The number of ships on the Lakes continued to increase until 1909 when the total number of registered Canadian and U.S. vessels leveled off at almost 6,000 ships.[38] By the time the Portsmouth Range lights were constructed, some forty-four lighthouses and light towers had been built in and around eastern Lake Ontario, but there was little demand for additional fixed aids to navigation in the region. Instead, numerous lighthouses were being automated, discontinued or demolished.

Of the forty-four towers that had been built up to that time, more than a dozen had already been taken out of service. Wherever lighthouses were no longer needed for the safety and convenience of navigation, they were discontinued and usually torn down. Wherever they were difficult to access and expensive to maintain, keepers were dispensed with and the lights were automated.

The demolition process had started in Presqu'ile Bay. As a result of a change in the location of the deepest channel at the entrance to the bay, the role of the original Presqu'ile rear range light had been taken over by the Calf Pasture Shoal range light in 1879. The original lighthouse had remained active as daymark, but eventually it was discontinued and, in 1891, it was dismantled.[39]

In 1899, the wood-framed Murray Canal pier lights had been replaced with taller, more durable, galvanized iron "cabins".

In nearby Wellers Bay, shipping traffic had dropped off significantly after 1900. Even though for a number of years there had been two separate ports of call on the bay — one at the Pine Point railway pier near Gardenville used primarily for the export of ore brought down from the Marmora iron mines, and the other at the village of Consecon where barley, wheat and other agricultural products were loaded onto steamships and schooners bound for Kingston and lake ports in New York State — cargo carried on Canadian and American registered vessels had dropped from 8,986 tons in 1890, to less than half of that, 3,822 tons, in 1895.[40] By 1900, shipments out of Wellers Bay had dropped to a trickle. The rear range light, which had already been moved twice since 1876 in order to compensate for the shifting sands at the entrance channel from Lake Ontario into Wellers Bay, was discontinued in 1909 and demolished.[41] The next year, the front range light was closed and the keeper's dwelling along with the six acre lighthouse reserve were sold at auction.[42]

In 1911, the Marine and Fisheries Department decided to discontinue the Prince Edward Point (South Bay Point) lighthouse and the official "Notice to Mariners" was published to that effect.[43] However, demands from ship owners and others resulted in the lighthouse being "temporarily" re-activated in 1912.[44] The Prince Edward Point lighthouse was still in operation in 1941 when it was automated with a gas light, and it was finally de-commissioned in 1959 when it was replaced by a structural steel tower erected nearby.[45]

In April, 1913, the Salt Point lighthouse (Presqu'ile Front Range light) in Presqu'ile Bay was discontinued and demolished. Ever since the new Brighton Range lights had been built in 1891 to guide ships to and from the Murray Canal, the Salt Point lighthouse had not been used as a range light. Since that time, the Marine Department had tried several times to close the lighthouse but local fisherman and other owners of light draught vessels asked that it be kept active. However, by 1913, the Salt Point lighthouse had reached the end of its life and it was torn down after sixty-two years of service.[46]

One month later, the Salmon Point lighthouse was shut down and sold. Brief "Notices to Mariners" like the one announcing the closure of this lighthouse were becoming a more common sight in local newspapers:

NOTICE TO MARINERS

No. 40 of 1913.

ONTARIO

Position. — On Wicked point [Salmon Point].

Lat. N. 43° 51' 25", Long. W. 77° 14' 41"

Light to be discontinued. — The maintenance of this light will be discontinued on the 1st July 1913, without further notice.[47]

Larger ships requiring deeper water no longer sailed close enough to this lighthouse, so its usefulness was at an end.

In the early years of the 20th Century, advancements in lighthouse illumination technology made it feasible for the Marine Department to start automating lighthouses. No lighthouses in eastern Lake Ontario were still using sperm-oil, but many lamps were still being fueled by kerosene. A number of earlier experiments had also been conducted with other fuels including fish oils, colza (canola oil), and Pintsch gas. But the illuminant that showed the most promise was acetylene gas.

Acetylene had been discovered by Edmond Davy in 1836, and experiments with this gas over the following half-century were successful in proving its viability as a brilliant source of light ideally suited to lighthouses.[48] By the 1890's, Thomas Willson of Hamilton, Ontario, together with James Turner Morehead of Spray, North Carolina, had developed a process to inexpensively manufacture calcium carbide which, when dissolved in water, would produce acetylene gas. This led to the formation of the Union Carbide company. Shortly after the discovery, Willson sold his shares in Union Carbide and moved to Ottawa where he established the International Marine Signal Company to manufacture self-sustaining acetylene buoys.[49]

The St. Lawrence River above Montreal was one of the first areas where acetylene was used as an illuminant for aids to navigation. This is explained in the Marine and Fisheries Department's booklet, *Review of Improvements in Lighthouse and Coast Service*, published in 1904:

> Experiments with Acetylene Gas.
>
> The gas buoys in the St. Lawrence River, between Montreal and Kingston, have been fitted with acetylene gas burners and holders. This gas has proven a more satisfactory illuminant than Pintsch gas for buoys so far as intensity is concerned; the lights on the buoys can be seen from a much greater distance and acetylene has also an advantage over the Pintsch gas, as acetylene gas can be conveyed from one point to another by the buoy tenders.... The use of acetylene will enable the Department to locate gas buoys where it

has been impossible in the past, because of the almost insuperable difficulty of procuring the Pintsch gas outside certain limited localities.[50]

Pintsch gas, a distillate of the petroleum product, naphtha, burned very brightly but was difficult to generate and store. Willson's process of converting calcium carbide into acetylene by simply adding water was a much easier way of producing a gas which burned significantly brighter. This method was adapted for use in a gas generator that was placed on board the Marine and Fisheries lighthouse supply ship, *Scout*. Starting in 1904, the Department decided to install acetylene burners and pressurized storage tanks in forty-three lighthouses between Montreal and Kingston, including those at Snake Island Shoal, Centre Brother Island, and Nine Mile Point, and *Scout* was used to deliver acetylene gas to these lighthouses.[51]

(105) Dominion Government Steamer *Scout*, 1903. Photographer unknown.
The wooden-hulled *Scout* was used as a lighthouse and buoy tender on the St. Lawrence River and the Great Lakes. She carried an acetylene generator on board which was used to recharge acetylene buoys and to supply lighthouses that had been converted to acetylene lights. In 1905, the explosion of a buoy on board the Scout killed the captain and three crew members. The ship was rebuilt and remained in service until 1934.
[From "Annual Report of the Department of Marine and Fisheries, 1903", *Sessional Papers of the Dominion of Canada*, No. 21, Sess. 1904.]

The beginning of lighthouse automation came when Commissioner of Lights, J.F. Fraser, decided to remove lightkeepers from eleven of the acetylene-powered lighthouses on the St. Lawrence River and to place the lights in charge of two part-time caretakers. In his report to the Minister of Marine and Fisheries in 1904, Fraser noted that:

> Before the opening of navigation consideration will be given to the question of keepership in this division, and where a number of lights are in one locality it may be advisable to appoint a caretaker, as has been done in the vicinity of Gananoque and Lachine.[52]

Fraser's plan for the extensive destaffing of lighthouses was largely unsuccessful. Even though the lightkeepers did not have to tend to the lighting and extinguishing of the acetylene burners every day, there were other duties including polishing lenses and reflectors, cleaning lanterns and general building maintenance that required a human presence. There was also the matter of the extra expense incurred to recharge the acetylene tanks more frequently since the gas was burned both day and night. As a result, many keepers were re-instated along the St. Lawrence River.[53] By 1914, only a few lighthouses in that sector were completely unmanned, and several others shared a single keeper.

However, in 1907, the idea of lighthouse automation was revived as a result of an invention that would eventually reduce the role of the lightkeeper at many remote locations to a part-time custodian. The invention was the sun valve; a device created by Swedish scientist Gustaf Dalén, of Aktiebolaget Gasaccumulator (the AGA Company). The company's literature describes this simple invention:

> It consists of a central, blackened, light absorbing metal rod surrounded by three gilt light-reflecting metal rods. When dawn breaks the blackened rod absorbs light

energy and acquires a slightly higher temperature than the shiny rods. It becomes slightly longer than the shiny ones triggering a device which cuts off the gas and switches off the lighthouse light.[54]

In 1912, Dalen was awarded the Nobel Prize for Physics "... for his invention of automatic regulators for use in conjunction with gas accumulators for illuminating lighthouses and buoys."[55] After 1914, AGA sun valves were installed in a number of lighthouses including the Scotch Bonnet Island lighthouse which became a fully automated light in 1919, after which a permanent lightkeeper was no longer required at this remote station.[56]

(106) AGA sun valves. Photographer unknown.
The sun valve, invented by Swedish scientist Gustaf Dalen in 1907, was used to automate lighthouses and lighted buoys. When the sun shone on it, the valve would expand and cut off the supply of gas. At sunset, the valve would open and allow acetylene gas to flow past a pilot light thereby lighting the lamp.
[Courtesy of Chance Brothers Lighthouses Engineers, Australia]

As other lighting technologies developed, more lighthouses were automated and destaffed. The widespread use of electric lights and remote monitoring systems later in the 20th Century would result in the complete elimination of all lightkeepers in the eastern Lake Ontario region by 1978.[57]

By the end of 1913, it appeared that the era of the traditional lighthouse, with its large lantern atop a tall enclosed tower, was over. The use of new materials and new forms for fixed aids to navigation was accelerating in the early years of the 20th Century. Not only was the classic form of lighthouse quickly becoming a relic of the past, many of the existing lighthouses were either being automated or demolished as they were no longer needed.

The era of the traditional, iconic lighthouse was rapidly coming to an end.

CHAPTER 10

The Last of Its Kind

Octagonal tower, with sloping sides; polygonal lantern
("Notice To Mariners," 1914)

In the early years of the 20th Century, lighthouses all along the shores of Lake Ontario were being discontinued, destaffed and demolished. Few new fixed aids to navigation were still being designed along the traditional lines of the familiar monolithic tower topped by a gallery and an enclosed lantern. Instead, simple masts, steel frames and various hybrid forms of light towers were being erected.

Just when the days of the iconic lighthouse appeared to be over, a controversial decision by the Government of Canada concerning the country's evolving transportation policy would lead to the construction of Lake Ontario's tallest and most magnificent lighthouse. The controversy was over whether to enlarge the existing Welland Canal or to establish a new, more direct canal route to the West along the Ottawa River to Georgian Bay.

From the time of the establishment of the Internal Navigation Commission by the Province of Upper Canada back in 1821, successive Canadian governments had supported a transportation policy that relied heavily on canals connecting the Great Lakes with Montreal and its outlet to the sea. While railways had also become an important part of this policy after the middle of the 19th Century, ships were still acknowledged as being the most cost effective mode of transportation for bulk freight such as lumber, iron ore, coal and wheat.

(107) Steamer *Seguin*, 1891. Photographer unknown.
Built in 1890 for the Parry Sound Steamship Company, the *Seguin* was 207 feet long. She was later sold to Canada Steamship Lines and served until 1944. Ships of this type were designed as "canallers" to carry bulk cargo from the upper Great Lakes through the Welland Canal to Kingston where smaller ships and barges would carry the cargo onward to Montreal. Larger ships referred to as "lakers", were confined to the upper lakes because they exceeded the allowable dimensions for canal passage until the enlarged Welland Ship Canal was completed in 1932.
[Courtesy Library and Archives Canada, PA-139102]

The Welland Canal had been a major contributing factor to Canada's economic growth from the time that the first ships had passed through its locks in 1829. Initially accommodating vessels with a draught of up to six feet, the canal and its locks had been periodically widened and deepened until the 1880's when a third major upgrade was performed. This larger canal allowed ships up to 270 feet long drawing 12 feet of water to pass through the locks with cargoes from as far west as Duluth and Port Arthur (now Thunder Bay) on Lake Superior en route to trans-shipment terminals at Kingston and

Prescott. At these ports, freight was offloaded onto barges or smaller ships for the passage through the St. Lawrence canal system to Montreal where it was again transferred to ocean-going steamers.[1]

(108) Entrance to the Welland Canal at Port Dalhousie, c.1910. Photographer unknown. A "canaller" approaches Lock No. 1 at Port Dalhousie. Ships up to 270 feet long drawing up to 12 feet of water could pass through the Welland Canal. One of the Port Dalhousie Range lights can be seen at centre in the background.
[Postcard in author's collection]

Even though successive Canadian governments had invested heavily in the Welland Canal, new and more direct routes from Montreal to the West were constantly being proposed. The circuitous Trent River route from the Bay of Quinte through to Lake Simcoe and down the Severn River to Georgian Bay had been under development since the 1830's. However, progress had been very slow and, by the beginning of the 20th Century, there was little hope that ships of any substantial size would ever be able to use that route.[2] For a time in the 1840's and then again in the 1860's, a route from Toronto north to Lake Simcoe and then to Georgian Bay was surveyed, but only a short section of a canal from Lake Simcoe, south to Newmarket, Ontario, was ever built.[3]

A more promising route along the path that the fur traders had once followed in the 17th and 18th centuries — canoeing from

Montreal, up the Ottawa River and across the French River to Georgian Bay — was examined by engineers and government officials at great length. Canals and locks had already been built along the lower Ottawa River at Ste. Anne's, Grenville, and Carillon so that barges and steamboats could access the Rideau Canal at Ottawa. Two locks comprising the Culbute Canal had also been constructed further upriver in the 1870's,[4] but dredging of long sections of the Ottawa River above the capital and cutting a canal to Georgian Bay would be an enormous undertaking that was projected to take many years and cost millions of dollars.

By 1900, with rising demand for iron ore and wheat, shipbuilders on the upper lakes had continued to build vessels of a larger class to carry heavier loads. It did not take long before these larger ships, known as "lakers", exceeded the dimensions of the locks of the third Welland Canal, so that only smaller ships, "canalers", could continue to use the canal for transporting goods to Kingston or directly to Montreal. Soon, millions of bushels of wheat loaded at Port Arthur every year were carried by lakers either to Port Colborne, where they were the transferred onto canalers that could pass through the Welland Canal, or to Buffalo where canal boats were loaded for passage through the Erie Canal to New York City. With a view to removing the bottleneck at the Welland Canal and keeping more of the shipping business in Canada, two opposing schemes surfaced as possible solutions to these problems: increasing the size of the Welland Canal, and digging the Ottawa/Georgian Bay Canal.

In 1900, the government appointed engineer John L. Weller to study the feasibility of constructing the Welland Ship Canal to allow lakers to sail non-stop from Lake Superior through to Kingston or, with some improvement of the St. Lawrence Canals, all the way to Montreal. John Weller had transportation in his blood. Sixty years earlier, his father, William Weller had run a successful stagecoach service between the Bay of Quinte and Toronto, and his father's cousin, Asa Weller, was one of the first settlers at The Carrying Place where he ran a portage service to haul logs and bateaux between the Bay of Quinte and Wellers Bay.[5] John himself started his career as a military engineer, having graduated from the Royal Military College at Kingston in 1883. He soon gained canal experience working on the Trent, Murray and Cornwall canals, and in 1900, he was appointed Superintending Engineer of the Welland Canal.[6]

Weller devised a plan to straighten the path of the Welland Canal and to make the locks longer and deeper to accommodate ships up to 800 feet long drawing up to 30 feet of water. This plan was supported by the communities along the route of the proposed ship canal as well as by interests in Hamilton, Toronto and Kingston.

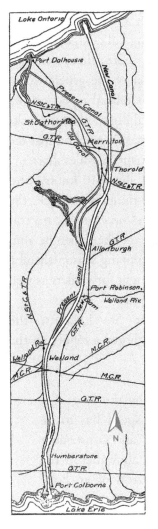

(109) Proposed route of the new Welland Ship Canal, 1914. Department of Railways and Canals, Canada. The new ship canal proposed by Superintending Engineer John Weller, shortened the route as well as making it accessible to much larger ships. [From "Report of the Department of Railways and Canals, 1914", *Sessional Papers of the Dominion of Canada*, Session 1915]

Meanwhile, groups of business men and ship owners at Port Arthur, Ottawa and Montreal, in favour of the more direct route between Lake Superior and the sea, were lobbying for the construction of a new canal along the Ottawa River/Georgian Bay route. From 1856 onward, the proposed Georgian Bay Ship Canal had been surveyed in detail and debated session after session in the Canadian House of Commons.[7] The government continually refused to commit funds to such an undertaking, usually citing the need to divert money to that important project of national unity: the trans-continental railway system. Until such time as the railways required less federal government funding, the existing Welland Canal/St. Lawrence River route with all of its limitations would have to be used for transporting bulk cargoes.

The Georgian Bay Canal was certainly a more direct route to the riches of "The Great West". An examination of the general route map included in the Public Works Department's official report on the proposed Georgian Bay Canal, shows that it would have 21 fewer locks than the existing St. Lawrence River/Welland Canal system, and that the Ottawa River/Georgian Bay route was some 250 nautical miles shorter.

Given that a laker had an average speed of about 10 knots,[8] and would experience an average delay of forty-five minutes per lock, the Georgian Bay Canal could save almost three days on every return trip between Montreal and Thunder Bay. This meant that a single ship could make up to six extra return trips every shipping season thereby increasing profits for shipping companies and freight forwarders as well as for farmers who were producing wheat for export.

This analysis is confirmed by Arthur St. Laurent, the Superintending Public Works Engineer who authored a report on the proposed Georgian Bay Ship Canal:

> Time of Transit — This is affected by the length of restricted channels on the route, where speed has to be reduced, and by the number of lockages and consequent delays. A close computation of the speed allowable in the different stretches, with about three-quarters of an hour delay for passage at each lock, gives about 70 hours, as time of transit from Georgian Bay to Montreal.

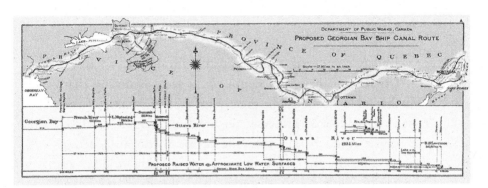

(110) Proposed Georgian Bay Ship Canal Route, 1908. Department of Public Works, Canada.

The Georgian Bay Canal was proposed as a shorter, faster alternative to the Welland Canal/St. Lawrence River route for shipping bulk cargo to Montreal from ports on Lake Superior. Ships loaded with grain at Thunder Bay would enter the canal system where the French River emptied into Georgian Bay. They would follow the river to Lake Nippising and then connect to the Mattawa and Ottawa rivers to Montreal. More than 24 locks and a series of artificial channels were planned for this proposed waterway.

[Courtesy Library and Archives Canada, NMC7409]

With the advantage of shorter distance between terminal harbours, it is computed that the route will be from 1 to 1½ days faster than any other existing water route, under present conditions from the head of the Great Lakes to an ocean port, apart from also having an enormous superiority as to carrying capacity.[9]

St. Laurent, however, cautioned that these advantages could readily be removed by improvements along the competing Welland Canal/St. Lawrence River route:

But as compared with a possible improved system of St. Lawrence canals to a depth of 22 feet, assuming that number of locks would be greatly reduced and some of the channels widened, probably no practical benefit in time of transit could be claimed, the saving in distance being nearly offset by the longer stretches of lake and wide river navigation which exist through the Lake Erie and Lake Ontario route, where higher speeds would be permissible.[10]

The debate was carried on in newspapers and pamphlets for several decades and it usually pitted the St. Lawrence/Welland Canal route squarely against the Ottawa/Georgian Bay route. If large sums of money were to be spent on Weller's plan to improve the Welland Canal, then St. Laurent's Georgian Bay Canal would not be needed. Conversely, if the Georgian Bay Canal were established, there would be no need to upgrade the Welland Canal.

In its pamphlet, *Canada's Canal Problem and Its Solution*, published in 1911, the Toronto Board of Trade summarized the argument in favour of the existing Welland Canal/St. Lawrence route:

As to the importance to Canada of retaining the control of traffic seeking its way to the world markets from the West and North-West, by the route of the Great Lakes, there is practically unanimity of opinion in the

Dominion. Canadians are agreed that this is essential to our commercial independence.... As to the best way to ensure this commercial independence, however, there is not the same unanimity of opinion....

Our neighbors in the State of New York realize quite as clearly as we do the importance of the control of the water-borne traffic of the West and North-West, and with splendid and entirely admirable energy they are doing all that nature will permit to divert that trade into channels of their own. They are enlarging and improving the Erie Canal, and, when completed, it will be without exception the finest barge canal in the world....

It is then, absolutely essential that Canada's canal system shall be able, by reason of its capacity and speed, to carry grain to tide-water more cheaply and advantageously than will be possible by the New Erie.... Standing still or even delay would for Canada be suicidal.... The new Canadian water-route must be in every way superior to the Erie, and it must be completed as soon or nearly as soon. As the Erie will be the best barge canal in the world, ours must be the best freshwater ship canal....

It seems clear that only by deepening and improvement of the complete Welland-St. Lawrence route can Canada assure to herself her proper control of the water-borne traffic from the Great Lakes to the seaboard.[11]

The Great Waterways Union of Canada, a lobby group formed to promote the Welland/St. Lawrence route,[12] agreed with the Toronto Board of Trade's viewpoint and added:

The St. Lawrence - Welland deep waterway is a national necessity. The French River development and Georgian Bay Canal are only a contractors' project, commercially impracticable and condemned by the Government engineers' report.[13]

On the other side of the debate, the Montreal-Ottawa & Georgian Bay Canal Company, a private corporation formed in 1894, published their own pamphlet in 1910 outlining a number of strong arguments for the new canal along the Ottawa River/Georgian Bay route:

> Two systems of canals have been constructed to secure through water navigation from the Great Lakes to the Atlantic, one by the Canadian Government to Montreal to overcome the rapids and obstructions in the Niagara and St. Lawrence Rivers, the other, known as the Erie Canal, by the State of New York from Lake Erie at Buffalo and Lake Ontario at Oswego to the Hudson River at Albany. Both of these systems were inadequate for the demands of commerce when completed. The Canadian system has been enlarged three times and the Erie Canal once, with the second enlargement now partially completed; and still like a narrow gauge railroad, their dimensions are too small to form a satisfactory or even approximately adequate link between the larger transportation routes which they connect....
>
> The present dimensions of these canals, more especially as regards depth, do not meet the requirements of the modern economic Lake freight carrier, and such requirements can only be obtained by constructing a waterway of dimensions which will conform to the depths and widths of the controlling channels on the Great Lakes themselves....
>
> The Montreal Ottawa & Georgian Bay Canal will be a deep waterway from the Great Lakes to the Sea capable of accommodating the largest type of lake freight carrier or ocean-going ship drawing up to a maximum of 20 feet of water....
>
> Such a canal will take any steamer, that can be made to profitably navigate the Lakes, right down to the seaboard without any trans-shipment or obstruction....
>
> This Canal will have five chief advantages over any other route which can be possibly opened up:

(1). It is the shortest route by which it is possible to construct a deep waterway from the head of the Great Lakes to tidewater, either through Canadian or United States territory, having an advantage of 270 miles [437 kms] over any other possible route....

(2). It will be the quickest route to navigate from the Great Lakes to an ocean port by 26 hours.

(3). It is the cheapest route by which freight can be carried from the Great Lakes to seaboard.

(4). This route will open up for development more natural resource than any other route.

(5). It is the only route through Canadian Territory which cannot be used by the United States to assist in their canal schemes for capturing Canadian traffic.[14]

A pamphlet written for the Port Arthur Board of Trade in favour of the Georgian Bay Canal, added:

The question to ask oneself in this great national problem, one of the greatest that the people of Canada have ever had before them, for it means the holding or losing by Canada of the transportation from these twin ports to the seaboard of her western freight is:

"Will the contemplated improvements of the Welland Canal retain to Canada her trade in her own channels to the seaboard, without any possibility of diversion to the United States?"

Then apply the same question to the Georgian Bay Canal and investigate. These are the two questions I considered and investigated, and the evidence I gathered was overwhelmingly, to my mind, in favor of the Georgian Bay Canal....

The Toronto papers say, build the Welland Canal first and then the Georgian Bay Canal. If the Welland Canal is deepened there will be no Georgian Bay Canal, for the damage to Canadian transportation will have been done, and it cannot be undone....

Canada only needs one deep water canal, and let her see to it that this canal is the one which retains to her the absolute control, for nearly eight months of each year, of the freight of half a continent, namely, the Georgian Bay Canal; which will, without a doubt, under the guidance of a wise government, make possible the development of Canadian shipping and the mineral resources of this country to their fullest extent.[15]

The debate truly polarized opinion in central Canada along North/ South lines. Those living north of about 45°N latitude, the area that would benefit most from the new canal, favoured the all-Canadian, northern route through Georgian Bay, along the French River, across Lake Nipissing, over to the Ottawa River and down to Montreal. Those living south of that line in the area that would continue to benefit from the existing waterway, favoured the southern route much of which was shared with the United States through lakes Huron, St. Clair and Erie, along the Welland Canal, across Lake Ontario and down the St. Lawrence River.

In an attempt to appease both sides in the debate, Prime Minister Sir Wilfrid Laurier held out hope that both routes would eventually be developed. He would not commit his government to one route over the other as indicated in this 1909 newspaper report:

During the past week Sir Wilfrid Laurier made a couple of very important announcements before large and influential deputations. First, he stated that the Government were alive to the necessity of improving our national waterways. Second, that the Welland Canal should be deepened and the work commenced without delay; and last that the Georgian Bay Canal must be constructed, as the commerce of the Great Lakes demand this additional outlet.

The Premier then took occasion to allude to the Georgian Bay Canal, "There is no rivalry," he said, "between the St. Lawrence canal system and the Georgian Bay canal. Both will be needed. We have no idea of the future of this country. We will soon have to handle 250,000,000 bushels of grain, and the Georgian Bay canal must come." The Premier made it very clear that he was aware of the necessity of an advanced transportation policy. "A commencement must be made on the Welland canal. Montreal must be placed in a position where it can compete with New York with more than success."[16]

While the Canadian Government wavered on funding either canal route, the State of New York's Erie Canal Commission had earlier begun examining the possibility of converting their relatively small canal into a much larger ship canal. By 1903, the state legislature had approved a plan of enlarging the existing canal to accommodate large barges. While the new Erie Barge Canal would not allow ocean-going ships to directly access the Great Lakes, it would still greatly increase the freight-carrying capacity of the old Erie Canal and divert more of the shipping trade to New York City and away from the port of Montreal.[17]

This decision put more pressure on Canadian legislators to commit funds for one or both of the competing Canadian routes, yet the Laurier government refused to vote the public monies required for either project.

The General Election of 1911 seemed to settle the question and end the debate over which route would be given precedence by the government. Sir Wilfrid Laurier's Liberals were defeated for the first time in fifteen years and the Conservatives, under the leadership of Robert Borden, formed a new majority government in Canada's Parliament. The new government decided to proceed first with upgrading the existing southern route and to fully fund John Weller's plan for the new Welland Ship Canal as soon as possible. However, since Borden's victory over the Liberals had largely been won on his stance against reciprocity with the United States and his emphasis on Canadian sovereignty and nationalism,[18] the all-Canadian Georgian

Bay Canal was not abandoned altogether and a token amount of money was promised for further studies and surveys of the northern route.

The newspaper, *Toronto World*, reported on the situation in March 1912:

> At an all day session of the cabinet on Saturday, the supplementary estimates [for the federal budget] were completed and will be presented to the house [the Canadian House of Commons].... Among some of the more important items will be one for a liberal sum to start work on the new Welland canal and for preliminary work on the Georgian Bay canal....
>
> It is the intention of the government to push work on the new Welland canal. Supt. Weller, who has been placed in charge of the work on the new canal, is in Ottawa conferring with Hon. Frank Cochrane [Minister of Railways and Canals] and a definite announcement as to the route which has been adopted will be made in a few days. Mr. Weller favors what is known as the Ten-Mile Creek route, and his recommendation will likely be followed. Work will start this spring.
>
> It is the intention to build a canal which will be ultimately thirty feet deep and will be able to accommodate the largest boats on the great lakes. The construction of the canal will, it is believed prevent western wheat going via the Erie Canal to New York, and will mean a saving to western farmers of two to four cents a bushel.[19]

While a small amount of money was promised for preliminary work on the Georgian Bay Canal, in the spring of 1912 Parliament voted $2,200,000 as the first installment towards the construction of the new Welland Ship Canal.[20] A larger Welland Canal with longer and deeper locks meant that larger ships from the Upper Lakes would soon start sailing across Lake Ontario with enormous cargoes of grain destined for storage elevators at Kingston and Prescott. These larger vessels, drawing in excess of twenty feet of water, would be unable to pass through the Murray Canal with its maximum twelve foot depth. The huge lakers would be obliged follow the old route with its many hazards that would take them into the open waters of Lake Ontario around the Prince Edward Peninsula and past The Ducks. The traditional shipping lanes at this point, however, passed close by False Ducks Island where there was insufficient depth of water for these larger ships. As a result, new shipping lanes were established which passed through deeper water just to the east of Main Duck Island where shoals and reefs in the immediate vicinity of the island were a danger to passing ships.

(110.1) Grain elevator in Kingston harbour, c.1910. Photographer unknown.
Grain shipped from Thunder Bay was stored in elevators at Kingston and Prescott awaiting transshipment onto smaller vessels for passage through the St. Lawrence canals to Montreal where it could be transferred to ocean-going ships. After the St. Lawrence Seaway was opened in 1959, large ocean vessels were able to sail directly into the Great Lakes and many elevators like this were no longer needed.
[Postcard in author's collection]

In the end, it was the decision to construct the Welland Ship Canal first and to defer work on the Georgian Bay Canal that was the major factor in the decision to build the Main Duck Island lighthouse.

Main Duck Island Lighthouse (1914)

Even before the government decided in 1912 to move forward with the Welland Ship Canal, the Lake Ontario Coal Carriers' Association had petitioned the newly formed Lighthouse Board of Canada for a light on Main Duck Island.[21] The Coal Carriers were well aware of the dangers in the vicinity of The Ducks where numerous ships had been grounded or lost over the past several decades. By the early 20th Century, coal had replaced wood as the primary fuel used for running factories and heating homes. Most of the coal used in Ontario was mined in Pennsylvania and had to be shipped across lakes Erie and Ontario aboard old schooners that had been converted to barges. Steamships would tow as many as three of these barges at a time across the lakes. When these unwieldy processions were caught in a storm at the eastern end of Lake Ontario, thousands of dollars of coal, as well as other cargoes such as wheat, flour and lumber, could be lost when these vessels were stranded or wrecked on Main Duck Island.

(111) Steamer towing barges, 1907. Photographer unknown.
By the end of the 19th Century, this would have been a common sight on the Great Lakes; a steamer with a large deck-load of lumber in addition to having its cargo holds full, towing a number of schooners that had been converted to cargo-carrying barges. If the steamer captain found himself in a dangerous situation due to severe weather, he would often cut the barges loose and their crews would have to set sail and fend for themselves.
[Courtesy of Deseronto Archives, HMR1-09-24]

In May 1903, the schooner *Acacia* bound Oswego for Kingston with a cargo of 350 tons of coal had gone ashore at Main Duck Island.[22] Three years later, in December 1906, there was a fire on board a coal-carrying steam barge sailing from Oswego to Belleville. In the ensuing confusion, the ship was wrecked on Main Duck Island. The alarming incident was reported in the *Buffalo Evening News*:

> Belleville, Dec. 5 — Grave fears are entertained here that the steam barge *Hickox*, owned and commanded by Capt. Smith of this place and carrying a total crew of five, is lost in Lake Ontario
>
> The vessel left Oswego with coal on Sunday and has not been accounted for... it is hoped that the *Hickox* is sheltered or icebound, but the worst is feared.[23]

The next day brought news that, although the ship had been lost, the captain and crew were saved:

> HICKOX MYSTERY CLEARED
> Crew Got to Safety in a Yawl — The Vessel a Total Loss — Unfortunate Capt. Smith Belleville. Dec. 6. There was much satisfaction here when it became known that the mystery of the missing steamer *Hickox* had been cleared up. The news first came through a telephone message from Capt. Smith himself, who announced his safety to his wife....
>
> Capt. Smith says his vessel is a total loss, as is also the cargo of 350 tons of coal.[24]

As reported in the trade journal, *Railway and Marine World* in 1911, the Coal Carriers' petition to the Lighthouse Board was eventually endorsed by the influential government lobby group, the Dominion Marine Association's Committee on Aids to Navigation:

> At its first meeting the committee had refused to endorse a petition from the Lake Ontario Coal Carriers'

Association for a light on the Main Duck in Lake Ontario, but in November ... asked that if a light is placed there it should be placed in such a location as to serve the traffic up and down the lake as well as the parties asking for its erection. The [Lighthouse] Board points out that on account of recent soundings and discovery of more shoal water between the islands than was indicated on the charts, vessels of deep draft which will come down Lake Ontario through a new Welland Canal will require to keep over well towards the Main Duck.[25]

In earlier decades, many other ships had also been grounded or wrecked at Main Duck Island. In 1864, the schooner *Jenny Lind,* carrying more than one thousand barrels of apples from Sodus to Kingston, ran aground on the island. The crew and much of her cargo were saved, but the ship was a total loss to the amount of $2,500.[26] One unfortunate ship, the *William Elgin,* had been reported ashore at Main Duck Island twice over a period of ten years:

[October 1871] ASHORE — The schooner *William Elgin* is reported ashore on the Ducks. She is laden with barley from the Bay of Quinte to Oswego.[27]

[September 1881] During a dense fog on Saturday night the schooner *William Elgin,* loaded with iron ore for Cleveland, ran ashore on the Ducks. A tug and lighter have gone to her assistance.[28]

At least ten other ships suffered the same fate in the four decades leading up to the establishment of the Main Duck Island lighthouse.[29] It is difficult to say whether or not a lighthouse on the island would have prevented these and other wrecks and groundings, however, the Dominion Marine Association argued that a lighthouse at that location would be a benefit both to the smaller steamers and schooners sailing from port to port on Lake Ontario as well as to the larger lakers that would gain access to Lake Ontario through the new Welland

Canal. This lighthouse would certainly be essential for warning ships away from the reefs immediately surrounding Main Duck Island as well as for guiding the deep draught lakers along the new shipping lanes which crossed the Duck Galloo Ridge close to the island.

Just after the Conservative government took office in 1911, the Marine and Fisheries Department started planning for a lighthouse on Main Duck Island. In December, a preliminary "Notice to Mariners" was published to announce the closure of the Prince Edward Point (South Bay Point) lighthouse and the proposed construction of the Main Duck Island lighthouse:

NOTICE TO MARINERS

No. 23 of 1911

(Inland Notice No. 51)

ONTARIO

(344) Lake Ontario — South Bay Point Light

discontinued — Proposed light on

Main Duck Island

The light heretofore maintained on South Bay point, Prince Edward county, lake Ontario, has been permanently discontinued.

It is proposed next year to establish instead thereof a lighthouse on the west extremity of Main Duck island, of which further notice will be given.

A. JOHNSTON

Deputy Minister.

Department of Marine and Fisheries,

Ottawa, Canada, 12th December, 1911.[30]

That winter, Marine and Fisheries Chief Engineer William Anderson would have started drawing plans for the new Main Duck Island Lighthouse. He would first have to consider what type of tower would be best for that location: the lighthouse would have to be tall enough so that its light could be seen as far as possible out into Lake Ontario; the light itself would have to be very bright, and the entire structure would have to be strong enough to contain a large and powerful lighting apparatus.

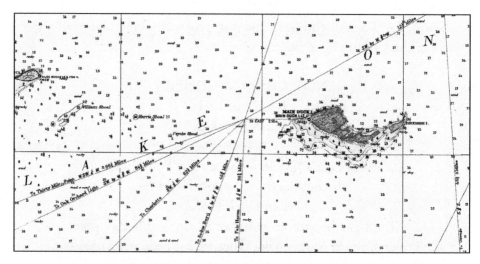

(112) Main Duck Island. Detail of *Coast Chart No. 1 - Lake Ontario, Survey of the Northern and Northwestern Lakes*, U.S. Corps of Engineers, 1913.

Seven shipping lanes are shown converging just two miles west of Main Duck Island where the lighthouse under construction is marked "Main Duck I. Lt.(bldg)". Extensive reefs project into the lake from one side of the island. To the west can be seen other obstacles to navigation including three marked shoals and False Ducks Island. (Near-shore depths in feet, offshore depths in fathoms.)

[Courtesy of NOAA's Office of Coast Survey Historical Map & Chart Collection http://historicalcharts.noaa.gov, LS21-09-1913]

Anderson calculated that the tower should be seventy feet tall from its base to the platform on which the lantern and lighting apparatus would be placed. For the light, he chose to use a huge 3rd Order Fresnel lens fitted with a single petroleum vapour lamp instead of a traditional array of kerosene lamps and reflectors. To house this dioptric apparatus along with the mechanism required to rotate the lens to give the lighthouse its characteristic flash once every ten seconds to distinguish it from other lights nearby, a ten foot tall cast iron lantern weighing more than seven tons would have to be built.

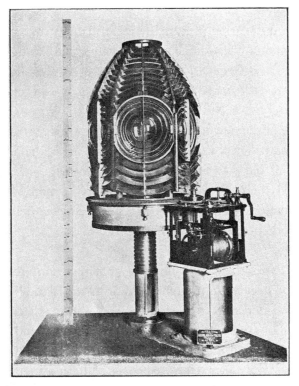

(113) 3rd-**Order Fresnel lens.** Department of Marine and Fisheries, 1910.
The Main Duck Island lighthouse was designed to accommodate a large dioptric apparatus similar to this one standing more than 2 meters tall. After it was wound by the lightkeeper, the clockwork mechanism next to the light would allow the entire apparatus to revolve unattended giving the light its characteristic one flash every ten seconds.
[From "Annual Report of the Department of Marine and Fisheries, 1910", *Sessional Papers of the Dominion of Canada*, No.24, Session 1911]

To build such a lighthouse with an overall height of eighty feet —
taller than any other lighthouse on Lake Ontario — and capable of
supporting such a massive lantern, would require a tower that had a
base of more than thirty feet across and a structure that was very solid;
a structure that would not be affected by the high winds and severe
weather to which Main Duck Island was often subjected in its exposed
location in the middle of Lake Ontario.

For some time, the Marine and Fisheries Department had
recognized the necessity of larger and stronger towers. This policy had
been summarized in a departmental publication in 1909:

> The installation of more powerful lights at many of the
> most important stations along the Atlantic and Pacific coasts,
> the Gulf and River St. Lawrence, Bay of Fundy and Great
> Lakes, made it necessary for the department to build more
> expensive and a better class of towers. The greater weight
> and size of the new lanterns required more stable structures,
> where new towers were erected, and the strengthening and
> raising of old towers. It was imperative to guard against
> vibration as far as possible, and this led to the more extensive
> use of masonry and the introduction of concrete reinforced
> with steel, instead of wooden structures.[31]

It was this relatively new building material, reinforced concrete,
that Anderson decided to use for the Main Duck Island lighthouse.

Reinforced concrete, or ferro-concrete, is the general term used
for a mixture of sand and gravel combined with Portland cement and
water which is poured into forms containing iron reinforcing bars. It is
these iron bars which give reinforced concrete greater strength over solid
concrete. As a viable building material, concrete had been in use since the
1850's.[32] For use in lighthouse construction, the material had been used as
early as 1874 when the thirty-five foot tall lighthouse at La Corbiere had
been built on Britain's Jersey Island in the English Channel.[33]

The development of reinforced concrete and its adaptation to
buildings of all sorts had been led by civil engineer Ernest Ransome.

In his article "Concrete Construction – Its Practical Application", published in the December 1894 issue of the trade journal *Canadian Architect and Builder,* Ransome had written that:

> The tensile strength of concrete is comparatively little, and by reason of the gradual though slight shrinkage that takes place in all concrete structures that age in dry situations, should not be relied upon in any important work.
>
> For giving tensile strength to concrete, all modern works of note now use iron in some form or other.
>
> Angular iron bars, cold-twisted, commend themselves in many ways, and on this continent [North America] they have been more largely used than any other form in concrete iron construction.[34]

As a qualified civil engineer as well as a charter member and past president of the Canadian Society of Civil Engineers founded in 1887,[35] William Anderson would have been familiar with Ransome's work. Under Anderson's technical leadership, Canada's Marine and Fisheries Department had begun using solid concrete for lighthouse foundations in the 1890's.[36] Starting in 1908, cast iron towers encased in concrete were being constructed on Canada's Atlantic coast. External buttresses were incorporated into the designs to provide extra support for these reinforced concrete structures. Soon, cast iron plates were replaced with iron reinforcing bars (rebar) and "flying buttresses" were being used to support ever taller concrete towers with their massive lanterns and lighting apparatus. In 1912, the reinforced concrete lighthouse on Lake Superior's Caribou Island was built to a height in excess of one hundred feet supported by flying buttresses.

By the time Anderson began designing the Main Duck Island lighthouse in 1912, his department had constructed more than a dozen buttressed, reinforced concrete lighthouses from Nova Scotia to British Columbia. These externally-supported towers ranged in height from less than thirty feet to more than one hundred feet. The tallest lighthouse built in Canada to that time <u>without</u> buttresses had been the seventy foot tall Point Mitis lighthouse on the St. Lawrence River east of Rimouski, Quebec. By designing the Main Duck Island lighthouse to be eighty feet tall with no buttresses, William Anderson was pushing the limits of this new building technology.

(114) External buttresses on the Caribou Island lighthouse, Lake Superior, c.1912. Department of the Interior.
"Flying" buttresses like these were used as external supports for the early reinforced concrete lighthouses built in Canada. Later designs for reinforced concrete towers dispensed with buttresses altogether.
[Courtesy of Library and Archives Canada, PA-043433]

Given Anderson's hands-on approach to his work — as evidenced in his annual reports to the Minister of Marine and Fisheries describing the minute attention he gave to all details of the construction, maintenance and administration of the lighthouses under his care — it is likely that he personally chose the site for the Main Duck Island lighthouse in the spring of 1912 while conducting his annual inspection tour of Great Lakes light stations aboard the Canadian Government Steamer *Lambton*. The *CGS Lambton* was one of four ships, including *Scout*, *Reserve* and *Simcoe*, that the government had purchased for lighthouse maintenance, construction and supply service on the Great Lakes to replace private vessels that had previously been hired on a seasonal contract basis.[37] With a steel hull and overall length of only 108 feet, *Lambton* was a small ship ideally suited to anchoring in shallows close to a lighthouse to run supplies to shore aboard the ship's boat.

(115) Canadian Government Steamer *Lambton*. Department of Marine and Fisheries, 1910. This 108 foot steel-hulled steamer was built for the department in 1909. Until his retirement in 1919, Marine and Fisheries Chief Engineer, William P. Anderson, spent part of each summer aboard the *Lambton* conducting his annual inspection tour of the lighthouses on the Great Lakes. The *CGS Lambton* was lost with all hands off of Caribou Island in 1922.
[From "Annual Report of the Department of Marine and Fisheries, 1909", Sessional Papers of the Dominion of Canada, No.21, Session 1910]

The site the chief engineer chose for the new lighthouse was adjacent to Canadian Hydrographic Survey Station "Ash", a triangulation station which had been established at the western tip of Main Duck Island three years earlier for the purpose of charting Lake Ontario.[38] Since the entire 740 acre island was owned by Claude "King" Cole of Cape Vincent, New York, who used it as a base for his commercial fishing operations, the Marine and Fisheries Department expropriated two acres of land for the lighthouse and keeper's dwelling, and Cole was given $200 in compensation.[39]

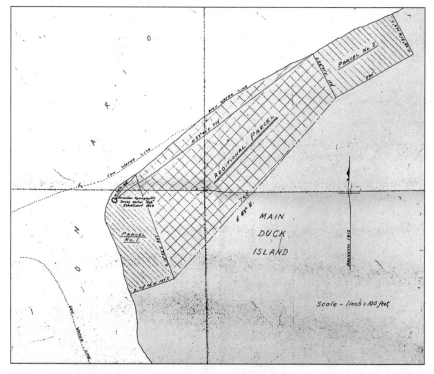

(116) Survey of Main Duck Island, 1912. Surveyor unknown.
The western point of the island was expropriated from the island's owner, Claude "King" Cole in 1913. This survey shows Hydrographic Survey Station "Ash" which was erected in 1909 on "Parcel No. 1" as a triangulation site to enable the Department of Marine and Fisheries to conduct a thorough survey of Lake Ontario. It was adjacent to this site that the Main Duck Island lighthouse was built. The duplex lightkeepers' dwelling was constructed on "Parcel No. 2".
[Courtesy of County of Prince Edward Public Library and Archives, A1982.152]

Since the 1890's, the Marine and Fisheries Department had instituted the practice of assigning two lightkeepers to remote locations instead of forcing the keeper to rely on his wife or children or a hired hand as an assistant, none of whom were directly responsible to the department. Located as it is almost ten nautical miles from the Canadian mainland, Main Duck Island was such a location, so the new lightstation would require accommodation for two keepers along with their families. To house them, a standard-pattern duplex keepers' dwelling of the type already in use at many light stations across Canada was specified.

The call for tenders for the lighthouse, keepers' dwelling and boathouse was published in August, 1913:

TENDERS

TENDERS addressed to the undersigned at Ottawa, and endorsed on the envelope, "Tender for Main Duck Island, Ont.," will be received up to noon of the Sixteenth day of September, 1913, for the construction of a reinforced concrete tower, wooden dwelling, boathouse and oil store at Main Duck Island, Lake Ontario, in the Province of Ontario....

Plans and specifications can be seen and forms of tender procured from this department, Ottawa, and at the post offices at Kingston, Picton, Bath, Deseronto, Trenton and Gananoque....

The department does not bind itself to accept the lowest or any tender.

ALEX JOHNSTON,
Deputy Minister of Marine and Fisheries,
Department of Marine and Fisheries,
Ottawa, 8th Aug., 1913.[40]

By September, all tenders had been submitted, and the following month, the contract for $17,000 was awarded to engineer and contractor, Alexander T.C. McMaster of Toronto.[41] In spite of the lateness of the construction season, McMaster immediately had his construction crew commence work on the Main Duck Island lighthouse. The only natural harbour on the island was at Schoolhouse Bay where fishermen had established a seasonal fishing village some two kilometers from the construction site; so one of the first tasks undertaken by McMaster's crew would have been the construction of a wharf and boat landing[42] so that building materials could be brought ashore directly at the lighthouse site. In some four weeks of hard work that autumn, the builders managed to construct the wharf and boat landing, lay the foundation and pour the concrete for the base of the tower before the weather became too cold to work. By the beginning of November, McMaster and his crew had left the island.[43] They would return the next spring to complete the job.

Within a month of the halt of construction, yet another ship had gone ashore on Main Duck Island. On December 4, there were reports that the steam barge *Navajo* was stranded on a reef on the south side of the island.[44] *Navajo* had gone to the rescue of another ship, the barge *Ceylon,* which was going to pieces near Poplar Point on the Prince Edward County shore with 55,000 bushels of wheat on board. Originally built on Garden Island as a schooner by the Calvin company for use in the lumber trade, *Ceylon* had recently been sold to the Montreal Transportation Company and converted to a barge to haul grain that was trans-shipped from lakers at Port Colborne. The barge had been under tow by the tug *Bartlett* bound for Montreal when they were caught in a late October gale. When *Ceylon* began to founder, *Bartlett* rescued the crew and abandoned the tow. *Ceylon* was blown into shallow waters near Poplar Point but a relentless string of gales that November thwarted many attempts to salvage the cargo.[45] Finally, the *Navajo* was able to reach the stranded barge in the first week of December and lighter some of her cargo. However, *Navajo* herself then ran into difficulties and was wrecked on Main Duck Island within sight of the partially completed lighthouse. In spite of an attempt by another steamer, the *Cornwall,* to pull the stricken vessel off the reef, *Navajo* could not be refloated and she eventually went to pieces.[46]

(117) Wreck of the steam barge *Navajo*, 1913. Photographer unknown.
The *Navajo* had made several unsuccessful attempts in the fall of 1913 to salvage part of the grain cargo from the barge *Ceylon*, which had gone ashore east of Point Petre in Prince Edward County. Finally, in December, the *Navajo* was able to load some of the salvaged grain into her holds. However, on her return to Kingston, she was wrecked on a shoal just off Main Duck Island, within sight of the lighthouse then under construction there.
[Courtesy of Prince Edward County Mariners Park Museum]

———∽∿∘৹⚬৹⚬∘∿∽———

Even as the first concrete was setting at the Main Duck Island lighthouse, there were further calls for the establishment of the Georgian Bay Canal. The *Toronto World* reported in November 1913 that:

> The Georgian Bay Canal has once more been brought into the limelight by the Montreal Board of Trade, this time in view of recent indications that the government is contemplating the appointment of a commission to enquire into the commercial feasibility of the project....
>
> They consider the question of the most vital importance to Canada at the present moment in view of the increasing shipments of grain from the Canadian west being made

thru American waters. It is their opinion that a great portion of this traffic could be rediverted to Canada thru the saving in distance the construction of a canal from Georgian Bay would mean, eliminating as it would the long trip south thru Lake Erie.[47]

In the end, the Georgian Bay Canal was never built. The canal's promoters had been right when they predicted that the deepening of the Welland Canal would mean that the Georgian Bay Canal would never become a reality. The St. Lawrence River/Welland Ship Canal route remained the primary shipping route for western grain, and this route itself was later upgraded as part of the St. Lawrence Seaway which was opened in 1959.

———— ~wo~oↄ☾◦☾◦☾☉◦☉◦oↄ~w◦ ————

In the spring of 1914, McMaster and his crew were back on Main Duck Island to finish pouring the concrete for the tower. Scaffolding was erected and a tapering octagonal wooden form was built around the iron reinforcing bars that had been spliced onto the bars that had been left protruding from the tower's base when the previous season's work had ended. The form was then filled with a precise mixture of Portland cement, sand, gravel and water to form concrete. Once the concrete had cured, the lower portion of the form would be pulled away and a new form, an octagon slightly smaller in diameter than the previous one to compensate for the taper of the tower, would be built around the next group of reinforcing bars.[48]

The forms for the lowest courses and for the uppermost courses were the most complex as they had to be crafted to include the classical architectural details that William Anderson had incorporated into the design. The forms also had to allow for the six window openings on each of two sides of the octagon that the design called for. At intervals, beams would be stretched across the open octagon along with a grid of reinforcing bars which were tied to the bars in the tower walls. A wooden form would be built around the grid and the concrete poured into the form to create a solid floor with an opening left for the stairway that was added later.

(118) Main Duck Island lighthouse under construction, 1914. Photographer unknown. The lighthouse was designed by William P. Anderson and constructed by the Toronto engineering firm of Alexander T.C. McMaster. Unlike earlier reinforced concrete lighthouses, the tower on Main Duck Island was built without external buttresses. When the tower was finished in September, 1914, it was one of the world's tallest, free-standing reinforced concrete structures.
[Courtesy of Library and Archives Canada, P-165799]

(119) The Main Duck Island lighthouse nearing completion, 1914. Photographer unknown. Families from the island's fishing village at Schoolhouse Bay would often spend leisure time at the lighthouse.
[Courtesy of Sue Fraser, Prince Edward County, Ontario]

In this way the construction of the tower proceeded throughout the summer of 1914. Periodically, supply ships from the mainland would anchor offshore and their cargoes of building materials and supplies for the construction crew would be lightered ashore. Toward the end of the summer, the flaring platform was poured to complete the top of the tower. Once the concrete of the platform had set, the seven-ton, twelve-foot diameter, cast iron lantern that had been fabricated by the Victoria Foundry Company in Ottawa[49] was carefully hoisted into place. Next came the huge 3rd order Fresnel lens,[50] 1.5 meters tall and a meter in diameter. Inside the hollow lens, a single petroleum vapour lamp was fitted. The entire apparatus was mounted on a rotating platform floating in a bath of mercury and controlled by a clockwork mechanism that gave the lighthouse its unique flashing characteristic. Its 100,000 candle-power light would be visible more than thirteen nautical miles out into Lake Ontario in clear weather. To complete the lighthouse, the lantern was glazed with twelve large panes of glass.

(120) The duplex lightkeepers' dwelling under construction on Main Duck Island, 1914. Photographer unknown.
The Main Duck Island light station was staffed with two lightkeepers. A duplex dwelling, built according to a standard pattern for similar dwellings at light stations all across Canada, was constructed to house the keepers and their families.
[Courtesy of Library and Archives Canada, PA-165798]

While carpenters put the finishing touches on the nearby duplex keepers' dwelling in August, 1914, the official "Notice to Mariners" was published announcing the establishment of the Main Duck Island lighthouse:

NOTICE TO MARINERS
No. 94 of 1914.
(Inland No. 33)
ONTARIO
(297) Lake Ontario — Main Duck Island —
Lighthouse established

Date of establishment — On or about 15th September, 1914, without further notice.

Position — On west extremity of Main Duck Island

Lat. N. 43° 55' 52", Long. W. 76° 38' 19".

Character — Flashing white light, showing one bright flash every ten seconds

Elevation — 74 feet

Visibility — 14 miles by all points of approach by water.

Power — 100,000 candles.

Order — Third dioptric.

Illuminant — Petroleum vapour, burned under an incandescent mantle.

Structure — Octagonal tower, with sloping sides; polygonal lantern

Colour — White; lantern roof, red.

Material — Tower, reinforced concrete; lantern, iron.

Height — 80 feet, from its base to the vane on the lantern.

N. to M. N. 94 (297) 27-8-14

    Department of Marine and Fisheries,

    Ottawa, Canada, 27th August, 1914.[51]

At eighty feet high, the Main Duck Island lighthouse was the tallest lighthouse on Lake Ontario. Its petroleum vapour lamp and 3rd Order Fresnel lens made it one of the brightest aids to navigation on the lake.

While Anderson's tall, unbuttressed design was a significant engineering achievement in its time, Anderson himself quickly surpassed this feat just two years later by designing the eighty-six foot tall Long Point lighthouse on Lake Erie. Before he retired in 1919, William Anderson would also design other reinforced concrete lighthouses at a number of locations across Canada including the highly ornate Point Abino lighthouse on Lake Erie and the now-famous Peggy's Point lighthouse at Peggy's Cove, Nova Scotia. Anderson died in 1927, but many of the hundreds of lighthouses that he built still stand as a memorial to his contribution to the safety and convenience of navigation in Canada.

(121) The completed Main Duck Island lighthouse, c.1915. Photographer unknown.
The lighthouse complete with its cast iron lantern. The crude structure in front of the
lighthouse is the triangulation tower of Hydrographic Survey Station "Ash".
[Courtesy of Sue Fraser, Prince Edward County, Ontario]

CONCLUSION

The completion of the Main Duck Island lighthouse in 1914 truly marked the end of the era of the traditional, iconic lighthouse. With the exception of a few minor lights, no new light stations were established on Lake Ontario after 1914. By then, more than a dozen of the forty-five staffed light towers and lighthouses that had been constructed on Canadian shores at the eastern end of the lake since 1828, had already been demolished or discontinued.

Over the next sixty years, a number of factors would combine to continue this trend of deactivation, destaffing and demolition of the region's traditional lighthouses. These factors included fewer, more seaworthy ships sailing the lakes; better methods of weather forecasting and communication of storm warnings; the closing of many harbours as ports of call for commercial vessels; significant navigation improvements including the availability of accurate charts and the adoption of onboard electronic navigation systems, and the use of modern, more durable and less expensive materials together with simpler, utilitarian tower designs to replace those fixed aids to navigation that were still useful to the recreational boating community.

After the total number of ships on the Great Lakes peaked at almost 6,000 in the early years of the 20th Century, every decade afterwards saw fewer and fewer vessels on the Great Lakes. Competition from railroads drew much of the freight traffic and passenger traffic away from ships. By the 1960's, further competition from transport trucks, commercial airlines and private passenger vehicles would further reduce the number of cargo ships sailing the Lakes. Those ships that continued to operate successfully did so by transporting large, bulk loads of grain, iron ore and other materials that were too expensive to move by other modes. By 2014, fewer than 300 commercial vessels continued to ply the Lakes: barely five percent of the peak number of ships a century earlier.[52]

(122) The steamer *Passport* shooting the Lachine rapids. Photograph by William Notman, 1891.
The *Passport* was built at Kingston in 1846, and saw service on the Bay of Quinte, Lake Ontario and the St. Lawrence River as far as Montreal. Her name was changed to *Caspian* in 1898. She had a composite iron hull sheathed in wood, an ideal combination for running the rapids of the St. Lawrence. While iron was generally more durable than wood, it was also very brittle. Eventually, steel replaced both iron and wood for commercial ship hulls.
[Courtesy of Library and Archives Canada, PA-028819]

Most ships built during the 20th Century were more seaworthy than their 19th Century counterparts so generally, they were better able to weather the types of storms that had been so destructive in the 1800's. Using modern construction materials and methods, wooden hulls were eventually replaced by iron. The first iron-hulled steamer on Lake Ontario was the *H.M.S Mohawk*, a gunboat built at the Kingston naval dockyard in 1843. She was followed by other iron-hulled vessels such as steamer *Kingston*, built at Montreal in 1855,[53] and composite ships like the *Passport* built with an iron hull sheathed in wood,[54] and the iron-framed wooden hulled *India* built by D.D. Calvin in 1899.[55] Even more durable than iron, steel-hulled ships like the *Monkshaven* and the *Spokane* first appeared on the Great Lakes in the 1880's.[56] These innovations were used in virtually every ship built in the 20th Century with the addition of features such as double bottoms, watertight bulkheads and watertight hatches,[57] all of which made ships safer and less susceptible to damage caused during a storm.

393

With the development of the science of meteorology in the latter half of the 19th Century, the weather itself was becoming less of a risk factor for mariners. No longer would ship captains have to rely solely on the barometer and weather vane for general weather predictions. In 1870, the United States government had established a weather forecasting and storm-signal service on the Great Lakes.[58] Government weather forecasters in Washington D.C., having gathered weather reports from all around the Great Lakes region, would use the latest in communication technology, the telegraph, to send storm "probabilities" to ports all along the lakes. Storm-signal flags would be hoisted at the ports to indicate the direction and severity of any forecasted storms and ship captains could then make an informed decision about whether to set sail or to wait until the storm passed. This service is reported to have had a sixty percent accuracy rate in its predictions of storms and it is credited with reducing the total number of ship casualties on the Great Lakes by two-thirds, from a high of more than one thousand incidents in 1869, to just over three hundred by 1872.[59]

The Canadian government started its own meteorological service in 1870,[60] and soon followed the lead of the Americans in establishing a storm signal service using a series of drums hoisted on a mast at various stations throughout the Great Lakes. The *British Whig* announced in November, 1871 that a signal station would soon be set up at Kingston:

> A Storm Signal Station
> The Dominion Government are about to connect Canada with the storm signal system of the United States. Meteorological stations are to be established at Montreal, Kingston, Port Stanley, Toronto, Goderich, Collingwood, Halifax, St. John and Quebec.... The Kingston station is to be one of the chief ones.... At the opening of next season, the proper signals will be displayed in some conspicuous point.[61]

However, it was August, 1873, before the signal station was finally operational:

In the month of August a signal drum was sent from Toronto, and it has been placed under charge of W. Power, Esq., at the end of whose wharf an apparatus for hoisting has been prepared. Since that time fourteen storm warnings have been forwarded, and it serves to demonstrate the utility of the science, that eleven of these warnings were found correct.[62]

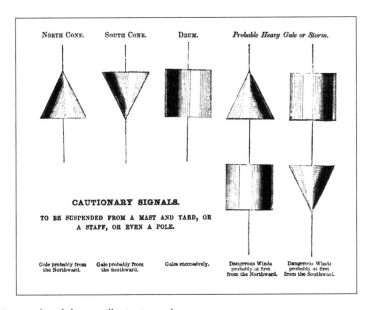

(123) Storm signal drums. Illustrator unknown.
American ports on the Great Lakes started communicating storm warnings in 1870 using a series of flags. By 1873, a similar system was in place at Canadian ports using a series of drums hoisted on a mast.
[From Fitzroy, *The Weather Book*, 1863]

Signal stations were also set up at Picton, Deseronto, Trenton and Presquile.[63] The storm signal system remained in place until early in the 20th Century by which time most ships had radio sets installed on board and radio broadcasts of marine forecasts could be sent directly to the ships. This gave navigators a chance to avoid storms by making course changes while underway. Ship-to-shore radios themselves also contributed to vessel safety as this technology allowed captains to call for help in the event of trouble.

While these developments were going on, many commercial harbours were being closed. The large, deep-draught bulk carriers sailing across Lake Ontario no longer stopped at ports along the Inside Passage and, with the opening of the St. Lawrence Seaway in 1959 with its larger locks and deeper canals, these ships could sail from Lake Superior to the Atlantic Ocean without stopping at any of the smaller harbours that had once relied heavily on shipping for their prosperity. The lighthouses in these harbours were eventually removed or replaced with simpler towers solely for the benefit of recreational boaters.

Navigational systems too saw a great deal of improvement. By the beginning of the 20th Century, accurate navigational charts were being published and frequently updated by the United States Lake Survey, the British Admiralty and the Canadian Hydrographic Service. The use of electronic navigation systems to supplement or replace lighthouses had begun in the 1950's with the implementation of onboard radar[64] as well as onboard radio direction finding equipment working in conjunction with land-based radio beacons installed at a number of lighthouses including Main Duck Island and Point Petre in 1957.[65] By the end of the 20th Century, radio beacons were superseded by other navigation technologies such as LORAN and later by Global Positioning Systems coupled with onboard computers.[66] The use of these new technologies meant that captains and navigators no longer had to rely on sighting a lighthouse in order to confirm their position.

The use of electric lights and remote monitoring systems, many of them powered by batteries charged by solar panels, meant that lightkeepers were no longer needed, and eastern Lake Ontario's last lightkeeper left Main Duck Island in 1978.[67] A quick visit by helicopter carrying a small Coast Guard crew once a year or so is now usually enough to check the lights, clean the solar panels and replace any faulty batteries. The old masonry towers and wood-framed towers are no longer being repaired. Instead, the Coast Guard's practice is either to replace these traditional lighthouses with a small electric beacon atop a simple steel cylinder or skeleton tower, or to discontinue the aid to navigation altogether.

The combination of all of these changes — fewer ships, fewer commercial harbours, better weather forecasting, onboard communications and navigation systems, and smaller, simpler replacement towers — mean that lighthouses are now, in the 21st Century, no longer essential for the safety and convenience of vessels sailing the Great Lakes, and these traditional aids to navigation have largely been relegated to a secondary role at best.

Between 1828 and 1914, more than forty-five lighthouses and light towers were built in the Canadian waters of eastern Lake Ontario from Presqu'ile Bay to Kingston harbour. This remarkable network of aids to navigation once helped to guide thousands of ships to their destinations, and it played a significant role in the history and development of Canada. Today, only seven of the original forty-five towers are still standing as monuments to a rich marine heritage that is on the verge of being lost forever.

PART III

EPILOGUE

PART III – EPILOGUE

CHAPTER 11

The 11ᵗʰ Hour

*It is felt that it will be more economical
to construct a new tower at this time.*

(J.S. Barrick, 1964)

B y 1914, only twenty-nine of the original forty-five lighthouses and
light towers that had been built in the Canadian waters of eastern
Lake Ontario were still in active service. Some, like the first Belleville
Harbour lighthouse had been unintentionally destroyed. Others, like
those at Salt Point and Wellers Bay had outlived their usefulness and
had been demolished or, like the Salmon Point lighthouse, boarded up
and sold off.

Over the next fifty years, with fewer ships on the Great Lakes;
all of them equipped with the latest onboard navigation and
communication systems and stopping at fewer harbours along their
routes, another twenty pre-1915 lighthouses and light towers in the
region were either demolished, discontinued or replaced by simpler,
automated aids to navigation.

(124) Demolition of the Pleasant Point lighthouse, 1956. Photographer unknown.
The steel skeleton tower on the far left held an electric light and a day-beacon as the replacement for the lighthouse. As soon as the 90-year old lighthouse was pulled down, it was set ablaze. Many lighthouses in the eastern Lake Ontario region suffered a similar fate in the latter half of the 20th Century.
[Courtesy of Mariners Park Museum, Prince Edward County, Willis Metcalfe collection]

Only six of the region's original forty-five fixed aids to navigation were still in active service in 1965. These included eastern Lake Ontario's four original stone towers from the 19th Century — False Ducks Island, Point Petre, Nine Mile Point and Presqu'ile Point — plus two early 20th Century lighthouses; the second Pigeon Island light and Main Duck Island. Although discontinued many years earlier, the lighthouses at Salmon Point and Prince Edward Point were still intact and, in spite of being abandoned in the 1940's, the stone tower and attached keeper's dwelling remained on Scotch Bonnet Island. In all, only nine of the original forty-five lighthouses and light towers were still standing in mid-1960's. Even these vestiges of the past were under threat of destruction. Ongoing advancements in navigation technology and illumination technology, as well as the use of more durable building materials and the simplification of tower design, would result in further changes to the few remaining lighthouses.

In 1964, the Government of Canada's Department of Transport, then responsible for Canada's lighthouses, decided to replace the aging stone tower on False Ducks Island with a new reinforced concrete light tower and attached fog-alarm building. The old lighthouse was becoming too costly to maintain and, according to the District Marine Agent at Prescott, its structural integrity was questionable:

> The lighthouse tower at False Ducks Island was constructed in 1828 and is now showing signs of serious deterioration. The mortar in the old stonework is dead and washes out easily with rain. Mortar on the interior of the tower is also crumbling.
>
> Consideration has been given to repairing this tower by encasing it in a foot of concrete, but eventually the old stonework will have to be removed.
>
> Hence, it is felt that it will be more economical to construct a new tower at this time.... It is estimated that this tower will cost $25,000.00 and permission is requested for this Agency to call for tenders and proceed with this work, as it is felt another winter may make the tower unsafe for climbing.[1]

A substantial crack had appeared in the lighthouse after it had been struck by lightning sixty years earlier. The lightning had also jumped from the tower to the keeper's dwelling and the keeper and his family had to flee the burning building.[2] The dwelling was quickly replaced, but the damage to the tower was never successfully dealt with.

In 1965, the Department of Transport allocated funds for the construction of a new light tower on False Ducks Island, and the Fort Construction Company of Prescott, Ontario, was contracted to do the work. The new False Ducks Island light tower, a unique hexagonal concrete structure surmounted by a flaring steel-framed watchroom with an electric beacon on the roof, was constructed near the old lighthouse. Attached to the new tower was a wood-framed fog-alarm building to house the diesel generators used to power the fog horn.[3]

(125) 2ⁿᵈ False Ducks Island lighthouse, 1965. Photographer unknown.
The new hexagonal reinforced concrete tower with its distinctive red stripes replaced the region's first lighthouse that had been built in 1828. In between the two towers can be seen the lightkeeper's dwelling.
[Courtesy of Mariners Park Museum, Prince Edward County, Willis Metcalfe collection]

Before demolishing the old stone tower, the heritage structure was offered to the Historic Sites Branch of the Department of Indian Affairs and National Resources (the precursor to today's Parks Canada). Interdepartmental correspondence on this subject indicated a complete lack of concern for the heritage value of the old lighthouse:

[January 13, 1965. letter from A.K. Laing, Chief Aids to Navigation to J.S. Barrick, District Marine Agent, Prescott, Department of Transport]

I have your letter of January 11ᵗʰ, 1965, asking whether or not the Department of Northern Affairs and National Resources has given its consent to the removal of the present tower.

I discussed this matter with the Chief, Historical Sites Division today and he has not had enough staff to cope with the work to be done and, therefore, has not made any inspection of the False Ducks Tower.

However, he said that they would raise no objection if we demolish the structure because the new one would have similar appearance on the horizon.

[May 11, 1965. Letter from J.R.B. Coleman, Director, Natural and Historic Resources Branch, Department of Northern Affairs and National Resources to A.K. Laing, Chief, Aids to Navigation, Marine Works Branch, Department of Transport]

... in view of the dangerous condition of the building, there was no point in delaying the disposal for historical reasons.[4]

The following April, the Department of Transport also contacted the Township of South Marysburgh in whose municipality the lighthouse stood. The reeve and council of the township wanted no part of the heritage lighthouse. The Transport Department's District Marine Agent wrote that "... the Township officials indicated that they have no interest in the old structure and would not consider taking over the maintenance of it."[5]

The local Prince Edward Historical Society had asked that the lighthouse's lantern and Fresnel lens be salvaged so that the historical society could preserve it. The original 1828 lantern, built in Brownville, New York, and equipped with Lewis lamps, had been replaced in 1885 by a lantern fabricated in Montreal by the E. Chanteloup company and equipped with a 3rd Order dioptric lens from Chance Bros. of Birmingham, England.[6] It was this later lantern that the Department of Transport agreed to give to the Historical Society who placed it atop a short. masonry-faced concrete-block tower at South Bay in Prince Edward County, now the site of the Mariners Park Museum.[7]

However, as neither the Historic Sites Branch, the guardian of Canada's built heritage, nor the local municipality had any interest in the rest of the old False Ducks tower, the Coast Guard dealt with it as described by Willis Metcalfe:

> The old stone tower which was weakened at the base by government workers, was pulled to the ground by the Canadian Lighthouse tender *Simcoe*[*II*], under Capt. Angus Morphet at 2:15pm, Friday, June 3rd, 1966.[8]

Joseph Swetman had climbed the spiraling stone staircase 137 years earlier to light the False Ducks Island lighthouse for the first time. Since then, the light had shone from the top of the masonry tower to guide ships past "the most dangerous point of the lake." Now it was a heap of rubble scattered along the shore. One hundred and thirty-seven years of Canadian marine history had been destroyed in a few hours.

That same year, the Department of Transport was considering a similar project at Nine Mile Point. However, the Department's District Engineer, C.A. Margison, determined that the Point Petre lighthouse was a better candidate for replacement as recommended in January, 1966:

> Re: Point Petre Proposal
>
> In lieu of building a new tower at Nine Mile Point as originally planned for 1966-67, it is proposed to erect a concrete reinforced tower at Point Petre as the old tower there is in a worse state of deterioration than the one at Nine Mile.
>
> The new tower is to be located approximately 700 feet from the old location adjacent to the dwellings and other buildings.
>
> The old tower and fog alarm building could be offered as is with equipment and site to the Historical Society for their

use as a complete system. Leaving it there would not affect the operation of the new light and fog alarm in any way.

A slender cylindrical reinforced concrete tower is proposed with a Crouse-Hinds DCB-10 as optic mounted on the flat top of the tower.[9]

(126) 2ⁿᵈ Point Petre lighthouse, c.1970. Photographer unknown.
The new tower at Point Petre was erected in 1967. The old stone lighthouse, built in 1833, was dynamited in 1970.
[Courtesy of Queen's University Archives, V142-14.9]

The Fort Construction Company was contracted to build the new cylindrical concrete light tower which was completed in 1968. However, in spite of Margison's assessment that the old tower "would not affect the operation of the new light", the District Marine Agent, J.S. Barrick, was complaining, even before the new aid to navigation was activated, that the old lighthouse would be an obstruction:

> The new tower at Point Petre was built because the old tower and associated buildings are unsafe and beyond repair.
>
> Further, the top section of the old tower will obscure the new light in a critical direction and our plan is to demolish it completely immediately the new light is commissioned.
>
> To assure that obstructions to our new light do not get built, we intend to level the site and retain it as part of our lightstation property.[10]

The District Marine Agent was informed by his superior that government policy stated that, before it could be demolished, the lighthouse had first to be offered to the Historic Sites Branch. This was done in February 1970, and the Historic Sites Branch replied a month later that the Point Petre lighthouse was "... not of historic or architectural significance."

> Ottawa, March 19, 1970
>
> The Point Petre lighthouse, which you advised in your letter of February 11 is slated for demolition, was placed on the agenda of the February 19th and 20th meeting of the Historic Sites and Monuments Board of Canada.
>
> In 1966 the Board had prepared for it a comprehensive survey of lighthouses on the Great Lakes system, among which was that at Point Petre. Documentation of this structure was sufficiently complete for the Board to establish that it is not of historic or architectural significance.
>
> The Minister has now approved the Board's recommendation and I would advise that this Department has no further interest in the lightstation at Point Petre. [11]

On April 1, Barrick communicated that, "... arrangements will be made to demolish the structure as time and personnel permit".[12]

In the meantime, the Prince Edward Historical Society together with the Township of Athol in Prince Edward County had sent a letter to the Department of Transport "... asking that the proposed demolition be delayed until some overall plan for the entire property could be established."[13] Unfortunately, that request was either ignored or overlooked. With no regard for the wishes of local stakeholders, and with no public consultation of any sort, demolition specialists entered the lighthouse on the morning of Friday, May 1, 1970, and set dynamite charges around the base of the tower. A few hours later, the 137-year-old Point Petre lighthouse was a pile of rubble.[14]

When asked about the request to delay the demolition, the Department of Transport claimed that dynamiting the lighthouse had been a mistake. The Historical Society strongly disagreed and suggested that the lighthouse be rebuilt as a Public Works project.[15] There is no record of the government's response to this last suggestion.

The nine original lighthouses that had survived into the 1960's had been reduced to only seven. By the time complete destaffing of Canadian lighthouses on Lake Ontario had been accomplished in the 1970's, the future of the remaining lighthouses was uncertain.

For the next two decades, lighthouse preservation organizations across Canada tried to convince the federal government to enact legislation to protect the dwindling number of traditional lighthouses. Some local groups were successful in their attempts to preserve individual lighthouses that were being disposed of by the Government of Canada, one at a time, at various locations across the country, but it was not until 2000 that the Canadian Senate introduced the Heritage Lighthouse Protection Act (HLPA) that promised to provide some limited measure of protection for those lighthouses that were still owned by the federal government. It took another eight years before the Act was passed by the Canadian House of Commons. In

2008, Bill S-215, received royal assent and the Heritage Lighthouse Protection Act came into force in 2010.[16]

The legislation was quickly hailed by heritage organizations as a positive step toward preserving these historic structures. Just as quickly, though, the Canadian Department of Fisheries and Oceans (DFO), which was then in charge of Canada's lighthouses, announced that more than 500 active lighthouses and light towers were "surplus to operational requirements"[17] and would be disposed of by the federal government so that DFO would not have to bear the costs of preserving them as stipulated by the HLPA. As surplus lighthouses, they could only be preserved if a province, a community organization or a private group were willing to acquire one or more of them and show that they had a viable plan to finance the conservation of the lighthouses over the long-term.[18]

In spite of this attempt by the government to undermine its own legislation, 348 lighthouses across Canada were nominated for heritage designation under the HLPA. These included the Nine Mile Point lighthouse (1833), the Scotch Bonnet Island lighthouse (1856), the Prince Edward Point lighthouse (1881) and the Main Duck Island lighthouse (1914). The modern light towers at False Ducks Island and Point Petre were also nominated. However, as of April, 2015, only 16 lighthouses have been designated under the Act and none of those is on Lake Ontario. The deadline for heritage designation as imposed by the Act is May, 2015.

Neither the Presqu'ile Point lighthouse nor the Salmon Point lighthouse is covered by the HLPA since they are not owned by the Government of Canada. The Presqu'ile Point lighthouse (1840) is located in Presqu'ile Provincial Park and is owned by the Government of Ontario and it has some limited heritage protection under the Ontario Heritage Act.[19] Nevertheless, this lighthouse is in poor condition and it has been estimated that at least one million dollars is required to conserve the tower.[20] The Salmon Point lighthouse has been privately owned for a century and the various owners have attempted to preserve the structure. However, located as it is on prime real estate, there is nothing to prevent the current owner from modifying, moving or demolishing the lighthouse. The County of Prince Edward has the authority to designate the lighthouse as a property of heritage value or significance under the Ontario Heritage Act, but the county has refused to take any steps that could help preserve this historic building.[21]

The nearby Scotch Bonnet Island lighthouse (1856) is in ruins. The outline of the masonry tower and the attached keeper's dwelling can still be seen, but the structure is rapidly crumbling. The island itself has been designated as a National Wildlife Area and the lighthouse has not been declared surplus by its owners, Environment Canada. The lighthouse has been nominated under the HLPA, but it has not yet been designated as a heritage lighthouse. Until that happens, the federal government has no intention to spend any money on conserving this heritage structure.

The Prince Edward Point lighthouse (1881), known locally as the Point Traverse lighthouse, is in a similar situation. It is located in the Prince Edward Point National Wildlife Area and has been owned by Parks Canada since 1975. In spite of being owned by the guardian of Canada's built heritage, very little has been done to conserve the lighthouse and the wooden structure is rotting away.

The lighthouses at Nine Mile Point (1833), Main Duck Island (1914), False Ducks Island (1965) and Point Petre (1968) have all been declared surplus by DFO, and local organizations[22] are in the process of trying to acquire the lighthouses from Government of Canada so that they can be conserved under the terms of the HLPA.

The Pigeon Island lighthouse (1909) is also a surplus lighthouse, but it has not been petitioned under the HLPA, and no organizations have expressed any interest in preserving the tower on this remote island in Lake Ontario.

The table below summarizes the status of the Canadian lighthouses in the eastern Lake Ontario region as of March 2015.

(Table 1) Status of remaining lighthouses – March 2015

Lighthouse	Active	Type	Current Owner	Notes
Nine Mile Point	1833 to present	Cylindrical stone	Fisheries and Oceans Canada	- condition fair - declared surplus - petitioned under HLPA*
Presqu'ile Point	1840 to present	Octagonal stone	Ontario Ministry of Natural Resources	- condition poor - limited protection under the Ontario Heritage Act
Scotch Bonnet Island	1856 to 1959	Cylindrical stone with attached dwelling	Environment Canada	- in ruins - petitioned under HLPA*
Salmon Point (Wicked Point)	1871 to 1913	Pyramidal wood	Privately owned	- condition fair - no heritage protection
Prince Edward Point (Point Traverse)	1881 to 1959	Pyramidal wood	Parks Canada	- condition poor - petitioned under HLPA*
2nd Pigeon Island	1909 to present	Structural steel	Fisheries and Oceans Canada	- condition fair - declared surplus - no heritage protection - can be purchased for $1.
Main Duck Island	1914 to present	Octagonal reinforced concrete	Fisheries and Oceans Canada	- condition fair - duplex keeper's dwelling condition poor - declared surplus - nominated under HLPA*
New False Ducks Island light tower	*1966 to present*	*Hexagonal reinforced concrete*	*Fisheries and Oceans Canada*	*- condition fair* *- declared surplus* *- nominated under HLPA**
New Point Petre light tower	*1968 to present*	*Cylindrical reinforced concrete*	*Fisheries and Oceans Canada*	*- condition fair* *- declared surplus* *- nominated under HLPA**

HLPA - Heritage Lighthouse Protection Act

The remarkable network of lighthouses and light towers that once stretched along the Canadian shores of eastern Lake Ontario is no more to be seen. Here and there, modern mariners may be able to catch a glimpse of an isolated lighthouse on a lonely point or on a remote island. These are the only hints that, at one time, forty-five of these essential aids to navigation dotted the shores and helped to guide ships and their passengers and crews to safety. The few lighthouses that are still standing are the only monuments remaining to a rich heritage of marine commerce and a history of economic growth which had once relied so much on lighthouses to ensure that ships arrived safely at their destinations.

Ranging in age from less than fifty years, to more than one hundred eighty years, these lighthouses are the last of their kind. Lighthouses are no longer being built, and all of the remaining towers in eastern Lake Ontario are being allowed to deteriorate until such time as they will become victims of "demolition by neglect". In spite of federal legislation like the Heritage Lighthouse Protection Act and provincial legislation such as the Ontario Heritage Act, these iconic structures are now more at risk of disappearing than ever before. There is great reluctance at all levels of government to take any steps to preserve these important monuments of our national marine heritage. The cost of conservation of many of these lighthouses, some situated in very remote locations, can be daunting. Lighthouses in other parts of Canada have been saved by being repurposed as museums, or inns, or simply preserved out of a sense of local pride as historic landmarks.[23] Some examples of the adaptive re-use of lighthouses in Canada can be seen in Appendix 4.

In the eastern Lake Ontario region, volunteers with organizations such as Save Our Lighthouses, the Hastings Prince Edward Land Trust, Presqu'ile Point Lighthouse Preservation Society, Nine Mile Point Lighthouse Preservation Society and many others are spending countless hours in an attempt to save the few heritage lighthouses that remain. To date, however, little progress has been made, and the future of these historic monuments, and the future of heritage lighthouses all across Canada, remains uncertain.

For want of a lighthouse in the 19ᵗʰ Century, ships were lost.
For want of a lighthouse in the 21ˢᵗ Century, our heritage will be lost.

You can help save these lighthouses and others that may be in your own area. Speak to your elected representatives, get involved with a local heritage organization, visit a lighthouse, or contact a local lighthouse preservation society.

All profits from the sale of this book will be donated
toward the preservation of lighthouses in Canada.

Contact Marc Seguin...
email: lighthouses@ontariohistory.ca
telephone: 613-394-0897
mail: RR3, Consecon, Ontario, Canada K0K 1T0

APPENDICES

Appendix 1
List of Lighthouses and Light Towers, Eastern Lake Ontario, 1829-1914

(italics = discontinued before 1914)   *(* = still standing in 2015)*

Official Name (Other Name)	Year Activated	Designer (Builder)	Style (material)	First Keeper	First Light	Overall Height	Status as of 2015
Barriefield Common Range Front	1892	Canada Bridge Co. (Dept. Marine & Fisheries)	tripod framework (iron)	A. Milligan	locomotive lamp	48 ft	Demolished
Barriefield Common Range Rear	1892	Canada Bridge Co. (Dept. Marine & Fisheries)	tripod framework (iron)	A. Milligan	locomotive lamp	75 ft	Demolished
(Bath wharf light)	c.1900	unknown	unknown	unknown	unknown	unknown	Demolished
Belleville Harbour(1ˢᵗ) (Belleville railway pier)	*1851*	*unknown*	*unknown*	*unknown*	*unknown*	*30 ft*	*Destroyed by fire 1879*
Belleville Harbour (2nd) (Belleville harbour pier)	1881	(Northcott & Alford)	pyramidal (wood)	J. Covert	anchor light	36 ft	Destroyed by fire 1941
(Billa Flint's wharf light)	1835	unknown	on building	unknown	unknown	unknown	Demolished

417

Appendix 1

List of Lighthouses and Light Towers, Eastern Lake Ontario, 1829-1914

(italics = discontinued before 1914)   *(* = still standing in 2015)*

Official Name (Other Name)	Year Activated	Designer (Builder)	Style (material)	First Keeper	First Light	Overall Height	Status as of 2015
Brighton Range Light No. 1	1891	(W. Alford)	pyramidal (wood)	H. V. Simpson	unknown	30 ft	Demolished
Brighton Range Light No. 2	1891	(W. Alford)	pyramidal (wood)	H. V. Simpson	unknown, red	47 ft	Demolished
Brighton Range Light No. 3	1891	(W. Alford)	pyramidal (wood)	H. V. Simpson	unknown	30 ft	Demolished
Centre Brother Island (Middle Brother Island)	1890	(N.J. Leonard)	pyramidal, dwelling attached (wood)	R. Filson (*asst. keeper Richards*)	dioptric	31 ft	Demolished
Deseronto Harbour (Rathbun Co. wharf)	1885	(Rathbun Co.)	pyramidal, on building (wood)	Rathbun Co.	anchor light	46 ft	Discontinued 1916, demolished

Appendix 1

List of Lighthouses and Light Towers, Eastern Lake Ontario, 1829-1914

(italics = discontinued before 1914)   (* = still standing in 2015)

Official Name (Other Name)	Year Activated	Designer (Builder)	Style (material)	First Keeper	First Light	Overall Height	Status as of 2015
False Ducks Island (Outer Drake, Swetman Island)	1829	T. Rogers (R. Matthews & W. Scott)	conical (stone)	F. Swetman	catoptric, 15 Lewis lamps	62 ft	Demolished and replaced 1966
(Garden Island)	c.1900	(Calvin Co.)	on building	unknown	unknown	unknown	Demolished
Kingston harbour (*Kingston marine railway wharf*)	*1846*	(*Sidney Scobell*)	*unknown*	*G. Clark*	*unknown*	*unknown*	*Demolished*
*MAIN DUCK ISLAND	1914	W.P. Anderson (A.T.C. McMaster)	octagonal (concrete)	J. Clark	dioptric 3rd Order, flashing	80 ft	ACTIVE *
Murray Canal East Pier Light (1st)	1891	(Dept. Railways & Canals)	pyramidal framework (wood)	F. Fitzgerald	copper pier lamp, red	12 ft	Demolished
Murray Canal West Pier Light (1st)	1891	(Dept. Railways & Canals)	pyramidal framework (wood)	C.A. Harries	copper pier lamp, red	12 ft	Demolished

Appendix 1

List of Lighthouses and Light Towers, Eastern Lake Ontario, 1829-1914

(italics = discontinued before 1914)   (* = still standing in 2015)

Official Name (Other Name)	Year Activated	Designer (Builder)	Style (material)	First Keeper	First Light	Overall Height	Status as of 2015
Murray Canal East Pier Light (2nd)	1899	(Dept. Railways & Canals)	Hexagonal cabin (galvanized iron)	unknown	dioptric	27 ft	Demolished
Murray Canal West Pier Light (2nd)	1899	(Dept. Railways & Canals)	Hexagonal cabin (galvanized iron)	unknown	dioptric	27 ft	Demolished
The Narrows Shoal (Nigger Island Shoal, Makatewis Island)	1894	Dept. Marine & Fisheries	pyramidal (wood)	C. Jeffrey	dioptric 7th Order	27 ft	Demolished
***NINE MILE POINT** (Gage's Point, Point Yeo)	1833	T. Rogers (R. Matthews)	conical (stone)	W. Sparham	catoptric, 10 Lewis lamps	40 ft	ACTIVE *

Appendix 1

List of Lighthouses and Light Towers, Eastern Lake Ontario, 1829-1914

(italics = discontinued before 1914)   (= still standing in 2015)*

Official Name (Other Name)	Year Activated	Designer (Builder)	Style (material)	First Keeper	First Light	Overall Height	Status as of 2015
Onderdonk Point (Onderdonk bluff)	1911	(T.H. Brewer, Dept. Marine & Fisheries)	square (wood)	E. Bryant	dioptric 7th Order	20 ft	Discontinued 1941, demolished
Pigeon Island (1st)	*1870*	*(R. Cameron)*	*school-house (wood)*	*J. Eccles*	*catoptric, 2 lamps*	*41 ft*	*Demolished and replaced 1870*
★**PIGEON ISLAND (2nd)**	1909	Goold, Shapley & Muir Co. (M.J. Egan, Dept. Marine & Fisheries)	pyramidal framework (steel and wood)	J.H. Davis	dioptric 4th Order, flashing	65 ft	ACTIVE *
Pleasant Point (Point Pleasant, Upper Gap, Indian Pt.)	1866	F.P. Rubidge (Public Works Dept.)	octagonal (wood)	J. Prinyer	catoptric	52 ft	Demolished 1956
Point Petre (Long Point, Peter's Point)	1833	T. Rogers (R. Matthews & W. Scott)	conical (stone)	O. Richards	catoptric, 11 Lewis lamps	60 ft	Replaced 1966, demolished 1970

Appendix 1

List of Lighthouses and Light Towers, Eastern Lake Ontario, 1829-1914

(italics = discontinued before 1914)   (* = still standing in 2015)

Official Name (Other Name)	Year Activated	Designer (Builder)	Style (material)	First Keeper	First Light	Overall Height	Status as of 2015
Portsmouth Harbour (1st) (*Portsmouth pier*)	*1880*	*unknown*	*unknown*	*unknown*	*unknown*	*unknown*	*Destroyed by storm Feb. 1887*
Portsmouth Harbour (2nd) (*Portsmouth pier*)	*1887*	*unknown*	*unknown*	*unknown*	*unknown*	*unknown*	*Destroyed by storm Oct. 1887*
Portsmouth Range Front (Little Cataraqui Bay)	1912	(T.H. Brewer, Dept. Marine & Fisheries)	pyramidal (wood)	E. Graham	dioptric 4th Order	33 ft	Demolished
Portsmouth Range Rear (Little Cataraqui Bay)	1912	Goold, Shapley & Muir Co. (M.J. Egan, Dept. Marine & Fisheries)	pyramidal framework (steel and wood)	E. Graham	catoptric	64 ft	Demolished
Potters Island (temporary light)	1892	(Dept. Marine & Fisheries)	pole light	Frank Dempsey	tubular lantern	20 ft	Removed 1894

Appendix 1

List of Lighthouses and Light Towers, Eastern Lake Ontario, 1829-1914

(italics = discontinued before 1914)   (* = still standing in 2015)

Official Name (Other Name)	Year Activated	Designer (Builder)	Style (material)	First Keeper	First Light	Overall Height	Status as of 2015
*PRESQU'ILE POINT (Presqu'Isle Main)	1840	N.H. Baird (J. McLeod)	octagonal (stone)	W.J. Swetman	catoptric, 11 lamps	67 ft	ACTIVE *
Presqu'ile Range Front (Salt Point)	*1851*	*(T. Lee, J. Newman & J. Smith)*	*pyramidal (wood)*	*W. Swetman Jr.*	*catoptric, 2 lamps*	*16 ft*	*Discontinued 1913, demolished*
Presqu'ile Range Rear (1st)	*1851*	*(T. Lee, J. Newman & J. Smith)*	*pyramidal (wood)*	*W. Swetman Jr.*	*catoptric, 1 lamp*	*16 ft*	*Discontinued 1891, demolished*
Presqu'ile Range Rear (2nd) (Calf Pasture Shoal)	*1879*	*(R. Cameron)*	*pyramidal (wood)*	*W. Swetman Jr.*	*catoptric, red*	*22 ft*	*Moved to Brighton Range No.1 1891*
*PRINCE EDWARD POINT (Point Traverse, South Bay Point)	1881	(J.W. Fegan)	pyramidal, dwelling attached (wood)	D.McIntosh	catoptric, red	36 ft	Discontinued, INACTIVE *

423

Appendix 1

List of Lighthouses and Light Towers, Eastern Lake Ontario, 1829-1914

(italics = discontinued before 1914)   (* = still standing in 2015)

Official Name (Other Name)	Year Activated	Designer (Builder)	Style (material)	First Keeper	First Light	Overall Height	Status as of 2015
SALMON POINT (*Wicked Point*)	1871	(R. Cameron)	pyramidal, dwelling attached (wood)	Lewis Hudgins	unknown, red	40 ft	Discontinued 1913, INACTIVE *
*SCOTCH BONNET ISLAND (Egg Island)	1856	unknown	conical (stone)	J. Giroux	catoptric, 8 lamps	54 ft	Automated 1919, IN RUINS *
Snake Island Shoal (1st)	1858	unknown	square (stone)	L. Wartman	catoptric, 3 lamps, red	35 ft	Demolished
Snake Island Shoal (2nd)	1900	(W.H. Noble, Dept. Marine & Fisheries)	octagonal (wood)	W.B. Orr	dioptric 7th order	39 ft	Moved to Four Mile Point 1918
Telegraph Island	1870	(R. Cameron)	School-house (wood)	J. Mason	catoptric	41 ft	Demolished

Appendix 1

List of Lighthouses and Light Towers, Eastern Lake Ontario, 1829-1914

(italics = discontinued before 1914)   (* = still standing in 2015)

Official Name (Other Name)	Year Activated	Designer (Builder)	Style (material)	First Keeper	First Light	Overall Height	Status as of 2015
Trenton Range Front (Trenton Harbour)	1905	(Dept. Marine & Fisheries)	mast	W. Fitzpatrick	Anchor light, red	20 ft	Demolished
Trenton Range Rear (Trenton Harbour)	1905	(Dept. Marine & Fisheries)	mast	W. Fitzpatrick	Anchor light, red	30 ft	Demolished
Wellers Bay Range Front	*1876*	*(Love and Harper)*	*pyramidal (wood)*	*R. Young (asst .keeper Silverson)*	*catoptric 1 lamp*	*22 ft*	*Discontinued 1910, demolished*
Wellers Bay Range Rear	*1876*	*(Love and Harper)*	*pyramidal framework (wood)*	*R. Young (asst .keeper Silverson)*	*catoptric 1 lamp*	*35 ft*	*Discontinued 1909, demolished*

425

Appendix 2

List of Lightkeepers, Eastern Lake Ontario, 1829-1914

Compiled by Marc Seguin, 2015

Lighthouse	Name of Keeper	Appointed	Salary	Note	Source
Barriefield Common	Milligan, Alex.	1892 Apr 25	$150		SP1893
	Murray, William	1900 May 17	$180		SP1911
Bath wharf	*unknown*	?	?	Private light	
Belleville Harbour (1*st*)	*unknown*	1851	?	Municipal light	
Belleville Harbour (2*nd*)	Covert, John	1881 Jun 1	$200		SP1900
	Weir, J.C.	1901 Apr 4	$240	Dismissed OIC-1912-0594	SP1911
	Smith, H.J.	1912 Apr 27	$275		SP1915
Belleville harbour pier	---	---	---	*(see 2nd Bellville Harbour)*	---
Belleville railway pier	---	---	---	*(see 1st Bellville Harbour)*	---
Brighton Range Lights	Simpson, Hedley V.	1888 May 11	$540	Started as keeper of Presqu'Isle Range Lights Became keeper of Brighton Range lights	SP1899
	McKenzie, Hugh H.	1907 May 7	$205		SP1911
Calf Pasture shoal	---	---	---	*(see Presqu'ile Rang Rear, 2nd)*	---
Centre Brother Is.	Filson, Robert	1890 Apr 27	$200	Filson hired asst. Richards 1890-91	SP1891

Appendix 2

List of Lightkeepers, Eastern Lake Ontario, 1829-1914

Lighthouse	Name of Keeper	Appointed	Salary	Note	Source
Centre Brother Is.	O'Rourke, Michael	1894 Jun 18	$200	Replaced Filson by OIC 1894-1547	SP1900
	Wemp, Daniel	1901 Jan 9	$240		SP1911
	Miller, J.	1913 Oct 30	$260		SP1915
Deseronto Harbour	Rathbun Lumber Co.	1884 Oct. 14	$200		SP1915
	Canadian Northern Railway	1914 June 6	$200		SP1916
Egg Is.	---	---	---	(*see Scotch Bonnet Is.*)	---
False Ducks Is.	Swetman, Joseph	1833		- as of 1859	SP1860
	Swetman, Frederick	1863?	$435	- as of 1865	SP1865
	Lane, Wm Hazelton	1886 Jun 28	$350	*Vice* Fred Swetman, superannuated	SP1887
	Farington, Philip	1889 ?	?		RDC
	Hudgins, James M.	1894 Apr 28	$350		SP1900
	Dulmage, Dorland	1903 May 19	$800		SP1911
	Hudgins, J.W.	1912 May 3	$905	Light and fog alarm	SP1915
Gage's Pt.	---	---	---	(*see Nine Mile Pt.*)	---
Garden Is.	*unknown*	?	?	Private light	
Hatter's Bay	---	---	---	(*see Portsmouth Harbour*)	---

Appendix 2

List of Lightkeepers, Eastern Lake Ontario, 1829-1914

Lighthouse	Name of Keeper	Appointed	Salary	Note	Source
Indian Pt.	---	---	---	*(see Pleasant Pt.)*	
Kingston harbour	Clark, G.	1847	?		BW1847
Kingston marine railway	---	---	---	*(see Kingston Harbour)*	---
Long Pt.	---	---	---	*(see Point Petre)*	---
Main Duck Is.	Clark, J.	1914 Oct	?	- first keeper	CSQW
	Bongard, Fred	1915	$600	- listed as *Temporary*	SP1916
Makatewis Is.	---	---	---	*(see Narrows Shoal)*	---
Middle Brother Is.	---	---	---	*(see Centre Brother Is.)*	---
Murray Canal East Pier	Fitzgerald	1890 Aug 22	25¢ per day	to Nov 30, 1890	SP1892
	Harries, Peter	1891 Apr 15	50¢ per day	to June 30, 1891	SP1892
	Harris, P.	1892	$129.50	259 days at 50¢ per day (same person as Harries above?)	SP1893
	Johnson, H.	1898	50¢ per day	March 30 to Dec. 6	SP1899
Murray Canal West Pier	McAuliff, M.	1891 Aug 22		to Sep 16, 1891	SP1892
	Harries, C.A.	1891 Sep 17	50¢ per day	to Nov 30, 1891	SP1892
	Talmage, A.	1898		March 30 to Dec. 6 – 50¢ per day	SP1899
The Narrows Shoal	Jeffrey, Carson	1894 Apr 28	$200		SP1900
Nigger Island Shoal	---	---	---	*(see Narrows Shoal)*	---

Appendix 2

List of Lightkeepers, Eastern Lake Ontario, 1829-1914

Lighthouse	Name of Keeper	Appointed	Salary	Note	Source
Nine Mile Pt.	Sparham, Thomas.	1833	£26.5.7	– as of 1856 – succeeded by J. Dunlop	JLA1835
	Dunlop, John	1855	£86.17.6		JLA1857
	Dunlop, Albert	1872 Feb 28			SP1873
	Veech, Stannes	1894 Mar 7	$450	Lightkeeper and engineer of fog alarm	SP1900
	Moreland, F.	1895 Apr 1	$200		SP1900
Onderdonk Pt.	Bryant, E.	1911 Mar 6	$140		SP1912
	Allison, W.	1912 Apr 25	$150		SP1915
Outer Drake	---	---	---	(*see False Ducks Is.*)	---
Peter's Pt.	---	---	---	(*see Point Petre*)	---
Pigeon Is. (1ˢᵗ)	Eccles, James	1870 Nov 1	$300		SP1872
	Davis, J.W.	1872 Mar 5		– drowned with 5 others, 4 Nov 1873	SP1873
	Davis, Mary	1873	$300	Widow of J.W. Davis – acting keeper for 11 years	SP1880
	Davis, Richard	1884 Feb 15	$300		SP1885
	Davis, John H.	1896 May 6	$350		SP1900
Pigeon Is. (2ⁿᵈ)	Davis, John H.	1896 May 6	$350		SP1911

Appendix 2

List of Lightkeepers, Eastern Lake Ontario, 1829-1914

Lighthouse	Name of Keeper	Appointed	Salary	Note	Source
Pleasant Pt.	Prinyer, John	1867 Jan 4	$300	Point Pleasant	SP1899
	Connors, Frank	1898 Oct 13	$200	- dismissed by OIC-1912-1573	SP1900
	Gordon, Mrs. M.	1913?	$380	(temporary)	SP1914
	Carson, S.C.	1913 Apr 18	$380		SP1915
Point Petre	Richards, Owen	1833	£65	Colonel Owen Richards – age 65	UC1848
	Palen, William A.	1843	$435 in 1859	superannuated May 1, 1876 at $281.40 per annum –	SP1877
	Burlingham, James	1876 May 1	$650	Also Fog Alarm – (OIC-1891-0415)	SP1900
	Scott, J.G.	1901 Jun 6	$800	or Guy F. Scott	SP1911
	Farrington, T.A.	1913 Jan 25	$905	light and fog alarm	SP1915
Point Pleasant	---	---	---	*(see Pleasant Pt.)*	---
Point Yeo	---	---	---	*(see Nine Mile Pt.)*	---
Point Traverse	---	---	---	*(see Prince Edward Pt.)*	---
Portsmouth Harbour (1st & 2nd)	*unknown*	?	?	Municipal light	
Portsmouth Range	Graham, E.	1912 Apr 27	$230		SP1915
Presqu'Isle Main	---	---	---	*(see Presqu'ile Pt.)*	

Appendix 2

List of Lightkeepers, Eastern Lake Ontario, 1829-1914

Lighthouse	Name of Keeper	Appointed	Salary	Note	Source
Presqu'ile Pt.	Swetman, W.J	1840 June 10	$325	W. Swetman Sr. of the town of Kingston (SP1860)	UCH1840
	Simpson, G.B.	1870 Jan 28	--- $700	Appointed 15 May 1873 to the charge of the 3 lights (Main plus 2 range lights), buoys and timber	SP1871 SP1874
	Sherwood, Wm H.	1874 Apr 29	$375	Presqu'Isle, main light in place of G.B. Simpson who was appointed keeper of the range lights and guardian of the peninsula	SP1875
	Smith, H. E.	1898 Apr 29	$350	- lightkeeper	SP1911
	Ainsworth, W.B.	1907 Oct 12	$600	- engineer	
	Cornwall, F.T.	1912 May 24	$380	- lightkeeper	SP1915
	McColl, H.C.	1914 Feb 27	$600	- engineer	SP1915
Presqu'ile Range	Swetman, W. Jr	1840	£62.7.6		JLA1857
	Cummins, James	1856?	$250		SP1866

Appendix 2

List of Lightkeepers, Eastern Lake Ontario, 1829-1914

Lighthouse	Name of Keeper	Appointed	Salary	Note	Source
Presqu'ile Range	Simpson, G.B.	1873 May 15	$700	- in charge of the 3 lights (main light plus range lights), buoys and timber on the peninsula - W.H Sherwood took over the main light 1874	SP1874
	Simpson, Hedley V.	1888 May 11	$540	Succeeded G.B Simpson, deceased (SP1889)	SP1899
Prince Edward Pt.	Fegan, Thomas	1881 June 3	$200	Temporary charge of light, June 3rd to Oct 3rd, 1881	SP1883
	McIntosh, Daniel	1881 Oct 1	$200		SP1900
	Vorce, Marcellus	1902 Nov 21	$240		SP1911
	Hudgins, W.	1912 Jun 15	$275		SP1915
Rathbun Co. wharf	---	---	---	(*see Deseronto Harbour*)	---
Salmon Pt.	Hudgins, Lewis	1871 Oct 23	$300	- includes remuneration for his services in connection with the lifeboat stationed there under his charge	SP1873
	Huff, Peter	1876 Jun 27	$300	- in the room of Mr. Lewis Hudgins, superseded	SP1877
Salmon Pt.	Hudgins, Lewis	1879 Mar 23	$300	He was also the keeper 1871-76	SP1880

Appendix 2

List of Lightkeepers, Eastern Lake Ontario, 1829-1914

Lighthouse	Name of Keeper	Appointed	Salary	Note	Source
	McDonald, Amos	1897 Jul 12	$400		SP1900
	Short, Anson	1909 Oct 13	$300		SP1911
	Cavanagh, James	1911 Mar 21	$395	Dismissed 1912 – OIC-1912-0822	SP1913
	Clark, A.	1912 May 13	$380		SP1914
Salt Pt.	---	---	---	(*see Presqu'île Range*)	---
Scotch Bonnet Is.	Giroux, John	1856	?		JLA1857
	Wilson, Samuel	1859?	326.25		SP1860
	Vandusen, H.	1865?	$435		SP1866
	Bentley, Wilson	1868	?	H. Vandusen retired	SP1869
	Bentley, Lafayette	1874 Sep	?	Wilson Bentley died – temporarily in charge of his son	SP1875
	Pye, Robert	1877 Apr 6	$400	in place of Mr. Wilson Bentley, deceased	SP1878
	Farley, William	1896 Feb 19	$350		SP1899
	Spencer, D.O.	1898 Aug 8	$350		SP1900
Scotch Bonnet Is.	Spencer, Cyrus R.	1903 Apr 7	$425	Dismissed by OIC-1912-0821	SP1911

Appendix 2

List of Lightkeepers, Eastern Lake Ontario, 1829-1914

Lighthouse	Name of Keeper	Appointed	Salary	Note	Source
	Cunningham, B.Y.	1912 May 9	$460	Plus $25 for operating fog horn or bell	SP1915
Simcoe Is.				*(see Nine Mile Pt.)*	
Snake Is. (1st)	Wartman, Lewis	1858	$108.75		SP1860
	Lamb, Geo and Herchmer, Lawrence	1859?	322.29		SP1860
	Orr, Nathaniel T.	1868 Oct 2	?		SP1870
	Orr, Wm Breden	1888 Jul 2	$350	Succeeded N.T. Orr, deceased	SP1889
Snake Is. (2nd)	Whitmarsh, John	1900 Jul 18	$375	Dismissed 1912 – OIC-1912-0339	SP1911
	Sudds, C.V.	1912 Mar 16	$275	Plus $25 to operate fog horn or bell	SP1915
South Bay Pt.	---	---	---	*(see Prince Edward Pt.)*	---
Swetman Is.	---	---	---	*(see False Ducks Is.)*	---
Telegraph Is.	Mason, John	1870 Nov 12	$200		SP1872
	Mrs. Mason	?	?	John Mason's widow	CSQW
	Rowe, Geo. Albert	1895 Oct 25	$200		SP1899
	Benn, M.	1912 Dec 10	$275		SP1915
Trenton Harbour	---	---	---	*(see Trenton Range)*	---

Appendix 2

List of Lightkeepers, Eastern Lake Ontario, 1829-1914

Lighthouse	Name of Keeper	Appointed	Salary	Note	Source
Trenton Range	Fitzpatrick, William	1906 Jan 27	$120	Trenton Harbour	SP1909
	Spicer, C.W	1909 May 5	$120		SP1911
	McHenry, J.H.	1912 Jun 5	$190	(or J.A. McHenry)	SP1915
Upper Gap	---	---	---	*(see Pleasant Pt.)*	---
Wellers Bay Range	Young, Reuben	1876 Aug 16	$150	Edward Silverson was the assistant keeper 1876-89	SP1877
	Orser, William	1889 Feb 16	$150	Dismissed for political partisanship OIC-1898-2426	SP1890
	Chase, H.J.	1898 Nov 4	$150		SP1900
Wicked Pt.	---	---	---	*(see Salmon Pt)*	---

BW = Board of Works, Canada

CSQW = Metcalfe, *Canvas and Steam on Quinte Waters*,1979

JLA = Journal of the Legislative Assembly, Canada

LAC RG-12 vol. 1507-7958 = Memo, Marine and Fisheries, 1891

OIC = Order-in-Council

RDC = Rochester Democrat, 18 September 1932

SP = Sessional Papers, Canada

UC = Upper Canada

UCH = Upper Canada Herald

APPENDIX 3

Specification - Presqu'ile Point Lighthouse
N.H. Baird, 1837

"Specification for the erection of a Light House on
Presque Isle point"

[Source: Archives of Ontario. "Baird Papers. Specifications sent to Commissioner Donald Campbell, Colborne, 10 Aug 1837." Other Projects, Presqu'ile Lighthouse, Miscellaneous Documents, 1837 - 1842. E-5, Box 18, Env. 1.] Punctuation has been added for clarity. (Plans are shown in image 33)

General description. 69 feet from foundation to top of blocking course. Basement to be 8 feet in height 30 feet square. Tower Octagon 23 ft.-6 in. at Base, 17 feet at top.

The Light House to be erected on the Site as marked out on the point by a trial pit dug thereon to the solid rock at a distance of 75 feet from the Lake shore as shewn on the accompanying elevation.

The Foundation for the building to be excavated thro' the sand and made to the solid Rock and one foot into the same leaving an irregular but level foundation for a base which shall be 30 feet square, 3 feet of which shall be solid masonry laid in water cement including the foot under surface of the rock: from the rock surface the Base to be 7 feet to the sill cornice of the Tower which shall be one foot in diameter with a semidiameter projection of 6 Inches. From the bottom of the sill course to the top of the capital to be 62 feet which shall be of an Octagon figure as per plan & Elevation. At 3 feet from the top of the cornice to contract to 23 feet 6 Inches Diameter to a radius of 4 feet as shewn, from which point the Tower to be carried up in a straight batter of 3 feet on the side to the bottom of blocking course or capital at which point the building will consequently contract the Shaft to 17 feet on the outer side Capital to be 18 Inches in thickness as shewn on Elevation accompanying.

As the set off (3 feet above cornice), the wall to be 6 feet in thickness which with the batter already mentioned will leave a thickness of 2 feet 6 In. at the full height saving the gathering to the inside diameter of Lanthorn [lantern] of 6 courses leaving a clear well hole of 8 feet diameter. The inside of walls being carried up perpendicularly to a radius of 5 feet 9 In. making a wall of 11 ft. 6 In. diameter surmounted by a substantial coping corresponding to moulding of capital upon which a Lanthorn of Cast Iron from work 10 feet in diameter & 11 feet in height with a corresponding as shewn on detailed elevation to be glazed with best plate glass

Lanthorn to be also Octagon the details of which will be more particularly given at a future period but to be estimated on the most approved principal now in use on Lake Ontario. Lanthorn to be surrounded by a maleable Iron railing 4 feet in height of bars of 1 inch square Iron properly let into the capital and run with lead — to have a hand railing of hard wood properly secured to an iron coping which shall be rivetted to the uprights or may be at the option of the Contractors rivetted into an Iron sill & coping with principales as in manner as shewn on the Elevation properly secured at each angel of the Octagon and run with Lead and batte down. Coping in Capital stones to be properly batted to each other by two bales in each — of Iron 2 ½ Inch by ½ Inch run with Lead. For manner of inserting Lanthorn see section by which the sill is let in its own thickness or flush with coping in white lead & flannel on Fur & plaiding — secured to the building by eight 1 ½ Inch bolts of Swedish Iron.

The well to have six floorings laid thereon in manner shewn per plan & section — joints to be 14 In. by 5 In. built into the side walls half through the same and laid with 2 Inch flooring having a well hole in each furnished with 2 inch trap doors with wrot Iron hinges and a ring bolt sufficient to allow a man to pass conveniently up and down by the wooden stairs as shewn, having the bridles so placed as to allow sufficient head room. Beams to [be] of red pine. The steps of stairs of Oak 2 inches thick, sides red pine. Outside door to be substantial Oak — door 2 Inches thick cross band & rivetted with a good substantial double lock. Masonry of the building to be of good hammer dressed courses one or two of which to correspond with one of the corner quoins which are not to be less than 15 Inches in thickness and to be properly dressed Ashler of proportional dimensions no thicker to be less in breadth of bed at the narrowest part than the thickness of the courses done half M — to be not less than 3 feet in length to be laid alternately and in band. Attention must be paid to have the body of the wall in one or two regular courses to correspond with the Ashler into which it is to band. All stones must be laid on their natural beds and one header for every two stretchers alternately — header must not be less in length of face than twice its thickness and not less in depth into the walls than three time is own thickness — stretchers not less in breadth of bed than one & a half times the thickness of course or less in length than 3 times the thickness — and no stone to break band less than 9 Inches — the [hearting] of the wall to be carefully laid flush in their well made mortar till it oozes out and each course well packed and grotted before another is commenced — The latticed windows to be done according to plan & section but should the Commissioners thro' their Engineer deem it adviseable to introduce Gothic windows 2 feet 6 inches in width over the door, the same to form no extra charge with the exception of the framing & Glazing the lintels of the lattices to have a projection weather barge of 1 ½ Inch worked out of the lintel as per elevation.

The Oil room to be provided with a double trap door on Iron hinges and otherwise properly secured of sufficient dimensions to admit a puncheon of Oil to be provided with a trap &c. Floor of oil room to be paved with 4 Inch flags or pavement properly laid. The masonry of solid basement to [be] done in manner described for the rest of the work but to be properly grooted, each course with hot lime & cement mixed. The whole of the masonry to be laid in well made mortar. The courses and blocking courses to be laid in water Lime, best clear coarse grit sand to be used

Lime not to be slacked and exposed to air more than necessary before using. Shells to be kept in temporary sheds and allowed to fall by the action of the air. The water not to be applied till the day it is used — Could Iron stone dust be procured, the water cement may be dispensed with by mixing the common hot mortar with a proportion of the dust and sharp clear sand in which case the mixture should be used throughout the entire building.

The outside courses, beds & joints to be neatly pointed and drawn. The beds of Quoins to have a rustic or champher to be taken off both beds 2 ½ inches on the face and ¾ of and inch on the bends to have a tooled margin of one & half inch round the head & face of the stones. Centre of stone to be stripped with a narrow tool 2 inches asunder or neatly boucharded — End joints to be worked full to the [quarel] at least to ¾ the breadth of bed — the inside or well hole to receive 3 coats of plaster of best quality. Woodwork to have 3 coats best white lead. Lanthorn &c. to be painted in same manner ordnance blue [probably similar to French blue]. The ceiling of the floors and beams to be white washed with hot lime

The whole of the work to be done in a substantial workman like manner and to the satisfaction of the Commissioners and the Engineer....

The whole to be completed by the 1ˢᵗ Sept 1838.

APPENDIX 4

Examples of Lighthouse Reuse in Canada

Sources: - DFO, "Alternate Use Study Surplus Lighthouses, Canada". March 2011
              - web: http://www.lighthousefriends.com

Lighthouse	Prov.	Current Owner	Reused as...	Notes
Point Atkinson	BC	Joint mgmt - City of West Vancouver & Govt of Canada	Landmark in nature reserve	Designated a Nat. Historic Site in 1994
Campbellton	NB	Community org.	Youth hostel	
Dalhousie Wharf	NB	-Private	Storage shed	Building moved to new site No public access
Green's Point	NB	Community org.	Seasonal rental & museum	
Head Harbour	NB	Community org.	Museum	$12K, grant from Prov.
Wilmot Bluff	NB	-Private	Storage shed	No public access
Cape Anquille	NL	Joint mgmt – Linkum Tours & DFO	B&B	
Ferryland Head	NL	HLPA surplus Community org	Museum and hiking trails	Lighthouse Picnics
Long Point	NL	Joint mgmt – Local tourism org. & Town of Twillingate	Gift shop – Plans for artist studio and restaurant	Funding from ACOA and Prov.
Quirpon Island	NL	Joint mgmt – Linkum Tours & DFO	B&B	
Rose Blanche	NL	Community organization	Museum	When Prov. funding stopped, the museum closed
Cape d'Or	NS	Local economic dev. org.	B&B	
Cape Forchu	NS	Munic. of Yarmouth	Museum & tea room Comm. org. handles day-to-day operations. Munic. funds the preservation	Initial funding of $2.7M from ACOA and Federal Stimulus Fund in 2000
Fort Point	NS	Joint mgmt - Town of Liverpool & Local Tourism org.	Museum	
Port Medway	NS	Local municipality	Landmark in park	Funding from 3 levels of govt.

Lighthouse	Prov.	Current Owner	Reused as...	Notes
Sambro	NS	HLPA surplus	- petition resulted in local MP introducing Bill C-588	Est. 1758 – oldest continuously operated lighthouse in the Americas
Sandy Point	NS	Joint mgmt – Local munic. & community org	Landmark	$65,000 initial grants in 2008 Community org. now responsible for conservation
Cove Island	ON	HLPA surplus	Museum	Located on remote island.
Flowerpot Island	ON	Parks Canada	Seasonal rental	$100/day fee for "Lightkeeper" program
Gibraltar Point	ON	City of Toronto	Conserved as a heritage landmark	Oldest remaining lighthouse on Great Lakes
Hope Island	ON	Community org.	unknown	
L'Orignal	ON	Private	none	No public access
Lake Superior – various	ON	Coalition of community organizations	Various – museums, tourist information, landmarks	Some lighthouses located on remote islands.
Long Point Cut	ON	Private	Private cottage	No public access
Manitoulin Island - various	ON	Local munic. and organizations	Museums and/or tourist information	
McKay Island, Bruce Mines	ON	Private	*Seasonal rental*	No public access
Point Abino	ON	City of Fort Erie	unknown	Sold keeper's dwelling to fund preservation.
Port Burwell	ON	Local municipality	Museum/tourist information	
Port Dalhousie	ON	Joint mgmt – City of St. Catharines and Niagara College	Classroom for sailing school	College pays City rental fee. City maintains the building.
Presqu'ile Point	ON	Government of Ontario	Conserved as a heritage landmark	$1,000,000 currently required for restoration
Salmon Point	ON	Private	unknown	No public access
PEI – various	PE	Various Private/Public Partnerships	B&B	
Pointe a la Renommée	QC	Joint mgmt – Munic. of Gaspé & local Dev. Agency	Museum	Annual fundraising campaign and Prov. grants

END NOTES

Abbreviations Used:

AJHA - Appendix to the Journal of the House of Assembly of Upper Canada

AJLA - Appendix to the Journal of the Legislative Assembly of the Province of Canada

DCB - Dictionary of Canadian Biography Online

LAC - Library and Archives Canada

M&F Report - Annual Report of the Department of Marine and Fisheries, for the fiscal year ending June

SP - Sessional Papers of the Dominion of Canada

Introduction

1. The term "graveyard of Lake Ontario" was first coined by the *Syracuse Herald* (13 March 1926) referring to the waters around Main Duck Island. This term is also used in the *United States Coast Pilot* (No. 6, 2014, p. 178) to refer to Mexico Bay in the extreme south-east corner of Lake Ontario

2. The population of Upper Canada in 1806 was estimated at 70,718. Joseph Bouchette. *The British Dominions in North America*, Vol. 2. London 1831. p. 235. The U.S. Census of 1800 shows a combined population of 107,646 in Michigan Territory, Ohio, and the counties of western New York State within 100 kilometers of the Great Lakes. United Status Census Office. *Census Reports*, Vol. I., *Twelfth Census of the United States*. Washington, 1901.

3. See: J.R. Robertson, *Landmarks of Toronto*, vol. 2. Toronto, 1896. Also see: J.B. Mansfield, *History of the Great Lakes*, vol. 1. Chicago, 1899.

4. Census of Canada, 1901 shows the population of Ontario as 2,182,947. United Status Census Office. *Census Reports*, Vol. I., *Twelfth Census of the United States*. Washington, 1901, shows the population of western New York, plus Ohio and Michigan as 8,274,197

5. There were 1,508 registered Canadian vessels in the Province of Ontario, and 2,855 U.S. vessels (sailing ships plus steamboats) on the Northern Lakes for a total of 4,363. Mansfield, *ibid*, pp. 423 & 439.

Part I – The Setting

Chapter 1   Lake Ontario

1. J.B. Mansfield. *History of the Great Lakes*, vol. 1. Chicago, 1899. p. 81

2. J.R. Robertson. *Landmarks of Toronto*, vol. 2. Toronto, 1896. pp. 818-820

3. Lord Dorchester, *An Ordinance, For promoting the Inland Navigation*, Quebec, 1788

4. Government ships *Caldwell*(sloop), *Mississaga*(schooner), *Mohawk*, and *Onondaga* (schooner). Merchant ship *York*. Robertson, ibid. pp. 821-824.

5. Isaac Weld, *Travels Through the States of North America and the Provinces of Upper and Lower Canada During the Years 1795, 1796 and 1797*, London, 1799, p. 284

6. *Treaty of Amity, Commerce and Navigation*. Philadelphia, 1795

7. Mansfield, *History of the Great Lakes*, p.127

8. U.S. Census of 1800 shows a combined population of 107,646 in Michigan Territory, Ohio, and the western New York counties within 100 kilometers of the Great Lakes. United Status Census Office. *Census Reports*, Vol. I., *Twelfth Census of the United States*. Washington, 1901

9. Isaac Weld. *ibid*. p. 281

10. Population estimated at 70,718. Joseph Bouchette. *The British Dominions in North America*, Vol. 2. London 1831. p. 235

11. See: *Treaties and Agreements Affecting Canada, 1814-1913*. Ottawa, 1914, pp. 22-26

12. See: Robertson, *ibid,* and Mansfield, *ibid,* for detailed discussions on the numbers of ships on the Great Lakes in the 19th Century

13. John Collins, quoted by William Caniff, *History of the Settlement of Upper Canada*, Toronto, 1869, p. 149

14. Isaac Weld. *ibid.*

15. Elizabeth Simcoe, *The Diary of Mrs. John Graves Simcoe*, annot. By J. Ross Robertson, Toronto, 1911

16. Kingston Chronicle, 15 Sep 1820, p. 3

17. Edward Allen Talbot, *Five Years' Residence in the Canadas*, London, 1824, p. 98

18. Kingston Chronicle, Dec. 24, 1819

19. *Mark L. Thompson. Graveyard of the Lakes.* Detroit, 2000. pp, 210-212. Also see: "Return... on the subject of meteorological observations and weather reports, 1872", *SP No. 53, Sess. 1872. Ottawa, 1872*

20. Orland French. Wind, Water, Barley & Wine. Belleville 2013. p. 32

21. *Kingston Gazette.* 12 April, 1817. Kingston 1817

22. John Howison. *Sketches of Upper Canada*. Edinburgh, 1821. p.54

23. Montreal Gazette, May 21, 1832. p. 2

24. Canadian Hydrographic Service. *Great Lakes Pilot Vol. 1, 6th ed.* Ottawa 1967. p.xxxviii

25. NOAA. *Bathymetry of Lake Ontario* map. National Geophysical Data Center, National Environmental Data and Information Service & Great Lakes Environmental Research Laboratory, Office of Oceanic and Atmospheric Research. U.S.A 1999.

26. NOAA. *United States Coast Pilot 6: Great Lakes, 2014* (44th Edition). Washington 2014. p. 178

27. *ibid*

28. See: *Shipwreck: A Comprehensive Directory of Over 3,700 Shipwrecks on the Great Lakes.* Boyne City Michigan 1992. Also see: "The David Swayze Great Lakes Shipwrecks File".

29. Data analysis by the author based on "The David Swayze Great Lakes Shipwrecks File". *ibid.*

30. Mark Monmonier, *Lake Effect: Tales of Large Lakes, Arctic Winds, and Recurrent Snows.* Syracuse, NY 2012. pp. 1-5

31. *The Globe.* Toronto, Nov. 28, 1860

32. *The Daily British Whig*, Kingston, Nov. 27, 1860. p. 2.

33. D.D. Calvin and T.R. Glover. *A Corner of Empire.* Toronto 1937. p. 66

34. Francis F. Atkin. *Atkin's Pocket Compass.* Oswego, 1871. p. 56.

35. Howard Patterson. *Patterson's Illustrated Nautical Dictionary,* New York 1891

36. Richard Palmer. "Lake Ontario's First Chartmaker". http://www.ancestry.com/s33216/t11564/grid1003/rd.ashx

37. "Letter from Augustus Ford to U.S. Congress", 1842. http://freepages.genealogy.rootsweb.ancestry.com/=twigs2000/chartmaker.html

38. "Dictionary of Canadian Biography". http://www.biographi.ca/en/bio/owen_william_4E.html. Also see: http://www.biographi.ca/en/bio/bayfield_henry_wolsey_11E.html

39. *Catalogue of Admiralty Charts, Plans, and Sailing Directions.* London 1898. p. 80

40. Oswego County Whig, May 30, 1838, p.2

41. The R.C.Y.C was founded in 1852 as the Toronto Yacht Club. Hodder was the club's Commodore from 1856 to 1859, 1862 to 1872, and 1874 to 1877. C.H.J. Snider. *Annals of the Royal Canadian Yacht Club.* Toronto, 1937

42. Edward Hodder, *The Harbours and Ports of Lake Ontario.* Toronto 1857. p. 4

43. Atkin. *ibid.* pp. 3-4

44. Arthur M. Woodford. *Charting the Inland Seas.* Detroit 1991. p. 14

45. *ibid.* p. 37

46. See chart: *Lake Ontario.* United States Corps of Engineers. New York 1877

47. Patterson, *ibid,* p. 270

48. Hydrographic Survey Office, Department of Naval Service. *Sailing Directions for Canadian Shores of Lake Ontario.* Ottawa 1921. p. 11

49. "Compass Bearings on Lake Ontario", *The Marine Record,* 26 September 1895. Cleveland 1895. p. 8

50. "The Recent Disaster on Lake Ontario", *Daily Ontario.* Belleville, 20 Nov 1879. p. 2

51. Willis Metcalfe. *Canvas and Steam on Quinte Waters.* Prince Edward County, 1979. endsheet.
    Paul Ackerman's *Lake Ontario Dive Chart* confirms at least twenty wrecks that have been located and identified by scuba divers, see: Midwest Explorer's League. *Lake Ontario Dive Chart.* Chicago, 1983

52. Save Ontario Shipwrecks. *Wrecks of Eastern Lake Ontario* map. Henderson Printing Inc. Brockville, Ontario 2004

53. "The David Swayze Great Lakes Shipwreck File", compiled by Brendon Baillod from the research of David Swayze. http://www.ship-wreck.com /shipwreck/swayze/

54. *The Provincial Statutes of Upper Canada*. York, 1818. p. 158

55. Larry & Patricia Wright. *Great Lakes Lighthouses Encyclopedia*. Erin, Ontario, 2006. pp. 50 and 58.

Chapter 2   The "Inside Passage

1. William Smyth, *A Short Topographical Description of His Majesty's Province of Upper Canada in North America*, London, 1799, p. 16

2. Heriot, George. *Travels Through the Canadas*. London, 1805, p. 58

3. Bouchette, Joseph. *The British Dominions in North America*. London, 1831. pp. 79-80

4. Richard Bonnycastle. *Canada and the Canadians, Vol. II.* London, 1846. pp. 222-228

5. Michael Smith, *A Geographical View of the Province of Upper Canada*, Trenton, N.J., 1813. pp.33-34. Also see: Seventh Town Historical Society. *7ᵗ Town/ Ameliasburgh Township Past & Present.* Bloomfield, 1984. pp 55-63

6. William Canniff. *History of the Settlement of Upper Canada*. Toronto, 1869. p. 142. See also

7. See: G.P. de T. Glazebrook. *A History of Transportation in Canada*. Toronto, 1938. pp. 118-124. See also: Edwin C. Guillet. *Pioneer Travel in Upper Canada*. Toronto, 1966. pp. 132-151.

8. David William Smyth. *A Map of the Province of Upper Canada*. London, 1800.

9. Swayze, *ibid DETAILS OF RESEARCH !!!*

Part II – The Lighthouses

1. The U.S. Census of 1820 counted a total 1,003,292 people in Michigan Territory, Ohio and the counties of western New York State located within 100 kilometers of Lake Ontario. U.S. Census Office. *ibid*

2. The General Census of Upper Canada for 1824 counted 156,886 people in the province. *AJHA*. Toronto 1828. App. 5

3. Robertson, *ibid*, p. 983

4. *Reports of the Commissioners of Internal Navigation*. Kingston, 1826

5. See: Bogart, Ernest L. "Early Canal Traffic and Railroad Competition in Ohio", *Journal of Political Economy,* Vol. 21. Chicago, 1913.

6. *Statutes of Upper Canada*, York, 1824, p. 93,

7. 1830 U.S. Census, 1,595,178 people. U.S. Census Office. *ibid*

8. Population Returns for 1828 counted 197,925 people in Upper Canada. *AJHA*. Toronto 1829. App. 4

Chapter 3   First Light

1. *Loyalist*, December 16th, 1826 — quoted from Robertson's Landmarks of Toronto: vol. 2, J. Ross Robertson, Toronto, 1896.

2. "Report of the Select Committee to whom was referred the petition of certain ship owners and others praying for a light-house upon the False Ducks Island", *AJHA, Sess. 1826-27*. York, 1827. App. Q

3. Robert L. Saunders. "Robinson, Sir John Beverly - Dictionary of Canadian Biography". URL: http: //www.biographi.ca /en/bio/ robinson_john_beverley_9E.html

4. "Report of the Select Committee... False Ducks Island", *ibid*.

5. DCB Vol VIII

6. *Kingston Chronicle*. Kingston, Nov. 29 1822. p. 3

7. *Kingston Gazette*. Kingston, Dec. 7, 1816, p.3

8. *Kingston Gazette*. Kingston, Dec. 14, 1816, p. 3

9. "Chart of the Bay of Quinté and of the South shore of Prince Edwards County Lake Ontario. Surveyed by the Hydrographic Department under the direction of Captain Fitz William Owen Royal Navy in the years 1815 and 1816". Drawn, 1846. The National Archives, UK, MR1/848/22.

10. "Report of the Select Committee... False Ducks Island", *ibid*.

11. "Report of the Commissioners appointed to superintend the erection of a Light House on the False Ducks Island", *AJHA 1829*. York, 1829. p 29

12. Walter Lewis. "McKenzie, James - Dictionary of Canadian Biography." URL: http://www.biographi.ca/en/bio/mckenzie_james_1832_6E.html

13. "Report of the Select Committee... False Ducks Island", *ibid.*

14. *Statutes of His Majesty's Province of Upper Canada, 4th Sess, 9th Parliament.* York. 1828. pp. 13-14.

15. Thomas L. Brock. "Barrie, Sir Robert", *Dictionary of Canadian Biography.* URL:http://www.biographi.ca/en/bio/barrie_robert_7E.html

16. *Statues of His Majesty's Province of Upper Canada 1827.* York, 1827. p 28

17. Robert L. Fraser. "Macaulay, John", *Dictionary of Canadian Biography.* URL:http://www.biographi.ca/en/bio/macaulay_john_8E.html

18. T.R. Millman. "Macaulay, William - Dictionary of Canadian Biography". URL:http://www.biographi.ca/en/bio/macaulay_william_10E.html

19. Jane Errington. "Kirby, John - Dictionary of Canadian Biography". URL:http://www.biographi.ca/en/bio/kirby_john_7E.html

20. "Rogers, Thomas - Biographical Dictionary of Architects in Canada 1800-1950". URL: http://dictionaryofarchitectsincanada.org/architects/view/1414

21. Letter from J.W. Macaulay to G. Gillier, Kingston, May 12, 1828. LAC RG5-A1, vol. 89, reel C9823, pp. 48977-48978

22. "Report of the Commissioners appointed to superintend the erection of a Light House on the False Ducks Island, in Lake Ontario, Dec. 24, 1828". *Appendix to the Journal of the House of Assembly of Upper Canada.* York, 1829, p. 32

23. "Report of the Commissioners... False Ducks Island", *ibid.*

24. George Lothropp Starr. *Old St. George's.* Kingston, 1913. p. 42

25. "Report of the Commissioners... False Ducks Island". *ibid.* p. 29

26. Peter Nicholson. *Practical Masonry, Bricklaying, and Plastering.* London 1841. p. 191

27. "Report of the Commissioners... False Ducks Island". *ibid.* p. 29

28. "Report of the Commissioners... False Ducks Island". *ibid.*

29. "Report of the Commissioners... False Ducks Island". *ibid.*

30. Appendix to the XVIIth volume of the Journals of the House of Assembly of the province of Lower Canada. Quebec, 1809. App No. 8

31. "Report of the Commissioners... False Ducks Island". *ibid.*

32. Francis Ross Holland Jr., *America's Lighthouses: An Illustrated History.* New York, 1972. pp. 15-16

33. See: Alan Stevenson. *A Rudimentary Treatise on the History, construction, and Illumination of Lighthouses.* London, 1850. pp. 66-69

34. Alan Stevenson. *On the Theory and Construction of Lighthouses*. Edinburgh 1857. p. 464

35. Holland, *ibid.*

36. "Report of the Commissioners... False Ducks Island". *ibid.*

37. "Report of the Commissioners... False Ducks Island". *ibid.* p. 30

38. *Kingston Chronicle*, 15 Sep 1820

39. "Report of the Commissioners... False Ducks Island". *ibid.* p. 29

40. "Report of the Commissioners... False Ducks Island". *ibid.* p. 30

41. URL:http://en.wikipedia.org/wiki/List_of_tallest_buildings_in_ Montreal#Timeline_of_tallest_buildings, URL:http://en.wikipedia.org/wiki/ Michigan_State_Capitol#First_state_capitol

42. "Report of the Commissioners... False Ducks Island". *ibid.*

43. "Report of the Commissioners... False Ducks Island". *ibid.*

44. "Report of the Commissioners... False Ducks Island". *ibid.*

45. "Report of the Commissioners... False Ducks Island". *ibid.*

46. *The Statues of the Province of Upper Canada*. Kingston, 1831. p. 509

47. *Kingston Chronicle*, Kingston. April 11, 1829. p.2

48. "Report of the Commissioners... False Ducks Island". *ibid.* pp. 30-31

49. "Petition of Joseph Swetman". *Appendix to the Journal of the House of Assembly of Upper Canada, 1833-34*. Toronto 1834. p. 218

50. *Pioneer Life on the Bay of Quinte*. Toronto, 1904. p. 742

51. Willis Metcalfe. Canvas and Steam on Quinte Waters. South Bay, 1979. p. 156

52. This description of the watchroom of the False Ducks Island lighthouse is based on an on-site examination conducted by the author in 2013 of the nearly-identical Nine Mile Point lighthouse.

53. *Upper Canada Herald*. Kingston, July 29, 1829. p. 3

Chapter 4   A Chain of Stone

1. "Report of the Select Committee on the Petition of G. Chalmers and Others", *Appendix to the Journal of the House of Assembly of Upper Canada, 1836-1837*. Toronto, 1837, App. 33, p. 2

2. "Captain Joseph Whitney". *Chronicle and Gazette*, Nov. 3, 1841. Kingston 1841. p.2

3. Chisholm was in the shipping and lumbering business and had substantial land holdings at the mouth of the Sixteen Mile Creek where the town of Oakville was established. See: Walter Lewis, "Chisholm, William". Dictionary of Canadian Biography, http://www.biographi.ca/en/bio/chisholm_william_7E.html

4. "REPORT of the Select Committee on the Petition of Captain Whitney and others, on the subject of a Light House on Long Point", *Appendix to the Journal of the House of Assembly of Upper Canada,1831-32.* Toronto 1832. pp. 174-175

5. Ronald J. Stagg. "McIntosh, John". Dictionary of Canadian Biography. url: http://www.biographi.ca/en/bio/mcintosh_john_1796_1853_8E.html

6. Robertson. *Landmarks*, ibid. Ch. 241

7. "Canadian Geographical Names, Long Point". Natural Resources Canada. http://www4.rncan.gc.ca/search-place-names/unique/FCASI, accessed 3 October 2014

8. Statutes of His Majesty's Province of Upper Canada. 2nd Session, 11th Parliament. York, 1832. pp. 94-95

9. Simeon (aka Simon) Washburn. See: Ruth McKenzie. "Washburn, Simon Ebenezer", Dictionary of Canadian Biography. URL:http://www.biographi.ca/en/bio/washburn_simon_ebenezer_7E.html

10. J.K. Johnson & P.B. Waite. "Macdonald, Sir John Alexander." Dictionary of Canadian Biography. URL:http://www.biographi.ca/en/bio/macdonald_john_alexander_12E.html

11. See: "Early Canadiana Online", http://eco.canadiana.ca/search?q=%22john+marks%22+-brunswick&field=&so=oldest&df=1825&dt=1868&collection=gvp

12. "Report of the Commissioners for Superintending the Erection of a Light-House on Point Peters", *Appendix to the Journal of the House of Assembly, 1832-33.* York 1833. p. 215

13. Note: The local pronunciation of "Point Petre" is PEETER, not PEE-TREE. This likely stems from the original name of the point being Point Peters, or Peter's Point, and the name was later misprinted on a map of Prince Edward County. While the misprint became the officially accepted spelling, the pronunciation of the original spelling was maintained.

14. "Report of the Commissioners... Point Peters", *ibid.*

15. *ibid.* p. 218"

16. "Kingston Mechanics' Institution", *Chronicle and Gazette.* Kingston, April 13, 1836. p.2

17. F.A. Burrall. *Asiatic Cholera.* New York, 1866. p. 25

18. "Cholera at Quebec and Montreal", *Free Press.* Hallowell, June 19, 1832

19. Extract from the *Kingston Watchman* appearing in the *Free Press*, Hallowell June 26, 1832. p. 2

20. Carroll Dunham. *Cholera.* New York 1866. pp6-7

21. David A Sack, R. Bradley Sack, G. Balakrish Nair, AK Siddique. "Cholera", *The Lancet.* Oxford, 17 January 2004 (Vol. 363, Issue 9404,. pp. 223-233

22. *Free Press.* Hallowell, June 26, 1832. p. 2

23. "Report of the Kingston Board of Health", *Free Press.* Hallowell July 3 and July 17, 1832

24. *Upper Canada Herald.* Kingston, August 29, 1832, p. 3

25. "Report of the Commissioners... Point Peters", *ibid. p. 218*

26. *ibid.* p. 215"

27. J. Baby. "Report from Inspector General on Light-houses on Point Peter", *AJHA 1832-3.* pp. 213-214

28. "Report of the Commissioners... Point Peters", *ibid.* p. 215"

29. J. Baby. "Report from Inspector General...", *ibid.*

30. LAC RG9 I-B-1, Letters Received, Vol. 19, 18822

31. *Chronicle and Gazette.* Kingston, Dec. 9, 1843. p. 2

32. "M&F Report", *SP No. 5, Sess. 1877.* Ottawa, 1877. p. xiii

33. *Journal of the House of Assembly of Upper Canada,* from the thirty-first day of October, 1832 to the thirteenth day of February, 1833. York,1833. p.94

34. "Western Steamboat", *Kingston Chronicle.* Kingston, Oct. 22, 1831, p. 2

35. Statutes of Upper Canada, 3rd Session, 11th Provincial Parliament. York, 1833. ch. 36, pp. 147-148

36. *Report of the commissioners appointed to superintend the erection of a penitentiary in Kingston.* Kingston, 1833.

37. J.R. Robertson. Robertson's Landmarks of Toronto, vol. 5, Toronto, 1908.

38. http://www4.nrcan.gc.ca/earth-sciences/geography-boundary/geographical-name/search/unique.php? output=xml&id=FCOKY

39. *The Provincial Statutes of Upper Canada.* York, 1818. p. 158

40. Barbara Wall Laroque. *Wolfe Island: A Legacy in Stone*, 2009. p. 52

41. "Report of the Commissioners for constructing a Light House on Nine Mile Point near Kingston", *AJHA 1833-1834*. Toronto, 1834. p. 184

42. *ibid.*

43. *Journal of the House of Assembly of Upper Canada,1836-1837*. Toronto, 1837. p 537

44. "Report of the Commissioners... Nine Mile Point ". *ibid.*

45. "Letter to the Editor", *Kingston Spectator*. Kingston, Nov. 19, 1833. p. 2

46. *Chronicle and Gazette*. Kingston, Oct 31, 1835. p. 3

47. "Report... Point Peters'. *ibid*

48. "An act to provide for the payment of light house keepers... and for other purposes", *Statutes of His Majesty's province of Upper Canada*, 1ˢᵗ Sess. 13ᵗʰ *Parliament*. Toronto, 1837. p. 388

49. "Report of the Board of Works", *Appendix to the third volume of the journals of the Legislative Assembly of the Province of Canada, Session 1843*. Kingston, 1844. App. Q

50. *Chronicle and Gazette*. Kingston, May 4, 1844. p.3

51. "AN ACT granting to His Majesty a sum of Money for the erection of certain Light-houses, within the Province", *Statutes of Her Majesty's Province of Upper Canada*. Toronto, 1837. p. 386

52. *Kingston Chronicle*. Kingston, 15 Dec 1820, p.3

53. Robert Gourlay. *Statistical Account of Upper Canada*. London, 1822. p. 94.

54. *Chronicle & Gazette* (Kingston, ON), 4 Oct 1834, p.2

55. *ibid.*

56. *British Whig*, "The Editors Trip, part 3", 2 Dec 1834. Kingston., p.3 and *British Whig*, "The Editors Trip, part 4", 9 Dec 1834. Kingston. p.3

57. Journal of the House of Assembly of Upper Canada, 1ˢᵗ Sess., 12ᵗʰ Parl., Feb 5. 1835, p. 99

58. *AJHA, Sess. 1836*. Toronto, 1836. p.17. also, *Journal of the House of Assembly of Upper Canada, 1836*. Toronto, 1836. p. 82. Many of the petitioners, including John Steele, would become shareholders of the Colborne Harbour Company, formed in 1837. see, *Statutes of His Majesty's province of Upper Canada, 1837*. Toronto, 1837. p. 202.

59. *Journal of the House of Assembly of Upper Canada*, from the 15ᵗʰ day of January, to the 16ᵗʰ day of April 1835, Toronto, 1835. p. 191

60. *Journal of the House of Assembly of Upper Canada, 1836.* Toronto, 1836. p. 330

61. ibid, p. 331

62. Journal of the Legislative Council of Upper Canada, second session of the twelfth Parliament, Toronto, 1836. p 169

63. J.K. Johnson. *Becoming Prominent.* Montreal, 1989. p. 151

64. *Journal of the House of Assembly of Upper Canada, from the eighth day of November, 1836, to the fourth day of March, 1837.* Toronto, 1837. p. 226

65. ibid, pp. 236-237

66. Statutes of His Majesty's province of Upper Canada, passed in the first session of the thirteenth Parliament of Upper Canada ... Toronto G. Tiffany, 1837. pp 386-388

67. *ibid.*

68. John Witham. "Baird, Nicol Hugh", in *Dictionary of Canadian Biography,* vol. 7, University of Toronto/Université Laval, 2003–, accessed September 22, 2014, http://www.biographi.ca/en/bio/baird_nicol_hugh_7E.html.

69. "Report of the Commissioners for Erecting Presqu'Isle Light-House", *Appendix to the Journal of the House of Assembly of Upper Canada,* 4th Session, 13th Parliament. Toronto, 1841. p. 303

70. *The Patriot.* Toronto, Aug. 11, 1837. p. 4

71. "Report... Presqu'Isle Light-House", *ibid.*

72. *ibid*

73. In 1840, the lightkeeper was only paid £37,5s,6d of the normal £65 salary. This would indicate that the keeper was paid for just over half of the shipping season, meaning that the light did not go into service until sometime in July, 1840. See: "Statement of Supplies, Appendix C", *Appendix to the first volume of the journals of the Legislative Assembly of the province of Canada : session 1841.* Kingston, 1842

74. "Report of the Chairman of the Board of Works", *Appendix to the fifth volume of the journals of the Legislative Assembly of the Province of Canada.* Montreal, 1846. App. N

75. *The Provincial Statutes of Canada: 1st Session of the 1st Provincial Parliament of Canada.* Kingston, 1841. pp. 266-269

76. *The Provincial Statutes of Canada: 1st Session of the 1st Provincial Parliament of Canada.* Kingston, 1841. pp. 220-223

77. *Ordinances made and passed by His Excellency the Governor General and special council for the affairs of the Province of Lower Canada.* Quebec, 1839. pp. 624-626

78. "An Act for the organization of the Department of Marine and Fisheries of Canada", 22 May 1868, *Statutes of Canada, Part Second, 1868.* Ottawa, 1868. p. 162.

Chapter 5   Harbour Lights

1. Robert Gourlay. *Statistical Account of Upper Canada.* London, 1822. pp. 97-99

2. Bonnycastle, *ibid.* pp. 281, 288

3. *Chronicle and Gazette.* Kingston., 21 October, 1840. p. 3

4. Thomas E. Appleton, *Usque Ad Mare: A History of the Canadian Coast Guard and Marine Services.* Ottawa, 1968. p. 304

5. *Report of the Board of Works : December, 1844.* Montreal, 1845. p. 65

6. *Kingston Herald.* Kingston, 18 August 1846. p.3

7. "City Council", *The British Whig.* Kingston, April 13, 1847. p. 2

8. *The British Whig and General Advertiser for Canada West.* Kingston, May 25, 1847. p. 2

9. "Our Walk", *British Whig.* Kingston, ON), 25 Mar 1848. p.2

10. Hydrographic Office. *Admiralty List of the Lights on the Coasts and Lakes of British North America.* London 1864. p. 12

11. Edward Hodder. Harbours and Ports... pp. (Kingston pages)

12. *Daily News.* Kingston, Dec. 14, 1866. p. 2

13. See: Gerald E. Boyce. *Historic Hastings.* Belleville, 1967

14. "Belleville Light House", *The British Whig.* Kingston, June 9, 1835. p. 2

15. Larry Turner, "Flint, Billa", *Dictionary of Canadian Biography*, vol. 12. Accessed May 23, 2014, http://www.biographi.ca/en/bio/flint_billa_12E.html.

16. Upper Canada Land Petitions, "B" bundle 5, Pt. II, 1848-1850. LAC microfilm RG1, L3, vol. 77

17. *ibid*

18. See, Hasting County Historical Society reprint of "Bird's Eye View of Belleville Ontario Canada, 1874." Belleville, 1974. Also see, Francis Atkin. *Atkin's Pocket*

Compass of the Harbors, Ports, Lighthouses and Buoys of Lake Ontario and River St. Lawrence,

19. In 1871, Belleville shipped 167,940 tons, Kingston shipped 599,658 tons and Toronto shipped 414,959 tons. "Statement by Province of the Canadian and American Tonnage", Sessional Papers of the Dominion of Canada, Vol. 3, Sess. 1872. Ottawa, 1872. p. 4-39

20. Atkin. *ibid.* pp. 69-72

21. Robert Gourlay. *Statistical Account of Upper Canada*. London, 1822. p. 94.

22. Hodder, *ibid.* p. 13.

23. "Report of the Board of Works, December 1844", *Appendix to the fourth volume of the journals of the Legislative Assembly of the Province of Canada,* Sess. 1844-45. Montreal, 1845. p. 17

24. "Report of the Commissioners of Public Works, 1847", *Appendix to the 6th Volume of the Journals of the Legislative Assemble of the Province of Canada.* Montreal, 1847. p. QQ6

25. "Notice to Mariners", *Daily British Whig.* Kingston, 26 Apr 1851. p. 2

26. Howard Patterson, *Patterson's Illustrated Nautical Dictionary*, New York, 1891. p. 144

27. Holland, America's Lighthouses, New York, 1972. p. 80

28. Hodder, *ibid.*

29. LAC RG43 vol.2550, File 17, Part 1, Specification & agreement of Thomas Lee, James Newman and James Smith for building Range lighthouse Towers at Presque Isle harbour. 30th September 1850. (No. 1424 J In Vol. J. page 101)

30. "Annual Report of the Department of Marine and Fisheries, 1873", *Sessional Papers Volume 3, First Session of the Third Parliament of the Dominion of Canada, Session 1874.* Ottawa, 1874. pp. v-vi

Chapter 6   Strengthening the Chain

1. In 1848, the population of Canada West was 723,292, (from "Tabular Statement of the Population of Upper Canada" Appendix to the Journals of the House of Assembly of the Province of Canada, Sess. 1849, App. B). In 1850,

the population of Western New York was 775,202, Ohio 1,980,329, Michigan 397,654 (from U.S. Census, *ibid*)

2. In 1871, the population of Canada West was 1,620,8511 ("Population, 1871-1931", *Seventh Census of Canada 1931*. Ottawa, 1934. Table 1). In 1870, the population of Western New York was 1,102,726, Ohio 2,665,260, Michigan 1,184,959 (from U.S. Census, *ibid*)

3. Canada: "Trade and Navigation", *Appendix to the Journals of the Legislative Assembly of the Province of Canada, Sess. 1850*. Toronto, 1850. App. A, No. 17. U.S.A: Mansfield, *ibid*. pp. 438-439

4. "Trade & Navigation, 1849", *AJHA, Sess. 1850*. Toronto, 1850. App. A, No. 7. Imports into the Province of Canada (Canada East and Canada West combined) from the United States, plus exports from Canada to the United States totaled more than £1.8 million (approximately $7.1 million), most of which would have been carried by ships on the Great Lakes. In addition, there was another £2 million of trade with Great Britain, a portion of which would have been handled by Great Lakes' ships.

5. "General Report of the Commissioner of Public Works, 1859", *Sessional papers of the Province of Canada, Sess. 1860*. Quebec, 1860. App. 11. In 1859 the number of British and American vessels afloat on the Inland Lakes were as follows: Steamers-132, Propellers-197, Schooners-1,007, Brigs-93, Barques-59, Sloops-4. Combined registered tonnage of all these ships was 390,201.

6. "Tables of Trade and Navigation", *SP No. 3, Sess. 1871*. Ottawa, 1871. p. 46

7. Lachine 13.7 km, 5 locks. Beauharnois 18.1 km, 9 locks. Cornwall 18.5 km, 7 locks. Farran's Point 1.2 km, 1 lock. Rapide Plat 6.4 km, 2 locks. Galops 12.3 km, 5 locks. See: G.P. de T. Glazebrook. *History of Transportation in Canada*. Toronto, 1938.

8. "Trade & Navigation, 1849", *ibid*. In 1849, exports to Great Britain included more than 200,000 barrels of flour, some 30,000 barrels of potash and pearl ash, 4 million barrel staves, 18,000 barrels of corn meal, 120,000 bushels of beans and peas, and 74,000 bushels of wheat. A large portion of each of these products would have come from the Great Lakes region.

9. *ibid*. In 1849, imports from Great Britain included 3.3 million pounds of sugar, $130,000 worth of liquors, 476,000 pounds of tea, 100,000 gallons of wine, 300,000 bushels of salt, and $20,000 worth of fruits and spices.

10. "Statement of the Canadian and American Tonnage", Sessional Papers of the Parliament of the Province of Canada, Sess. 1860. No. 23, pp. 274-275. In 1859, Kingston had a combined total of 2,496 ships inbound and outbound making the average number of ships calling there at 1,248. Those numbers would increase every year until late in the 19th Century.

11. *Kingston Chronicle*, 30 Nov. 1833. p.3

12. Appendix to Journal of the House of Assembly, 1833-1834, Toronto : R. Stanton, 1834, p.219

13. *Report of the Board of Works, Dec. 1844*. Montreal 1845. p. 17

14. *Daily News*. Kingston, Oct. 10, 1851. p.2

15. "The Lakes, Canals, and Rivers", *The Daily British Whig*. Kingston, June 21, 1853. p. 2

16. "Report of the Commissioners of Public Works, 1854", *AJLA, Sess. 1854 to 1855*. Quebec, 1855. Appendix O

17. *Daily News*. Kingston, Nov. 16, 1854, p. 2. Also see: URL- http://www.ship-wreck.com/shipwreck/swayze/swayzedbdetail.php?HKEY=1401. Note: One source states that there was a single survivor. *The Democracy*. Buffalo, Nov. 18, 1854

18. *The Globe*. Toronto, Dec. 7, 1854. *The Democracy*. Buffalo, Dec. 11, 1854. URL-http://www.ship-wreck.com/shipwreck/swayze/swayzedbdetail.php?HKEY=1217

19. "Report of the Commissioners of Public Works, 1855", *AJLA, Sess. 1856 to 1855*. Toronto, 1856. App. 31.

20. Hodder. *ibid*. p. 14

21. See: LAC RG12 File 8010-1466, Scotch Bonnet. H.E. Poland, "Inspection Scotch Bonnet", July, 1947. "The tower is constructed of outer walls of heavy rough or uncut stone and lined with several thicknesses of brick work... The wall of the body of this tower is some four foot, six inches in thickness..."

22. "Public Accounts for the Province of Canada, 1857", *AJLA, Sess. 1858*. Toronto, 1858. Statement No. 12.

23. "Appendix 29", AJLA Sess. 1857.

24. "Report of the Commissioner of Public Works, 1861", *Sessional Papers of the Province of Canada, Sess. 1862*. Quebec, 1862. No. 3, p. 40

25. *Kingston News* (Kingston, ON), 7 Aug 1845. p.3

26. *Kingston Herald*. Kingston, 24 March 1846. p.2

27. Copy of a letter from Tomas Maxwell to T.A. Begley, Esq., May 27, 1854. *Appendix to the Journals of the House of Assembly of the Province of Canada*, 1855. Appendix RRR, No. 25.

28. "Report of the Commissioners of Public Works for the Year Ending 31st December 1855", *Appendix to the fourteenth volume of the journals of the Legislative Assembly of the Province of Canada*. Toronto, 1856. Appendix 31, p. 10

29. See: URL http://images.maritimehistoryofthegreatlakes.ca/ results?q=snake+isl and&bl=phrase&st=kw&fz=0&da= 1840&db=1857&dt=&dtfz=&lc=&grd=& itype=&sort= dateOldest+asc&rows=40

30. An act for granting to Her Majesty certain sums of money required for defraying certain expenses of the civil government for the year 1856, Toronto, 1856. p.10

31. "General Report of the Commissioners of Public Works, December 1857", *Appendix to the Journals of the Legislative Assembly of the Province of Canada, Sess. 1858*. Toronto, 1858. App. 19, p. 15

32. Composite description from *1861 Report of Commissioners of Public Works, 1864 Admiralty List of Lights,* and *1871 Marine and Fisheries Department List of Lights*

33. See: URL http://images.maritimehistoryofthegreatlakes.ca/results?q=snake+isl and+aground&bl=and&st=kw&fz=0&da=1859&db=1899&dt=&dtfz=&lc=& grd=&itype=&sort=dateOldest+asc&rows=40

34. See: *Tables of Trade and Navigation 1858*. Toronto, 1859. Table No. 28. Also see: *Tables of Trade and Navigation 1899*. Ottawa, 1900. Table No. 52

35. Maxwell to Begley, *ibid*

36. *Tables of the Trade and Navigation of the Province of Canada, 1865*. No. 29. Note: 109,020 tons of cargo were carried to and from the ports of Picton, Belleville and Trenton in 1865. A total of 795 ships were recorded entering those Bay of Quinte ports that year. Some ships would have called at more than one of these ports on a single trip, and some would have sailed through the North Channel directly to or from Kingston thus bypassing the Upper Gap. Therefore, the total number of ships that would have sailed past Pleasant Point was something less than 795.

37. Letter, Thomas Maxwell to T.A. Begley, Appendix RRR, No. 25. Note: The geographic name Pleasant Point in Prince Edward County was officially assigned in 1976 to distinguish it from Point Pleasant which is 25 kilometers

away within the bounds of the City of Kingston. [http://www4.rncan.gc.ca/search-place-names/unique/FCHPI]. Indian Point is a separate feature that is 800 meters north-west of Pleasant Point.

38. "General Report of the commissioners of Public Works, June 1854", *Appendix to the Journals of the Legislative Assembly of the Province of Canada, Sess. 1854-55.* Quebec, 1855. App. O.

39. Journals of the Legislative Assembly of the Province of Canada, Sess. 1857. Toronto, 1857. 6th June, p. 658

40. This is based on a calculated exchange rate of £1 = $3.976. This is the rate that was used in 1828 to pay Winslow Lewis for lamps and supplies used in the False Ducks Island lighthouses. See: "Report of the Commissioners... False Ducks, 1829", *ibid.*

41. *The Daily British Whig.* Kingston September 16, 1857. p. 2

42. "Appendix to the Report of the Commissioner of Public Works, 1865", *Sessional Papers of the Parliament of the Province of Canada, Sess. 1866.* Ottawa, 1866. App. 14

43. $108.16. *ibid.* App. 1, Statement 3

44. *Journals of the Legislative Assembly of the Province of Canada from March 16 to May 18, 1861.* Quebec, 1861. 5th April, p. 64

45. LAC, Political papers. Letterbooks textual record (MG26-A). Microfilm reel C-23. Aug. 12, 1864

46. *Daily British Whig.* Kingston, Oct 26, 1864. p2

47. "Appendix to the Report of the Commissioner of Public Works, 1865", *Sessional Papers of the Parliament of the Province of Canada, Sess. 1866.* Ottawa, 1866. App. 14

48. "Statement Showing the Cost of Construction", *General Report of the Commissioner of Public Works, 1867.* Ottawa, 1868. App. 62

49. *ibid.* App. 10

50. Loris S. Russell, "GESNER, ABRAHAM," in *Dictionary of Canadian Biography*, vol. 9, University of Toronto/Université Laval, 2003–, accessed October 19, 2014, http://www.biographi.ca/en/bio/gesner_abraham_9E.html

51. Henri Erni. *Coal Oil and Petroleum: Their Origin, History, Geology and Chemistry.* Philadelphia, 1865. p. 88

52. Russell, *ibid.* By 1869, sperm-oil was no longer being used in any lighthouses in Canada. ["M&F Report, 1869", *SP 1870, No. 11, Sess. 1870.* Ottawa, 1870]

53. *ibid,* Microfilm reel C-23. Feb. 10, 1865 and Microfilm reel C-24. Aug. 23, 1865

54. See: "Among Lighthouses", *British Whig.* Kingston, 29 Jul 1889. p. 1. "We had on board with us from Montreal, Mr. John Prinyer, collector of customs at the cove, a genial old gentleman, staunchly conservative and patriotic.... At Prinyer's Cove, our party landed and visited the homestead, where we were entertained in the heartiest way. I had a glass of milk punch - "a genuine conservative drink," our host averred - but as its effects are rather confusing I would hardly like to consider it as such. In the parlors of the pretty homestead were portraits of Sir John Macdonald and Sir Alex. Campbell.

55. *Grenville Gazette.* Prescott, Dec. 3, 1846. p. 2

56. *Buffalo Daily Republic.* Buffalo, Sept. 17, 1853

57. *Daily News.* Kingston, Oct. 13, 1862. p. 2

58. *Buffalo Commercial Advertiser.* Jan. 20, 1864

59. "Casualty List for 1866", *Commercial Advertiser.* Buffalo, Feb. 26, 1867

60. "3rd Annual Report of the Department of Marine and Fisheries", *Sessional papers of the Dominion of Canada, Sess. 1871.* Ottawa, 1871. No.5, p. 11

61. "M&F Report, 1871", *SP No. 5, Sess. 1872. Ottawa, 1872. p. 5*

62. "Fourth Annual Report of the Department of Marine and Fisheries", *Sessional papers of the Dominion of Canada, Sess. 1872.* Ottawa 1872. No. 5, pp. 5-6

63. *ibid.*

64. *Daily News.* Kingston, Sept. 6, 1871. p.2

65. *Daily News.* Kingston, Sept. 7, 1871. p.2

66. *Daily News.* Kingston, Nov. 7, 1873. p. 2

67. *The Democracy.* Buffalo, May 31, 1855

68. Robert Thomas. *Register of the Ships of the Lakes and River St. Lawrence, 1864.* Buffalo, 1864. p. 56

69. *The Intelligencer,* Belleville, Nov. 4, 1870. p.2

70. Recollection of Amos McDonald appeared in *Canvas & Steam on Quinte Waters,* (rev. ed), Willis Metcalfe, South Bay, Ontario, 1979. pp 88-89

71. *Daily News,* Kingston, ON, 31 Oct 1870

72. *ibid*

73. "Statement of Wrecks and Casualties", "M&F Report, 1870". *SP No. 5, Sess. 1871.* Ottawa, 1871. Appendix 19.

74. "Third Annual Report of the Department of Marine and Fisheries", 31 December 1870, from *Sessional Papers of the Dominion of Canada, vol. 3, fourth session, first Parliament.* Ottawa, 1871. pp.2-3

75. *Daily News*, Kingston, 17 Nov 1870. p. 2

76. *Daily News*, Kingston, 23 Nov 1870. p. 2

77. "Third Annual Report of the Department of Marine and Fisheries", 31 December 1870, ibid. p. 3

78. *Parliamentary debates, Dominion of Canada*, fourth session, 33 Victoriae, 1871 Ottawa : Ottawa Times Print. & Pub. Co., 1871. p. 330

79. Journals of the House of Commons of the Dominion of Canada from 15th February to 14th April, 1871, Ottawa : Hunter, Rose, 1871. p. 274

80. "M&F Report, 1872", *SP No. 8, Sess. 1873*. Ottawa, 1873. App. 9

81. Annual Report of the Department of Marine and Fisheries for the year ending the 30th June, 1872, *Sessional Papers of the Dominion of Canada*, Ottawa, 1873. p. 6

82. Annual Report of the Department of Marine and Fisheries for the year ending the 30th June, 1871, *Sessional papers of the Dominion of Canada* : volume 4, fifth session of the first Parliament, session 1872, Ottawa, 1872, p. 53

83. See: *Francis' Metallic Life-Boat Company.* New York, 1852. Also see: Clayton Evans. *Rescue at Sea.* London, 2003.

Chapter 7   More Harbours, More Lights

1. In 1871, the government spent in excess of $350,000 on canals, harbours and lighthouses in the Great Lakes region. See: "General Report of the Minister of Public Works, 1871", *SP No. 4 Sess. 1872*. Ottawa, 1872. Also see: "M&F Report, 1871", *SP No. 5, Sess. 1872*. Ottawa, 1872.

2. "Canal Commission, 1871", *SP No. 54, Sess. 1871*. Ottawa, 1871. 481 ships with registered in Ontario in 1867 with a total tonnage of 66,959 tons (see p. 170) and 2,171 American lake vessels in 1866 with a total tonnage of 547,267 tons (see p. 161). In addition, 1,124 ships were registered in the Province of Quebec, many of which would have traded on the Great Lakes.

3. *ibid*. p.55. The Canal Commissioners estimated that a total of $19,170,000 would have to be spent on improving or constructing canals and waterways in Canada including the Sault Ste. Marie Canal, Welland Canal, Lower Ottawa, Chambly Canal, deepening the St. Lawrence River, Bay Verte Canal, St. Lawrence Canals and work on the upper St. Lawrence River.

4. *Daily News*, Kingston, 6 Nov 1867. p. 2 Note: This *Mary Ann* was probably the schooner built in 1857 and not Captain Mosier's *Mary Ann* of fifty years earlier. [http://images.maritimehistoryofthegreatlakes.ca/55359/data?n=3]

5. "Information respecting proposed Canal between Lake Ontario and Bay of Quinte, December 1867." *Sessional papers of the Dominion of Canada : volume 9, session 1867-68*. Ottawa, 1868. pp. 5 & 10

6. *Journals of the House of Commons, Session 1867-8, Vol. I*. Ottawa, 1868. p. 272

7. "General Report of the Minister of Public Works, 1874", *Sessional papers of the Dominion of Canada, Sess. 1875, No. 7*. Ottawa 1875. App. 14, p. 58

8. "Third Annual Report of the Department of Marine and Fisheries," *Sessional papers of the Dominion of Canada: volume III, session 1871*, Ottawa, 1871.

9. "Fourth Annual Report of the Department of Marine and Fisheries", *Sessional papers of the Dominion of Canada: volume 4, session 1872*. Ottawa, 1872. p. 5

10. Annual Report of the Department of Marine and Fisheries for the year ending the 30th June, 1871, *Sessional papers of the Dominion of Canada* : volume 4, fifth session of the first Parliament, session 1872, Ottawa, 1872. App. 1

11. For more information about the Pugwash harbour lighthouse, see http://www.lhdigest.com/Digest/database/uniquelighthouse.cfm?value=1607. A similar design was used for another Nova Scotia lighthouse, the Cranberry Islands lighthouse, built in 1929. See http://www.nslps.com/light-detail.aspx?ID=100&M=IP&N=1

12. See: Larry and Patricia Wright, *Great Lakes Lighthouses Encyclopedia*. The Boston Mills Press, 2006.

13. LAC RG2, Privy Council Office, Series A-1-a. OIC 1871-0971

14. "Auditor General's Report 1894-95, Part K, Marine and Fisheries Department", *SP No.1 Sess.1896*. Ottawa, 1896. p. 16

15. "M&F Report", *SP No. 21 Sess. 1899*. Ottawa, 1899.

16. *Canada Gazette 1867-1946 (Dominion of Canada)*, volume 10, number 9. Ottawa 1876. p. 15

17. See: Orland French. *Wind, Water, Barley and Wine*. Belleville, 2013.

18. N.H. Baird, "Report on the Construction of the Murray Canal, 16 November 1833". *Appendix to the Journal of the House of Assembly of Upper Canada 1833-1834*. Toronto, 1834. pp. 188-189

19. *Cobourg Sun*, Tue July 1, 1856

20. *Daily News*, Kingston, July 3, 1856

21. *Daily British Whig.* Kingston, Nov. 10, 1856. See also: "Casualty List", *Commercial Advertiser.* Buffalo, Jan. 31, 1857

22. "The Late Gale on Lake Ontario", *Port Hope Guide.* Port Hope, Nov. 15, 1856. Note: The same schooner, *Ann Jane Brown,* had nearly been wrecked at Wicked Point two years earlier. [*Daily News.* Kingston, Dec. 20, 1854]

23. *Journals of the Legislative Council of the Province of Canada, Sess. 1857.* Toronto, 1857. Petitions were received from Samuel Muckleston and others of Kingston, Joseph Lee and others of Trenton, William Johnson and others of Consecon, Misters Donaldson, Austin and others of St. Catharines, George Gillespie and others of Picton, Gage Hagaman and others of Oakville, and Mr. B. King

24. LAC – quoted from: url http://images.maritimehistoryofthegreatlakes. ca/40687/data?n=1

25. *Daily News.* Kingston, 10 Feb 1857. p.2

26. *General Report of the commissioners of Public Works for the Year Ending 31st December 1857.* Toronto, 1858. p. 20

27. *ibid*

28. "Weller's Bay and Its Advantages", *Daily News*, Kingston. April 16, 1857. p.2

29. Daily News (Kingston, ON), 15 Feb 1858. p. 3

30. Daily News (Kingston, ON), 25 Jul 1860. p. 2

31. LAC microfilm. RG11-B-1-b, File no. 52725, Subject No. 126, 24 April 1861

32. "General Report of the Commissioner of Public Works for the Year Ending 31st December, 1861", *Sessional papers, first session of the seventh Parliament of the Province of Canada, session 1862.* Quebec, 1862. pp. 107-108

33. "General Report of the Commissioner of Public Works for the Year Ending 31st December, 1862", *Sessional papers, second session of the seventh Parliament of the Province of Canada, session 1863.* Quebec, 1863. pp. 37-38

34. Appeared in *Daily News* (Kingston, ON), 25 Dec 1862. p. 2

35. LAC. MG26-A, vol. 519, pp. 566-567

36. *Journals of the House of Commons of the Dominion of Canada from the 4th February to the 8th April, 1875.* Ottawa, 1875. p. 167

37. "Light Houses", *Daily News.* Kingston, March 8, 1876. p. 2

38. "Penny Wisdom", *The British Whig.* Kingston, March 28, 1876. p. 3

39. "M&F Report, 1876", *SP No. 5, Sess.1877.* Ottawa, 1877. Appendix, p. 22

40. *ibid.*

41. *ibid.* Appendix, pp. 5-9

42. Order-in-Council Number: 1876-0771. Reference: RG2, Privy Council Office, Ottawa. 1876

43. See: LAC, RG42-C1, file 21792K, vol. 517. Letter Alex Norris to Sir Charles Tupper, Jan 31, 1889, and Letter W.P. Anderson to William Smith, Feb 2, 1889

44. LAC - Order-in-Council 1889-0313, RG2 Series A-1-a

45. *ibid*

46. *Daily News.* ibid

47. "Consecon", *Trenton Courier.* Trenton, Oct. 24, 1889. p. 1

48. Gerald E. Boyce. *Historic Hastings.* Belleville, 1967. pp. 65 and 157

49. *The Canada Gazette.* Ottawa, April 20, 1889. p. 1983

50. "Notice To Mariners No. 40 or 1892", *The Canada Gazette.* Ottawa, Dec. 17, 1892. p. 1123

51. "The Lakes, Canals, and Rivers", *The Daily British Whig.* Kingston, June 21, 1853. p. 2

52. "General Report of the Minister of Public Works, 1867 to 1882, Part II", *Sessional Papers of the Dominion of Canada, Sess. 1883, No. 10.* Ottawa, 1883. App. 43, p. 1229.

53. Copy of letter from William Quick, Presqu'ile Harbour to the Secretary of the Board of Public Works, Ottawa, 29 August 1868. Order-in-Council 1869-0128. Feb. 20, 1869

54. "General Report of the Minister of Public Works, 1871", *Sessional Papers of the Dominion of Canada, Sess. 1872, No. 4.* Ottawa, 1872. p. 23

55. See: "Order in Council 1871-1369", LAC RG2 Series A-1-a. Also see: "General Report of the Minister of Public Works, 1867 to 1882, Part I", *Sessional Papers of the Dominion of Canada, Sess. 1883, No. 10.* Ottawa, 1883. p. 260.

56. "Eleventh Annual Report of the Department of Marine and Fisheries, June 1878", *Sessional papers of the Dominion of Canada, Session 1879.* Ottawa, 1879. p. xii

57. "Sixth Annual Report of the Department of Marine and Fisheries", *Sessional Papers of the Dominion of Canada, Sess. 1874, No. 4,* Ottawa, 1875. p. vi

58. "Tables of Trade and Navigation, 1878", *Sessional Papers of the Dominion of Canada, Sess. 1879, No. 2*. Ottawa, 1879. Statement No. 26. These vessels shipped 7,860 tons of cargo from Brighton that year. By 1890, there were fewer ships trading into the bay, but they were each carrying more cargo; the net result being that the amount of goods shipped out of the port of Brighton stayed roughly the same. 54 ships carried 7,318 tons of cargo from Brighton that year. See: "Tables of Trade and Navigation, 1890", *Sessional Papers of the Dominion of Canada, Sess. 1891, No. 4*. Ottawa, 1891. Statement No. 23.

59. "Report of the Superintendent of Lights", "Annual Report of the Department of Marine and Fisheries, 1878", *Sessional papers of the Dominion of Canada, Sess. 1879*. Ottawa, 1879. App. No. 3, pp. 105-121

60. *ibid.*

61. "Improvement of Kingston", *Chronicle & Gazette*. Kingston, 21 Aug 1839. p.3

62. "Improvements of Kingston - Its Harbour and Neighbourhood", *Chronicle & Gazette*. Kingston, 7 Mar 1840. p.2

63. "A Walk to Hatter's Bay. No. VIII", *Daily British Whig*. Kingston, 28 May 1849. p.2

64. *Census of Canada 1880-81, Vol I*. Ottawa, 1882. Table I, pp. 65-65

65. *British Whig*. Kingston, 9 Jun 1880. p. 3

66. British Whig (Kingston, ON), 26 Feb 1887. p.8

67. British Whig (Kingston, ON), 24 Oct 1887. p. 8

68. *The Daily British Whig*. Kingston September 16, 1857. p. 2

69. "Report M&F, 1881", *SP No. 5, Sess. 1882*. Ottawa, 1882. p. xi

70. *British Whig*, June 4, 1880. Kingston. p. 2

71. *British Whig*, Oct.1, 1880. Kingston. p. 3

72. *ibid.* "Report M&F, 1881"

73. *ibid.*

74. SP1883 Appendix 8. p. 111

75. SP 1882, *ibid*

76. "Annual Report of the Department of Public Works, 1882, *SP No. 10, Sess. 1883*. Ottawa 1883. p. 26

77. See: Theresa Levitt. *A Short Bright Flash*. New York, 2013

78. See: Edward F. Bush. "The Canadian Lighthouse", *Canadian Historic Sites: Occasional Papers in Archaeology and History, No. 9*. Ottawa, 1975.

79. Order-in-Council Number: 1881-0813 Date Introduced: 1881/05/19 Considered Date: 1881/05/20 Approved Date: 1881/05/20 Reference: RG2, Privy Council Office, Series A-1-a, For Order in Council See: volume 402, Reel C-3334, Register Number: Series A-1-d, Volume 2763

80. SP 1883, Appendix 1. p. 3

81. This larger bay is now officially called Prince Edward Bay, and the smaller, inner bay is called South Bay. (Decision of the Geographical Name Board, March 1,1932.)

82. Hodder. *ibid.* p. 16

83. *Sessional papers of the Dominion of Canada : volume 6, second session of the fourth Parliament, session 1880.* Ottawa, 1880. Appendix 9, p.312

84. *British Whig.* Kingston, 16 Feb 1880. p.3

85. *Journals of the House of Commons of the Dominion of Canada. Sess. 1879.* Ottawa :1879. p. 340

86. "Twelfth Annual Report of the Department of Marine and Fisheries, June 1879", *Sessional papers of the Dominion of Canada : volume 6, second session of the fourth Parliament, session 1880.* Ottawa,1880. Appendix 9, p. 12

87. "Thirteenth Annual Report of the Department of Marine and Fisheries, June 1880", *Sessional papers of the Dominion of Canada : volume 6, third session of the fourth Parliament, session 1880-81.* Ottawa,1881.

88. Belden's Atlas pg.

89. "Fourteenth Annual Report of the Department of Marine and Fisheries, June 1881", *Sessional papers of the Dominion of Canada : volume 4, fourth session of the fourth Parliament, session 1882.* Ottawa,1882. p. 110

90. *Ibid.*

91. "A Member Speaketh", *British Whig.* Kingston, 6 Oct 1881. p.3

Chapter 8   The Completed Inside Passage

1. Seventh Town Historical Society. *7ᵗʰ Town/Ameliasburgh Township Past & Present.* Bloomfield, 1984. pp 55-63

2. "Report of R.B Sullivan, Commissioner of Crown Lands, Toronto, January 7, 1840", *Journals of the Legislative Assembly of the Province of Canada from the 28th day of November 1844, to the 29th day of March, 1845*. Montreal, 1845. p. 301

3. Macaulay, Gordon & Jones. *Reports of the Commissioners of Internal Navigation*. Kingston, 1825. p. 88

4. *ibid*

5. See: Stryan & Taylor. *This Great National Object*. Montreal, 2012

6. Baird. "Report of a proposed line of Canal to connect the Bay of Quinte with Presque Isle Harbour", *Appendix to the Journal of the House of Assembly 1833-34*. Toronto, 1834. pp. 188-190

7. Journal of the House of Assembly of Upper Canada, from the 14th day of January to the 20th day of April, 1836. Toronto : 1836 p.77 — Jan 28, 1836

8. $33,325,044.63 of government funding subsidized 2,188.25 miles of track. S.J. McLean. "The Early Railway History of Canada", *The Canadian Magazine*. Toronto, March 1899. p. *March 1899*. pp. 424-425.

9. "An Act to Incorporate the Ontario and Bay of Quinte Canal Company", *Statutes of the Province of Canada, first session of the fifth Parliament of Canada*. Quebec 1854. pp. 796-807

10. Montreal Board of Trade, "Improvement of Inland Navigation", from "Report of the Special Committee on the Murray Canal, *Journals of the Legislative Assembly of the Province of Canada from June 8 to August 15, 1866, 5th session of the 8th Provincial Parliament of Canada*. Ottawa,1866. Appendix 3, p. 2.

11. URL- http://www.ship-wreck.com/shipwreck /swayze/swayzedbdetail.php?HKEY=1401

12. This is a conservative estimate of losses during storms on Lake Ontario, 1798 to 1889 and does not include losses due to fire or losses that occurred in harbours. Data analysis by the author based on WEB: "The David Swayze Great Lakes Shipwrecks File".

13. John Gordon, et al. *Report of the Commissioners appointed to consider the defences of Canada, 1862*. London 1862. p. 19

14. *Journals of the House of Commons of Canada from April 15th to June 22nd 1869 ... being the second session of the first Parliament of Canada, session 1869*. Ottawa, 1869. p. 56

15. *ibid*. pp. 185-186

16. "General Report of the Minister of Public Works, 1871", *Sessional papers of the Dominion of Canada : volume 3, fifth session of the first Parliament, session 1872.* Ottawa, 1872. Sessional Paper No. 4, p. 4

17. *ibid.* "Report of the Canal Commissioners", *Sessional papers of the Dominion of Canada : volume VI, fourth session of the first Parliament, session 1871.* Ottawa, 1871. Sessional Paper No. 54, p. 40

18. *Journals of the House of Commons of the Dominion of Canada, Sess. 1879.* Ottawa, 1879. p. 198

19. *Daily Ontario*, Belleville, November 19, 1879, p.2. See also: *Oswego Palladium.* Oswego, Nov. 18, Nov. 19 and Nov. 21, 1879.

20. *Daily Ontario. ibid.*

21. *Daily Ontario*, Belleville, November 20, 1879, p.2

22. Debate, April 27, 1880. *Debates of the House of Commons of the Dominion of Canada : second session, fourth Parliament.* Ottawa,1880. pp. 1793-1794

23. *ibid.* p. 1795

24. ibid. p.1803

25. Debate, March 10, 1881. *Debates of the House of Commons of the Dominion of Canada : third session, fourth Parliament ... comprising the period from the second day of February 1881, to the twenty-first day of March, 1881.* Ottawa, 1881. p. 1322

26. Resolution 17, March 16, 1881. *Journals of the House of Commons of the Dominion of Canada from the 9th December, 1880, to the 21st March, 1881.* Ottawa, 1881. p.332. Resolution 19, March 18, 1881. *ibid.* p. 381. Note: Two separate appropriations of $25,000 each were voted.

27. "Annual Report of the Minister of Railways and Canals, July 1880 to June 1881". *Sessional papers of the Dominion of Canada : volume 5, fourth session of the fourth Parliament, session 1882.* Ottawa, 1882. p. xl.

28. LAC — MG26-A, vol. 384, "Prince Edward Insulted"

29. "Table of all tenders received for the construction of the Murray Canal", *Sessional Papers of the Dominion of Canada, Sess. 1883, No. 83.* Ottawa, 1883. pp. 3- 5

30. LAC — Order-in-Council 1882-1081, RG2, series A-1-a

31. *Oswego Palladium*, 2 Sep 1882

32. Boyce, ibid. pp. 274-275

33. "Tables of Trade and Navigation, 1884", Sessional Papers of the Dominion of Canada, Sess. 1885, No. 2. Ottawa, 1885, Statements No. 22 & 23

34. "Seventeenth Annual Report of the Department of Marine and Fisheries, June 1884", *Sessional papers of the Dominion of Canada : volume 6, third session of the fifth Parliament, session 1885*. Ottawa, 1885. p. xii

35. "Notice to Mariners", Canada Gazette, volume 19, number 12, 19 September 1885. Ottawa 1885. p. 6

36. "Annual Report of the Department of Marine and Fisheries 1885", *Sessional papers of the Dominion of Canada* : volume 9, fourth session of the fifth Parliament, session 1886. Ottawa 1886. App. 8 p. 126

37. House of Commons debate July 11, 1885, *Official report of the debates of the House of Commons of the Dominion of Canada : third session, fifth Parliament to the twentieth day of July, 1885* Ottawa, 1885. p. 3303

38. "Annual report of the Minister of Railways and Canals to June 1885", *Sessional papers of the Dominion of Canada : volume 10, fourth session of the fifth Parliament, session 1886*. Ottawa, 1886. p. lxiv

39. Debate, May 10, 1886. *Official report of the debates of the House of Commons of the Dominion of Canada* : fourth session, fifth Parliament, to the second day of June, 1886. Ottawa, 1886. p. 1453

40. "*Official Report of the Debates of the House of Commons of the Dominion of Canada, 1889. Vol. XXVIII.* Ottawa, 1889. p. 1206.

41. "Notice to Mariners", *Canada Gazette* volume 25, number 16, 17 October 1891. Ottawa 1891. p. 28

42. Letter from T.P Keeler, Superintendent Murray Canal to A.P. Bradley, Secretary Dept. Railway and Canals, Ottawa, Appendix 14, "Annual Report of the Minister of Railways and Canals to 30th June 1890", *Sessional papers of the Dominion of Canada : volume 11, first session of the seventh Parliament, session 1891*. Ottawa 1891.

43. Canal Statistics for Season of Navigation 1891, *Sessional papers of the Dominion of Canada : volume 8, second session of the seventh Parliament, session 1892*. Ottawa 1892. pp. 9C-132-133, 9A-134-135

44. *British Whig 6 Oct 1881*, Kingston, 1881. p. 3

45. Debate April 13, 1882, *Official debates of the House of Commons of the Dominion of Canada : fourth session, fourth Parliament ... comprising the period from the ninth day of February to the seventeenth day of May, 1882*. Ottawa 1882. p. 867

46. LAC RG-12 vol. 1507-7958. Petition, July 1887

47. *ibid.* Letters from E.W. Rathbun and D.W. Allison.

48. *ibid.* Marginal comments in letter, Sept. 28, 1888

49. 1889 Annual Report of the Department of Marine, *Sessional papers of the Dominion of Canada : volume 12, fourth session of the sixth Parliament, session 1890* Ottawa 1890. p. 5

50. LAC — "Copy of Schedule of Tenders for construction of Light on Centre Brother Island". Sir John A. Macdonald Papers, vol. 482.

51. LAC RG-12 vol. 1507-7958. Letter from Leonard to Smith. July 3, 1890

52. *ibid.* Letter Patrick Harty to John Hardie, July 9, 1890.

53. "M&F Report, 1890", *SP No. 7 Sess. 1891*. Ottawa, 1891. pp. 5-6.

54. 1891 Report of the Auditor General, *Sessional papers of the Dominion of Canada : volume 1, second session of the seventh Parliament, session 1892*. Ottawa 1892. p. D-29

55. ibid, p. D-18

56. LAC RG-12 vol. 1507-7958. Memorandum for the Minister, from William Smith, Deputy Minister, 16 Sep 1891

57. *ibid..* Memo from W.P. Anderson to W. Smith, June 24, 1891.

58. *ibid.* margin notes, 26 June 1891

59. *ibid.* W.P. Anderson to William Smith, 14 Sept. 1891

60. *ibid.* Letter to Uriah Wilson, 21 Sept. 1891.

61. Order-in-Council 1894-1547

62. 1890 Annual Report of the Department of Marine, *Sessional papers of the Dominion of Canada : volume 7, first session of the seventh Parliament, session 1891*. Ottawa 1891. p. 7

63. 1891 Annual Report of the Department of Marine, *Sessional papers of the Dominion of Canada : volume 8, second session of the seventh Parliament, session 1892*. Ottawa 1892. pp. 10-11

64. "Notice to Mariners, No. 56 of 1891", *Canada Gazette, Oct. 17, 1891*. Ottawa 1891. pp. 664-665

65. M&F Report, 1888. *SP No. 7 1889*. Ottawa 1889

66. "Canal Statistics", "Annual Report of the Department of Railways and Canals, 1894", Dominion of Canada Sessional Papers, Ottawa, 1895

67. "Canal Statistics", "Annual Report of the Department of Railways and Canals", Dominion of Canada Sessional Papers, 1892 to 1901. Note: Registered tonnage (also called net registered tonnage) is the volume of a ship measured in units

of 100 cubic feet (2.83 cubic meters) to the registered ton, but does not include the space occupied by boilers, engines, fuel storage and crew quarters. Registered tonnage is used to figure taxes, canal tolls and port charges. This should not be confused with the maximum weight of cargo that a ship can carry. See: Board of Trade. *Instructions as to the Tonnage Measurement of Ships.* London, 1913

68. NRCAN website ???

69. "Report on the Bay of Quinte from Thos. S. Rubidge, Engineer to John Page, Chief Engineer, Dept of Railways and Canals, Feb. 1, 1882", *Sessional papers of the Dominion of Canada : volume 12, first session of the fifth Parliament, session 1883.* Ottawa 1883. p. 25

70. "Twenty-fifth Annual Report of the Department of Marine and Fisheries, 1892", *Sessional Papers of the Dominion of Canada, Sess. 1893, No. 10.* Ottawa, 1893. p. 6

71. "Notice to Mariners, No. 20 of 1892", *Canada Gazette.* Ottawa, July 30, 1892. p. 166

72. "M&F Report, 1898", *SP No. 11, Sess. 1899.* Ottawa 1899. p. 138

73. "Report of the Chief Engineer, M&F Report, 1893", *SP No. 11, Sess. 1894.* Ottawa, 1894. App. 29

74. 1893 Annual Report of the Department of Marine and Fisheries, *Sessional papers of the Dominion of Canada : volume 9, fourth session of the seventh Parliament, session 1894.* Ottawa 1894. p. iv

75. 1894 Notice to Mariners No. 21 of 1894, *Canada Gazette* volume 28, number 4, 28 July 1894. Ottawa 1894. p. 13

76. Auditor-General's Report *Sessional papers of the Dominion of Canada : volume 1, fifth session of the seventh Parliament, session 1895.* Ottawa 1895. Part J, p. 129

77. Report of the Department of Marine and Fisheries. Ottawa 1899. p. 163

78. "M&F Report, 1892", *SP No. 10, Sess. 1893.* Ottawa 1893. p. 3

79. "32nd Annual Report of the Department of Marine and Fisheries, 1899", *Sessional Papers of the Dominion of Canada, Sess. 1900, No. 13.* Ottawa, 1900. p. 33

80. LAC, Order-in-Council 1877-0904, RG2 Privy Council Office Series A-1-a

81. Chart, *Lake Ontario, Survey of the Northern and Northwestern Lakes.* Corps of Engineers, War Department, 1904

82. Department of Marine and Fisheries. *Port Directory of Principal Canadian Ports and Harbours.* Ottawa 1913 & 1914. p. 203

83. See: D.D. Calvin III. *A Saga of the St. Lawrence.* Toronto, 1945.

84. *ibid.* pp. 146-147

85. "Tables of Trade and Navigation", *Sessional Papers of the Dominion of Canada, Session 1901, No. 11.* Ottawa, 1901. Tables 52 & 53. Note: In 1900, 4,605 ships arrived and departed Kingston. The Canadian and U.S registered ships carried a total of 203,006 tons of cargo. Freight tonnage of British ships is not given. Total registered tonnage of all ships was 1,326,562 tons, for an average registered tonnage of 288 tons.

86. Department of Marine and Fisheries. "List of Vessels on the Registry Books of the Dominion of Canada, 1898", *Sessional Papers of the Dominion of Canada, Sess. 1899, No. 11B.* Ottawa, 1899, Parts I & II.

87. *British Whig* (Kingston, ON), 2 Aug 1884 and *British Whig* (Kingston, ON), 5 Aug 1884

88. "Where the Shoals Are", *British Whig* (Kingston, ON), 8 Nov 1886. p. 8

89. "Chief Engineer's Report", *Report of the Department of Marine and Fisheries.* Ottawa 1898. p. 34

90. "Notice to Mariners", *The Canada Gazette*, Ottawa July 29, 1899. p. 191

91. "M&F Report, 1899", *SP No. 11, Sess. 1900.* Ottawa, 1900. p.35

92. "Notice to Mariners", *The Canada Gazette.* Ottawa, April 14, 1900. p. 2214.

93. J.H. Meacham & Co. *Illustrated Historical atlas of the counties of Frontenac, Lennox and Addington, Ontario.* Toronto, 1878. http://digital.library.mcgill.ca/countyatlas/showrecord.php?PersonID=11922, accessed 3 October 2014

Chapter 9   The End of an Era?

1. "Marine Intelligence", *British Whig.* Kingston, 25 Aug 1890. p. 1

2. Notice to Mariners No. 55 of 1891. Canada Gazette, October, 1891. Ottawa 1891. p. 28

3. Report of the Auditor-General, 1891. Sessional papers of the Dominion of Canada : volume 1, second session of the seventh Parliament, session 1892. Ottawa 1892. Appendix E

4. *ibid.* p. 17

5. "Annual Report of the Department of Railways and Canals, 1896", *SP No. 10, Sess. 1897.* Ottawa, 1897, p. 133

6. "Report of the Superintending Engineer, Murray Canal", "Annual Report of the Department of Railways and Canals, 1899", *SP No. 10, Sess. 1900.* Ottawa, 1900. p. 230.

7. "M&F Report, 1899", *SP No. 11, Sess. 1900.* Ottawa, 1900. p. 35

8. G. Drysdale Dempsey. *Rudimentary Treatise. Tubular and other Iron Girder Bridge.* London, 1850, p. 2

9. *British Whig.* Kingston, 11 Dec 1890. p.1

10. *ibid.* 1891 Marine Dept. Report. p. 11

11. "Tables of Trade and Navigation, 1885, No. 22", *SP No. 1, Sess. 1886.* Ottawa, 1886

12. 4,898 ships in 1895. "Tables of Trade and Navigation, 1895, No. 24", *SP No. 6, Sess. 1896.* Ottawa, 1896.

13. See: "General Report of the Minister of Public Works", 1876 and 1885.

14. "Report of the Auditor General, 1892", *SP No. 1, Sess. 1892.* Ottawa, 1892. p.

15. Annual Report of the Minister of Marine, *Sessional papers of the Dominion of Canada : volume 7, third session of the seventh Parliament, session 1893.* Ottawa 1893. pp. 3-4

16. *ibid.* p. 9

17. "Notice to Mariners, No. 24 of 1892", *The Canada Gazette.* Ottawa July 30, 1892. p. 168.

18. "Annual Report of the Department of Marine and Fisheries, 1892", *Sessional Papers Volume 7, Third Session of the Seventh Parliament of the Dominion of Canada, Session 1893.* Ottawa, 1893 Changes in Light-Keepers (table - p. 35)

19. "General Report of the Minister of Public Works from 30th June 1867 to 1st July 1882", *Sessional Papers of the Dominion of Canada, Sess. 1883, No. 10.* Ottawa 1883. p. 112

20. "Notice to Mariners, No. 104 of 1905", *The Canada Gazette.* Ottawa, Nov. 11, 1905. p. 1000.

21. "M&F Report, 1908", *SP No. 21, Sess. 1909. p.*

22. See: *Minutes of the Proceedings of the Society of Civil Engineers.* January 1927. pp. 376 to 377. Also see: "Col. Anderson is Dead After Long and Useful Life", *The Ottawa Evening Citizen.* Feb. 2, 1927.

23. Order-in-Council 1908-1470. LAC, RG2, Privy Council Office, Series A-1-a, volume 954

24. Order-in-Council 1908-2162. LAC, RG2, Privy Council Office, Series A-1-a, volume 962

25. "Report of the Department of Marine and Fisheries, 1909", *Sessional Papers of the Dominion of Canada, No. 21, Session 1910*. Ottawa, 1910. p. 64

26. F. Douglas Reville. *History of the County of Brant*. Brantford, 1920. pp. 684-685

27. "Notice to Mariners No. 80 of 1909". *Canada Gazette, September 25, 1909*. Ottawa 1909. p. 823

28. The Windsor Evening Record, Feb. 13, 1909. Windsor, Ontario. p 5

29. "Notice to Mariners No. 75 of 1909". *The Canada Gazette*, September 18, 1909. Ottawa, 1909. p. 758

30. *Railway and Marine World*, March 1911. Toronto 1911. p. 269

31. "M&F Report, 1911", *SP No. 21, Sess. 1912*. Ottawa, 1912. p. 62

32. "Notice to Mariners, No. 5 of 1911", *The Canada Gazette*. Ottawa, Feb 4, 1911. p. 2531

33. "M&F Report, 1913-14", *SP No. 21, Sess. 1915*. Ottawa, 1915. App. 2

34. "Auditor General's Report, 1911-12," *SP. No. 1, Sess. 1913*. Ottawa, 1913. p. N-99

35. Department of Marine and Fisheries Annual Report, SP 21. Ottawa, 1913.

36. "Notice to Mariners, No. 19 of 1912", *The Canada Gazette*. Ottawa, April 27, 1912. p. 4004

37. "M&F Report, 1913-14", *ibid.*

38. This number included steamships, sailing ships and barges (usually schooners converted into towable cargo vessels) on all of the Great Lakes. Some larger ships, because of their extreme length and draught, were unable to pass from the upper lakes through the Welland Canal so they would not have sailed on Lake Ontario until the enlargement of the canal after 1913. See, "List of Vessels on the Registry Books of the Dominion of Canada, 1912", *Sessional Papers of the Dominion of Canada, Sess. 1913, No. 21b*. Ottawa, 1913. p. vii. Also Mansfield, *ibid.* p. 439. Note: The number 6,000 vessels is an estimate based on the actual Canadian registry numbers plus double that number of U.S ships which was the typical ratio of Canadian to American vessels on the Great Lakes.

39. "Notice to Mariners No. 56 of 1891", *The Canada Gazette*. Ottawa, Oct. 17, 1891. p. 664

40. "Tables of the Trade and Navigation of the Dominion of Canada, 1895", *Sessional Papers of the Dominion of Canada, Sess. 1896, No. 6*. Ottawa, 1896. Table No. 52

41. "Forty Second Annual Report of the Department of Marine and Fisheries, 1909", *Sessional Papers of the Dominion of Canada, Sess. 1910, No. 21*. Ottawa, 1910, p. 64

42. "Forty Third Annual Report of the Department of Marine and Fisheries, 1910", *Sessional Papers of the Dominion of Canada, Sess. 1911, No. 21*. Ottawa, 1911, p. 103

43. "Notice to Mariners No. 123 of 1911", *The Canada Gazette*. Ottawa, Jan. 13, 1912. p. 2715

44. "Notice to Mariners No. 33 of 1912", *The Canada Gazette*. Ottawa, June 8, 1913. p. 4606

45. LAC RG12 File 8010-1449, Prince Edward Point

46. "Notice to Mariners No. 35 of 1913", *The Canada Gazette*. Ottawa, June 14, 1913. p. 4606

47. "Notice to Mariners No. 40 of 1913", *The Canada Gazette*. Ottawa, June 14, 1913. p. 4629

48. William E. Gibbs. *Lighting by Acetylene*. New York, 1898, p. 4

49. Thomas Carpenter. *Inventors: Profiles in Canadian Genius*. Camden East, Ontario, 1990. pp. 83-99. See: Albert Ross. *Report on the Use of Acetylene Gas by the Canadian Government as an Illuminant for Aids to Navigation*. Washington, 1907.

50. Department of Marine and Fisheries. *Review of Improvements in Lighthouse and Coast Service*. Ottawa, 1904. p 15

51. "Thirty-seventh Annual Report of the Department of Marine and Fisheries", *Sessional Papers of the Dominion of Canada, 1905, No. 21*. Ottawa, 1905, pp. 58-63

52. *ibid*. p. 63

53. See: Annual Report, SP No. 21, Sess 1915, Ottawa 1915. Encl. No. 2, "Statement of lightstations and names of lightkeepers, etc, in the Dominion"

54. WEB:http://www.aga.com/international/web/lg/aga/like35agacom.nsf/docbyalias/aga_history

55. Elisabeth T. Crawford. *The Beginnings of the Nobel Institution*. Cambridge, 1984. p. 166

56. LAC, File No. 8010-1466. Letter from J.N. Arthurs, Supt. of Lights, Feb. 23, 1944.

57. Brian Johnson. "The Last Lighthouse Keeper", *The Kingston Whig-Standard*. Kingston, Dec. 29, 2010.

Chapter 10   The Last of Its Kind

1. See: Roberta M. Styran and Robert R. Taylor. *This Great National Object*. Montreal, 2012

2. See: James T. Angus. *A Respectable Ditch*. 1998

3. See: *Report of the Select Committee on Georgian Bay and Lake Ontario Ship Canal*. Quebec, 1864. Also see: (ref for Newmarket canal!!!)

4. David Lee. *Lumber Kings and Shantymen*. Toronto, 2006. p. 47

5. Seventh Town Historical Society. *7th Town/Ameliasburgh Township Past & Present*. Bloomfield, 1984. pp 55-63

6. WEB: "Major John Laing Weller, 1862-1932". Royal Military College of Canada website. URL: http://www.rmc.ca/cam/wh-mh/whc-cmh/weller-jl-eng.php

7. See: Marcus Smith. *Report on the Montreal, Ottawa and Georgian Bay Canal*. Ottawa, 1895

8. S.J.P. Thearle. "The Evolution of the Modern Cargo Steamer", *Transactions of the Institution of Naval Architects*. London, 1907. p. 100

9. *Interim Report, Georgian Bay Ship Canal*. Ottawa, 1908. p. 2

10. *Ibid*

11. The Board of Trade of the City of Toronto. *Canada's Canal Problem and Its Solution*. Toronto, 1911. pp. 1-11

12. LAC finding aid "D.B. Detweiler, 1902-1920", http://data2.archives.ca/pdf/pdf001/p000001430.pdf link from http://collectionscanada.gc.ca/pam_archives/index.php?fuseaction =genitem. displayItem&lang=eng&rec_nbr=97887

13. Great Waterways Union of Canada. *The Inland Waterways of Canada*. Berlin Ontario, 1913. title page

14. The Montreal-Ottawa and Georgian Bay Canal Company. *From the Great Lakes to the Atlantic.* Ottawa, 1910. pp. 7-21.

15. Joseph Redden. *The Welland Canal or Georgian Bay Canal. Which?* Port Arthur, 1913. pp.

16. "Needs of Growing Commerce", *Newmarket Era.* Newmarket, Dec. 3, 1909. p. 2

17. See: Roy G. Finch. *The Story of the New York State Canals.* Albany, 1925

18. See: Heath Macquarrie. "Robert Borden and the Election of 1911", *The Canadian Journal of Economics and Political Science.* August, 1959. pp.271-286

19. "Start Soon on Welland Canal", *Toronto World*, March 25, 1912. Toronto 1912. p. 7

20. "Estimates for the Fiscal Year Ending March 31, 1914", *Sessional Papers of the Dominion of Canada, Sess. 1912-13, No. 3a.* Ottawa, 1913. p. 52

21. "Aids to Navigation on the St. Lawrence and the Great Lakes". *Railway and Marine World*, March 1911. Toronto 1911. p. 269 Note: The Canadian Lighthouse Board was established in 1904 to "... consider all applications for the improvement of the Lighthouse Service, the establishment of additional aids to navigation, and such matters as tend to the protection of life and property of those engaged in the mercantile marine of the Dominion." ("M&F Report, 1904", *SP No. 21, Sess. 1905.* Ottawa 1905. p. 1.)

22. *Buffalo Evening News.* Buffalo, Dec. 5, 1903. ???

23. *ibid.* ???

24. *The Evening Record*, Dec. 6, 1906. Windsor, Ontario. p. 1

25. "Aids to Navigation on the St. Lawrence and the Great Lakes". *Railway and Marine World*, March 1911. Toronto 1911. *ibid.*

26. *Toronto Globe*, Nov. 23 1864

27. *Buffalo Commercial Advertiser*, Oct. 26 1871

28. *Cleveland Herald*, Sep. 15 1881

29. Ships reported aground at Main Duck Island 1856 to 1910:
    Lord Elgin, propeller, 1 Oct. 1856
    Caroline, schooner carrying flour, 27 May 1857
    Jenny Lind, schooner, 1 Nov 1864
    Glad Tidings, schooner carrying lumber, 1 Oct 1869
    William Elgin, schooner carrying barley, 1 Oct 1871
    Star, schooner carrying railroad iron, 1 Nov 1874
    Gardiner, propeller towing three barges, 1 Sep 1880

Folger, schooner carrying coal, 28 Oct 1880

William Elgin, schooner carrying iron ore, 10 Sep 1881

City of Montreal, propeller carrying flour and whiskey, 10 June 1883

St. Lawrence, schooner carrying grain, 17 Nov 1884

Canada, propeller, 11 Jun 1889

Nirvana, steam yacht, 24 Jun 1890

Acacia, schooner carrying coal, 4 May 1903

Hickox, steam barge carrying coal, burned 5 Dec 1906

Jeska, steam barge carrying coal, 13 May 1910

See: http://images.maritimehistoryofthegreatlakes.ca /results?q=main+duck&b
l=phrase&st=kw&fz=0&da =1856&db=1910&dt=&dtfz=&lc=&grd=&itype=
&sort =dateOldest+asc&rows=40

30. "Notice to Mariners No. 123 of 1911", The Canada Gazette, Jan. 13 1912. p. 2715

31. Department of Marine and Fisheries. *Port Directory of Principal Canadian Ports and Harbours.* Ottawa, 1909. p. 19

32. Frederick Rogers. "Concrete Buildings", *Specifications for Practical Architecture.* London, 1886

33. Ray Jones. *The Lighthouse Encyclopedia.* Guildford, Connecticut, 2004. pp. 199-200.

34. Ernest L. Ransome. "Concrete Construction — Its Practical Application", *Canadian Architect and Builder,* Dec. 1894. Toronto, 1894. p. 158

35. *Minutes of the Proceedings of the Society of Civil Engineers.* January 1927. pp. 376 to 377.

36. "Notice to Mariners No. 10 of 1897", Canada Gazette. Ottawa, May 1, 1897. p. 2174

37. "M&F Report, 1914-15", *SP. No. 21, Sess. 1916.* Ottawa, 1916. pp. 15-16. In April 1922, while transporting lightkeepers to their stations on Lake Superior, *Lambton* lost with all hands near Caribou Island in Lake Superior. See: Appleton. *Usque Ad Mare. ibid. p. 192.*

38. PEC Archives. A1982.152, Box 122B. Survey of Main Duck Island

39. PEC Archives. Land Registry, South Marysburgh, Main Duck Island, folio 260, 18 March 1913.Claude W. Cole had purchased the island from the Government of Canada in 1905 for $1,200. *ibid.*

40. "Tenders", *Toronto World*, Aug. 26, 1913. Toronto 1913. p. 13

41. LAC RG2 Series A-1-a, Order-in-Council No. 1913-2496, Oct. 8, 1913. In 1901, McMaster graduated from the University of Toronto, Faculty of Engineering. and later formed his own engineering and contracting company. See: The University of Toronto Engineering Society. Also see: *Applied Science, Vol. X.* Toronto 1916.

42. The original tender did not include the construction of a wharf or boat landing. However, these items are listed, along with an oil shed, in the summary of expenses for new aids to navigation that appears in "M&F Report 1915-16", *SP No. 21, Sess. 1917.* Ottawa, 1917. p. 50.

43. We know that the building crew had left the island by November 1, 1913 because of the following incident: Arthur T. Thompson, the Marine and Fisheries resident engineer at Prescott hired a boat on Sunday, November 2, to take him and two others to Main Duck Island so that he could check on the progress of construction. A storm came up while they were on the island and they were stranded for three days. "They had but a scanty supply of food and suffered much from cold and hunger." before being rescued by the Calvin Company's steamer *Cornwall*. (*Toronto World*. Nov. 6, 1913. p. 7). Also see: *The British Whig*. Kingston, Nov. 5, 1913. p.1.

44. *British Whig*. Kingston, Dec. 4, 1913, p. 8

45. "Barge Did Not Sink", *British Whig*. Kingston, Oct. 24, 1913, p. 1.

46. *British Whig*. Kingston, Dec. 8, 1913, p. 5. Many authors, including Swayze and Metcalfe, list *Navajo* as being wrecked in December 1914 although newspaper accounts clearly indicate that she was lost in 1913.

47. "Georgian Canal Project Urged at Montreal", *Toronto World*, Nov. 6, 1913. Toronto 1913. p. 1 and p. 7

48. The construction methodology used is a re-creation based on examination of the Main Duck Island lighthouse in September 2011, and from an interview with engineer and architectural historian Ernest Margetson in November, 2014.

49. One 10ft. lantern complete. $675. "Report of the Auditor General, 1914-15", *SP No. 1, Sess. 1916.* Ottawa, 1916 p. O-86

50. The source of the Fresnel lens for the Main Duck Island lighthouse is not indicated, although it was probably manufactured by Chance Bros. & Co. Ltd. of Birmingham, England from whom the Marine and Fisheries Department

purchased one 3rd Order single flashing optic (500mm focal length) for $4,335.23 in the 1913-14 fiscal year. "Report of the Auditor General, 1913-14", *SP No. 1, Sess. 1915*. Ottawa, 1915. p. O-94

51. "Notice to Mariners No. 94 of 1914", *The Canada Gazette*. Ottawa, Sep. 19, 1914. p. 924.

52. Mansfield, *ibid*, pp. 423 & 439

53. 302 cargo ships and passenger ships of all types with a capacity of 400 tons of cargo or more were sailing on the Great Lakes in 2014. Many of these ships had a gross tonnage of more than 30,000 tons, and a few were in excess of 80,000 tons. Roger LeLievre. *Know Your Ships 2014*. Ann Arbor Michigan, 2014.

54. Swayze database, http://www.ship-wreck.com/shipwreck/swayze/ *ibid.*

55. "Steamers On Lake Ontario", *Daily News*. Kingston, No. 30, 1870. p. 2

56. Swayze database, http://www.ship-wreck.com/shipwreck/swayze/ *ibid.*

57. *ibid.*

58. See: F.B. Webster(ed.). *Shipbuilding Cyclopaedia*. New York, 1920.

59. Mark L. Thompson. *Graveyard of the Lakes*. Detroit, 2000. pp. 210-212

60. [From the *Cleveland Leader*] In order to make more apparent the value of the weather signals to mariners, let us compare the disasters on the lakes alone for three years previous to the establishment of the Storm-Signal Service with those of the three years after the system was in operation. The total number of disasters reported was:

    In 1867, 931
    In 1868, 983
    In 1869, 1,002
    Total 2,916

    The Storm Signal Bureau established stations along the lakes in 1870. Mark the record of the years which succeeded:

    For 1870 971
    For 1871 750
    For 1872 314
    Total 2,035

    There is an instructive point in these last figures.
    "Storm Signal Service", *Daily News*. Kingston, Feb. 11, 1874.

61. See: "Return... on the subject of meteorological observations and weather reports, 1872", *SP No. 53, Sess. 1872*. Ottawa, 1872

62. "A Storm Signal Station", *Weekly British Whig*. Nov. 16, 1871. p. 2

63. "Auditor General's Report 1885, Part II", *SP No.3, Sess.1886*. Ottawa, 1886. p. 400

64. "Storm Signal Service, *Daily News. ibid*

65. Thompson. *Graveyard of the Lakes. ibid*. p. 76

66. LAC. RG12, Vol. 5134, File 1465

67. Fisheries and Oceans Canada. *Sailing Directions, CEN 300, General Information, Great Lakes*. Ottawa, 1996. pp. 13-14

Part III – Epilogue

Chapter 11   The 11th Hour

1. LAC, RG12. Letter from J.S. Barrick, District Marine Agent, D.O.T., Prescott to W.J. Manning, Director, Marine Works, D.O.T., Ottawa. Aug. 12, 1964

2. LAC, RG42-C1, file 21754K, vol. 515, correspondence Nov. and Dec. 1905.

3. The wood-framed fog-alarm building was later replaced with the current hexagonal concrete-block building attached directly to the light tower.

4. LAC, RG12, Vol. 5134, File 8010-1448

5. *ibid*.

6. "M&F Report, 1886", *SP No. 15, Sess. 1887*. Ottawa, 1887. App. 2, p. 6. Also see: "Notice to Mariners No. 39 of 1885, II", *Canada Gazette*. Ottawa, Jan. 2, 1886. p. 3

7. LAC, RG12, Vol. 5134, File 8010-1448

8. Metcalfe. *ibid*. p. 156

9. LAC, RG12, Vol. 5134, File 8010-1448, Letter from C.A. Margison to J.S. Barrick, Jan. 26, 1966

10. *ibid*. Letter J.S. Barrick to T.J. Kew, Sep. 5, 1968

11. *ibid*. File 8010-1465, Letter from Peter H. Bennett to J.S. Barrick, Mar. 19, 1970

12. *ibid*. Barrick to Kew, Ap. 1, 1970

13. *Picton Gazette.* Picton, Ontario, May 8, 1970

14. *ibid*

15. *ibid*

16. *Canada Gazette, Part III.* Ottawa, July 24, 2008. p. 5

17. ref for 500 surplus lighthouses ???

18. "Heritage Lighthouse Protection Act" ref ???

19. See: "Ontario Heritage Act", http://www.e-laws.gov.on.ca/ html/statutes/ english/elaws_statutes_90o18_e.htm

    Also see: Ontario Ministry of Tourism and Culture. *Standards and Guidelines for Conservation of Provincial Heritage Properties.* Toronto, 2010.

20. The Presqu'ile Point Lighthouse Preservation Society is currently trying to raise $1,000,000 for the restoration of the lighthouse. See: http://www.koppla.ca

21. "Ontario Heritage Act". *ibid.*

22. The Nine Mile Point Lighthouse Preservation Society has submitted a proposal to DFO to acquire the lighthouse.

    The Hastings Prince Edward Land Trust has submitted proposals to DFO to acquire the lighthouses at False Ducks Island, Point Petre and Main Duck Island.

23. See: Fisheries and Oceans Canada. "Alternate Use Study, Surplus Lighthouses Canada". Ottawa, March 2011.

BIBLIOGRAPHY

Archival Sources

Archives of Ontario
C1 Thomas Burrows Fonds
C130-6 Marsden Kemp Fonds
F32 Macaulay Family Fonds
F645 Baird Family Fonds
RG1-50-3 Land Orders-in-Council

Deseronto Archives
Picture collections
(https: //www.flickr.com/photos/deserontoarchives/sets/)
    DESNAVCO
    HMR1

Hastings County Archives
Picture collection

Library and Archives Canada
MG26-A, Sir John A. Macdonald Papers, vol. 384, 482, 519
NMC, Microfiche Collection.
PA, Picture Collection.
R11630, Admiralty Records, Admiralty Charts.
R6390-0-5-E, Topley Studio Records
RG1, Executive Council Records. L3, vol. 77, Upper Canada Land
    Petitions, "B" bundle 5, Pt. II, 1848-1850.

RG13, Department of Justice Records.

RG2, Privy Council Records. Series A-1-a, Orders-in-Council.

RG5-A1, Records of Provincial and Civil Secretaries. Upper Canada Sundries, vol. 89, reel C9823.

RG9, Militia and Defence Records. I-B-1, Letters Received, Vol. 19, 18822.

RG10M, Indian Affairs Records, Maps and Plans of Indian Reserves.

RG11-B-1-b, Public Works Records, Canals.

RG11-B-1-b, Public Works Records, Harbours and Piers.

RG11-B-1-b, Public Works Records, Lighthouses.

RG11M, Marine Engineering and Architectural Drawings.

RG12, Department of Transport Records, Lighthouses, fog alarms and beacons - Operation - Construction, repairs and maintenance. File No. 8010.

RG12, Department of Transport Records, Aids to Navigation - General - Fixed structures establishment and operation

RG12, Department of Transport Records, Aids to Navigation - General - Fixed structures – Sites. File No. 8012.

RG42-C1, Department of Marine Records, Aids to Navigation, Construction.

RG42-C1, Department of Marine Records, Aids to Navigation, Keepers.

RG43 Department of Railways and Canals Records, Correspondence.

Marine Museum of the Great Lakes

Transport Canada Fonds, DocPictorial. Canadian Coast Guard. Accession series 1984.0028 and 1982.0156

National Archives – United Kingdom

UK, MR1/848/22. "Chart of the Bay of Quinté and of the South shore of Prince Edwards County Lake Ontario. Surveyed by the Hydrographic Department under the direction of Captain Fitz William Owen Royal Navy in the years 1815 and 1816". Drawn, 1846.

Prince Edward County Archives
A1982.152, Box 122B. Main Duck Island
Land Registry. South Marysburgh, Main Duck Island. Folio 260.

Queen's University Archives
V108.1. George Vosper Collection
V23. Kingston Picture Collection
V25.5. George Lilley Fonds
0110. Village of Portsmouth Fonds.

Books and Pamphlets

Ainsworth, William (ed.) *All Round the World: An Illustrated Record of Voyages, Travels and Adventures.* Second Series. London, 1871.

Angus, James T. *A Respectable Ditch: A History of the Trent-Severn Waterway 1833-1920.* Montreal & Kingston, 1998

Appleton, Thomas E. *Usque Ad Mare: A History of the Canadian Coast Guard and Marine Services.* Ottawa, 1968.

Armstrong, Frederick H. *Handbook of Upper Canadian Chronology.* Toronto, 1985.

Association of Canadian Lake Underwriters. *Lake Vessel Register, 1866.* Toronto, 1866.

Atkin, Francis F. *Atkin's Pocket Compass of the Harbors, Ports, Lighthouses, and Buoys of Lake Ontario and River St. Lawrence.* Oswego, 1871.

Baird, David. *Northern Lights: Lighthouses of Canada.* Toronto, 1999.

Barton, James L. *Commerce of the Lakes.* Buffalo, 1847.

Board of Trade of the City of Toronto. *Canada's Canal Problem and Its Solution.* Toronto, 1911.

Board of Trade. *Instructions as to the Tonnage Measurement of Ships.* London, 1913

Bonnycastle, Richard. *Canada and the Canadians, Vol. II.* London, 1846.

Bouchette, Joseph. *The British Dominions in North America*, Vol. 2. London 1831.

Boyce, Gerald E. *Historic Hastings.* Belleville, 1967.

Burrall, F.A. *Asiatic Cholera.* New York, 1866.

Bush, Edward F. "The Canadian Lighthouse", *Canadian Historic Sites: Occasional Papers in Archaeology and History, No. 9.* Ottawa, 1975.

Calvin, D.D. *A Saga of the St. Lawrence.* Toronto, 1945.

Calvin, D.D. and T.R. Glover. *A Corner of Empire.* Toronto 1937.

Camu, Pierre. *Le Saint-Laurent et les Grand Lace au Temps do la Voile 1608-1850.* LaSalle, Quebec. 1996.

Canadian Federation of Boards of Trade and Municipalities. *Canada's Canal Problem and Its Solution.* Ottawa, 1912.

The Canadian Who's Who. London, 1910.

Caniff, William. *History of the Settlement of Upper Canada,* Toronto, 1869.

Carpenter, Thomas. *Inventors: Profiles in Canadian Genius.* Camden East, Ontario, 1990.

Catalogue of Admiralty Charts, Plans, and Sailing Directions. London 1898.

Chance Brothers & Co., Ltd. *A Few Notes on Modern Lighthouse Practice.* Birmingham, 1910.

Chance, James T. *On Optical Apparatus Used in Lighthouses.* London, 1867.

Conlon, Thomas. *The St. Lawrence Route: Its Past and Future.* Thorold, Ontario, 1909.

Craig, Gerald M. *Upper Canada: The Formative Years 1784-1841.* Toronto, 1963.

Crawford, Elisabeth T. *The Beginnings of the Nobel Institution.* Cambridge, 1984.

Croil, James. *Steam Navigation and Its Relation to the Commerce of Canada and the United States.* Toronto, 1898.

Crompton, Samuel Willard and Michael J. Rhein. *The Ultimate Book of Lighthouses.* San Diego, 2001.

Dawson, W.F. *Procedure in the Canadian House of Commons.* Toronto, 1962.

Dempsey, G. Drysdale. *Rudimentary Treatise. Tubular and other Iron Girder Bridges.* London, 1850.

Donaldson, Gordon. *Eighteen Men: The Prime Ministers of Canada.* Toronto, 1985.

Dunham, Carroll. *Cholera.* New York 1866.

Erni, Henri. *Coal Oil and Petroleum: Their Origin, History, Geology and Chemistry.* Philadelphia, 1865.

Evans, Clayton. *Rescue at Sea: An International History of Lifesaving, Coastal Rescue Craft and Organisations.* London, 2003

Finch, Roy G. *The Story of the New York State Canals.* Albany, 1925.

Fitzroy, Rear Admiral. *The Weather Book: A Manual of Practical Meteorology.* London, 1863.

Forman, Debra. *Legislators and Legislatures of Ontario: A Reference Guide, Vol. 1., 1792-1866.* Toronto, 1984.

Francis' Metallic Life-Boat Company. New York, 1852.

French, Orland. *Wind, Water, Barley & Wine: The Nature of Prince Edward County.* Belleville, 2013.

Gesner, Abraham. *A Practical Treatise on Coal, Petroleum, and other Distilled Oils.* New York. 1861.

Gibbs, William E. *Lighting by Acetylene.* New York, 1898.

Glazebrook, G.P. de T. *History of Transportation in Canada.* Toronto, 1938.

Glazebrook, G.P. de T. *Life in Ontario: A Social History.* Toronto, 1968.

Gordon, Alexander. *Lighthouses of the British Colonies and Possessions Abroad.* London, 1848.

Gourlay, Robert. *Statistical Account of Upper Canada.* London, 1822.

Grant, George Monro. *Picturesque Canada: The Country as it was and is.* Toronto, 1882.

Great Waterways Union of Canada. *The Inland Waterways of Canada.* Berlin Ontario, 1913.

Guillet, Edwin C. *Pioneer Days in Upper Canada.* Toronto, 1964.

Guillet, Edwin C. *Pioneer Travel in Upper Canada.* Toronto, 1966.

Heap, Major D.P. *Ancient and Modern Light-Houses.* Boston, 1889.

Heriot, George. *Travels Through the Canadas.* London, 1805.

Hodder, Edward. *The Harbours and Ports of Lake Ontario.* Toronto 1857.

Holland, Francis Ross, Jr. *America's Lighthouses: An Illustrated History.* New York, 1972.

Howison, John. *Sketches of Upper Canada.* Edinburgh, 1821.

Hunter, William S. *Hunter's Panoramic Guide from Niagara Falls to Quebec.* Boston, 1857.

Institution of Naval Architects. *Transactions of the Institution of Naval Architects.* London, 1907.

Johnson, J.K. *Becoming Prominent: Regional Leadership in Upper Canada, 1791-1841.* Montreal, 1989.

Jones, Ray. *The Lighthouse Encyclopedia: The Definitive Reference.* Guilford, Connecticut, 2004.

Koeppel, Gerard. *Bond of Union: Building the Erie Canal and the American Empire.* Cambridge, Massachusetts, 2009.

Lafreniere, Normand. *Lightkeeping on the St. Lawrence: The End of and Era.* Toronto, 1996.

Laroque, Barbara Wall. *Wolfe Island: A Legacy in Stone.* 2009.

Lee, David. *Lumber Kings and Shantymen.* Toronto, 2006.

Lefroy, J.H. *Diary of a Magnetic Survey of a Portion of the Dominion of Canada, executed in the years 1842-1844.* London, 1883.

LeLievre, Roger. *Know Your Ships 2014.* Ann Arbor Michigan, 2014.

Levitt, Theresa. *A Short Bright Flash: Augustin Fresnel and the Birth of the Modern Lighthouse.* New York, 2013

Lunn, Richard & Janet. *The County: The First Hundred Years in Loyalist Prince Edward.* Prince Edward County Council, 1967.

Mansfield, J.B. *History of the Great Lakes,* vol. 1. Chicago, 1899.

Metcalfe, Willis. *Canvas and Steam on Quinte Waters.* Prince Edward County, 1979.

Metcalfe, Willis. *Marine Memories.* Picton, Ontario, 1975.

Monmonier, Mark. *Lake Effect: Tales of Large Lakes, Arctic Winds, and Recurrent Snows.* Syracuse, NY 2012.

Montreal-Ottawa and Georgian Bay Canal Company. *From the Great Lakes to the Atlantic.* Ottawa, 1910.

Nicholson, Peter. *Practical Masonry, Bricklaying, and Plastering.* London 1841.

Oleszewski, Les. *Great Lakes Lighthouses American & Canadian.* Gwinn, Michigan, 1998.

Patterson, Howard *Patterson's Illustrated Nautical Dictionary.* New York, 1891.

Pioneer Life on the Bay of Quinte. Toronto, 1904.

Redden, Joseph. *The Welland Canal or Georgian Bay Canal. Which?* Port Arthur, 1913.

Rhein, Michael J. *Anatomy of the Lighthouse.* New York, 2000.

Reville, F. Douglas. *History of the County of Brant.* Brantford, 1920.

Richardson, Hugh. *Steam Navigation on Lake Ontario.* York, 1825.

Robertson, J.R. *Robertson's Landmarks of Toronto, vol. 2.* Toronto, 1896.

Robertson, J.R. *Robertson's Landmarks of Toronto, vol. 5,* Toronto, 1908.

Rogers, Frederick. *Specifications for Practical Architecture.* London, 1886

Scott, George. *Scott's New Coast Pilot for the Lakes.* Detroit, 1892.

Seventh Town Historical Society. *Gunshot and Gleanings of the Historic Carrying Place, Bay of Quinte.* Bloomfield, Ontario, 1987.

Seventh Town Historical Society. *7ᵗʰ Town/Ameliasburgh Township Past & Present.* Bloomfield, Ontario, 1984.

Simcoe, Elizabeth. *The Diary of Mrs. John Graves Simcoe,* annot. by J. Ross Robertson, Toronto, 1911.

Smith, Marcus. *Report on the Montreal, Ottawa and Georgian Bay Canal.* Ottawa, 1895.

Smith, Michael. *A Geographical View of the Province of Upper Canada,* Trenton, N.J., 1813.

Smith, William. *The Lighthouse System of Canada.* 1884.

Smyth, William. *A Short Topographical Description of His Majesty's Province of Upper Canada in North America,* London, 1799.

Snider, C.H.J. *Annals of the Royal Canadian Yacht Club 1852-1937.* Toronto, 1937.

Society of Civil Engineers. *Minutes of the Proceedings of the Society of Civil Engineers.* January 1927.

Starr, George Lothropp. *Old St. George's.* Kingston, 1913.

Stevenson, Alan. *A Rudimentary Treatise on the History, Construction, and Illumination of Lighthouses.* London, 1850.

Stevenson, Alan. *On the Theory and Construction of Lighthouses.* Edinburgh 1857.

Stonehouse, Frederick. *Great Lakes Lighthouse Tales.* Gwinn, Michigan, 1998.

Styran, Roberta M. and Robert R. Taylor. *This Great National Object: Building the Nineteenth-Century Welland Canals.* Montreal, 2012.

Swayze, David. *Shipwreck: A Comprehensive Directory of Over 3,700 Shipwrecks on the Great Lakes.* Boyne City Michigan, 1992.

Talbot, Edward Allen. *Five Years' Residence in the Canadas.* London, 1824.

Thomas, Robert. *Register of the Ships of the Lakes and River St. Lawrence, 1864.* Buffalo, 1864.

Thompson, Mark L. *Graveyard of the Lakes.* Detroit, 2000.

Thompson, Thomas S. *Thompson's Coast Pilot and Sailing Directions for the North-Western Lakes.* Detroit, 1878.

Thompson, Thomas S. *Thompson's Coast Pilot for the Upper Lakes on Both Shores.* Detroit, 1869.

Townshend, Robert B. *Tales from the Great Lakes.* Toronto, 1995.

Townshend, Robert B. *When Canvas Was King: Quinte and Prince Edward.* Carrying Place, Ontario, 2001.

Walker, Augustus. "Early Days On The Lakes, With An Account Of The Cholera Visitation Of 1832", *Publications of the Buffalo Historical Society V.* Buffalo, 1902.

Webster, F.B. (ed.). *Shipbuilding Cyclopaedia.* New York, 1920.

Weld, Isaac. *Travels Through the States of North America and the Provinces of Upper and Lower Canada During the Years 1795, 1796 and 1797.* London, 1799.

White, Randall. *Ontario 1610-1985: A Political and Economic History.* Toronto, 1985.

Woodford, Arthur M. *Charting the Inland Seas: A History of the U.S. Lake Survey.* Detroit 1991.

Wright, Larry & Patricia. *Great Lakes Lighthouses Encyclopedia.* The Boston Mills Press, 2006.

Young, Anna G. *Great Lakes' Saga.* Owen Sound, Ontario, 1965.

Charts and Maps

Ford, Augustus. *Chart of Lake Ontario from Actual Survey.* New York, 1836. [Library and Archives Canada]

Hasting County Historical Society. *Bird's Eye View of Belleville Ontario Canada, 1874* (reprint). Belleville, 1974.

Labroquerie. *Carte du Lac Ontario, 1757.* [British Library]

Midwest Explorer's League. *Lake Ontario Dive Chart.* Chicago, 1983.

NOAA. *Bathymetry of Lake Ontario* map. National Geophysical Data Center, National Environmental Data and Information Service & Great Lakes Environmental Research Laboratory, Office of Oceanic and Atmospheric Research. U.S.A 1999.

Smyth, David William. *A Map of the Province of Upper Canada.* London, 1800.

United States Corps of Engineers. *Lake Ontario.* New York 1877.

United States Corps of Engineers, War Department. *Lake Ontario, Survey of the Northern and Northwestern Lakes.* 1904

Government Publications

Dominion of Canada (1867 to present)

"Annual Report of the Department of Marine and Fisheries for the fiscal year ending 30th June...

...1870", *Sessional Papers of the Dominion of Canada No. 5, Sess. 1871.* Ottawa, 1871.

...1871", *Sessional Papers of the Dominion of Canada No. 5, Sess. 1872.* Ottawa 1872.

...1872", *Sessional Papers of the Dominion of Canada No. 8, Sess. 1873.* Ottawa, 1873.

...1873", *Sessional Papers of the Dominion of Canada No. 4, Sess. 1874.* Ottawa, 1874.

...1876", *Sessional Papers of the Dominion of Canada No. 5, Sess. 1877.* Ottawa, 1877.

...1878", *Sessional Papers of the Dominion of Canada No. 3, Sess. 1879.* Ottawa, 1879.

...1879", *Sessional Papers of the Dominion of Canada No. 9, Sess. 1880.* Ottawa, 1880.

...1880", *Sessional Papers of the Dominion of Canada No. 11, Sess. 1880-81.* Ottawa, 1881.

...1881", *Sessional Papers of the Dominion of Canada No. 5, Sess. 1882.* Ottawa, 1882.

...1884", *Sessional Papers of the Dominion of Canada No. 9, Sess. 1885.* Ottawa 1885.

...1885", *Sessional Papers of the Dominion of Canada No. 11, Sess. 1886.* Ottawa 1886.

...1886", *Sessional Papers of the Dominion of Canada No. 15, Sess. 1887.* Ottawa 1887.

...1888", *Sessional Papers of the Dominion of Canada No. 7, Sess. 1889.* Ottawa 1889.

...1889", *Sessional Papers of the Dominion of Canada No. 16, Sess. 1890* Ottawa 1890.

...1890", *Sessional Papers of the Dominion of Canada No. 7, Sess. 1891.* Ottawa, 1891.

...1891", *Sessional Papers of the Dominion of Canada No. 10, Sess. 1892.* Ottawa 1892.

...1892", *Sessional Papers of the Dominion of Canada No. 10, Sess. 1893.* Ottawa, 1893.

...1893", *Sessional Papers of the Dominion of Canada No. 11, Sess. 1894.* Ottawa, 1894.

...1897", *Sessional Papers of the Dominion of Canada No. 11, Sess. 1898.* Ottawa 1899.

...1898", *Sessional Papers of the Dominion of Canada No. 11, Sess. 1899*. Ottawa 1899.

...1898", "List of Vessels on the Registry Books of the Dominion of Canada, 1898", *Sessional Papers of the Dominion of Canada No. 11b, Sess. 1899*. Ottawa, 1899.

...1899", *Sessional Papers of the Dominion of Canada No. 11, Sess. 1900*. Ottawa, 1900.

...1905", *Sessional Papers of the Dominion of Canada No. 21, Sess. 1905*. Ottawa, 1905.

...1908", *Sessional Papers of the Dominion of Canada No. 21, Sess. 1909*. Ottawa, 1909.

...1909", *Sessional Papers of the Dominion of Canada No. 21, Sess. 1910*. Ottawa, 1910.

...1910", *Sessional Papers of the Dominion of Canada No. 21, Sess. 1911*. Ottawa, 1911.

...1910", *Sessional Papers of the Dominion of Canada No. 21, Sess. 1911*. Ottawa, 1911.

...1911", *Sessional Papers of the Dominion of Canada No. 21, Sess. 1912*. Ottawa, 1912.

...1912", *Sessional Papers of the Dominion of Canada No. 21, Sess. 1913*. Ottawa, 1913.

...1912", "List of Vessels on the Registry Books of the Dominion of Canada, 1912", *Sessional Papers of the Dominion of Canada No. 21b., Sess. 1913*. Ottawa, 1913.

...1913", *Sessional Papers of the Dominion of Canada No. 21, Sess. 1915*. Ottawa, 1915.

...1914", *Sessional Papers of the Dominion of Canada No. 21, Sess. 1916*. Ottawa, 1916.

...1915", *Sessional Papers of the Dominion of Canada No. 21, Sess. 1917*. Ottawa, 1917.

"Annual Report of the Minister of Railways and Canals to 30th June...

...1881". *Sessional Papers of the Dominion of Canada No. 8, Sess. 1882*. Ottawa, 1882.

...1882", *Sessional Papers of the Dominion of Canada No. 8, Sess. 1883*. Ottawa 1883.

...1885", *Sessional Papers of the Dominion of Canada No. 13, Sess. 1886.* Ottawa, 1886.

...1890", *Sessional Papers of the Dominion of Canada No. 10, Sess. 1891.* Ottawa 1891.

...1892", *Sessional Papers of the Dominion of Canada No. 9, Sess. 1893.* Ottawa, 1893.

...1893", *Sessional Papers of the Dominion of Canada No. 10, Sess. 1894.* Ottawa, 1894.

...1894", *Sessional Papers of the Dominion of Canada No. 10, Sess. 1895.* Ottawa, 1895.

...1895", *Sessional Papers of the Dominion of Canada No. 10, Sess. 1896.* Ottawa, 1896.

...1896", *Sessional Papers of the Dominion of Canada No. 10, Sess. 1897.* Ottawa, 1897.

...1897", *Sessional Papers of the Dominion of Canada No. 10, Sess. 1898.* Ottawa, 1899.

...1898", *Sessional Papers of the Dominion of Canada No. 10, Sess. 1899.* Ottawa, 1899.

...1899", *Sessional Papers of the Dominion of Canada No. 10, Sess. 1900.* Ottawa, 1900.

...1900", *Sessional Papers of the Dominion of Canada No. 10, Sess. 1901.* Ottawa, 1901.

...1901", *Sessional Papers of the Dominion of Canada No. 10, Sess. 1902.* Ottawa, 1902.

"Auditor General's Report...

...1885, "*Sessional Papers of the Dominion of Canada No. 3, Sess. 1886.* Ottawa, 1886.

...1891. *Sessional Papers of the Dominion of Canada No. 1, Sess. 1892.* Ottawa 1892.

...1892", *Sessional Papers of the Dominion of Canada No. 1, Sess. 1892.* Ottawa, 1892.

...1894", *Sessional Papers of the Dominion of Canada No. 1, Sess. 1895.* Ottawa 1895.

...1894-95", *Sessional Papers of the Dominion of Canada No.1 Sess.1896.* Ottawa, 1896.

...1911-12, *"Sessional Papers of the Dominion of Canada No. 1, Sess. 1913.* Ottawa, 1913.

...1913-14", *Sessional Papers of the Dominion of Canada No. 1, Sess. 1915.* Ottawa, 1915.

...1914-15", *Sessional Papers of the Dominion of Canada No. 1, Sess. 1916.* Ottawa, 1916.

Canada Gazette 1867-1946 (Dominion of Canada), volume 10, number 9. Ottawa 1876. p. 15

Canada Gazette, Part III. Ottawa, July 24, 2008. p. 5

Canadian Hydrographic Service. *Great Lakes Pilot Vol. 1, 6ᵗʰ ed.* Ottawa 1967.

"Canal Commission, 1871", *Sessional Papers of the Dominion of Canada No. 54, Sess. 1871.* Ottawa, 1871. 481 ships with registered in Ontario in 1867 with a total tonnage of 66,959 tons (see p. 170) and 2,171 American lake vessels in 1866 with a total tonnage of 547,267 tons (see p. 161). In addition, 1,124 ships were registered in the Province of Quebec, many of which would have traded on the Great Lakes.

"Canal Statistics for Season of Navigation 1891, *Sessional Papers of the Dominion of Canada : volume 8, second session of the seventh Parliament, session 1892.* Ottawa 1892. pp. 9C-132-133, 9A-134-135

Census of Canada 1880-81, Vol I. Ottawa, 1882.

Census of Canada 1901. Ottawa, 1902

The Civil Service List of Canada, 1886. Ottawa, 1887.

Debates of the House of Commons of the Dominion of Canada : second session, fourth Parliament. Ottawa,1880.

Debates of the House of Commons of the Dominion of Canada : third session, fourth Parliament ... comprising the period from the second day of February 1881, to the twenty-first day of March, 1881. Ottawa, 1881.

Department of Marine and Fisheries. *Canada: Her Natural Resources Navigation Principal Steamer Lines and Transcontinental Railways.* Ottawa, 1912.

Department of Marine and Fisheries. *List of Lights and Fog Signals on the Coasts, Rivers and Lakes of the Dominion of Canada. 1878.* Ottawa, 1879.

Department of Marine and Fisheries. *Port Directory of Principal Canadian Ports and Harbours.* Ottawa, 1909.

Department of Marine and Fisheries. *Port Directory of Principal Canadian Ports and Harbours.* Ottawa 1913 & 1914.

Department of Marine and Fisheries. *Review of Improvements in Lighthouse and Coast Service.* Ottawa, 1904.

Department of Transport, Marine Services. "Canada Rules and Instructions for Lightkeepers and Fog Alarm Engineers and Rules Governing Buoys and Beacons." Ottawa. 1953

"Estimates for the Fiscal Year Ending March 31, 1914", *Sessional Papers of the Dominion of Canada No. 3a, Sess. 1912-13.* Ottawa, 1913.

Fisheries and Oceans Canada. *Alternate Use Study, Surplus Lighthouses Canada.* Ottawa, March 2011.

Fisheries and Oceans Canada. *Sailing Directions, CEN 300, General Information, Great Lakes.* Ottawa, 1996.

General Report of the Commissioner of Public Works, 1867. Ottawa, 1868.

"General Report of the Minister of Public Works to 1st July...

...1871", *Sessional Papers of the Dominion of Canada No. 4 Sess. 1872.* Ottawa, 1872

...1874", *Sessional Papers of the Dominion of Canada No. 7, Sess. 1875.* Ottawa 1875.

...1876". *Sessional Papers of the Dominion of Canada No. 6, Sess. 1877.* Ottawa, 1877.

...1882", *Sessional Papers of the Dominion of Canada No. 10 Sess. 1883.* Ottawa 1883.

...1885". *Sessional Papers of the Dominion of Canada No. 12, Sess. 1886.* Ottawa, 1886.

Hydrographic Survey Office, Department of Naval Service. *Sailing Directions for Canadian Shores of Lake Ontario.* Ottawa 1921.

"Information respecting proposed Canal between Lake Ontario and Bay of Quinte, December 1867." *Sessional Papers of the Dominion of Canada : volume 9, session 1867-68.* Ottawa, 1868.

Interim Report, Georgian Bay Ship Canal. Ottawa, 1908.

Journals of the House of Commons, Session 1867-8, Vol. I. Ottawa, 1868.

Journals of the House of Commons of Canada from April 15th to June 22nd 1869 ... being the second session of the first Parliament of Canada, session 1869. Ottawa, 1869.

Journals of the House of Commons of the Dominion of Canada from 15th February to 14th April, 1871. Ottawa 1871.

Journals of the House of Commons of the Dominion of Canada from the 4th February to the 8th April, 1875. Ottawa, 1875.

Journals of the House of Commons of the Dominion of Canada, Sess. 1879. Ottawa, 1879.

Journals of the House of Commons of the Dominion of Canada from the 9th December, 1880, to the 21st March, 1881. Ottawa, 1881.

Monro, Thomas. *Report of the Chief Engineer of Public Works on the Enlargement of the Welland Canal.* Ottawa, 1872.

"Notice to Mariners" published in *The Canada Gazette.* Ottawa, –Sep. 19 1885. –Apr. 20 1889. –Oct. 17 1891. –July 30 1892. –Dec. 17 1892. –July 28 1894. –May 1 1897. –July 29 1899. –Apr. 14 1900. –Nov. 11 1905. –Sep. 18 1909. –Sep. 25 1909. –Feb. 4 1911. –Jan. 13 1912. –Apr. 27 1912. –June 8 1913. –June 14 1913. –Sep. 19 1914.

Official debates of the House of Commons of the Dominion of Canada : fourth session, fourth Parliament ... comprising the period from the ninth day of February to the seventeenth day of May, 1882. Ottawa 1882.

Official report of the debates of the House of Commons of the Dominion of Canada : third session, fifth Parliament to the twentieth day of July, 1885 Ottawa, 1885.

Official report of the debates of the House of Commons of the Dominion of Canada : fourth session, fifth Parliament, to the second day of June, 1886. Ottawa, 1886.

Official Report of the Debates of the House of Commons of the Dominion of Canada, 1889. Vol. XXVIII. Ottawa, 1889.

Parliamentary debates, Dominion of Canada, fourth session, 33 Victoriae 1871. Ottawa, 1871.

Report of the Board of Works, 1844. Montreal 1845

"Report of the Canal Commissioners", *Sessional Papers of the Dominion of Canada No. 54, Sess. 1871*. Ottawa, 1871.

"Return... on the subject of meteorological observations and weather reports, 1872", *Sessional Papers of the Dominion of Canada No. 53, Sess. 1872*. Ottawa, 1872.

Seventh Census of Canada 1931. Ottawa, 1934.

Statutes of Canada, Part Second, 1868. Ottawa, 1868.

"Tables of Trade and Navigation...

...1870", *Sessional Papers of the Dominion of Canada No. 3, Sess. 1871*. Ottawa, 1871.

...1871", *Sessional Papers of the Dominion of Canada N.o 3., Sess. 1872*. Ottawa, 1872.

...1878", *Sessional Papers of the Dominion of Canada No. 2, Sess. 1879*. Ottawa, 1879.

...1884", *Sessional Papers of the Dominion of Canada No. 2, Sess. 1885*. Ottawa, 1885.

...1885", *Sessional Papers of the Dominion of Canada No. 1, Sess. 1886*. Ottawa, 1886.

...1890", *Sessional Papers of the Dominion of Canada No. 4., Sess. 1891*. Ottawa, 1891.

...1895", *Sessional Papers of the Dominion of Canada No. 6, Sess. 1896*. Ottawa, 1896.

...1900", *Sessional Papers of the Dominion of Canada No. 11, Sess. 1901*. Ottawa, 1901.

Tables of Trade and Navigation 1899. Ottawa, 1900.

Treaties and Agreements Affecting Canada, 1814-1913. Ottawa, 1914.

Other Governments

Great Britain. Admiralty Hydrographic Office. *Admiralty List of the Lights on the Coasts and Lakes of British North America*. London 1864.

Great Britain. Ryder, Captain Alfred P., RN. *Heads of Inquiry into the State and Conditions of Lighthouses.* extracted from *The Royal Commission on Lighthouses, Buoys, and Beacons, 1861.* London, 1863.

Lower Canada. *Appendix to the XVIIth volume of the Journals of the House of Assembly of the province of Lower Canada.* Quebec, 1809.

Province of Ontario (1867 to present). Ministry of Tourism and Culture. *Standards and Guidelines for Conservation of Provincial Heritage Properties.* Toronto, 2010.

Province of Quebec (1774-1791). *An Ordinance, For promoting the Inland Navigation*, Quebec, 1788.

State of New York. *Report of the Commissioners to Explore the Route on an Inland Navigation.* New York, 1811.

U.S.A. Light-House Board. *List of Lights on the Northern Lake and River Coasts of the United States.* Washington, 1873.

U.S.A. NOAA. *United States Coast Pilot 6: Great Lakes, 2014* (44th Edition). Washington 2014.

U.S.A. *Papers on the Comparative Merits of the Catoptric and Dioptric or Catadioptric Systems of Lighthouse Illumination.* Washington, 1861.

U.S.A. *Public Statutes at Large of the United States of America.* Boston, 1848.

U.S.A. Ross, Albert. *Report on the Use of Acetylene Gas by the Canadian Government as an Illuminant for Aids to Navigation.* Washington, 1907.

U.S.A. *Treaty of Amity, Commerce and Navigation.* Philadelphia, 1795.

U.S.A. Treasury Dept., U.S. Coast Guard. *List of Lights and Other Marine Aids Vol. IV: Great Lakes, United States and Canada, 1961.* Washington, 1961.

U.S.A. United Status Census Office. *Census Reports*, Vol. I., *Twelfth Census of the United States.* Washington, 1901.

U.S.A. United States Hydrographic Office. *Sailing Directions for the Great Lakes and Connecting Waters.* Washington, 1896.

United Province of Canada (1841-1867)

Appendix to the Journals of the Legislative Assembly of the Province of Canada...

    Sess. 1841. Kingston, 1842.

    Sess. 1843. Kingston, 1844.

Sess. 1844-45. Montreal, 1845.

Sess. 1846. Montreal, 1846.

Sess. 1847. Montreal, 1847.

Sess. 1850. Toronto, 1850.

Sess. 1854 to 1855. Quebec, 1855.

Sess. 1855 to 1856. Toronto, 1856.

Sess. 1856. Toronto, 1856.

Sess. 1857. Toronto, 1857.

Sess. 1858. Toronto, 1858.

General Report of the commissioners of Public Works for the Year Ending 31st December 1857. Toronto, 1858.

Journals of the Legislative Assembly of the Province of Canada from the 28th day of November 1844, to the 29th day of March, 1845. Montreal, 1845.

Journals of the Legislative Assembly of the Province of Canada, Sess. 1857. Toronto, 1857.

Journals of the Legislative Assembly of the Province of Canada from March 16 to May 18, 1861. Quebec, 1861.

Journals of the Legislative Assembly of the Province of Canada, 5th session of the 8th Provincial Parliament of Canada. Ottawa,1866.

Provincial Statutes of Canada: 1st Session of the 1st Provincial Parliament of Canada. Kingston, 1841.

Report of the Board of Works : December, 1844. Montreal, 1845.

Report of the Commissioners appointed to consider the defences of Canada, 1862. London 1862.

Report of the Select Committee on Georgian Bay and Lake Ontario Ship Canal. Quebec, 1864.

Sessional papers of the Province of Canada, Sess. 1860. Quebec, 1860.

Sessional papers, first session of the seventh Parliament of the Province of Canada, session 1862. Quebec, 1862.

Sessional papers, second session of the seventh Parliament of the Province of Canada, session 1863. Quebec, 1863.

Sessional Papers of the Parliament of the Province of Canada, Sess. 1866. Ottawa, 1866.

Shanley, Walter. *Report on the Ottawa and French River Navigation Project*. Montreal, 1863.

Statutes of the Province of Canada, first session of the fifth Parliament of Canada. Quebec 1854.

Tables of Trade and Navigation of the Province of Canada, 1858. Toronto, 1859.

Tables of Trade and Navigation of the Province of Canada, 1865. Quebec, 1865.

Upper Canada (1791-1841)

Appendix to the Journal of the House of Assembly of Upper Canada...
    1826-27. York, 1827.
    1828. York, 1828.
    1829. York, 1829.
    1831-32. York, 1832.
    1832-33. York 1833.
    1833-1834. Toronto, 1834.
    1836. Toronto, 1836.
    1836-1837. Toronto, 1837.
    1840. Toronto, 1841.

First Report from the Select Committee Appointed to Inquire into the State of the Trade and Commerce of the Province of Upper Canada. Toronto. 1835

Journal of the House of Assembly of Upper Canada...
    1833. York, 1833.
    1835. Toronto, 1835.
    1836. Toronto, 1836.
    1836-1837. Toronto, 1837.
    1837. Toronto, 1837.
    1836. Toronto, 1836.

Ordinances made and passed by His Excellency the Governor General and special council for the affairs of the Province of Lower Canada. Quebec, 1839.

Provincial Statutes of Upper Canada. York, 1818.

Report of the commissioners appointed to superintend the erection of a penitentiary in Kingston. Kingston, 1833.

Reports of the Commissioners of Internal Navigation. Kingston, 1825.

Statutes of Upper Canada. York, 1824,

Statues of His Majesty's Province of Upper Canada 1827. York, 1827.

Statutes of His Majesty's Province of Upper Canada, 1828. York, 1828.

Statues of the Province of Upper Canada. Kingston, 1831.

Statutes of His Majesty's Province of Upper Canada,1832. York, 1832.

Statutes of Upper Canada, 1833. York, 1833.

Statutes of His Majesty's province of Upper Canada, 1837. Toronto, 1837.

Internet Sources

AGA. "AGA History", http://www.aga.com/international/web/lg/aga/ like35agacom.nsf/docbyalias/aga_history (accessed 5 Nov. 2014)

Baillod, Brendon. "Great Lakes Shipwreck Research", http://www. ship-wreck.com

Baillod, Brendon. "The David Swayze Great Lakes Shipwreck File", http://www.ship-wreck.com /shipwreck/swayze/

Brock, Thomas L. "Barrie, Sir Robert" in "Dictionary of Canadian Biography", http://www.biographi.ca/en/bio/ barrie_robert_7E.html

Canadian Coast Guard. *List of Lights Buoys and Fog Signals.* http://www.notmar.gc.ca/go.php?doc=eng/services/list/ inland-waters-2009

Canadiana.org. "John Marks" search in "Early Canadiana Online", http://eco.canadiana.ca/search?q=%22john marks%22 -brunswick &field=&so=oldest&df=1825&dt=1868&collection=gvp

Errington, Jane. "Kirby, John" in "Dictionary of Canadian Biography", http://www.biographi.ca/en/bio/kirby_john_7E.html

Fraser, Robert L. "Macaulay, John" in "Dictionary of Canadian Biography", http://www.biographi.ca/en/bio/ macaulay_john_8E.html

Government of Canada. "Natural Resources Canada, Query by Geographical Name", http://www4.rncan.gc.ca/search-place-names/search?lang=en

Hill, Robert G. "Biographical Dictionary of Architects in Canada 1800-1950", http://dictionaryofarchitectsincanada.org/architects/view/1414

Ingersoll, L.K. "Owen, William" in "Dictionary of Canadian Biography", http://www.biographi.ca/en/bio/owen_william_4E.html

Johnson, J.K. and P.B. Waite. "Macdonald, Sir John Alexander" in "Dictionary of Canadian Biography", http://www.biographi.ca/en/bio/macdonald_john_alexander_12E.html

Lewis, Walter. "Maritime History of the Great Lakes", http://images.maritimehistoryofthegreatlakes.ca/

Lewis, Walter. "McKenzie, James" in "Dictionary of Canadian Biography", http://www.biographi.ca/en/bio/mckenzie_james_1832_6E.html

Library and Archives Canada. "D.B. Detweiler finding aid", file http://data2.archives.ca/pdf/pdf001/p000001430.pdf link from http://collectionscanada.gc.ca/pam_archives/index.php?fuseaction=genitem.displayItem&lang=eng&rec_nbr=97887

McGill University. "In Search of Your Canadian Past: The Canadian County Atlas Digital Project." J.H. Meacham & Co. *Illustrated Historical atlas of the counties of Frontenac, Lennox and Addington, Ontario.* Toronto, 1878. http://digital.library.mcgill.ca/countyatlas/showrecord.php?PersonID=11922

McKenzie, Ruth. "Bayfield, Henry Wolsey", in "Dictionary of Canadian Biography", http://www.biographi.ca/en/bio/bayfield_henry_wolsey_11E.html

McKenzie, Ruth. "Washburn, Simon Ebenezer" in "Dictionary of Canadian Biography", http://www.biographi.ca/en/bio/washburn_simon_ebenezer_7E.html

Millman, T.R. "Macaulay, William" in "Dictionary of Canadian Biography", http://www.biographi.ca/en/bio/macaulay_william_10E.html

Natural Resources Canada. "Canadian Geographical Names Database", http://www.nrcan.gc.ca/earth-sciences/geography/place-names/search/9170

O'Brien, Audrey and Marc Bosc, eds. "House of Commons Procedure and Practice. 2nd Ed., 2009" http://www.parl.gc.ca/procedure-book-livre/Document.aspx?Language=E&Mode=1&sbdid=7c730f1d-e10b-4dfc-863a-83e7e1a6940e&sbpid=976953d8-8385-4e09-a699-d90779b48aa0

Palmer, Richard. "Lake Ontario's First Chartmaker", http://freepages.genealogy.rootsweb.ancestry.com/~twigs2000/chartmaker.html

Presqu'ile Point Lighthouse Preservation Society. "Restoration", http://www.koppla.ca/restoration.html

Province of Ontario. "Ontario Heritage Act" in "e-Laws", http://www.e-laws.gov.on.ca/html/statutes/english/elaws_statutes_90o18_e.htm

Royal Military College of Canada. "Major John Laing Weller, 1862-1932", http://www.rmc.ca/cam/wh-mh/whc-cmh/weller-jl-eng.php

Russell, Loris S. "Gesner, Abraham" in "Dictionary of Canadian Biography", http://www.biographi.ca/en/bio/gesner_abraham_9E.html

Saunders, Robert L. "Robinson, Sir John Beverly" in "Dictionary of Canadian Biography", http: //www.biographi.ca /en/bio/robinson_john_beverley_9E.html

Stagg, Ronald J. "McIntosh, John" in "Dictionary of Canadian Biography", http://www.biographi.ca/en/bio/mcintosh_john_1796_1853_8E.html

Turner, Larry. "Flint, Billa" in "Dictionary of Canadian Biography", http://www.biographi.ca/en/bio/flint_billa_12E.html.

Wikipedia. "List of Tallest Buildings in Montreal", http://en.wikipedia.org/wiki/List_of_tallest_buildings_in_Montreal#Timeline_of_tallest_buildings

Wikipedia. "Michigan State Capitol", http://en.wikipedia.org/wiki/Michigan_State_Capitol#First_state_capitol

Witham, John. "Baird, Nicol Hugh" in "Dictionary of Canadian Biography", http://www.biographi.ca/en/bio/baird_nicol_hugh_7E.html.

Newspapers

The British Whig. Kingston,
–Dec. 2, 1834. –Dec. 9, 1834. –June 9, 1835. –Apr. 13, 1847.
–Mar. 215, 1848. –Mar. 28, 1876. –Feb. 16, 1880. –June 4, 1880.
–June 9, 1880. –Oct.1, 1880. – Oct. 6, 1881. –Aug. 2, 1884.
–Aug. 5, 1884. –Nov. 8, 1886. –Feb. 26, 1887. –Oct. 24, 1887.
–July 29 1889. –Aug. 25 1890. –Dec. 11 1890. –Oct. 24, 1913.
–Nov. 5, 1913. –Dec. 4, 1913. –Dec. 8, 1913
The British Whig and General Advertiser for Canada West. Kingston,
May 25, 1847
The Buffalo Daily Republic. Buffalo. Sep. 17, 1853
The Buffalo Evening News. Buffalo, May 5, 1903
The Buffalo Evening News. Buffalo, Dec. 6, 1906
The Chronicle & Gazette. Kingston,
–Oct. 4, 1834. –Oct. 31, 1835. –Apr. 13, 1836. –Aug. 21, 1839.
–Mar. 7, 1840. –Oct. 21, 1840. –Nov. 3, 1841. –Dec. 9, 1843.
–May 4, 1844
The Cleveland Herald. Cleveland, Sep. 15, 1881
The Cobourg Sun. Cobourg, July 1, 1856
The Commercial Advertiser. Buffalo, Jan. 20, 1864
The Commercial Advertiser. Buffalo, Feb. 26, 1867
The Commercial Advertiser. Buffalo, Oct. 26, 1871
The Daily British Whig. Kingston,
–May 28, 1849. –Apr. 26, 1851. –June 21, 1853. –Sep. 16, 1857.
–Nov. 27, 1860. –Oct 26, 1864
The Daily News. Kingston,
–Oct. 10, 1851. –Nov. 16, 1854. –July 3, 1856. –Feb. 10, 1857.
–Apr. 16, 1857. –Feb. 15, 1858. –Jul. 25, 1860. –Oct. 13, 1862.
–Dec. 25, 1862. –Dec. 14, 1866. –Nov. 6, 1867. –Oct. 31, 1870.
–Nov. 17, 1870. –Nov. 23, 1870. –Nov. 30, 1870. –Sep. 6, 1871.
–Sep. 7, 1871. –Nov. 7, 1873. –Feb. 11, 1874. –Mar. 8, 1876
Daily Ontario. Belleville, Nov. 19, 1879
Daily Ontario. Belleville, Nov. 20, 1879
The Democracy. Buffalo, Nov. 18, 1854

The Democracy. Buffalo, Dec. 11, 1854

The Democracy. Buffalo, May 31, 1855

The Evening Record. Windsor, Dec. 6, 1906.

The Farmers' Journal. Syracuse, Nov. 8, 1826.

The Free Press. Hallowell, June 19, 1832

The Free Press. Hallowell, June 26, 1832

The Free Press. Hallowell, July 3, 1832

The Free Press. Hallowell, July 17, 1832

The Globe. Toronto, Dec. 7, 1854

The Globe. Toronto, Nov. 28, 1860

The Globe. Toronto, Nov. 23, 1864

The Grenville Gazette. Prescott, Dec. 3, 1846

The Intelligencer. Belleville, Nov. 4, 1870

The Kingston Chronicle. Kingston,
  –Dec. 24, 1819. –Sep. 15, 1820. –Dec. 15, 1820. –Nov. 29, 1822.
  –Apr. 11, 1829. –Oct. 22, 1831. –Nov. 30, 1833

The Kingston Gazette. Kingston, Dec. 7, 1816

The Kingston Gazette. Kingston, Dec. 14, 1816

The Kingston Gazette. Kingston, April 12, 1817

The Kingston Herald. Kingston, Mar. 24, 1846

The Kingston Herald. Kingston, Aug. 18, 1846

The Kingston News. Kingston, Aug. 7, 1845

The Kingston Spectator. Kingston, Nov. 19, 1833

The Kingston Whig-Standard. Kingston, Dec. 29, 2010

The Marine Record. Cleveland, Sep. 26, 1895

The Montreal Gazette. Montreal, May 21, 1832

The Newmarket Era. Newmarket, Dec. 3, 1909

The Oswego County Whig. Oswego, May 30, 1838

The Oswego Palladium. Oswego, Nov. 18, 1879

The Oswego Palladium. Oswego, Nov. 19, 1879

The Oswego Palladium. Oswego, Nov. 21, 1879

The Oswego Palladium. Oswego, Sep. 2, 1882

The Ottawa Evening Citizen. Ottawa, Feb. 2, 1927

The Patriot. Toronto, Aug. 11, 1837

The Picton Gazette. Picton, May 8, 1970

The Syracuse Herald, Syracuse, Mar. 13, 1926

Toronto World. Toronto, Mar. 25, 1912

Toronto World. Toronto, Aug. 26, 1913

Toronto World. Toronto, Nov. 6, 1913

The Trenton Courier. Trenton, Oct. 24, 1889

The Upper Canada Herald. Kingston, July 29, 1829

The Upper Canada Herald. Kingston, August 29, 1832

The Weekly British Whig. Kingston, Nov. 16, 1871

The Windsor Evening Record. Feb. 13, 1909

Periodicals

"Aids to Navigation on the St. Lawrence and the Great Lakes". *Railway and Marine World.* Toronto, March 1911.

Barlow, William Henry. "On the Adaptation of Different Modes of Illuminating Lighthouses", *Philosophical transactions of the Royal Society of London. Vol. 127.* London, 1837

Bogart, Ernest L. "Early Canal Traffic and Railroad Competition in Ohio", *Journal of Political Economy,* Vol. 21. Chicago, 1913.

Mather, F.G. "Water Routes from the Great Northwest", *Harper's New Monthly Magazine".* New York, August, 1881.

Macquarrie, Heath. "Robert Borden and the Election of 1911", *The Canadian Journal of Economics and Political Science.* August, 1959.

McLean, S.J. "The Early Railway History of Canada", *The Canadian Magazine.* Toronto, March 1899.

McMaster, A.T.C. "A Psalm of Life at S.P.S.", *Applied Science and Transactions of the University of Toronto Engineering Society,* Vol. X. New Series, May 1915 to June 1916. Toronto 1916.

Ransome, Ernest L. "Concrete Construction — Its Practical Application", *Canadian Architect and Builder.* Toronto, Dec. 1894.

Sack, David A. and R. Bradley Sack and G. Balakrish Nair and A.K. Siddique. "Cholera", *The Lancet.* Oxford, 17 January 2004.

INDEX

CPSIA information can be obtained
at www.ICGtesting.com
Printed in the USA
LVOW04*2000051115
461253LV00015B/507/P